Impediments to the Prevention and Intervention of Genocide

Impediments to the Prevention and Intervention of Genocide

Genocide:
A Critical
Bibliographic Review
Volume 9

Samuel Totten
editor

Routledge
Taylor & Francis Group
LONDON AND NEW YORK

First published 2013 by Transaction Publishers

2 Park Square, Milton Park, Abingdon, Oxfordshire OX14 4RN
711 Third Avenue, New York, NY 10017

Routledge is an imprint of the Taylor & Francis Group, an informa business

First issued in paperback 2017

Library of Congress Catalog Number: 2012013892

Library of Congress Cataloging-in-Publication Data

Impediments to the prevention and intervention of genocide / Samuel Totten, editor.
p. cm.
Includes bibliographical references and index.
ISBN 978-1-4128-4943-2
1. Genocide—Prevention—International cooperation. 2. Genocide intervention—Political aspects. 3. Genocide (International law) 4. Convention on the Prevention and Punishment of the Crime of Genocide (1948) I. Totten, Samuel.
HV6322.7.I47 2013
364.151—dc23

2012013892

ISBN 13: 978-1-4128-4943-2 (hbk)
ISBN 13: 978-1-138-51084-5 (pbk)

Contents

Preface

Why No One Came?

Brent Beardsley

I was very honored when the renowned genocide scholar and my friend, Samuel Totten, asked me to write the preface to this work, which I believe will provide a deeper understanding of the crime of genocide. I am not a scholar, an academic, or a renowned author or activist of genocide. I am a retired soldier, who, in 1993–1994, had the opportunity and the privilege of serving as the Personal Staff Officer to Canadian Major-General Romeo Dallaire (the Force Commander of the United Nations Assistance Mission for Rwanda or UNAMIR) in Rwanda, both prior to and during the 1994 genocide. I was a privileged witness, periodic rescuer/helper, and in some ways a survivor of one of the fastest and deadliest genocides in modern history, which claimed the lives of an estimated 800,000 men, women, and children in a period of approximately 100 days. I therefore feel academically unqualified to introduce a scholastic work, but I can add a very human plea, a rallying cry if you will, to all who will read this book. It must be used, along with other works on the gross deprivation of human rights, to increase our understanding of the crime of genocide, to increase our motivation to become anti-genocide activists, and to learn from our failures and mistakes so that we never repeat them again. Let us finally give the promise of "Never Again" some real meaning and not have this rallying cry reduced to "Yet Again."

Unlike previous genocides, the 1994 Rwandan genocide was covered in near real time by television, radio, newspapers, call-in shows, and even the early Internet. Despite this exceptional exposure of the genocide to the connected world, the institutions of the international community and, in fact, most of humanity, witnessed the genocide, but chose to pick up the remote and change the channel, switch to a different radio station, glance over the articles in newspapers, and generally ignore what was taking place in Rwanda. While most in the connected world were apathetic at best, or hypocritical at worst, no one can "Pontius Pilate" themselves and truthfully claim that they did not know what was happening in Rwanda from April to July 1994. The Rwandan genocide was simply, and profoundly, ignored, *and* was allowed to run its deadly course as hundreds of thousands of our fellow human beings were brutally murdered. And no one came!

After a typical day of trying successfully, or too often unsuccessfully, to save human beings from the slaughter, trying to deliver humanitarian aid to our protected sites and shuttling between the lines to try and save lives and obtain a ceasefire, it would be around midnight that we would retire for a few hours before stand-to at dawn. In my bed, made of an old African hotel mattress with a curtain for a blanket, I tried to sleep with the INMARSAT (our only link to the outside world) telephone on one side of my head and the radio on the other. Each night in my thoughts, before I dozed off, were the memories of the sights, the sounds, and the smells of the ongoing slaughter: the mounds of bodies, especially the contorted faces of the young women murdered after they had been gang raped and the innocent children robbed of the innocence of youth; the cries and screams of the fearful, the sick, the wounded, and the injured as they went untreated and forgotten by the world; and the terrible, unforgettable, and unmistakable stench of death and the dying, which never left your nostrils—not the kind of thoughts that help one sleep.

These images and memories were always accompanied by a single question: "Why doesn't anyone come to help us end this?" And that single question was followed by a rush of subsequent questions:

- "Where are they?"
- "Can't they see what's happening?"
- "Don't they care?"
- "What about 'Never Again'?"
- "Why are they ignoring our reports, the media broadcasts and the wealth of information showering them from around the world?"
- "What has happened to humanity and the international community?"
- "Are they blind, deaf, mute, apathetic, hypocritical, ignorant, greedy or have they just lost the last ounce of basic humanity in themselves?"

How I hated the perpetrators for what they were doing, and the world, the United Nations, my country, and everyone else *for what they were not doing.* One evening, early in the genocide, during a conversation with a high military official in the United Nations, I got an answer when he said, "You have to be ready to leave the country by foot, vehicle and/or by road because no one is coming to back you guys up or to get you out!" That was us! UN soldiers from twenty-two nations, sent to Rwanda with the blessings of our countries, with a mandate from the United Nations Security Council (UNSC), representing the will of the international community on the behalf of humanity. While being expected to remain in Rwanda and try, without reinforcement or even basic essential support, to contain the violence, we were being written off by our respective nations, the United Nations, and by humanity. But even worse than this treatment of professional soldiers, what about the potential victims who could be saved and the survivors in hiding, and the tens of thousands of defenseless civilians in our protected sites? No mention of them, because they mattered even less than the approximately 450 soldiers and civilians who chose to stay and try to at least do something in Rwanda.

It became a nightly ritual that ended in a prayer (there are no atheists in foxholes or during a genocide), and with tears of frustration and pain, to commit ourselves to continuing on the next day, to do the best we could, with what little we had, and to save as many lives as we could. In the end we saved approximately 40,000, but we lost 800,000 in what most serious scholars, soldiers, and politicians have now, in hindsight, concluded was a preventable or easily suppressed genocide.

Why they (individual nations, the UN, and humanity) did not rally to halt the genocide —or, more to the point, why no help came during most genocides and massive crimes against humanity—is addressed in this volume, *Impediments to the Prevention and Intervention of Genocide: A Critical Bibliographic Review.* We can, if we are diligent, learn as much from our failures and our defeats as we do from our victories. There have been too many defeats in genocides to date and too few victories. Why we have failed—and continue to fail—is probed within these pages. It contains the insights of scholars who are dedicated to overcoming these failures and are committed, with others across the globe, to figuring out how major human rights violations can be addressed and stopped before they eventuate in crimes against humanity and/or genocide.

My experience with the mistakes, defeats, and a failed mission in Rwanda in 1994 taught me that there are five major factors in genocide prevention or suppression:

1. In order to develop and engage in genocide prevention, we need to have knowledge of the potential genocide area *before* the genocide is perpetrated.
2. We need to have the will to take risks to sustain a determined effort to achieve the goal of preventing or stopping a genocide.
3. We need to have a way or ways in the form of tools to prevent or stop a genocide.
4. We need the means, which will be found, if the will is present, to prevent and to stop this crime.
5. Finally, we need to have a more realistic view of the issue of time in the face of potential or actual genocide.

Address these five factors and the host of subfactors related to each and we could be well on our way to banishing the crime of genocide to the dustbin of history.

I congratulate Samuel Totten and the chapter authors for their dedication and their academic and scholastic abilities as displayed in this book. The challenge now is for readers to study this subject, further inform themselves with other seminal works, and then commit themselves to anti-genocide activism. If enough of us do so, then next time (and there will be a next time) perhaps we will finally give "Never Again" some real meaning.

Introduction

Samuel Totten

More than ever before, scholars, nongovernmental organizations, the United Nations, and individual nations are focused on the prevention and intervention of genocide. That is, more individuals, organizations, and states are engaged in examining how to make the prevention and intervention of genocide more of a reality than it has been in the recent past (meaning, more likely to be undertaken, period; more likely to be undertaken in a timely manner; and more likely to be undertaken in an effective manner with an adequate number of well-trained and well-armed troops attached to a mission with an adequate mandate and the resources to do the job). Both in the recent past and today, missions to prevent (or, as the case may be, to intervene in) crimes against humanity and/or genocide have variously been sporadic, erratic, under-resourced, undermanned, outgunned, and/or assigned a weak mandate (each of the latter certainly applies to UNAMIR in Rwanda in the early to mid-1990s and to both the former AU and the current UNAMID missions in Darfur), or, simply nonexistent (as is the case today vis-à-vis the crisis in the Nuba Mountains and Blue Nile in Sudan). The results have ranged from disastrous (e.g., the 1994 genocide in Rwanda in which between 500,000 and one million people, mainly Tutsi but also moderate Hutu, were murdered over a period of 100 days) to pathetic (the ongoing mission in Darfur where the UN mission has not been able to provide adequate protection for the over two million internally displaced peoples).

The contributors to this volume (Volume 9 in the series, *Genocide: A Critical Bibliographic Review*) tackle what they and the editor perceive as some of the major impediments to the prevention and intervention of genocide in today's world. It is an ideal time to focus on such impediments, for over the past decade or so the international community has undertaken a number of well-intentioned attempts to overcome the lackluster efforts of the past to prevent genocide or to intervene early on in an effective manner. A question that clouds such efforts—particularly as the violence in Darfur (Sudan) continues unabated, mass rape remains a common denominator of the crisis in the Democratic Republic of the Congo, Syria guns down (with impunity) thousands of its own people, and the Government of Sudan purposely prevents humanitarian aid from reaching some two to three hundred thousand severely malnourished people huddled in the caves and crevasses of the Nuba Mountains where they have sought sanctuary from both ground and aerial attacks the past thirteen plus months (July 2011 to present—August 2012)—is whether such efforts by individual and collective nations are more akin to wishful thinking and/or so much window dressing versus *a deep and abiding commitment to the prevention and intervention of genocide.*

Despite all of the talk, all the meetings and conferences, reports, position papers, and promises vis-à-vis the prevention of and intervention of genocide, one has to wonder whether, in the end, to paraphrase Shakespeare, it will all constitute little more than sound and fury signifying nothing. Of course, we all hope it is not, but it really does seem that the more we talk about prevention and intervention, the more we allow crimes against humanity and genocide to break out and continue unabated, only to be followed by half-witted, half-hearted, undermanned, under-resourced missions with weak mandates that leave tens, if not hundreds, of thousands or more in the lurch.

The contributors to this special issue are an eclectic group comprising second-, third-, and fourth-generation scholars of genocide from diverse fields (history, political science, philosophy, and peace studies) and countries (Australia, Canada, and the United States).

The volume begins with a powerful and insightful "Preface" by Major Brent Beardsley, a man who saw the 1994 Rwandan genocide up close. As the Personal Staff Officer to Major-General Romeo Dallaire, the Force Commander of the United Nations Assistance Mission for Rwanda (UNAMIR), Beardsley was in Rwanda prior to and during the genocide and has firsthand knowledge regarding a slew of impediments to the prevention of genocide.

Paul R. Bartrop, a historian based in Australia, and Samuel Totten lead off the volume with "*Realpolitik*: The Major Impediment to the Prevention and Intervention of Genocide." In their chapter, Bartrop and Totten argue that when all is said and done, *realpolitik* is *the* major factor that impedes efforts to prevent genocide and to intervene once it has broken out, and that it shall continue to be the inhibitor to timely, effective action even as individual nations and the international community work to implement The Responsibility to Protect and other recent innovations vis-à-vis prevention and intervention. Ultimately, it is *realpolitik*, they argue, that must be overcome but the question that remains is: Is that possible; and if so, how?

In Chapter 2, "Lack of Political Will," Kenneth J. Campbell, a political scientist at the University of Delaware, provides an interesting take on the issue of the lack of political will in relation to the prevention and intervention of genocide. He avers that no other problem has frustrated genocide scholars and the anti-genocide movement more than the chronic shortage of "political will" on the part of Western nations to stop genocide. He goes on to note that over the past two decades, Western nations that had solemnly pledged "never again" to allow genocide to occur have instead permitted it, again and again, in such places as Bosnia, Rwanda, Kosovo, and Darfur. He further examines why those nations with the power and means to prevent genocide lacked such political will; what can be done, if anything, to overcome the impediment posed by a lack of political will; and what, if anything, can genocide scholars and the anti-genocide movement do to help create the necessary political will within governments (and particularly within the US government), to employ national power to stop present and future genocides.

In a provocative chapter (Chapter 3) entitled "Denial of Ongoing Atrocities as a Rationale for Not Attempting to Prevent or Intervene," Henry C. Theriault, Professor of Philosophy at Worcester State College in Worcester, Massachusetts, focuses on the ways in which denial is an obstacle to the prevention and/or intervention of genocide. More specifically, Theriault declares that denial is a multifaceted phenomenon: "a verbal strategy consisting of assertions that events that constitute genocide are not happening or did not happen, or that the events in question are or were something other than genocide."

In Chapter 4, "The Wording and Interpretation of the UN Convention on the Prevention and Punishment of the Crime of Genocide: An Ongoing Impediment," Samuel Totten discusses past and current issues in regard to how the *United Nations Convention on the Prevention and Punishment of the Crime of Genocide* has been variously interpreted in both nonlegal and legal investigations of atrocity crimes and different court cases, and how such interpretations have, in various situations, hindered progress in stanching genocide and trying alleged genocidaries. He also draws attention to new and broader interpretations of various terms and phrases that have come out of court cases, mainly at the International Criminal Tribunal for Rwanda and the International Criminal Tribunal for the former Yugoslavia, that have resulted in important legal precedents.

In Chapter 5, "Data Limitations as an Impediment to Genocide Intervention," Cyanne E. Loyle, Assistant Professor of Comparative Politics in the Department of Political Science at West Virginia University, and Christian Davenport, Professor of Peace Studies at the University of Notre Dame, discuss how genocide intervention is impeded by a lack of reliable data on genocide violence once the violence is underway. They argue that "evidence suggests that even under optimal political conditions (i.e., genuine political will, multilateral coalitions, and sufficient resources) intervention can be hampered by the lack of accurate and efficient information regarding events on the ground, what Kuperman (2001) calls the 'physical impediments' to intervention" (p. viii). In their chapter, Loyle and Davenport basically argue that prior to carrying out an intervention, it is imperative for the intervener(s) to obtain "a minimum threshold of data on the actors and actions at work." They view these issues through the lens of what transpired in Rwanda during the 1994 genocide. In their conclusion, they present a series of recommendations aimed at assisting policymakers and others in overcoming some of the aforementioned limitations.

In Chapter 6, "Aspects and Components of the United Nations That Constitute Impediments to the Prevention and Intervention of Genocide," Samuel Totten addresses a host of ways in which the United Nations, itself, impedes timely and effective efforts to prevent genocide (and short of that, the intervention of genocide). Among the various issues he discusses are: debates over whether a conflict is genocidal or not; the bureaucratic structure of the United Nations; the composition and operation of the Permanent Five of the UN Security Council; inadequate donations of personnel, vehicles, weapons systems, and other resources by member states for preventive and interventive missions; naivety; and overshadowing everything, *realpolitik*.

In Chapter 7, "The Impact of the Media on Genocide Intervention: A Prod, an Impediment, or Both?" Isabelle Macgregor, a PhD candidate in international relations at the Australian National University, presents an overview of the influence of the media as it relates to the prevention and intervention of genocide. Macgregor's analysis is largely restricted to Western democracies, primarily those that have engaged in interventionary missions in the last thirty years, and touches on the genocidal events in Iraq, Rwanda, Bosnia, and Darfur (with a particular focus on the extent and quality of the media coverage of each crisis, how the victim group and its attackers were portrayed, and whether or not there was a consensus among political powerbrokers regarding interventionary policy).

In Chapter 8, "The International Arms Trade and the Prevention of Genocide: The Law and Practice of Arming Genocidal Governments," Hannibal Travis, Associate Professor of Law at Florida International University, examines a critical but often overlooked issue in regard to the perpetration of genocide: the impact of the global arms trade. As he notes in his introduction, "At each stage, genocide [has been] facilitated, and efforts at resistance were often thwarted, by the traffic in arms from mercantile centers and imperial capitals to peripheral, colonial, and client states in the Americas, Africa, and Asia." Continuing, he notes that "The Cold War period aggravated these trends as aircraft, tanks, howitzers, automatic weapons, and chemical and nuclear weapons proliferated to dictatorships around the world." Any examination of the kinds and numbers of weapons used in, for example, 1994 Rwanda and Darfur (2003–present) readily shows the ongoing and extremely detrimental impact of the global arms trade vis-à-vis genocide: both enabling its implementation and impeding the prevention and intervention of such.

In Chapter 9, "Do Criminal Trials Prevent Genocide? A Critical Analysis," Maureen S. Hiebert, Assistant Professor of Political Science and Law and Society at the University of Calgary, Calgary, Alberta, Canada, examines how international criminal prosecutions of atrocity crimes can possibly impede preventive efforts. In doing so, she discusses the case for deterrence, which is followed by a discussion of the argument that trials do not lead to effective genocide prevention. Hiebert concludes with an assessment of the critical challenges that "face the role of trials in wider genocide prevention strategies and the probability of progress toward effective genocide prevention through deterrence as a result of criminal trials."

In Chapter 10, "'Paved with Good Intentions': Attempts to Design Mechanisms to Prevent Genocide in the Twenty-First Century and Why They Have Not Succeeded," Herbert Hirsch, a political scientist at Virginia Commonwealth University, analyzes the strengths, weaknesses, and relative effectiveness of several major international and national prescriptions that have been developed over the course of the last decade in an attempt to delineate the mechanisms necessary to prevent genocide. In his introduction, Hirsch notes that as readers delve into the chapter, "it will become increasingly evident that the good intentions of those devoting so much energy to devising means to prevent genocide often come to naught as they only pay lip service to the lessons learned and thus never really overcome the primary impediments and obstacles to the prevention of genocide."

Many of the chapters in this volume are less sanguine about the future of the prevention and intervention of genocide than those that have appeared in previous volumes of *Genocide: A Critical Bibliographical Series* and, for that matter, in most books about genocide. That is, of course, due, at least in part, to the focus of this volume: impediments to the prevention and intervention of genocide. It is also due to the fact that the authors have taken their task seriously and not downplayed the power and pervasiveness of the impediments. And finally, it is true, at least in certain cases, due to the fact that some of the impediments seem intractable.

As each author duly notes, the impediments are complex and not easily dealt with, and none are likely to be ameliorated anytime soon—and certainly not without first facing the reality of such impediments, truly caring about the fate of those facing atrocity crimes, and then putting immense amounts of creative thought and time into the effort. While the world has seen dents punched into state sovereignty (a classic example is the general agreement over The Responsibility to Protect), they are just that, dents and not much more. While nations can, and have, signed on to The Responsibility to Protect, it is another matter altogether for them to implement its tenets when the time calls for it (i.e., in an area where horrific crimes are being committed against a group of people by a powerful nation or a nation that is a wild card, and no one really knows how it will react to an intervention). Furthermore, and this is directly tied to the latter, until the issues of *realpolitik* and a lack of political will are dealt with in an efficacious manner, the question remains: Will any innovation really result in a sea change in which the international community readily steps up in a bold and sincere way to prevent genocide and crimes against humanity in a timely and effective way?

1

Realpolitik: The *Major* Impediment to the Prevention and Intervention of Genocide

Paul R. Bartrop and Samuel Totten

Introduction

Over the past several decades, scholars and others have weighed in as to why the international community has allowed, time and again, genocide to be perpetrated across the globe. Among some of the many reasons that have been put forth are a lack of political will, a concern about the sanctity of sovereignty, a tentativeness to become involved in another nation's "internal affairs," *realpolitik*, the lack of an effective genocide early warning system, ineptitude within the United Nations, a fear of becoming embroiled in a war that governments feel their citizens might not support, so-called "compassion" or "intervention fatigue," and so forth. Undoubtedly, it is also true that the Cold War (between the latter half of the 1940s and 1991) dramatically impacted the way states reacted or, more accurately, did not react to potential and actual cases of genocide.

While all of the above factors certainly contributed to the international community's poor record vis-à-vis the prevention and intervention of genocide, herein, we argue that the overriding reason behind the poor record is *realpolitik*.[1] Indeed, all the talk about developing a sound and effective genocide prevention program counts for little if the international community, human rights activists, and scholars do nothing in regard to confronting the steel-like bulwark that *realpolitik* has become for those leaders of the international community and individual states who wish to do next to nothing (or, hypocritically, the barest minimum in order to make it seem as though their cosmetic approaches look as if they care and that they have attempted to ameliorate a deadly situation) when it comes to the prevention and intervention of genocide. What this may well mean in the "real world" is that the prevention and intervention of genocide will, at least for the foreseeable future, remain more of a hope than a reality.

Realpolitik and Its Impact

Believed to have been coined in the early nineteenth century by the Austrian statesman Prince Klemens von Metternich following the theoretical work of German political theorist Ludwig von Rochau, and then put to its most effective use by Prussian Chancellor Otto von Bismarck, the German term *realpolitik* effectively translates to "the politics of reality." In a short essay entitled "*Realpolitik:* Foreign Policy Based on Practical Rather than Ethical or Ideological Considerations," Robert Rauchhaus (n.d.), of the University of California, Santa Barbara, notes that

> Over the last century, two academic schools of thought have incorporated key elements of *realpolitik* thinking. In the realist tradition, E. H. Carr and Hans Morgenthau expanded on the concept of balance of power, citing human nature as the source of the quest for power. In contrast, Kenneth N. Waltz and other neorealists locate the source of state behavior not in human nature, but instead in the structure of the international system. Neorealists find that the lack of world government (anarchic international order) produces a self-help system that requires states to maximize their security by balancing internally (armaments) or externally (alliances). In keeping with the tradition of *realpolitik*, most realists and neorealists call for a cautious foreign policy.... (n.p.)

The term *realpolitik* is generally employed by political scientists for the purpose of identifying the reasons behind certain state behaviors relative to other states within the international community. The term effectively refers to an attitude whereby states do *not* have friends, but interests; accordingly, states work to secure those interests in a manner that is the least threatening and costly to themselves, and from which they can derive the greatest possible advantage. Thus, *realpolitik* sees states assessing every situation in accordance with its ultimate implications for state security, rather than with idealistic concerns that might place the state at risk politically or militarily.

Put slightly differently, the classical states system sees states as neither moral nor immoral; they are *amoral*, with all means—good and bad, ethical and unethical—seen as legitimate in the pursuit of state security. Humanitarian initiatives, of "doing the right thing" in the face of evil, have until very recently not been a satisfactory reason for states breaking away from a *realpolitik* approach to international relations, particularly if as a result they might find themselves involved in physical confrontation with other states. Every state that wages war, no matter how powerful, must reckon on the possibility of defeat, a situation that, obviously, does not serve the interests of the state or those who comprise it.

Despite these considerations, the idea of creating what might be called a global anti-atrocities regime is in fact not new. Two early twentieth-century beginnings in this regard were to be found in the Hague Conventions of 1899 and 1907, and in the establishment of the League of Nations in 1919.

The Hague Conventions arose out of two international conferences called to discuss issues relating to the conduct of states at war, and built on the earlier Geneva Conventions, a work-in-progress of four international treaties (and two protocols) initiated in 1864. These Conventions established the humanitarian standards by which nations should engage in war, and in which they should behave toward the individuals caught up in it, whether as combatants or as civilians. By the time of the Hague Conventions, it was recognized that alternatives to war should be sought prior to engaging in warfare, and that these alternatives could include such devices as disarmament and international arbitration. At base was an attempt to try to diminish the evils of war by revising, where possible, the general laws and customs that had, until then, regulated the nature of violent conflict. Once agreed to, the Conventions were signed by twenty-six countries, each of which agreed to restrain their behavior by delineating a set of actions that would henceforth be classified as war crimes.

Next to nothing, however, was developed in the early part of the twentieth century by way of an enforcement mechanism for states contravening the laws proscribed by the Hague treaties. Indeed, the Hague Conventions refrained from embracing the notion of any sort of international court in order to enforce its principles, preferring to retreat behind well-established tenets relating to the absolute sovereignty of nations. However, although they failed to prevent the outbreak of war in 1914, the Hague Conventions were successful in codifying the actions that could be considered war crimes, and they retained their attraction as an ideal to which states should aspire.

The principle of state sovereignty is the key to understanding how *realpolitik* works. Sovereignty, put simply, is the governing authority within a polity that renders a state to be independent and free from external control. Sovereign control means that a state has the right and ability to construct itself as its citizens deem appropriate, without outside interference. The notion of sovereignty has been the guiding principle of international relations since the Peace of Westphalia in 1648, and among the powers of a sovereign state ever since have been those of military defense, civil order, taxation, right to make war and peace independently, enter into treaties, and the like.

Ultimately, and until fairly recently, sovereignty was understood to mean that there was sovereign equality among states; that nonintervention in domestic jurisdiction was sacrosanct; and that sovereign immunity was guaranteed. This implied that within its borders a state ruled supreme, and that whatever it did within those borders constituted "internal affairs" that could under no circumstances be violated by another state. Moreover, "internal affairs" were invoked in discussions both throughout World War I and in its aftermath, and featured in the deliberations of the League of Nations throughout the next two decades.

All that said, it is still true that both the Geneva and Hague Conventions began the building of an infrastructure for the development of the new discipline of international humanitarian law, together with a slew of other such treaties initiated from 1948 onward. Notably, one of these was the *United Nations Convention on the Prevention and Punishment of the Crime of Genocide* (referred to hereafter as the UNCG).

The League of Nations was formally established in 1919, a direct consequence of World War I and the failure of international diplomacy to maintain the peace. In its attempts at creating a new order for the world based on open diplomacy, fairness, and rule of law, the League adopted a procedure based on dialogue, conferencing, and negotiation rather than multilateral intervention in order to reduce the risk of conflict. But the League found itself a prisoner of the very features of international life it was attempting to supersede. These included *realpolitik*, the states system, the secret diplomacy, and the impunity of states acting contrary to the common international good. The major problem the League faced was that none of its member states were ever prepared to surrender any portion of their sovereignty in favor of an international ideal that had never been attempted before.

Given this, such notions as multilateral intervention for the purpose of peacemaking, peace enforcement, or peacekeeping were neither suggested nor tried. It took the failure of the League, followed by World War II and the creation of a new international organization—the United Nations—to realize the necessity of cutting through the structures that had so impeded the League's earlier ability to act.

Interestingly, immediately after World War II new principles were developed that, rather than permitting international intervention for the purpose of stopping such phenomena as massive human rights violations and genocide, took responsibility for these acts away from states and placed them squarely at the feet of individuals. An example of this is to be found in the so-called Nuremberg Principles, a set of precepts adopted by the United Nations International Law Commission in 1950. The essential implication of these principles is that every *person* (rather than every state) is responsible for their own actions and, that, as a result, *no one* stands above international law.

The Nuremberg Principles have since been incorporated into a number of multilateral treaties, most notably The Rome Statute, which established the International Criminal Court (ICC). In the UNCG, Article IV refers to the establishment of "such international penal tribunals as may have jurisdiction" for the purpose of trying cases of genocide. By the Rome Statute of July 17, 1998, this notion became enshrined as international law. It had taken half a century of constant effort for human rights law to arrive at this point. By this treaty, it was agreed that the key crimes the ICC would address would be genocide, crimes against humanity, and war crimes. Once the Rome Statute was adopted, it was agreed that the ICC would become operational after sixty of the signatory states had ratified their accession within their home legislatures, and this was achieved in April 2002.

Time, circumstances, and changing views of how states should operate have thus, in certain but in very limited respects, slowly eroded the sanctity of sovereignty. Significantly, the question has arisen as to whether or not intervention (unilaterally, by a single state, or multilaterally, by a confederation of states) should take place against a sovereign state perpetrating genocide within its own borders, and thus far the issue has not yet been fully resolved. Put another way, the traditional understanding of the concept of sovereignty is slowly being rethought, as is the actual practice of sovereignty. That is not to say that sovereignty is not still firmly in place, for it very much is; but it can be said that how the concept is being thought about is undergoing change in some states—though in some serial human rights-offending states such as China, Sudan, Syria, Burma, Iran, and North Korea, no progress of any kind has been made along this line.

In this regard, the twenty-six-member alliance system known as NATO (North Atlantic Treaty Organization), which has recently worked closely with the United Nations in a number of highly volatile situations, is instructive. NATO's central objectives have undergone a transformation since the end of the Cold War, as the breakdown of bipolar international politics has given way to renewed hopes for the creation of a lasting peaceful order in the North Atlantic region.

With this in mind, NATO waged a successful military intervention in 1999 against Serbia, for the purpose of stopping ethnic cleansing and other violations of human rights in its southern province of Kosovo. More specifically, between March 24 and June 9, 1999, a massive air campaign was conducted by NATO to counteract Serbian military actions being undertaken against the civilian population of the province of Kosovo, at which time thousands of sorties were flown in which bombs or missiles were fired. The campaign provoked intense controversy, principally because NATO's intervention in Kosovo was not supported by a United Nations Security Council (UNSC) resolution. The intervention was, in reality, an act of aggressive war by the greatest military alliance in the world against a sovereign country, the Yugoslav Federation.[2]

For NATO and its supporters, the intervention was a major moral statement that Western countries would not tolerate a repetition of what had happened in Bosnia-Herzegovina between 1992 and 1995, and that genocide, in effect, would be stopped physically by a concerted effort on the part of nations that had looked on in the past and done little or nothing. Despite this, it is important to note that NATO is not an alliance that has as its primary intention the intervention in, or stopping of, genocide. Rather, its focus is on the maintenance of a peaceful Europe. Moreover, its action, when looked at from its most legalistic perspective, was a clear breach of sovereignty—and, ironically, did not serve any of the known principles of *realpolitik*. It was not in the vital national interests of any of the NATO states to go to war with Serbia–Yugoslavia, in what was an apparent instance of war carried out primarily for moral and humanitarian purposes.

Individual states almost always determine the degree to which they will involve themselves in the affairs of other states along *realpolitik* lines. Sometimes, the rationales offered for particular decisions do not make for pleasant reading, forming, as they do, the clearest expression of practical politics. For example, neither the United States, China, nor the Soviet Union stepped in to attempt to halt the genocide being perpetrated by the Khmer Rouge in Cambodia between 1975 and 1979. At that point, China supported the Khmer Rouge "for ideological reasons and as a counterweight to Vietnam" (Beigbeder 1999, 98). The United States looked the other way, even though President Jimmy Carter was hailed as "the human rights president," as the United States had just recently extricated itself from Vietnam by virtually acknowledging that it had lost the war there. And after Vietnam intervened in Cambodia, the United States supported the Khmer Rouge as it was not about to offer any type of support to Vietnam. The Soviet Union also backed the Khmer Rouge.[3] Following the overthrow of the Pol Pot regime in 1979, the United States, with *realpolitik* driving its morally wayward policy, supported the Khmer Rouge's effort to retain its seat at the United Nations, and supported the Khmer Rouge remnant as a way of offering resistance to the Vietnamese-installed regime in Cambodia.

Two other classic examples, again involving the United States, revolve around the most important human rights eruptions of the 1990s, Bosnia and Rwanda. Here, various statements, decisions, and actions provide classic examples of the use of *realpolitik* in the formation of policy priorities. Where Bosnia was concerned, then-Secretary of State James Baker asserted early on that the United States did "not have a dog in this fight," implying that the United States had no direct interests in the Balkans, and thus had no reason to get involved (quoted in Power 2002, 267). In a similar vein, six days into the Rwandan Genocide of 1994, Republican Senate Minority Leader Robert Dole commented that "I don't think we have any interest there. . . . The Americans are out, and as far as I'm concerned, in Rwanda, that ought to be the end of it" (quoted in Power 2002, 352). Similarly, as related by Samantha Power (2002), "when James Woods of the U.S. Defense Department's African Affairs Bureau suggested that the Pentagon add Rwanda-Burundi to its list of potential trouble spots, his bosses told him, in his words, 'Look, if something happens in Rwanda-Burundi, we don't care. Take it off the list. U.S. national interest is not involved and we can't put all these silly humanitarian issues on lists . . . Just make it go away'" (342).

The United Nations' record is no better. A classic example is the UN Security Council's stance vis-à-vis the contemporary crisis in Darfur, Sudan (ongoing since 2003). Time and again, the Security Council has considered, and in many cases, issued, resolutions regarding the crisis in Darfur and, in certain cases, even applied sanctions. However, when it has come to undertaking solid actions to halt the killing and rape of the black Africans of Darfur and destruction of their abodes, various members of the Permanent Five (P5) of the Security Council (the United States, Great Britain, France, Russia, and China) have used their power of veto to stymie any real efforts to accomplish any such favorable outcomes. All it takes is a single veto from one of the P5 to defeat a resolution or vote on a sanction.

China has huge petroleum interests in Sudan and significant weapons contracts, and thus it is not about to upset its relationship with the Government of Sudan (GoS) over Darfur. Russia, likewise, has a huge armaments contract with Sudan, and it is not likely to upset those financial relationships by censoring Khartoum. As for the United States, it has wavered between taking a tough stance regarding the intransigence of the GoS to adopting a hands-off approach. The latter is ostensibly due to the fact, at least in part, that the GoS has agreed to assist the United States in its so-called "global war on terror."

The point is, in regard to the issue of the prevention and intervention of genocide, the 1990s and early 2000s have proved, for the most part, not to be all that different from earlier years where the predominance of *realpolitik* trumped that of morality.[4]

Despite the fact that the international community and individual states have been increasingly involved in interventions since the 1990s, *realpolitik* still plays a major role in regard to who, if anyone, will intervene to stop genocide (as well, of course, when, where, and why) to what form such intervention will take. Indeed, those interventions that have taken place have for the most part all been characterized by diffidence, sluggishness, a lack of logistical or manpower deployment, and weak UN mandates.

Critical Challenges

The most critical challenge is how to effectively get around *realpolitik* so that the prevention and intervention of genocide is timely and effective in every way possible, which likely means either developing the means to sidestep *realpolitik* and/or change the way in which the United Nations—and, particularly, the P5 of the Security Council—operates.

Unfortunately, nothing along those lines is likely to change any time soon, meaning that *realpolitik*, founded as it is on nationalism, state sovereignty, and notion of the inviolability of a state's internal affairs, is likely to remain as the key arbiter of how individual states act and react to the world around them for a long, long while—despite the hopes held by some people around the world for the relatively new concept of the R2P. To think otherwise, we believe, is naïve.

It is not certain that a way can be found through this action/legality/effectiveness relationship anytime soon—unless there is a significant measure of rethinking the issue at the United Nations, and an accompanying set of reforms that will cut through the centuries-old principles that regard the primacy of the state sacrosanct—*or* the fear of states to abandon the principle of *realpolitik* that has dominated state actions since the seventeenth century. If states are truly committed to the creation of a genocide-free world, then anything short of the above will be inadequate.

What Is the Likelihood of the Challenges Being Met?

While common sense should dictate that the challenges imposed by *realpolitik* during the twenty-first century should be confronted as a matter of urgency, the mystique embedded in the term "national interest" would appear to be an all-powerful inhibition to any sort of action in the immediate future. This is a terribly significant and complex issue in that *realpolitik* certainly drives what some refer to as the failure of political will, which is characteristic of the nations of the world when it comes to sticking their necks out on behalf of others facing danger, be it crimes against humanity, ethnic cleansing, or genocide.

A very pessimistic view, we know. But, and there is no intentional play on words here, that is the reality of the situation. That said, over the past few years a number of initiatives that are intended to redress the situation have been suggested by politicians and scholars. These can be seen as a way of looking for some light amidst the gloom. (Some see them as watershed events, but we, respectively, decline to view them in that light.)

In November 2007, former US Secretary of State Madeleine Albright and former US Secretary of Defense William Cohen agreed to serve as cochairs of a new "Genocide Prevention Task Force," established jointly by the United States Holocaust Memorial Museum, the American Academy of Diplomacy, and the United States Institute for Peace.

The Task Force released its report, *Preventing Genocide: A Blueprint for US Policymakers*, on December 8, 2008. The report asserted that genocide is preventable, and that making progress toward doing so begins with leadership and political will. In its thirty-four recommendations, it laid out a comprehensive approach that recommended improved early warning mechanisms, early action to prevent crises, timely diplomatic responses to emerging crises, greater preparedness to employ military options, and action to strengthen global norms and institutions. The report was roundly criticized in several quarters, chiefly on the ground that it ultimately hid behind well-trodden paths relating to ultimate sovereign inviolability—and, thereupon, the ongoing dominance of *realpolitik* in the authors' fashioning of responses to genocide. (For a rather detailed critique of the Albright–Cohen report, see Volume 4, Issue Number 2, Summer 2009, of *Genocide Studies and Prevention: An International Journal.*)

More recently, an initiative emanating from Montreal's Concordia University has attempted to break through the *realpolitik* straitjacket via the nurturing of domestic political will in Canada and the United States that could prevent future mass atrocities and encourage intervention. The "Will to Intervene" (W2I) project is a campaign developed jointly by General Roméo Dallaire, the former Force Commander of the United Nations Assistance Mission for Rwanda (UNAMIR), at the time of the Rwandan Genocide in 1994, and Dr. Frank Chalk, of Concordia's Montreal Institute for Genocide and Human Rights Studies. The W2I project's 2009 policy report, *Mobilizing the Will to Intervene: Leadership and Action to Prevent Mass Atrocities*, contains concrete policy recommendations for the governments of Canada and the United States, as well as recommendations for journalists and civic groups to assist in advancing the ultimate objective of a genocide-free world. The report also details the long-term consequences to Canadian and American security, public health, and prosperity that result from mass atrocities, which, the authors argue, should make the prevention of such atrocities a major national interest of each nation. Similar arguments have been made in the past and have gone nowhere. Time will tell whether the "Will to Intervene" actually makes a concrete impact.

The most significant proposal to attempt to cut through the *realpolitik*-sovereignty conundrum has been the initiative known as The Responsibility to Protect, or R2P. In 2000–2001, Gareth Evans, a former Australian Minister for Foreign Affairs, and Mohamed Sahnoun, an Algerian diplomat, served as cochairs of a Canadian government initiative entitled the International Commission on Intervention and State Sovereignty (ICISS). The Commission's report, *The Responsibility to Protect,* was published in December 2001. R2P is based on a set of principles stating that sovereignty is not a privilege, but a responsibility, and part and parcel of that responsibility is that each and every nation must treat its citizens fairly and justly and neither commit atrocities nor allow others to perpetrate atrocities against them. More specifically, R2P's focus embodies the proposal that all states should attempt to prevent and stop four crimes (or categories of crime): genocide, war crimes, crimes against humanity, and ethnic cleansing. Building on the report, several years later, in 2008, Evans wrote *The Responsibility to Protect: Ending Mass Atrocity Crimes Once and for All,* in which he argued that R2P constituted a new international norm and could be effective in preventing a return to the killing fields of the twentieth century.

The idea behind R2P embodies a simple—and very powerful—concept, namely, that the primary duty of any state is the protection of its own people from crimes of mass atrocity. In other words, state sovereignty implies responsibility, not a license to kill. But when a state is unwilling or unable to halt or avert such crimes, the idea runs, the broader international community then has a collective responsibility to take whatever action is necessary to stop the killing. However, R2P emphasizes that prior to doing so, preventive action should first be sought at all costs. Such action includes, for example, seeking assistance from the international community to contain potential crises, and rebuilding a nation in the aftermath of a conflict and in doing so addressing the underlying causes that led up to and sparked the conflict. R2P's primary tools are persuasion and support, not military or other coercion, always proceeding from the premise that in a twenty-first-century environment the world cannot just stand by when lives are at stake.

Among the critics of R2P, and presumably other similar proposals that fail to take into account the sway that *realpolitik* has over nation states, Michael J. Glennon (2005), a professor of international law at the Fletcher School of Law and Diplomacy, Tufts University, provides the following, and quite devastating, critique of the United Nations' ready acceptance of R2P:

> . . . Today, more than ever before, the report [of the UN appointed "High-level Panel on Threats, Challenges and Change"] repeats, "threats are interrelated and a threat to one is a threat to all." But

> that is not the way that modern states assess threats. The reason that Rwanda, Darfur, Kosovo and other human tragedies generate mainly yawns within the United Nations is not that states fail to respond to genuine threats to their own security. The reason that states often do not respond to such humanitarian catastrophes is that they do not believe that such events really *are* threats to their own security. Yet the report prattles on in this vein in the seeming belief that the power of positive thinking can overcome that reality. "There is a growing recognition," the report asserts, "that the issue is not the 'right to intervene' of any State, but the 'responsibility to protect' of every State when it comes to people suffering from avoidable catastrophe." The report here borrows, once again, from Evans's Canadian group, which had initially come up with the idea of rhetorical relabelling as the solution to international divisions over humanitarian intervention. This panel resists confronting those underlying divisions, however, let alone the historic and geopolitical reasons, that states of the South and East have opposed Western suggestions that sovereignty ought not be permitted to shield intra-state genocide. Michael Ignatieff, a member of the Canadian group, got it right. Referring to the panel's report, Ignatieff told the *Financial Times* (August 30, 2003):
>
> On intervention, the conclusion I draw is that there is no consensus in the system for any change. The great majority of states are against it, come what may. . . . I remember talking to Jeremy Greenstock [the departing British UN Ambassador] and saying "We've got to get into a situation where the UN can intervene over ethnic massacres and occasions like that." And he said, "If you think that's a starter you don't know what planet you're living on."
>
> In response to such objections, the panel declares repeatedly that a new global consensus should somehow come into being, as though creating one is just one more item to be added to some to-do list. The panel never asks *why* the current consensus is what it is, how attitudinal patterns such as these develop, or why they change. It doesn't care what interests states view as countervailing or what incentives might need to be put in place to overcome them. States are simply at fault for having "a lack of political will to react firmly against genocide"; why they lack that will is a question that the panel neither asks nor answers. What planet we're living on is beyond the scope of its inquiry. (n.p.)

In the end, then, whether or not any of these initiatives—the Albright-Cohen, the Will to Intervene, or R2P are but three examples among many—are likely to work in the future will all depend on the states of the world agreeing to break through the boundaries imposed by *realpolitik* and the international behavior it demands. While this is difficult to foresee, it is nonetheless no reason to stop trying to seek ways to stop the killing that has been such a characteristic of the past century. Before that happens, though, one and all have to face the fact that *realpolitik* continues to drive the decisions and actions of states; and if that is conveniently overlooked or not addressed, then there is little to no hope that the prevention and intervention of genocide will become a standard operating procedure of the world community.

Notes

1. Yet another reason, as Totten has pointed out, is the simple but profound fact that many governmental and intergovernmental officials simply have not cared about certain crisis situations and/or the fate of the individuals and groups caught up in such.

   A classic action of such a lack of caring occurred at the beginning of the Rwandan Genocide in April 1994, when Secretary of State Warren Christopher, a member of the Clinton administration, cavalierly dismissed the tragedy unfolding on the ground. Purportedly, "Belgian foreign minister Willie Claes recalls trying to discuss Rwanda with his American counterpart and being told, 'I have other responsibilities'" (Power 2002, 352).

   There are those who are bound to assert that both a lack of care and *realpolitik* are essentially one and the same, but it is Totten's view that the lack of care constitutes, in a very real sense, an even more heartless and base element at work.
2. A criticism of the NATO intervention stemmed from the fact that as soon as the bombing began, Yugoslav President Slobodan Milošević took the opportunity the intervention presented to engage in "ethnic cleansing" against the Kosovar Albanian population. An estimated 800,000 Kosovars were expelled from Kosovo, as NATO's air attack was unable to halt Serb actions on the ground. The criticism was thus leveled at NATO for initiating the bombing campaign in the first place, as the forced expulsion (so the argument ran) would not have occurred without it.
3. Many other such examples exist. As Alvarez (2001) notes, "Just before Indonesia invaded East Timor in 1975 and began its brutal repression of the East Timorese population, the Australian ambassador to Indonesia wrote that Australia should assume 'a pragmatic rather than a principled stand,' because 'that is what national interest and foreign policy is all about.' American diplomats were similarly directed to avoid the issue of East Timor and, just days before the invasion, [US Secretary of State] Henry Kissinger and [US President] Gerald Ford met with Indonesia's president, Suharto, and essentially gave him the go-ahead for the invasion. Approximately two hundred thousand East Timorese were killed under the Indonesian occupation" (137).
4. If it is true that *realpolitik* considerations usually determine the extent to which states will or will not intervene in genocide, it must be borne in mind that a number of possibilities *do* exist for successful intervention to stop genocide—many of which do not necessarily involve military action such as bombing or invasion. While the former are softer options, they, nonetheless, can be effective in at least showing the world that *realpolitik* can be transcended and that the sovereignty principle can be breached.

Take, for example, the prospects presented by radio jamming. Rwandan Hutu extremist radio broadcasts were instrumental in stimulating and sustaining the genocide, and recommendations that measures be taken to stop these broadcasts were made throughout the spring of 1994, especially in the United States. Three possibilities were given serious consideration by US authorities:

1. The destruction of key transmitters in Rwanda;
2. Broadcasting so-called "counter-broadcasts" in order to negate the messages from Rwandan radio stations;
3. Using powerful airwave technology to jam the extremists' radio programs.

All these initiatives, though, were rejected by the US government. It was argued that such actions constituted an infringement of Rwanda's sovereignty; arguments were also proffered that these actions were cost-prohibitive, and that interfering with Rwanda's radio networks could be considered unconstitutional under US law on the grounds that it would constitute the abrogation of First Amendment Rights (freedom of expression). Ultimately, radio jamming technology was not tried as a strategy to help stop the killing in Rwanda, in another instance of an untried policy option that could have saved lives.

When all was said and done, though, *realpolitik* was the driving force behind the United States not taking action to halt the killing. The simple but profound—and unconscionable—fact is that the United States simply did not want to get involved, and thus any and all options were considered moot as soon as they were raised.

References

Alvarez, Alex. 2001. *Governments, Citizens, and Genocide: A Comparative and Interdisciplinary Approach*. Bloomington and Indianapolis: Indiana University Press.

Beigbeder, Yves. 1999. *Judging War Criminals: The Politics of International Justice*. New York: St. Martin's Press.

Chalk, Frank, Romeo Dallaire, Kyle Mathews, Carla Barqueiro, and Simon Doyle. 2010. *Mobilizing the Will to Intervene: Leadership to Prevent Mass Atrocities*. Montreal and Kingston: McGill-Queen's University Press.

Evans, Gareth. 2008. *The Responsibility to Protect: Ending Mass Atrocity Crimes Once and for All*. Washington, DC: Brookings Institution Press.

Glennon, Michael J. 2005. "Idealism at the UN." *Policy Review* no. 129, n.p.

Maogoto, Jackson Nyamuya. 2004. *War Crimes and Realpolitik: International Justice from World War I to the 21st Century*. Boulder, CO: Lynne Rienner Publishers.

Power, Samantha. 2002. *"A Problem from Hell": America and the Age of Genocide*. New York: HarperCollins.

Rauchhaus, Robert. n.d. "Realpolitik: Foreign Policy Based on Practical Rather than Ethical or Ideological Considerations." Accessed at: www.polsci.ucsb.edu/faculty/rauchhaus/.../Rauchhaus—Realpolitik.pdf.

Wayman, Frank W. and Paul F. Diehl, eds. 1994. *Reconstructing Realpolitik*. Ann Arbor, MI: University of Michigan Press.

Annotated Bibliography

Alvarez, Alex. *Governments, Citizens, and Genocide: A Comparative and Interdisciplinary Approach*. Bloomington and Indianapolis: Indiana University Press, 2001, 224 pp.

Includes a very short but insightful passage on the way *realpolitik* played out during the Indonesian attack on East Timor in 1975 and the 1994 Rwandan genocide.

Amnesty International. *Power and Impunity: Human Rights under the New Order*. London: Amnesty International, 1994, n.p.

In part, this book focuses on Indonesia's repression and extrajudicial executions in East Timor. The authors explicitly take the international community to task for deliberately acquiescing and allowing human rights abuses to be perpetrated in East Timor and other areas under Indonesian control. Further, they assert that the Cold War, along with perceptions of Indonesia's strategic and economic significance, resulted in a Western—and particularly a United States'—policy of support for the Suharto government regardless of its human rights record. They go on to note that in the post–Cold War period more attention was paid to the human right infractions by the West, but the latter still continued to sell weapons and provide huge amounts of economic assistance to Indonesia, as well as reject refugees fleeing Indonesian repression.

Ball, Howard. *Prosecuting War Crimes and Genocide: The Twentieth-Century Experience*. Lawrence, KS: University Press of Kansas, 1999, 288 pp.

Ball, Professor of Political Science at the University of Vermont, addresses the issue of *realpolitik* vis-à-vis the following: The Dayton Peace Treaty, the Rome Convention, the Rwandan genocide, among other issues.

Barash, David P. *Introduction to Peace Studies*. Belmont, CA: Wadsworth Publishing Co., 1991, 327 pp.

A short section (207–10) in chapter 9 ("The State Level") is entitled *Realpolitik* and *Raison D'Etat*. The former comprises the following subsections: *Realpolitik* and Power, *Realpolitik* and War, *Realpolitik* and Morality, and Status Quo versus Revisionist States.

Barnett, Michael N. *Eyewitness to a Genocide: The United Nations and Rwanda*. Ithaca, NY: Cornell University Press, 2002, 215 pp.

Barnett, Professor of Political Science at the University of Wisconsin, Madison, presents a detailed, highly informative, and thought-provoking discussion about how and why the United Nations reacted the way it did to the events on the ground in Rwanda prior to and during the 1994 Rwandan Genocide. Having served as a political officer at the US Mission to the United Nations from 1993 to 1994 during which he handled issues related to Rwanda, he presents a unique and troubling perspective into the inner workings of the United Nations and its bureaucratic culture. His findings have profound ramifications vis-à-vis current and future efforts (or lack thereof) by the United Nations in the field of humanitarian diplomacy and humanitarian assistance during periods of potential and/or actual genocidal activity.

Barnett, Michael N. "The Politics of Indifference at the United Nations and Genocide in Rwanda and Burundi." In *This Time We Knew: Western Responses to Genocide in Bosnia*, edited by Thomas Cushman and Stejepan G. Mestrovic, 128–62. New York: New York University Press, 1996.

This thought-provoking essay states, in part, that the reason the United Nations did little to nothing to prevent the 1994 genocide in Rwanda was due to the fact that its member states did not care enough to act—either because they assumed their own citizens did not care about the situation and/or in the belief that the effort to stop the genocide was not worth the attempt—especially in regard to the risks faced by their military personnel. But, he further argues, that is only part of the story. The other part is that the UN's indifferent response was "shaped and filtered through the organizational culture and bureaucratic interests of the United Nations. . . . [Put another way,] from the UN's perspective, the United Nations had more to lose by taking action and being associated with another failure (e.g., along the lines of Somalia) than it did by not taking action and allowing the genocide in Rwanda to take its course. The choice was straightforward: genocide was acceptable if the alternative would harm the United Nations' future. [In other words,] the bureaucratization of peacekeeping contributed to the indifference to the suffering of the very people that it was mandated to assist" (129, 130).

Concluding his essay, Barnett perspicaciously asserts that

> *. . . an assumption of the search for early warning indicators and the proposal for a UN standing army for preventive deployment suggest that knowledge brings action. There is an unwritten belief that with knowledge the international community will act. Yet it was not the lack of knowledge that halted action in either Bosnia or Rwanda—it was politics. In both cases, states and UN officials knew of but chose to ignore the war crimes that were being committed. In both cases UN Forces were on the ground and were eyewitnesses to acts of ethnic cleansing and genocide, and in both cases the rules of engagement prevented UN forces from coming to the active aid of civilians. More technologies and capabilities are no elixir and no substitute for a politics of engagement.* (italics added)

Bass, Warren. "The Triage of Dayton." *Foreign Affairs* 77, no. 5 (1998): 95–108.

Bass, an associate editor at *Foreign Affairs* and a Wexner Fellow in history at Columbia University, argues that The Dayton Accords—not a product of Wilsonian idealism but of a reluctant *realpolitik*—actually strengthened the hands of Serbia's Milosevic and Croatia's Tudjman. He also asserts that "[s]omehow, the United States had shifted from a determination not to be dragged into the Balkans to using US officials and computers to draw Bosnia's new frontiers. . . . To be sure, Dayton was a vast improvement over the muddle and bloodshed that preceded it, but the deal the administration helped cut edged ominously close to partition, writing an epitaph for Bosnia as a multiethnic state and ceding much of its territory to Bosnian Serbs" (95, 96). Tellingly, Bass writes that "In the end, the very policies that the [Clinton] Administration balked at in May 1993—using military force and firm leadership of the Europeans—were the ones that stopped the war in the autumn of 1995. According to Warren Zimmerman, the last U.S. Ambassador to Yugoslavia, *the cost of delay was more than 100,000 lives*" (italics added) (97).

Bassiouni, M. Cherif. "From Versailles to Rwanda in Seventy-Five Years: The Need to Establish a Permanent International Criminal Court." *Harvard Human Rights Journal* 10 (1997): 11–62.

In his introduction, Bassiouni, Professor of Law and President of the International Human Rights Law Institute at DePaul University, writes, in part, that

> The history and record of international criminal investigation and adjudication bodies, from the Treaty of Versailles to the International Criminal Tribunal for Rwanda, clearly demonstrate the need to establish a permanent international criminal court. In the absence of such a court, not only have many atrocities gone unpunished, but every one of the ad hoc tribunals and investigations that has been created has suffered from the competing interests of politics or the influence of a changed geopolitical situation. As the history of the United Nations' efforts to establish a permanent international criminal court and a code of crimes evince, this task is controversial and complex. Nevertheless, the lessons of the past seventy-five years dictate its fundamental importance.
>
> . . . If the lessons of the past are to instruct the course of the future, then the creation of a permanent system of international criminal justice with a continuous institutional memory is imperative. But such a system must be independent, fair and effective, in order to avoid the pitfalls experienced in the past. Above all, it must be safeguarded from the vagaries of *realpolitik. Compromise is the art of politics, not of justice.* (italics added) (11, 12–13)

This essay comprises the following parts and sections: Introduction; I. Ad Hoc International Investigative Commissions and International Criminal Tribunals since 1919 (A. The 1919 Commission of the Responsibilities of the Authors of War and on Enforcement of Penalties; B. The Allies' Failure to Establish Prosecutions Pursuant to the Treaty of Versailles; C. The Leipzig Trials; D. The 1943 United Nations War Crimes Commission; E. The International Military Tribunal of Nuremberg; F. Control Council Law No. 10; G. The Instrument of Surrender to Italy; H. The Far Eastern Commission and the International Military Tribunal for the Far East at Tokyo; I. Politics of Defendant Selection in the Far East; J. Comparison of the Legal Bases for Setting Up the IMT, IMTFE, and CCCL 10 and Far East Allied Military Prosecution; K. The Years of Silence: 1955–1992; L. The Commission of Experts Established Pursuant to Security Council Resolution 780 (1992); M. The International Criminal Tribunal for the Former Yugoslavia; N. The Rwanda Commission of Experts; O. The International Criminal Tribunal for Rwanda [ICTR]); II. The United Nations' Efforts to Establish an International Criminal Court and to Codify Certain International Crimes; and Conclusion: The Need for a Permanent System of International Criminal Justice.

Beres, Louis Rene. "Reason and *Realpolitik*: International Law and the Prevention of Genocide." In *Toward the Understanding and Prevention of Genocide:*

Proceedings of the International Conference on the Holocaust and Genocide, edited by Israel W. Charny, 306–23. Boulder, CO: Westview Press, 1984.

Beres, Professor of Political Science at Purdue University, argues that *realpolitik* overpowers the moral imperative expressed in the norms of international law, and because of the latter what is needed is the creation of a new world-order system in which anti-genocide efforts will be perceived by states as not only in the interest of all peoples across the globe but in the interest of the states themselves. More specifically, he argues for "a new world order system—a planetary network of obligations stressing cooperative global concerns over adversarial relationships, and a move away from 'the dying forms of *Realpolitik*' " (316).

Booth, Ken. *Realism and World Politics*. New York: Routledge, 2010, 350 pp.

This book contributes to the rethinking of realism through multiple analyses of the keys works of Kenneth Waltz, arguing that a sophisticated appreciation of realism is needed to truly understand world politics and International Relations.

The book comprises the following parts and chapters: Preface 1. Realism Redux: Contexts, Concepts, Contests by *Ken Booth.* Part 1: Political Ideas in Waltzian Realism; 2. Anarchy and Violence Interdependence by *Daniel Deudney*; 3. Bringing Realism to American Liberalism: Kenneth Waltz and the Process of Cold War Adjustment by *Michael Foley*; 4. Waltz, Realism and Democracy by *Michael C. Williams.* Part 2: Challenges to Structural Realist Theory; 5. Waltz's Theory of Theory by *Ole Wæver*; 6. Structure? What Structure? by *Nicholas Onuf*; 7. "Big and Important Things in IR": Structural Realism and the Neglect of Changes in Statehood by *Georg Sørensen*; 8. Reckless States and Realism by *John Mearsheimem*. Part 3: Realist Theories and Human Nature; 9. Structural Realism, Classical Realism and Human Nature by Chris Brown; 10. Human Nature and World Politics: Rethinking "Man" by *Neta Crawford*; 11. Women, the State, and War by *Jean Bethke Elshtain*. Part 4: War and Security, Causes and Consequences; 12. Understanding Man, the State and War by *Hidemi Suganami*; 13. Lost in Transition: A Critical Analysis of Power Transition Theory by *Richard Ned Lebow and Benjamin Valentino*; 14. Hegemony, Equilibrium and Counterpower: A Synthetic Approach by *Cornelia Beyer*; 15. Nuclear Weapons in Waltz's World: More Trust May Be Better by *Nicholas J. Wheeler*. Part 5: Continuity and Change in the International and in the World; 16. How Hierarchical Can International Society Be? by *Ian Clark*; 17. Waltz and World History: The Paradox of Parsimony by *Barry Buzan and Richard Little*; 18. Human Interconnectedness by *Andrew Linklater*. Part 6: Conclusion 19. International Politics: The Inconvenient Truth by *Ken Booth.*

Brus, Marcel M. T. A. *Third Party Dispute Settlement in an Interdependent World.* Boston: MA: Martinus Nijhoff Publishers, 1995, 262 pp.

In chapter 3 ("Coping with Analytical Complexity: A Systems Approach"), Brus cogently delineates the following problem vis-à-vis the prevention and intervention of genocide:

> With regard to the prohibition of genocide . . ., which [is] recognized as [a] fundamental value of the system in international conventions and declarations—it is evident that their application and interpretation depends to a large extent on political and economic factors. Although the Genocide Convention provides for settlement of dispute by the

International Court of Justice at the request of one party, consistent application and interpretation can hardly be guaranteed by the Court as many states have made a reservation concerning the compulsory jurisdiction of the Court. In a community perspective such reservations should be regarded as against the objective and purpose of the Convention and therefore prohibited. Several states have objected against these reservations as being against the object and purpose. (92–93)

Charny, Israel W. "Toward a Generic Definition of Genocide." In *Genocide: Conceptual and Historical Dimensions*, edited by George J. Andreopoulous, 64–94. Philadelphia, PA: University of Pennsylvania Press, 1994.

A section of this essay by the noted genocide scholar and Director of the Institute on the Holocaust and Genocide (Jerusalem) is entitled "Pressures to Exclude from the Definition of Genocide Certain Events for Purposes of *Realpolitik*" (70–72).

Cushman, Thomas. "Is Genocide Preventable? Some Theoretical Considerations." *Journal of Genocide Research* 5, no. 4 (2003): 523–42.

In a section entitled "The Normalcy of Genocide Versus the Prevention of Genocide," Cushman asserts (and then goes on to discuss his assertion) that "in spite of rhetorical commitments to peace, modern governments remain committed to *realpolitik* in international relations and the modern context has allowed for new forms of expression of *realpolitik* rather than a replacement of the latter by an ethic of 'perpetual peace' or morality in foreign relations" (535).

Falk, Richard A. *Human Rights Horizons: The Pursuit of Justice in a Globalizing World*. New York: Routledge, 2000, 288 pp.

Two chapters in this book—chapters 9 ("The Unmet Challenges of Genocide in Bosnia and Rwanda") and 10 ("The Challenge of Genocidal Politics in an Era of Globalization")—by a noted international law scholar at Princeton University deal specifically with genocide.

In chapter 9, Falk asserts that intervention to prevent genocide was never a genuine option for Bosnia and then discusses what he perceives as key to meeting the challenge of genocide (including democratic empowerment, criminal accountability, and globalizing citizenship). In chapter 10, he discusses such issues as "human wrongs as a world order challenge," genocidal politics (including the issue of *realpolitik*), and economic globalization.

Glennon, Michael J. "Idealism at the UN." *Policy Review*, no. 129 (2005): n.p.

Well worth reading! This is a hard-hitting, no nonsense, and thought-provoking article by a professor of international law at the Fletcher School of Law and Diplomacy, Tufts University, that appeared in the Hoover Institute's journal *Policy Review*. Glennon provides ample and painful evidence (as if such were really needed) that many at the United Nations, ironically and disturbingly, seem to hide from the fact that *realpolitik*, not idealism, drives the nations of the world.

Haas, Michael. *Genocide by Proxy: Cambodian Pawn on a Superpower Chessboard*. Westport, CT: Praeger, 1991, 385 pp.

The issue of *realpolitik* is mentioned/discussed throughout this book: the assertion that *realpolitik* was used by various actors as basically "an argument for genocide in Cambodia" (36); Prince Sihanouk's perspective on *realpolitik*

(44); Chinese *realpolitik* (64); U.S. policymaking in relation to *realpolitik* (75–76); and an entire section of chapter 29 is entitled "The Theory and Practice of *Realpolitik*" (301–4). At the end of the book the author calls for an end to *realpolitik* (208–310).

Jensen, Kenneth M. and Elizabeth P. Faulkner, eds. *Morality and Foreign Policy: Realpolitik Revisited.* Washington, DC: USIP Press Books, 1991, 96 pp.

Focusing on post–World War II American foreign policy and its intellectual architect, George Kennan, this volume explores the moral dimensions of *realpolitik* and the ethical dilemmas posed by present-day politics. Two of the key questions the authors ask are: "Is Kennan responsible for persuading the US foreign policy establishment that morality should go by the wayside? Or was Kennan right to regard as 'presumptuous' the idea that Americans should tell other societies how to behave?"

The book comprises the following: "Morality and National Security" by David Little; "Universal Morality" by Francis Deng; "What Kennan Really Said" by Theodore Weber; "Power and Ethics in the Third World" by Richard Joseph; and "Equal Necessity" by Dayle E. Powell. The individual chapters are followed by "A Discussion of Morality and Foreign Policy" and includes an appendix "Morality and Foreign Policy" by George F. Kennan, an article that originally appeared in *Foreign Affairs.*

Kaldor, Mary. *New & Old Wars: Organized Violence in a Global Era.* Stanford, CA: Stanford University Press, 2001, 206 pp.

Kaldor, Jean Monnet, Reader of Contemporary European Studies in the Sussex European Institute at the University of Sussex, discusses the issue of *realpolitik* in regard to the high-level talks that took place among outside negotiators vis-à-vis the situation in Bosnia-Herzegovina in the 1990s.

Lake, Anthony and Roger Morris. "The Human Reality of *Realpolitik.*" *Foreign Policy* Autumn, no. 4 (1971): n.p.

In this piece, Lake and Morris address *realpolitik* in relation to the US' government's policies and actions in Vietnam. In doing so, it raises a host of critical issues vis-à-vis *realpolitik* and its impact on governmental perspectives, decisions, and actions—and in that regard, extrapolation to the issue of genocide is instructive.

Basically the authors ask, how could good men who considered themselves moral have carried out a war that was so morally questionable? Replying, they argue that *realpolitik* revolves around "interests," "influence," and "prestige," and overrides concern for those who are impacted (often in deadly ways) by policymakers' decisions and actions.

Maogoto, Jackson. *War Crimes and Realpolitik: International Justice from World War I into the 21st Century.* Boulder, CO: Lynne Rienner Publishers, 2004, 267 pp.

Commenting on the focus of this book by Maogoto, Lecturer in the School of Law at the University of Newcastle, the publisher states the following:

> From the early stages in the development of international law, the nature of the state-centric international system has dictated that law play second fiddle to the hard realities of power politics. *War Crimes and Realpolitik* explores the evolution and operation of the international criminal justice system, highlighting the influences of politics.

> Maogoto takes the reader behind the scenes of the conflict between justice and *realpolitik*. Showing how states, in furthering their political agendas, sometimes hinder the enforceability of international criminal law, he delineates the state interests that often control international legal norms and institutions and even manipulate public perceptions. Ranging from the period just after World I to the recent establishment of the International Criminal Court, he provides a thorough exposition of the politics and processes of international penal institutions in the state-driven international system. (267)

The book comprises the following chapters: "Introduction"; 1. "Toward the Modern International Penal Process"; 2. "A False Dawn: The Failure to Enforce International Justice After World War I"; 3. "A New Dawn: The Birth of the Modern International Penal Process"; 4. "Cold War: International Justice in the Shadow of *Realpolitik*"; 5. "Crisis in the Balkans: Raising the Nuremberg Precedent"; 6. "Rwanda: Portrait of a Reluctant International Community"; 7. "The International Criminal Court: Challenges and Concessions to the State"; and 8. "International Justice: Retrospect and Prospect."

Midlarsky, Manus I. *The Killing Trap: Genocide in the Twentieth Century*. New York: Cambridge University Press, 2005, 423 pp.

Midlarsky, a professor of international peace and conflict resolution at Rutgers University, addresses *realpolitik* throughout his book. In doing so, he addresses such issues as a change in *realpolitik*, the definition of the geopolitical component of *realpolitik*, *realpolitik* and ethnic cleansing, cynical *realpolitik*, imprudent-brute force *realpolitik*, and prudent *realpolitik*.

Chapter 7 is entitled "*Realpolitik* and Loss," and is divided into the following sections: The Holocaust, The Armenians, The Tutsi, and Conclusion.

Morgenthau, Hans J. and Kenneth W. Thompson. *Politics among Nations: The Struggle for Power and Peace*. New York: McGraw Hill, 1985, 688 pp.

Considered a classic in the field, this book examines the issue of political realism and its perspective of the state as a rational and unitary actor that pursues, as its main goal, a self-interest whose ultimate aim is "the pursuit of power."

Rieff, David. "The Persistence of Genocide." *Policy Review* no. 165 (February 1, 2011): n.p., http://www.hoover.org › policy review

This is a hard-hitting discussion of The Genocide Prevention Task Force's *Preventing Genocide: A Blueprint for U.S. Policy Makers* (the Albright-Cohen Report). The Task Force and the report were cochaired and coauthored, respectively, by former US Secretary of State Madeleine Albright and former US Secretary of Defense William Cohen. Rieff takes the authors to task for not acknowledging the reality of the world, *realpolitik*, and the lack of political will, and instead, focusing on genocide prevention through rose-colored glasses, that is, because it is the right thing to do, and/or it can be done if the powers that be choose to do it.

Rieff states and then argues the following:

> . . . the authors begin by stating plainly that 60 years after the United Nations adopted the Genocide Convention and twenty years after it was ratified by the U.S. Senate, "The world agrees that genocide is

> unacceptable and yet genocide and mass killings continue." To find ways to match words and "stop allowing the unacceptable," Albright and Cohen write with commendable candor, "is in fact one of the most persistent puzzles of our times." . . . [L]ike most thinking influenced by the human rights movement, the task force seems imbued with the famous Kantian *mot d'ordre*: "Ought implies can." But to put the matter bluntly, there is no historical basis to believe anything of the sort, and a great deal of evidence to suggest a diametrically opposing conclusion.
>
> Of course, history is not a straitjacket, and the authors of the report, again echoing much thinking within the human rights movement, particularly Michael Ignatieff's work in the 1990s, do make the argument that since 1945 there has been what Ignatieff calls "a revolution of global concern" and what they call a "revolution in conscience." In fairness, if in fact they are basing their optimism on this chiliastic idea, then one better understands the degree to which the members of the task force came to believe that genocide, far from being "A Problem From Hell," as Samantha Power titled her influential book on the subject, in reality is a problem if not easily solved then at least susceptible to solution—though, again, only if all the international actors, by whom the authors mean the great powers, the UN system, countries in a region where there is a risk of a genocide occurring, and what they rather uncritically call civil society, make it a priority. (n.p.)

Rudolph, Christopher. "Constructing an Atrocities Regime: The Politics of War Crimes Tribunals." *International Organization* 55, no. 2 (2001): 655–91.

In his introduction, Rudolph, Visiting Fellow at the Center for International Studies at the University of Southern California, states that:

> I seek to identify and analyze the myriad political and procedural obstacles to establishing an effective atrocities regime by examining humanitarian norms, the strategic interests of powerful states, and bureaucratic factors. I also seek to determine how the emergent regime may or may not be effective in achieving its primary goal (individual conviction) as well as its secondary and perhaps more salient goal: to manage violent conflict and reduce the likelihood of future transgressions. I argue that although liberal humanitarian ideals have created the demand for political action, the process of dealing with brutality in war has been dominated by *realpolitik*—that is, furthering the strategic interests of the most powerful states. However, by understanding the political interests and procedural obstacles involved, the international community can make institutional adjustments in the design and implementation of an atrocities regime to bridge the gap between *idealpolitik* and *realpolitik*. (656)

The article comprises the following sections and subsections: Ideas, Interests, and Institutions; The ICTY in Bosnia; Genocide in Rwanda; The ICTY in Kosovo; Justice in Southeast Asia? (Cambodia, Indonesia, and East Timor); The International Criminal Court; Evaluating the Atrocities Regime

(Formation, Application, Expanded Goals, and Institutional Adjustments); and Conclusion.

Sadkovich, James J. "The Former Yugoslavia, the End of the Nuremberg Era, and the New Barbarism." In *This Time We Knew: Western Responses to Genocide in Bosnia*, edited by Thomas Cushman and Stjepan G. Mestrovic, 282–303. New York: New York University Press, 1996.

Arguing that the international community has entered into what he deems a "new age of barbarism," Sadkovich, Professor of History at the American University in Bulgaria, asserts that "the United Nations and other international and regional organizations act to contain and manage, not end or resolve, such phenomena as aggression and genocide" (282). He further argues that the proponents of state sovereignty and *realpolitik* rule the day. More specifically, he asserts the following: "The past four years [1991–1995] may have marked the victory of the proponents of state sovereignty and the practitioners of bureaucratic barbarism and power politics over the advocates of individual and collective rights" (282). Continuing, he argues that "in short, there has been a tendency to reassert the *realpolitik* of the nineteenth century without the humanistic principle of the period. So foreign policies are now less 'hypocritical' in that the naked self-interest of states is repeatedly invoked to justify action or inaction, but elites have become morally insensitive. Governments will not intervene to stop aggression or genocide so long as doing so presents any risk of serious conflict" (294).

Schoenfeld, C. G. "Psychoanalytic Dimensions of the West's Involvement in the Third Balkan War." In *Genocide after Emotion: The Postemotional Balkan War*, edited by Stjepan G. Mestrovic, 158–83. New York: Routledge, 1996.

While the issue of *realpolitik* is discussed throughout this essay, it is worth noting that one entire section of the essay is entitled "Morality, *Realpolitik*, and Yugoslavia."

Theriault, Henry C. "The Albright-Cohen Report: From *Realpolitik* Fantasy to Realist Ethics." *Genocide Studies and Prevention: An International Journal* 4, no. 2 (2009): 201–10.

A highly critical assessment of the Albright–Cohen report, *Preventing Genocide: A Blueprint for U.S. Policy Makers*. Essentially, Theriault argues that the report "sidesteps or omits entirely the core problems the U.S. faces in preventing and intervening against genocide globally: (1) The report mistakes a subset of genocides ('failed state' genocides) for the form of all genocides; even if its recommendations can improve the response to this form, they might well not address other forms; (2) The report fails to conceive accurately the true relationship of the United States to genocide; and (3) The report fails to take seriously the active abuse of what it proposes as key methods of genocide prevention and intervention" (207).

Totten, Samuel. "The Intervention and Prevention of Genocide: Sisyphean or Doable?" *Journal of Genocide Research* 6, no. 2 (2004): 229–47.

Among the issues Totten discusses herein is the thorny issue of *realpolitik* and how nations' practice of it deters efforts to prevent genocide from being perpetrated.

Volkan, Vamik. *Blood Lines: From Ethnic Pride to Ethnic Terrorism*. Boulder, CO: Westview Press, 1997, 280 pp.

Realpolitik is mentioned twice in *Blood Lines*. First, the author discusses the origin of the term and its evolution in meaning. Second, *realpolitik* is discussed in regard to a report that claimed British government officials (under then prime minister John Major) had allegedly "refused to turn over British intelligence that allegedly showed links between Slobodan Milosevic and the 1992 'ethnic cleansers' in Bosnia" (80).

Wayman, Frank W. and Paul F. Diehl, eds. *Reconstructing Realpolitik*. Ann Arbor, MI: University of Michigan Press, 1994.

This book comprises the following parts and chapters: Part 1. Introduction: "Realism Reconsidered: The Realpolitik Framework and Its Basic Propositions" by Frank W. Wayman and Paul F. Diehl; Part 2. An Overview of Military Force and *Realpolitik*: "Cannons and Capital: The Use of Coercive Diplomacy by Major Powers in the Twentieth Century" by Brian M. Pollins; Part 3. The Initiation of Military Conflict: "Accounting for Crises in Worldly Politics: *Realpolitik* versus Internal Processes" by Patrick James and Athanasios Hristoulas; "When Do States Take on Extended Deterrent Commitments? Cases from 1885 to 1994" by Paul Huth; "International Norms and Power Politics" by Gary Goertz and Paul F. Diehl; Part 4. Dynamics of Conflict Behavior: "Influence Techniques in Militarized Crises: *Realpolitik* versus Reciprocity" by Russel J. Leng; and "Power Relationships, Democratic Constraints and War" by Bruce Bueno de Mesquita and David Lalman.

Williams, Michael C. *The Realist Tradition and the Limits of International Relations*. New York: Cambridge University Press, 2005, 254 pp.

Williams provides a reexamination of the Realist tradition and its relevance for contemporary international relations. Examining three thinkers commonly invoked as Realism's foremost proponents—Hobbes, Rousseau, and Morgenthau—Williams argues that far from advocating a crude *realpolitik*, Realism's most famous classical proponents actually stressed the need for a restrained exercise of power and a politics with ethics at its core.

This book comprises the following: "Introduction"; 1. "Sceptical States: Hobbes"; 2. "Rousseau, Realism and *Realpolitik*"; 3. "Hans Morgenthau and the Historical Construction of Realism"; 4. "The Tyranny of False Polarities"; and 5. "The Ethic of Responsibility."

2

Lack of Political Will

Kenneth J. Campbell

Introduction

No other problem has frustrated genocide scholars and the anti-genocide movement more than the chronic shortage of "political will" on the part of Western nations to stop genocide. In recent years in Bosnia, Rwanda, Kosovo, and Darfur, Western nations that had solemnly pledged "never again" to allow genocide to occur have instead permitted it, again and again. Clearly, these nations, especially the United States, possess more than sufficient power to stop genocide in its tracks. What they lacked rather was the political will to use that power. Why has this been the case and what is to be done about it? How can genocide scholars and the anti-genocide movement help create the necessary political will within governments, particularly within the US government, to employ national power to stop present and future genocides? This chapter attempts to provide some answers to these challenging questions.

The Current State of Affairs

At the time of this writing, the Government of Sudan continues to perpetrate slow-motion genocide in Darfur. Estimates of the dead as a result of the Government of Sudan's actions range as high as 400,000 people, both from direct killing and other causes (starvation, lack of medical attention to serious injuries, dehydration, etc.). Mass atrocity crimes continue unabated in the Democratic Republic of Congo, Uganda, the Nuba Mountains of Sudan, Syria, and in other countries around the world. All of this is despite the international community's verbal commitment at the 2005 World Summit to the international norm of a state's "responsibility to protect" (R2P) its own citizens from mass atrocity crimes. The rhetoric at the Summit was pious but the action following it was weak. Today, there exists a large gap between the world's promise to "never again" permit the crime of genocide and the world's actual practice in preventing genocide. Alas, there is insufficient *political will* to honor the solemn pledge codified in the 1948 United Nations' Convention on the Prevention and Punishment of the Crime of Genocide (UNCG).

The United Nations Security Council (UNSC) agreed to some watered-down economic sanctions against the Khartoum government for its grave crimes in Darfur and the International Criminal Court (ICC) indicted Sudan's president, Omar Hasan al-Bashir, for war crimes, crimes against humanity, and genocide. However, Bashir remains at large and the genocide continues, as governments and leaders who slaughter their own people are not intimidated by peaceful gestures not backed by credible force. The UNSC did authorize the deployment of a United Nations–African Union (UN–AU) hybrid peacekeeping force, but the force has been largely ineffective as its mandate is restricted, its numbers are limited, and its resources are inadequate.

The US government, for its part, formally labeled the atrocities in Darfur "genocide" and pointed its finger at the Khartoum government. The United States pushed for UN sanctions against Sudan but has not gone beyond limited, nonlethal measures. The (George W.) Bush administration made it clear that US ground troops were off the table; the United States has been distracted and drained by the twin wars in Iraq and Afghanistan. The 2008 crash of the US stock market and deep economic recession that resulted through today (mid-2012) did not help matters, either.

The international humanitarian relief and human rights communities rallied to provide emergency relief to the victims of genocide in Darfur, and to document Khartoum's campaign of atrocities, but the Government of Sudan threw some of the world's leading relief organizations out of the country following al-Bashir's indictment, charging them with aiding the ICC's prosecutorial effort. The international community of genocide scholars also contributed to the international effort by teaching, researching, and publishing on the Darfur genocide. However, their efforts were somewhat hampered by chronic definitional differences over the application of the term "genocide" to the Darfur crisis.

Within the United States a powerful and diverse Save Darfur movement was built, consisting of human rights activists, humanitarian relief groups, religious organizations, political leaders, students, scholars, journalists, Hollywood celebrities, and so on. This grassroots movement put enormous pressure on US government officials on the issue of Darfur. Also important was the emergence of a group of elite foreign policy institutions and senior members of the foreign policy "establishment"; they entered the national debate over how to stop genocide and other mass atrocities and they urged the creation of the national political will, to use force if necessary, to stop genocide. The elite organizations included the United States Holocaust Memorial Museum, the United States Institute for Peace, the American Academy of Diplomacy, the United States Army, the Rockefeller Foundation, and the Carnegie Corporation. Prominent individuals leading this effort included former US Secretary of State Madeleine Albright, former US Secretary of Defense William Cohen, and former US Ambassadors Thomas Pickering and Morton Abramowitz.

Other Great Powers continued to play "the great game" of the primacy of national interests, with Russia opposing more forceful measures against the Khartoum government because of Russia's lucrative arms trade with Sudan, and China opposing more forceful measures because of their oil interests in Sudan. Many Third World nations also opposed more forceful measures against Sudan as they jealously guarded their hard-won sovereignty against possible Western imperial encroachment cynically dressed up in "humanitarian" garb. Meanwhile, the government of Sudan successfully rallied many Arab and Muslim countries against a possible new US-led military "crusade" into yet another Arab Muslim country.

Given the many levels and forms of obstruction, national and international, it is in some ways surprising that any progress at all was made in singling out the perpetrators and mitigating the suffering of the victims of the Darfur genocide.

Critical Challenges Facing the Field

The critical challenges facing the scholarly field of genocide studies regarding political will are many and massive. They are international and national, theoretical and practical, and academic and activist. Genocide scholars will need to build better connections not only to governments, intergovernmental organizations, and international nongovernmental organizations but also to civil society groups. It is time to end the sterile debate over whether or not it is "proper" for genocide scholars to work with anti-genocide activists, as though somehow engaging in practical anti-genocide activity will somehow ruin our scholarly "purity." Government officials, journalists, civil society activists, and the general public need our knowledge to understand genocide better.

Internationally, we need to reinforce "the responsibility to protect" and extend it to include "the responsibility to enforce." The victims of genocide and other mass atrocity crimes must be protected *and* the perpetrators of these crimes must be brought to justice. International society (however embryonic its form may now be) has a first-order responsibility to enforce international criminal law. The alternative is global lawlessness and barbarity.

We also need to rebut the cynics and critics who would paralyze us with unwarranted pessimism. True, we still live in a Westphalian international system, where the national interest is primary and the "international community" is suspect. *Realpolitik* is still a powerful political force in today's world, but so too is the power of public outrage. It is just as much a fact of life as *realpolitik* that the world's publics have a basic moral sense of right and wrong, and that political leaders, especially in Western democracies, are incapable of weathering a firestorm of public outrage, once the conscience of humanity has been shocked by genocide. President Bill Clinton learned this hard lesson in the immediate wake of the July 1995 massacre in Srebrenica. This then requires that the graphic reality of genocide be communicated—in photos and videos as well as audio and the printed word—as far and wide as possible. Hence, scholars and activists must build more and better connections to the news media—broadcast, print, and web (even at the risk of becoming a "tweeter").

The international system of early warning and early response needs improvement. We must develop better indicators of genocide and mass atrocities and improved international systems of early response. Preventive diplomacy must be strengthened as well, for it is better to prevent atrocities than to react to them. However, if early warning and prevention fail, the international community must be prepared to employ the "last resort": decisive force. This means that we must develop a UN quick-reaction force to serve at the Secretary-General's discretion and to be tasked to prevent an imminent genocide or stop genocide in its earliest stage. This force, of initially 5,000 well-trained, well-supported, well-led combat troops, will not be lightly armed, will not wait for an invitation from the host nation, and will not adopt a posture of impartiality toward the perpetrators and the victims. Instead, the special UN quick-reaction force will target the perpetrators and protect the victims. The UNSC will be duty bound to reinforce this unit with combat troops drawn from the Member States of the Security Council, if necessary.

Finally, international chapters of a worldwide anti-genocide coalition will need to be built in every nation around the world to pressure national leaders from the ground up to find the political will to stop genocide. The international community of genocide scholars can assist this effort by expanding its own membership into every country in the world.

Nationally, a dialogue on making the prevention of genocide a national priority must be organized. Within this national discussion, a special focus must be placed upon the question of the "impartiality" of international intervention and why such an approach to genocide is neither moral nor effective. A strong, well-supported argument must be made that to side with the victims of crime and against its perpetrators is to be biased in favor of the rule of law and civil society. Anti-genocide chapters must be organized in every political district in the nation, so as to win the maximum number of political allies to the cause of preventing genocide—or hold the feet of political vacillators to the proverbial fire until they see the wisdom of joining the side of the angels.

The Realistic Chances for Progress

When we talk about creating the political will to stop genocide, what we are talking about, fundamentally, is changing the calculus of genocide. And that is no quick and easy task; it will take much time, energy, wisdom, and patience—even though time is never on the side of the intended victims of genocide.

Genocide is a politically calculated crime, just as preventing genocide is a politically calculated remedy. In an ideal world, the moral imperative would be sufficient to stop genocide. But we do not live in an ideal world, which means that while we may try our best, we cannot be discouraged and defeated by natural imperfection. We must operate in, and continually adjust to, the realm of the paradox, which is defined as an apparent contradiction that is nevertheless true. For genocide scholars and activists, our paradox is that we must both be idealists and realists; we must believe in the moral argument and do the practical organizing—and accept the inevitable slowness of our progress, while never being satisfied with it.

How do we define "progress"? Progress in preventing genocide is changing the calculus of genocide in our favor. Perpetrators of genocide calculate the costs versus the benefits before they begin to carry out their crime; they seek to ensure that the political benefits of perpetrating genocide exceed the costs of perpetrating genocide, measured in terms of the probability that the international community will stop them and hold them accountable for their crime. The leaders of states in the international community, on the other hand, seek to ensure that the political benefits of doing nothing to stop the genocide exceed the costs of doing nothing, measured in terms of the probability that their domestic public will punish them politically for a profound failure of moral courage. The principal challenge for scholars and activists alike is to change the calculus of genocide by raising the costs for committing genocide *and* by raising the costs for doing nothing to stop it. The strategy and tactics for doing this are outlined above. However, changing the calculus of genocide will be an uphill battle, for in many ways it will require changing the very political culture of international relations from a fundamentally "self-help" state system to an interdependent global system (with states still centrally important). The good news is that on many other dimensions—economic, technological, scientific, social, etc.—this is already well under way. The bad news is that, especially regarding the politics of force, we humans tend to be politically backward and learn only by catastrophe—two world wars, the Holocaust, the Cuban missile crisis, Vietnam—and then only with great reluctance and the occasional backsliding.

The extent, intensity, and complexity of the learning, teaching, and organizing that will be necessary to change the genocide calculus and create political will is enormous. The process will have to occur on every level of national and international society and involve all elements of those societies. It will have little chance of achieving early, big success but much chance of continued incremental progress. And the international community of genocide scholars has a vital role to play in the process.

Conclusion

We must accept that government leaders are politicians who respond to political pressure. To be disappointed by this is to be disappointed that the sun is hot or the desert dry. This is how political will is created.

Annotated Bibliography

Abramowitz, Morton and Thomas Pickering. "Making Intervention Work: Improving the UN's Ability to Act." *Foreign Affairs* 87, no. 5 (2008): 100–108.

This important article, written by two of the most senior members of the US foreign policy establishment, addresses the need to go beyond the rhetoric of humanitarian responses to genocide and other mass atrocities. Noting that "states persecuting their own people are rarely responsive to peaceful gestures" (100), the authors call for the kind of major changes in the UN system that will provide the United Nations the ability to use military force to stop mass atrocities. However, they warn that such systemic changes will require non-governmental organizations (NGOs) and humanitarian groups to build the kind of political pressure capable of overcoming skepticism among Western publics about military intervention in distant, ambiguous conflicts, as well as the reluctance of government leaders, who "see little political benefit and high political costs in taking on large, long-term overseas projects fraught with uncertainty and danger" (102–3). Abramowitz and Pickering propose the reconsideration—it was first considered in 1945—of a small (initially 5,000 troops) autonomous UN rapid-deployment force to respond with "early and robust" force to genocide and other mass slaughters. By publishing this article, the authors hoped to trigger a serious debate within the American foreign policy community about creating effective international measures to prevent genocide.

Albright, Madeleine K. and William S. Cohen. *Preventing Genocide: A Blueprint for U.S. Policymakers.* Washington, DC: United States Holocaust Memorial Museum, American Academy of Diplomacy, and the Endowment of the United States Institute of Peace, 2008, 147 pp.

This is a report from the Genocide Prevention Task Force, established by three prestigious groups named above. The authors of the report were the Task Force's two cochairs: former US Secretary of State Madeleine K. Albright and former US Secretary of Defense William S. Cohen. The bipartisan Task Force members were former US Senator John Danforth, US Senator Tom Daschle, former US Ambassador Stuart Eizenstat, senior journalist and former presidential speech-writer Michael Gerson, former US Secretary of Agriculture Dan Glickman, former US Secretary of Housing and Urban Development Jack Kemp, former judge for the International Tribunal for the Former Yugoslavia Gabrielle Kirk McDonald, former US Ambassador Thomas Pickering, former director of USAID's Office of US Foreign Disaster Assistance Julia Taft, chairman of the National Endowment for Democracy Vin Weber, and retired US Marine Corps General Anthony Zinni. The report is dedicated to "the millions of innocent children, women, and men who have suffered and died from mass atrocities and genocide" (v). In the Foreword, the authors acknowledge that the United States could have and should have done more in the past to stop genocide and that unchecked genocide in fact threatens both American values and national interests. They further state that "(p)reventing genocide and mass atrocities is a purpose that transcends partisan lines and demands public support at all levels of society" (iv). They write that the report's fundamental goal is to "identify practical steps to enhance the capacity of the U.S. government to prevent and respond to genocide" (x). Their recommendations include the US president making the prevention of genocide and mass atrocities a national priority, assigning significant resources to the problem and developing a comprehensive policy approach that includes early warning, early prevention, preventive diplomacy, employing military options, and strengthening international norms and institutions. Regarding the *political will* to do this, the cochairs write: "Summoning political will requires leadership, not only after a crisis strikes, but also before one emerges. It means taking on inertia within the government, investing political capital, doing the heavy lifting of persuasion. Political will involves fending off critics and cynics. It means bucking the tides of caution. It means risking failure" (xxi).

Conley-Zilkic, Bridget and Samuel Totten. "Easier Said Than Done: The Challenges of Preventing and Responding to Genocide." In *Century of Genocide: Critical Essays and Eyewitness Accounts*, 3rd ed., edited by Samuel Totten and William S. Parsons, 609–36. New York: Routledge, 2009.

In this well-written essay, the authors identify several factors that contribute to a pattern of international indifference regarding the obligation to prevent genocide and other mass atrocities, including "an international system geared towards protecting national sovereignty, *realpolitik*, and lack of concern about abuses" (616). Regarding ways to increase political will, the authors write: "In addition to institutional and inter-institutional changes, there needs to be an informed and concerned public constituency who makes their voices heard" (617).

Daly, M. W. *Darfur's Sorrow: A History of Destruction and Genocide.* Cambridge: Cambridge University Press, 2007, 388 pp.

Daly is a distinguished Sudan scholar who has written a rich and fascinating book on the historical origins of the genocide in Darfur. He describes in great detail, through eleven chapters, the complex political, economic, and social development of Sudan, in general, and the Darfur region, in particular. He reviews the pre-Muslim period, the era of Sulayman, the Turco-Egyptian period, the Mahdist era, the Anglo-Egyptian period, and the legacies of colonialism and Cold War competition, including the internal power struggles following independence in 1956. In chapter 12, Daly details the recent destruction of the western region of Darfur by the Sudanese Army and their irregular allies, the *Janjawid.* He bemoans the amount of time and attention wasted over the past few years—to the advantage of the Khartoum government, he notes—in what he describes as "the dubious task of defining the unfolding carnage. Was it race war, ethnic cleansing, or genocide?" (285) He estimates that 350,000–400,000 people have been killed in and around Darfur in raids by the *Janjawid*–Sudanese Army alliance, and that an ineffective joint United Nations–African Union peacekeeping operation has allowed the worst humanitarian disaster in the world to continue unabated. In Daly's words: "As the world dithers and looks away, Darfur is again on the brink of the abyss of what Colin Powell in 2004 famously called 'genocide'" (1).

Davis, Rachel, Benjamin Majekodunmi, and Judy Smith-Hohn. *Prevention of Genocide and Mass Atrocities and the Responsibility to Protect: Challenges for the UN and the International Community in the 21st Century.* New York: International Peace Institute, 2008, 19 pp.

This report is based on a follow-up roundtable to the 2005 World Summit, where the concept of a "responsibility to protect" (R2P) populations from genocide and mass atrocities was allegedly "affirmed" by all member states of the United Nations. The Stellenbosch (South Africa) Policy Roundtable, convened in December 2007, aimed to address the large gap that had emerged between the World Summit rhetoric regarding the responsibility to protect and real action by the international community between 2005 and late 2007. The roundtable's thirty-member list of participants included Francis M. Deng, Special Adviser to UN Secretary-General for the Prevention of Genocide, and Edward C. Luck, Special Adviser to the UN Secretary-General. As the *rapporteurs* wrote regarding R2P: "(T)his significant development has not been matched by comparable progress in enhancing international machinery or national will to insure that the failures to protect in recent decades will not be repeated" (1). Though the acceptance of R2P was allegedly "universal," each state seemed to interpret the concept to its own advantage. Many smaller nation-states in the global South objected to any interpretation that might allow international military intervention to trump their national sovereignty. Apparently, they feared that the strong states of the world would cynically use the cover of "humanitarian intervention" against the weak states of the world for their own "ulterior motives" (e.g., the 2003 US invasion and occupation of Iraq). On the other hand, the authors pointed out that "Member States have been unwilling to commit to long-term protection efforts or to support early intervention into what are perceived as other states' internal affairs unless their own security is directly threatened (for example, through conflict spillover, outflows of refugees, or restricted access to key resources)" (7–8). Regarding the slow-motion genocide that continued to be perpetrated in Darfur, the authors wrote: "Even in advanced R2P situations, where genocide, crimes against humanity, war crimes, or ethnic cleansing may already be occurring, legal definitions are no guarantee of action. For instance, while the US announcement in September 2004 that the situation in Darfur constituted genocide may be considered a breakthrough after its reluctance to acknowledge the reality of the situation in Rwanda in 1994, this pronouncement did not produce any obvious change in US policy on the ground. International legal instruments and declarations provide an essential framework for genocide prevention and R2P, but they rely on political will for their implementation on the ground" (6). To close the gap between rhetoric and reality regarding R2P, the authors propose the following:

- refining a set of genocide/mass atrocity indicators;
- strengthening the UN's early warning system;
- improving the UN's assessment and evaluation capacity;
- reinforcing partnerships between the United Nations, states, and civil-society groups; and
- continuing to explore best practices among states, regional organizations, and civil-society groups.

Evans, Gareth. *The Responsibility to Protect: Ending Mass Atrocity Crimes Once and for All.* Washington, DC: Brookings Institution Press, 2008, 349 pp.

This book by one of the cochairs of the International Commission on Intervention and State Sovereignty (ICISS) is an elaboration and update of the ICISS's concept of the responsibility to protect (R2P). Over ten chapters,

Evans describes the problem of genocide and mass atrocities; explains the solution of moving from the right to intervene to the responsibility to protect; delineates the scope and limits of R2P; explores the tasks before, during, and after the crisis, including responding with military intervention; details the institutional preparedness necessary for each of the participating actors; explains how to build diplomatic, civilian, and military capability; and proposes how to mobilize the political will necessary to make all of this work. In chapter 10, "Mobilizing Political Will," Evans writes: "Without the exercise of political will, by the relevant policymakers at the relevant time, almost none of the things for which this book has argued will actually happen" (223). Pointing out to the reader that he has been both a civil society activist and a high government official for many years, Evans goes on to write: "To explain a failure as the result of lack of political will is simply to restate the problem, not provide an explanation or any kind of strategy for change. The need to generate the necessary will to do anything hard, or expensive, or politically sensitive, or seen for better or worse as not directly relevant to the national interest, is just a fact of public policy life. Political will is capable of creation and subject to change: its presence or absence is not a given. It is not a missing ingredient, waiting in each case to be found if we only had the key to the right cupboard or lifted the right stone. It has to be painfully and laboriously constructed, case by case, context by context. And all of us have a role in this respect. It is a matter of key officials in key governments, and those who can influence them directly, making the effort to persuade and mobilize their peers in the international community to take the necessary action in the UN Security Council and everywhere else that matters. It is also a matter of bottom-up mobilization: making the voices of ordinary concerned citizens heard in the corridors of power, using all the resources and physical and moral energy of civil society organizations all around the world to force the attention of policymakers on what needs to be done, by whom, and when" (224). Evans then lists the five key elements necessary to create political will: knowledge of the problem, concern to do something about it, confidence in the ability to make a difference, institutional processes capable of implementing action, and good moral and political leadership. This last element is in many ways the most important, Evans explains. "All the knowledge, concern, confidence, and process in the world will not count for much if there is inertia, indecisiveness, or hostility at the top" (239).

Feil, Scott, R. *Preventing Genocide: How the Early Use of Force Might Have Succeeded in Rwanda.* Washington, DC: Carnegie Commission on Preventing Deadly Conflict, 1998, 62 pp.

This report, written by a US Army officer, was produced by a conference jointly sponsored by the Institute for the Study of Diplomacy at Georgetown University, the Carnegie Commission on Preventing Deadly Conflict, and the US Army. The goal of the conference was to consider whether or not international military intervention could have stopped the 1994 Rwandan genocide at an earlier stage, thus saving perhaps hundreds of thousands of lives. The conclusion the conference arrived at was "yes," but that the United States and other UNSC members lacked the political will to intervene with such a robust military operation. As the author writes: "For this operation, conference panelists observed, the participation of the United States would be crucial. But the United States and other members of the UN Security Council were hesitant to become engaged again in Africa as they were still trying to absorb the lessons of the recent UN action in Somalia. There, casualties, a change in operations, and political pressure prompted U.S. withdrawal. Second, in 1993 and 1994 the UN, regional organizations, and major powers were trying to devise a solution to the ongoing violence in the former Yugoslavia. The strategic situation (some called it fatigue, caution, or fear of 'stretch') militated against the formation of political will to do anything in Rwanda in the spring of 1994" (22).

Fein, Helen. *Human Rights and Wrongs: Slavery, Terror, Genocide*. Boulder, CO: Paradigm, 2007, 279 pp.

In her most recent book, Helen Fein addresses the lack of political will to stop genocide. Regarding the 1994 genocide in Rwanda, she writes: "The questions repeatedly raised since then involve the ability and lack of will of the international community to anticipate and stop the genocide" (144). Of the ongoing genocide in Darfur, she wrote: "The failure of the international community to press the GoS (Government of Sudan) has been attributed to political and ideological divisions within the UNSC (UN Security Council) and fears of the United States and the European Union of sending in North American and European troops. Russia and China depend on the GoS for oil and oppose sanctions against other governments for repressing their minorities, fearing the use of sanctions against them (such as happened in Chechnya)" (150).

Cheadle, Don and John Prendergast. *Not on Our Watch: The Mission to End Genocide in Darfur and Beyond*. New York: Hyperion, 2007, 252 pp.

This is a "how to" book on organizing for the prevention of genocide, cowritten by a former US State Department official-turned-activist and a Hollywood celebrity-turned-activist. It attempts to encourage the reader to become an activist and direct that action toward building capacity and will to stop genocide. In the Foreword, Elie Wiesel writes: "I refuse to remain silent while leaders of the world make excuses for failing to protect the people of Darfur . . . Not to help, not to urge our elected officials to intervene and save innocent lives in any manner possible and needed is to condemn us on grounds of immorality. Our failure to speak out to end the ongoing genocide in Darfur would place us on the wrong side of history" (x–xi). The introduction is written by US Senators (now President) Barack Obama and Sam Brownback. They ask: "So what does it take to stop genocide? What does it take to make the world listen and respond? It takes a number of important tools, including diplomacy, financial resources, and effective security forces. And in a world where these resources are finite, it often takes pressure—pressure from ordinary individuals standing together for an extraordinary cause—to mobilize these resources. In short, it takes you." (xiii) The authors then present nine chapters in which they lay out the situation in Darfur, identify the obstacles to stopping the genocide, and offer concrete tactics for organizing pressure on elected officials to change policy, including examples of successful actions in the past. The authors ask: "Will the United States lead efforts to protect people when they are being systematically annihilated by predatory governments or militias? Will we punish the perpetrators of crimes against humanity? Will we promote peace processes with high-level envoys and other support? None of these options is beyond the realm of the possible; they are simply matters of political will" (9).

Human Security Centre. *Human Security Report 2005: War and Peace in the 21st Century.* Vancouver, BC: Human Security Centre, 2005, 158 pp.

This report, based on the best available empirical data from around the world, is the most comprehensive—indeed the only comprehensive—analysis of international conflicts such as wars, genocides, terrorism, and violent human rights abuses. Funded by the governments of Canada, the United Kingdom, Sweden, Switzerland, as well as the Rockefeller Foundation, its conclusions are somewhat counterintuitive: armed conflicts are down 40 percent since the 1990s, refugee flows from conflicts declined by 45 percent between 1992 and 2003, and genocides and politicides declined 80 percent between 1988 and 2001. (Of course, these figures include neither the US war in Iraq or the genocide in Darfur.) Regarding genocide and other mass atrocities, the report states: "(D)espite Rwanda, Srebrenica and a host of lesser massacres, the 1990s saw a steep worldwide decline in the number of mass killings of civilians" (40). For those waging the uphill battle to create the political will to stop genocide, these figures should give some encouragement as the historical trends seem not to be working against them. (To read one of the Human Security Centre's most recent reports, see *Modern Warfare: Armed Groups, Private Militaries, Humanitarian Organizations, and the Law* by Benjamin Perrin. It constitutes a timely examination of how modern armed conflicts have outpaced the laws designed to govern them, July 11, 2012.)

Gow, James. *Triumph of the Lack of Will: International Diplomacy and the Yugoslav War.* New York: Columbia University Press, 1997, 343 pp.

The author, a scholar of war studies at Kings College, London, argues that Western weakness enabled Serb "ethnic cleansing" to run rampant in Bosnia, thus forfeiting the opportunity to end the slaughter much earlier and saving hundreds of thousands of innocent lives. Regarding this absence of international political will, he writes: "In the final analysis, the critical factor in the failure of the Western countries to intervene was the refusal of the U.S. to put ground troops into the ring" (307).

Krain, Matthew. "International Intervention and the Severity of Genocides and Politicides." *International Studies Quarterly* 49, no. 3 (2005): 363–87.

In this article, the author takes on the question of what will be most effective in stopping genocide and other mass atrocities. Addressing the general concern over the repeated failure of the international community to produce the political will to stop genocide and other mass atrocities, he tests a half dozen theories regarding the potential effectiveness of overt military intervention in slowing or stopping mass slaughter. These theories are (1) "Bystander," or no intervention; (2) "Impartial," or classic peacekeeping; (3) "Witness," or symbolic presence; (4) "Balance-of-power," or aiding the perpetrator; (5) "Threat-based," or making the slaughter worse; and (6) "Direct challenge," or opposing the perpetrator or protecting the victims. Applying these theories to cases of genocide or "politicide" between 1955 and 1997, he concludes that only using military force to directly challenge the perpetrator or protect the intended victims held any real hope of mitigating or stopping the genocide or politicide. More specifically, Krain writes: "The results suggest that the most effective way for the international community to intervene militarily to reduce the severity of an ongoing genocide or politicide is to directly challenge the perpetrator or to aid the target of the brutal policy. Perhaps equally important, this study confirms that attempts by external actors to intervene as impartial parties seem to be ineffective. . . . While impartial interveners such as the UN can and should remain integral to military-led humanitarian interventions, their emphasis on impartiality may be best suited to rebuilding and reconciliation efforts after the genocide or politicide has been ended" (383).

Kristof, Nicholas. "What to Do about Darfur?" *The New York Review of Book* 56, no. 11 (2009): 32–34.

Kristof, a long-time advocate of suppressing genocide in Darfur, describes the Darfur issue as a complex and confusing problem with disagreements among scholars and bickering between activists within the Save Darfur movement. He concedes that much has been done by the international community of states, NGOs, and the "Movement" to mitigate the suffering in Darfur and draw attention to the atrocities, but that progress has stalled over the past couple of years as the rate of killing slowed and the Movement fizzled somewhat. He contends that the missing key ingredient in the effort to stop genocide in Darfur and elsewhere in the world is the political will among the most powerful states to halt these great crimes. He writes: "The lessons from places like Kosovo is that the most urgent need is less for sophisticated technical solutions than for political will to face the problem squarely" (34).

Organization of African Unity (OAU). "International Panel of Eminent Personalities (IDEP): Report on the 1994 Genocide in Rwanda and Surrounding Events (Selected Sections)." *International Legal Materials* 40 (2001): 140–235.

> In the abstract of this report, it is stated that The Organization of African Unity (OAU) formed the International Panel of Eminent Personalities [Panel] to investigate the Rwandan genocide and to contribute to the prevention of further conflicts in the region. The Panel endorsed the finding of the earlier Carlsson Inquiry report that "the U.N.'s Rwandan failure was systemic and due to a lack of political will." (140)
>
> The Panel found clear evidence that "a small number of major actors," including Belgium, France, and the United States, could have directly "prevented, halted, or reduced the slaughter." (140)

Power, Samantha. *"A Problem from Hell": America and the Age of Genocide.* New York: Harper Perennial, 2007, 620 pp.

Power's book in many ways is the best overview of the pattern of genocide and inadequate international response. On the failure of international political leadership, particularly American leadership, she wrote: "The real reason the United States did not do what it could and should have done to stop genocide was not a lack of knowledge or influence but a lack of will. Simply put, American leaders did not act because they did not want to. They believed that genocide was wrong, but they were not prepared to invest the military, financial, diplomatic, or domestic political capital needed to stop it" (508). On the political calculus of stopping genocide, Power wrote, "(O)fficials at all levels of government calculated that the political costs of getting involved in stopping genocide far exceeded the costs of remaining uninvolved" (509). Regarding the location of the failure of political will, she wrote, "The battle to stop genocide has . . . been repeatedly lost in the realm of domestic politics." (509) Finally, on the relationship between leaders and the public opinion when considering the chief responsibility for a lack of political will, domestically, Samantha Power wrote: "(T)he inertia of the governed cannot be disentangled from the indifference of the government. American leaders have both a circular and a deliberate relationship to public opinion. It is circular because their constituencies are rarely if ever aroused by foreign crises, even genocidal ones, in the absence of political leadership, and yet at the same time U.S. officials continually cite the absence of public support as grounds for inaction" (509).

Semelin, Jacques. *Purify and Destroy: The Political Uses of Massacre and Genocide.* New York: Columbia University Press, 2007, 443 pp.

This French scholar of genocide and mass atrocities addresses the lack of international political will to stop these crimes in the following way: "At this point an important question arises: what can be done by what is labeled the 'international community'? On what terms and with what means could it intervene in the crisis? Even though everyone agrees to use the term, it is a strange one: it is actually a wonderful example of an oxymoron. That which is international is in fact anything but a 'community,' such is the degree to which the interests of several nations can be contradictory. When we speak about the 'international community' it evokes above all the role of the great powers, that, precisely because they are powerful, can impose their law on smaller nations, or join forces against a nation posing a threat to make it see reason through pressure or force as required by armed might. Over and above this point of vocabulary, the question is absolutely crucial to the outcome of the crisis: could the said international community in some way put the brakes on, stifle, or contain the process of violence that is gaining ground? Once again, this would require on the part of the international community a clear perception of the issues and, using this analysis as a starting point, a strong will to do something about it. But in the crises examined in these pages it is singularly passive. How can we qualify this almost generalized passivity: indifference, ignorance, hypocrisy, cowardice? All these words fit—despite the moral connotations that apply to some of them—since we can observe for each crisis a more or less complex combination of these diverse attitudes" (126). To help move forward the effort to prevent genocide, Semelin proposes that the international community pursue the "responsibility to protect" (R2P) and that genocide scholars advise political decision-makers and engage in militant political activity. On advising political leaders, Semelin writes, "The decision-makers in question must, of course, have a will to do something, and whether they have this will, as I have insisted in these pages, may be quite another matter" (373).

Straus, Scott. "Rwanda and Darfur: A Comparative Analysis." *Genocide Studies and Prevention: An International Journal* 1, no. 1 (2006): 41–56.

This is a comparative study of genocide and international response using the African cases of Rwanda and Darfur. Regarding political will, the author argues that neither US nor UN officials wanted to deploy troops to stop the Rwanda genocide for fear the humanitarian intervention might turn into another disaster such as had occurred in Somalia six months earlier. There was also not much of a domestic coalition to put political pressure on US political leaders regarding intervention in Rwanda. On the other hand, Straus contends that the lack of political will to stop genocide in Darfur—despite the creation of, and action by, a powerful and diverse political coalition—can best be explained by the failure to gain international support for robust intervention. For Straus, "Darfur shows that domestic pressure may be necessary, but it is not sufficient" (52). Both Russia and China blocked any firm action against the Khartoum government and the West did not go around the UN Security Council, as it had done in the case of Kosovo in 1999 because, compared to Kosovo, Darfur was less important to the West, economically and strategically. The author's remedy then is to go beyond domestic political pressure and to begin building an international civic coalition capable of pressurizing the international community to stop genocide.

Weiss, Thomas G. "Halting Genocide: Rhetoric versus Reality." *Genocide Studies and Prevention: An International Journal* 2, no. 1 (2007): 7–30.

In this article, the author, the leading scholar on the politics of humanitarian intervention, compares the rhetoric of the commitment to protect the innocent from genocide and mass atrocities, particularly the "responsibility to protect," with the actual practice of the international community regarding real genocidal threats to defenseless populations, such as in Darfur. His pessimistic analysis employs words such as "charade" and "collective spinelessness." While he notes that there has been increased international support for the concept of the "responsibility to protect," he argues that such progress has not been matched by actual practice of stopping genocide in places such as Darfur. He points to an absence of political will as the major obstacle to implementing the R2P commitment.

Wyman, David S. *The Abandonment of the Jews: America and the Holocaust, 1941–1945*. New York: New Press, 1998, 458 pp.

This is a well-documented, carefully argued indictment of America's lack of political will to save the Jews of Europe from destruction during the Holocaust. Strategic tunnel vision (putting winning the war above all other considerations), placating an ally (the British insisted on restricting the number of Jews emigrating to Palestine), and plain old anti-Semitism combined to produce a pusillanimous policy of American indifference toward the plight of the European Jews. As Wyman explained: "It was not a lack of workable plans that stood in the way of saving many thousands more European Jews. Nor was it insufficient shipping, the threat of infiltration by subversive agents, or the possibility that rescue projects would hamper the war effort. The real obstacle was the absence of a strong desire to rescue Jews" (339).

3

Denial of Ongoing Atrocities as a Rationale for Not Attempting to Prevent or Intervene

Henry C. Theriault

Introductory Clarifications

This chapter focuses on the ways in which denial is an obstacle to intervention against and prevention of genocide. "Denial" is a verbal strategy consisting of assertions that events that constitute genocide are not happening or did not happen or that the events in question are or were something other than genocide. "Intervention" is action taken to stop or mitigate a genocide once it has started, while "prevention" efforts attempt to alter conditions so that events, which may be leading to genocide, are halted prior to actually becoming a genocide. Of course, claims about prevention are speculative, because it is impossible to prove that genocide definitely would have occurred in the absence of prevention efforts. Given this, "prevention" will not be employed as an absolute term herein but will be used to indicate actions that are likely to decrease the probability of genocide occurring.

In recent years, "intervention" has come to be understood as military action. But, military intervention is just one option and not necessarily the best (see Alvarez 2011). This chapter's treatment of intervention should not be mistaken to apply only to or to be a call for or endorsement of military intervention. Diplomatic pressure, withdrawal of political support, education of a perpetrator group, meaningful economic divestment, and many other options that promise much exist. As discussed below, perhaps most effective—more effective than military intervention—is the *withdrawal* of military support from those committing genocide.

From Stage to Constant Feature

There is a prevalent view among scholars of genocide that denial is the final stage of genocide (Stanton 1998). According to this view, after the killing and related destruction of the execution phase of a genocide, the perpetrators seek to escape accountability by covering up what they did. Denial also functions to destroy further the victim group, by wiping out even the memory that they existed as they did before genocide: if there was no genocide, then the people who were killed in fact were not killed and their present nonexistence means they did not exist in the first place, that is, they never existed; the victims' culture, social structures, economic wealth, political relevance, and so on that were destroyed were in fact not destroyed and their present nonexistence means that they in fact never existed; and so on. Denial transforms a partial success into a more total genocide, by denying the link of dispersed survivors, their culture, and social structures to the place where their group experienced genocide.

This analysis of the effects of denial is correct, but this does not entail that denial is exclusively a particular (the final) stage of genocide. Denial is a feature of at least three stages of genocide: execution, immediate aftermath, and long-term legacy. Presumably what holders of the mainstream view recognize is that denial characterizes the final stage of a genocide. But considering denial the essence of this stage not only prevents deeper analysis of the long-term aftermath of genocide but also obscures the important roles of denial in earlier stages of genocide. Attention to both these elements promises new avenues for prevention and intervention.

The view that different stages of genocide have denialist elements should not be confused with a charting of temporal developments and shifts in denial of a particular genocide as a phenomenon in itself. Some scholars have produced incisive accounts of long-term denial campaigns, recognizing external and internal academic, economic, political, geopolitical, and other forces that shape variations in denial over time (see, e.g., Yoshida 2000). While these accounts are invaluable to an understanding of denial, they generally focus on denial in the long-term aftermath of a genocide, and so do not capture fully the function of denial in different genocide stages.

Richard Hovannisian (1986) provides one of the few treatments of denial through the various stages of a genocide, in particular the execution phase, the short-term aftermath, and different points in the long-term aftermath of the Armenian Genocide. While not concerned explicitly with prevention or intervention, Hovannisian's approach provides a highly useful template for consideration of the role of denial in different stages of a genocide and its impact on intervention and prevention of the Armenian Genocide and other genocides.

Denial against Prosecution

Denial is clearly a feature of the short-term aftermath of genocide. It usually is meant to help perpetrators (Hovannisian 1986, 115–19; Stanton 1998) and bystanders[1] escape accountability for actions or nonaction, respectively. Denials can be total, asserting that what happened was not genocide, as Ratko Mladic has claimed since his recent arrest (Associated Press 2011; Channel 4 News 2011). Misconstruing events as civil war, unfortunate nonsystematic violence, or even self-defense can be particularly useful to major perpetrators who were not direct killers. Denial can also be partial, not questioning the general facts of a genocide but claiming that a specific person was not involved. For instance, Khieu Samphan, a former Khmer Rouge leader, has not denied the massive death toll during the Khmer Rouge regime, but answers the recent UN-tribunal indictment by claiming that he was not involved in the killing (BBC News 2009). Another example is Karl Blessing, who covered up his complicity in the Holocaust and membership in the Nazi party, and eventually presented himself, and was regarded, "as virtually an anti-Nazi Resistance hero," as he became one of the most important corporate leaders in Germany and the world by the 1960s (Simpson 1993, 225–27).

Prosecution of perpetrators is a crucial deterrent for would-be perpetrators and can be used as a threat against current perpetrators to push them to cease genocidal actions. At the same time, denial is not a key factor here. First, in the present age, there have been frequent enough prosecutions that past successful escapes do not necessarily outbalance them. Second, denial is usually less effective in legal than in political, scholarly, and journalistic contexts. In legal contexts, a decision is usually eventually made, based on evidence. It is expected that perpetrators will lie about what happened and/or their involvement, and unlike what is typical in academia, journalism, and politics, denials are treated skeptically and subjected to careful application of evidence standards. When perpetrators are not put on trial, the reason is usually not the success of denial, but geopolitical, economic, military, and other forces and factors that prevent the proper legal process. It is often precisely because denial will not succeed in a court that legal processes are prevented from occurring or truncated.

What is more, especially in recent years but also in Nuremberg and before, the charge of genocide is not essential to prosecution for genocidal acts. As some have argued recently, being charged with crimes against humanity or some other variant can be just as effective (Schabas 2009). That does not make such a reduced charge or this general approach ethically correct—far from it—but it does undermine the effectiveness of genocide denial as a protection for perpetrators.

Contemporaneous Denial

Denial happens not just after genocide, but *during*. It is a key perpetrator and bystander strategy with effects unnoticed when denial after genocide is the focus. Contemporaneous denial is a serious obstacle to intervention in a number of ways, as the following case studies show.

Contemporaneous denial occurs primarily to stop intervention or other interference. In the case of the Armenian Genocide, Ambassador Morgenthau relates discussions with Young Turk leaders, especially Talaat and Enver, about the many acts of genocide being reported to him by US consuls and others. These leaders routinely blamed Armenians for instigating violence and employed other denial arguments (see Morgenthau 2000, 211, 217–24, 227–31, 236, 239, 249). While the possibilities of direct US intervention were limited, the broader issue for Talaat was preventing public outrage in the United States, outrage that he was concerned would cause entry into the war, which would have had the potential to stop the Armenian Genocide and turn the balance of power decisively against Germany and Turkey. While it is impossible to determine the effectiveness of Talaat's denial, it is clear that at least some in the US government took the same approach, downplaying the violence to avoid public concern that might push the United States into the war (Payaslian 2003, 69).

Indonesia presented as a civil war the one-sided genocidal violence it orchestrated and perpetrated, starting in 1975, in order to annex East Timor (Dunn 2009, 281–82). What is more, those *outside* of Indonesia participated decisively in denial (Dunn 2009, 276). For instance, then-US

Ambassador to the United Nations Daniel Patrick Moynihan later admitted running interference very successfully to prevent UN action against the invasion of East Timor (Jardine 1996, 10–12). British government documents show that it engaged in a parallel denial effort, which included blaming the deaths of five British, Australian, and New Zealand journalists killed by Indonesian and pro-Indonesia proxy soldiers in 1975 on the journalists themselves rather than genocidal attacks by the Indonesian government. As with US denial, the goal was to stop UN action, but denial was also intended to preclude popular outcry from within the British population against Britain's ally because of its violence (Parry 2005).

The case of Rwanda represents a further shift from perpetrator to third-party denial. While it is true that in some cases *Interahamwe* leaders denied what they were doing in response to expressions of concern by foreign governments (Kovanda 2010, 199–200; Power 2002, 348), they were typically blatant in public calls for the extermination of the Tutsi (see, for instance, Power 2002, 339–40; Stanton 2009, 9–11). The crucial denials came instead from the United Nations, the US administration, and other governments as well as journalists (Kovanda 2010, 196–208; Power 2002, 358–64; Stanton 2009, 9–14). Despite having information to the contrary, they promoted the view that what was happening in Rwanda was not genocide, but an intractable ethnic conflict with deep, inscrutable, historical roots (Power 2002, 355–56).

External denial was present in the case of Serbian genocidal actions as well. For instance, in some policy circles in the United States, it was standard to assert, even to assume, that the violence occurring in Bosnia was mutual and atrocities were being committed "on all sides" (Power 2002, 207–10). While it is true that atrocities were documented on all sides, many genocide scholars agree that in Bosnia local and external Serbs pursued a policy of genocide. Again, the goal of this kind of denial was to justify lack of action as the genocide proceeded.

This motivation represents an interesting similarity and contrast to denial of the genocidal process in East Timor. In the latter case, denial and disavowal by outside powers was mainly to avoid the political problem of being exposed as supporting the genocidal Indonesian regime, in order to maintain beneficial military, political, and economic ties with Indonesia (Jardine 1996, 37–50). This appears to have been the French motivation, and in particular then-President Mitterrand's, in the Rwanda case (Kovanda 2010, 200, 201, 211). But the United Nations, the United States, and other international actors who accepted or pushed denialist lines regarding the former Yugoslavia and Rwanda appeared unconcerned about others intervening but instead were intent on justifying their own bystanding.

Serbs themselves also denied what they were doing in Bosnia to prevent intervention. While much Serbian denial was what might be called standard—claiming civil war not one-sided violence, asserting provocation by the Bosnian Muslims, etc., one form of contemporaneous denial bears special mention for two reasons. First, its target was not an external audience, but rather Serbs themselves. Second, rationalization intertwined with denial, as false claims of Serbian victimization directly negated true victimization of Bosnians. For example, Serbian television in Banja Luca showed films of Muslim or Croat women being raped by Serbs, but sham uniforms, fictitious commentaries, and other fabrications suggested that it was Serbian women being raped by Muslims or Croats. This reversal was used to exonerate Serbs while simultaneously whipping up anti-Muslim and -Croat sentiment, which helped fuel genocide (MacKinnon 1994, 76).

Complex denial can be seen in other cases as well. The Khmer Rouge kept tight control over all information exiting Cambodia, and so, at least initially, information about the Cambodian genocide was scant and denial unnecessary. However, as evidence of Khmer Rouge atrocities accumulated, the question of mass destruction (genocide) arose. As in the East Timor and Rwanda cases, the key denials came not from the perpetrators, but from outsiders. The dominant motives, however, were different from Rwanda. As Donald Beachler (2009) has shown, the US discourse on Khmer Rouge violence was not primarily a function of factual data, however limited, but positioning on the US political scene. In some sense, discourse on the genocide had little to do with Cambodia. Denial was prevalent among left-wing intellectuals and journalists who illegitimately fit Cambodian events into the legitimate critical framework they had developed regarding US military aggression in Southeast Asia. Critical of the US anticommunism that wreaked such destruction in Vietnam, Laos, and Cambodia, these figures refused to be critical of those they saw as the "other side." Thus, they became apologists for the Khmer Rouge as the genocide unfolded.

There is legitimate debate as to whether Russian actions in Chechnya over the past two centuries have genocidal elements, but it is possible to argue that partial genocide in the service of subjugation of Chechens has occurred (Russell 2005, 105). While there has been mutual violence, the brutality of the Russian military including targeting of civilians

(Russell 2005, 109), with civilian death tolls in the 1990s and 2000s at least in the 10,000s, and possibly in the 100,000s (Russell 2005, 114, note 1), shows that the violence has been generally one-sided. Denials of Russian culpability have taken the form of labeling all Chechens in opposition to Russia—no matter how legitimate their grievances—"terrorists" or some other negative term and attributing all Russian violence to self-defense against "terrorist" or otherwise objectionable Chechens (Russell 2005, 101–16). Denial in Chechnya has not just prevented intervention, but has stopped the violence from drawing anything like the level of attention focused on other cases, such as the similar situation in the former Yugoslavia in the 1990s. Denialist claims—especially that the Russians have been fighting Islamic terrorism—have been an alibi all too readily embraced by great powers eager to avoid confrontation with another great power.

In the Sudan case, the United Nations concluded that genocide was not perpetrated in Darfur (International Commission of Inquiry on Darfur 2005, 4, 124–32, 160–61), while the US government officially characterized the events in Darfur as genocide (VandeHei 2005). While one might engage in all sorts of definitionalism on this issue, Samuel Totten provides a powerful critique of the contents of and research methods behind the UN report on Darfur that makes a compelling case for characterizing these events as genocide (Totten 2009). In this case, the United Nations has accepted Sudanese denials apparently in order to resist what would otherwise be an imperative to intervene meaningfully.

The nature of Sudanese denial is telling and suggests an important critical point helpful to overcoming the legalistic embrace of denial by the United Nations and others in this case and others. As I have argued elsewhere, in the age of "international human rights," recent perpetrators seem cagey enough to mold their activities to just not quite fit the genocide definition unequivocally (Theriault 2010, 487–88). One can argue that it is precisely denial that confirms genocide here. The Sudan government insists that it has no control over the Janjaweed militia and to some extent Janjaweed operations are decentralized. But this appears to be precisely what the government wants in order to allow it to deny that it is committing genocide. Through its approach of allowing some decentralization, the government intentionally, and with eyes fully turned toward the UN definition of genocide, effected genocide with mechanisms that do not quite fit the genocide definition tightly. This "anticipatory" denial seems also to have been used by the Serbs in the former Yugoslavia (Theriault 2010, 487–88).

Consolidation of Genocide, Denial, and Prevention

If denial is not the final stage of genocide but characteristic of many stages, then what is the final stage? Unless directly addressed through substantive legal, political, economic, social, and/or cultural interventions, the long-term aftermaths of genocides are generally periods best captured by the term "consolidation" (Theriault 2009, 2011). After direct destruction, perpetrators, their supporters, and typically a critical mass of their progeny seek to consolidate the gains made through genocide. These include material benefits in land and moveable wealth; increased political, demographic, and military power; increased cultural and identity security and cohesion; and much more. Along with geopolitical pressure and exploitation of the weakened economic, political, social, and cultural position of victim groups, denial is a central tool for advancing consolidation.

The consolidation process not only fixes the gains as a new status quo, but through denial it preserves the same genocidal attitudes, practices, and even institutions that produced genocide initially. Indeed, when the consolidation process is challenged, these attitudes can spur increased oppression and renewed violence. An example is the challenge to consolidative denial of the Armenian Genocide in Turkey by Turkish–Armenian journalist Hrant Dink, who was assassinated in 2007 for writing publically about the Armenian Genocide in Turkey. Successfully overcoming consolidative denial, while dangerous, can expose the consolidation process and promote perpetrator group rehabilitation and, through reparations, material improvements in the situation of the victim group. In this sense, it can be seen as intervention against the extension of genocide through consolidation or prevention of renewed violence.

Challenging consolidative denial is, more generally, also an important prevention method. The lessons of successful consolidation, which depends on successful long-term denial, are clear for would-be perpetrators of other genocides. For instance, it cannot be lost on potential perpetrators today that, despite eventual negative effects for some leaders, the Bosnian Genocide resulted in Serbian territorial gains made permanent through the Dayton Accords.

Astute would be perpetrators understand that genocide is not simply one option for accomplishing domination, political advancement or preservation, and land and wealth expropriation, but quite often the preferable option to other forms of conquest and acquisition. A war leaves a defeated population that might be capable of significant military action in the future, as the dynamic of Germany and France in the nineteenth and twentieth centuries demonstrates. Even slavery, colonialism, and apartheid largely preserve oppressed populations who, history has shown, often rise against their oppressors. Genocide, which typically destroys at least a substantial part of the victim group and undercuts the viability of survivors, offers the best chance of permanent gain.

Explicit theorization of the consolidation of genocide and especially consolidative denial are new research territories. Yet, recently there have been novel analyses of the consolidation stages of specific genocides, some with an explicit focus on denial. Discussion of certain case studies here will help elucidate the tremendous historical success and thus genocide-fostering force of consolidation in a climate of denial.

Cutting-edge work by Uğur Ümit Üngör and Mehmet Polatel (Üngör and Polatel 2011) offers both broad, incontrovertible evidence and insightful analysis of the massive expropriation of Armenian property through the Armenian Genocide process.[2] The state and specific Committee of Union and Progress members as well as other genocide participants gained immensely from the theft of Armenian property. Reflecting the insights of Üngör and Polatel, Temel Demirer (2010) has argued that this so-called "abandoned property" taken from Armenians formed the economic basis of the Kemalist Turkish Republic. The discussion following Üngör's special presentation on "abandoned property" at the 2009 "Armenian Genocide and International Law" Conference at Haigazian University in Beirut, Lebanon, on September 4, 2009, added a crucial dimension, by highlighting that family fortunes of many elites in Turkey today can be traced back to the Armenian Genocide and explaining that this is a significant factor in contemporary denial of the genocide. Denial here functions not only conceptually, to preserve a pure image of the Young Turks and Turkey more broadly, but in a much more material way, to protect perpetually the property expropriations of this genocide.

This is not to suggest that the conceptual dimension of consolidation is not important. Clearly the preservation of national self-image is a significant motivation—not simply to erase memory of the victims but to rehabilitate the image of the perpetrators and the perpetrator group's identity. For example, Colin Tatz (2011) argues that Australian denial of the genocidal nature of the physical killings of Aborigines and forced removals of Aboriginal children from their homes preserves a self-image according to which Australian identity is not genocidal and its colonialism was "decent." Interestingly, Tatz also suggests the material dimension of consolidative denial when he notes Prime Minister John Howard's refusal to admit that the genocide of Australia's Aborigines was motivated by a fear of reparations.

One can see both aspects of consolidation in the case of the overall Native American genocide.[3] For instance, many US citizens, including leaders, refuse to recognize the genocide of various Native American groups as an overarching historical process. While, on the one hand, this is explicitly linked to a rejection of a stain on American identity, it also clearly supports consolidation of land gains through genocide, the latter coming after the major execution phase of physical destruction (ending with the Wounded Knee Massacre of 1890). Steve Russell's (2004) work on twentieth-century expropriation of Native American land exposes a consolidation phase that extended the land thefts through direct killing and deportation in prior centuries. Such techniques as federal laws mandating individual ownership of land, coupled with various unethical practices by land speculators, produced a second wave of land expropriations. These clearly depended on the failure to recognize the wrongness of federal legal control over Native Americans as the product of genocide and denialist rejection of a moral imperative for the United States to restore land and dignity to Native Americans rather than increasing their losses.

Consolidation of the US Native American Genocide has had other important dimensions as well. Andrea Smith (2005) demonstrates a multifaceted continuing victimization of Native American women under US rule. This includes the rendering "rapeable" of Native American women by whites (60 percent of the perpetrators of violence against Native American women are white). It also includes internment in the twentieth century of Native girls (and boys) in boarding schools where they were subjected to brutal suppression of their identities, sexual abuse, and other forms of torture and degradation. The upshot is that Native American genocide in the United States has resulted in a continuing, deep, and brutal domination relation of whites (white men) over Native American women and girls (Smith 2005, 1–54).

Researchers and the Smithsonian Institution have over the past century radically underestimated the number of indigenous people living in North America prior to the European invasion, often by a factor of ten. The effect of this demographic denial is to render invisible the great pre-European Native American presence, in order to validate the view of North America as empty wilderness legitimately settled by Europeans, rather than a heavily populated land that was conquered and depopulated through genocide (Churchill 1997, 131–37). This, in turn, makes much less tenable contemporary land claims by Native Americans and thus supports perpetual maintenance of the state of affairs produced through genocide, including a material status quo that represents injustice toward Native Americans made permanent.

Walter Delrio, Diana Lenton, Marcelo Musante, Mariano Nagy, Alexis Papazian, and Pilar Pérez argue that denial of genocide against indigenous people in Argentina is central to the historical narrative of Argentine national identity. Claims of genocide are perceived as an assault on that identity. What is more, land expropriation was and continues to be at the core of Argentine state policies toward indigenous peoples, and denial of the history of genocide and its impact today preserves past gains by preventing material and symbolic reparation (Delrio et al. 2010).

Consolidative denial can be particularly twisted in some cases. While not a case of genocide, the Japanese military's enslavement of approximately 200,000 girls and women from 1931 to 1945 for use as "sexual slaves" was a major human rights violation of the twentieth century that included extensive murder and rape as well as other physical and psychological abuse and torture. Japanese governmental and nongovernmental denial in the case of the "Comfort Women" serves a clear consolidative purpose. In the 1990s, a number of surviving Comfort Women from various countries came forward to demand an apology from Japan and reparation for the harms done to them, often desperately needed to address resulting physical ailments. The Japanese government refused. Because the crimes against the women in question have not been taken as identity issues by their national or ethnic groups and because in many cases the women could not have families because of the physical and psychological damage to them, the women themselves represent the affected community (Gibson 1999; Yoshiaki 2002). With their passing, the reparative challenge will be gone, if for no other reason than there will be no one left to receive reparations. Within a few years there will be no surviving Comfort Women and consolidative denial will have been completely successful.

While too often it is believed that the Holocaust has been resolved through perpetrator trials, restitution, universal recognition, and creation of the state of Israel, it, too, has had a complex consolidative phase. As Israel Charny (1992) has noted, denial functions typically in the long aftermath of a genocide as a renewed psychological attack on the victim group. Holocaust denial is thus an expression of anti-Semitism in solidarity with the perpetrators. In this sense, it is an attempt to reverse the outcry against anti-Semitism evoked by the Holocaust; that is, it works to hold on to the conceptual gains against Jews made through the Holocaust, the actual lowering of the status of Jews that was one feature of the Holocaust and that persists, despite the view that widespread condemnation of the Holocaust signals a decrease in anti-Semitism.

Selective denial is also part of Holocaust consolidation. Filmmaker Slawomir Grunberg (2005) documents the dual role of denial of the specifically local Polish responsibility for the destruction of the Jewish population of Jedwabne, to preserve both a false view of local Poles as nonperpetrators and their hold on expropriated Jewish property.

Critical Challenges Facing the Field

Challenge 1: If it were just a matter of pointing out the problem of contemporaneous denial, then, in the aftermath of the Rwanda Genocide, the problem would have been solved. But, with Sudan, Congo, and other current cases, denial mechanisms have worked with the same efficiency as before. Contrary to Bill Clinton's self-defensive remarks (Bradshaw and Loeterman 1998), denial is not a function of ignorance; it is a culture that shapes our perceptions of the world and provides a psychological and political alibi to our desire *not* to care about those being unjustly victimized. To end the effectiveness of contemporaneous denial, it is not enough to refute the arguments; it requires changing the pervasive underlying cognitive framework that supports denial.

Contemporaneous denial can have many intended audiences. Central for the purposes of this chapter is the targeting of external agents to dissuade them from intervention. Denial is unlikely to affect those who approach the situation and its data objectively and critically. But, as Terrence Des Pres' (1986) important work indicates, for those who are on the fence, it can reinforce their indecision and uncertainty, thus preventing them from taking a stand against genocide—while for those who are looking for a good reason not to consider what is going on genocide, denial arguments provide the cover (519–22). Once there is a dispute by different parties over the facts on the ground, it is always possible to say that the situation is uncertain—even if this is factually wrong. It is this relativist tendency that constitutes crucial support for contemporaneous denial.

Despite decades of excellent scholarship on denial, the trend has been toward its increased legitimacy in political, journalistic, and even academic contexts. Through naïve and muddled concepts of critical thinking, relativist neutrality in the face of clear one-sided violence has come to grant equal status to—and even to generate—"the other side of the story" (Des Pres 1986), which is typically denialist. Indeed, this has created a political and journalistic culture of "universal denial," in which the default "truth" of any conflict over facts in a case of violence is that it is the result of mutual agency, not one-sided destruction (Theriault 2001).

Though the focus of policy and scholarly discussions in recent years has been on external intervention, *internal* intervention might in some circumstances have greater potential impact. Though historically the genocidal component of the perpetrator society has dealt harshly and effectively with those who oppose it, internal dissent can be an important force against genocide. Crucial to the balance of power within a perpetrator group is the typically sizable segment of the population without a strong initial commitment in either direction. Denial can quell uneasiness in this segment and can even motivate their passive or active participation.

Challenge 2: Reparative justice remains an afterthought in mainstream genocide studies. For instance, Charny (1992) discounts Armenian Genocide reparations as implausible and any desire for them as much a function of frustration over Turkish denial as anything else (291–92). Most discussions of the long-term aftermath of genocide focus on psychological legacies, recognition of the fact of the genocide, and conciliation, not the virtually unrecognized issue of consolidation. Out of geopolitics or "national interest," that is, fear of their own state being held accountable for past crimes, major-power policymakers avoid the issue of reparations. As the examples of consolidation above indicate, genocide after genocide is consolidated without serious political or academic opposition.

The problem of consolidative denial is twofold. First, as a function of the relativist cognitive framework discussed above, denial remains an acceptable form of historical discourse. Second, even where genocides are recognized in popular and political discourse, there is pervasive denial of the *obvious* impacts of the past on the present.

For example, stark Native American poverty is not linked to genocide and subsequent land thefts, social and psychological destruction in boarding schools, and continuing oppression, but treated as a discrete contemporary phenomenon. Similarly, the frail, desperate economic poverty and military vulnerability of the tiny, landlocked Armenian Republic is not recognized as the direct result of population destruction, massive wealth expropriation, and land theft through genocide (see McCalpin et al. 2010, 10–13, 56–58).

The Probability of Progress

Despite the dismal track record of intervention and prevention and the resilience of denial as a key obstacle, there are hopeful signs of possible change and clear paths to improvement.

US Representative James P. McGovern (Massachusetts' 3rd Congressional District) has offered important insights into the way that the Clinton administration contributed to stopping further genocide in East Timor in 1999, as the UN-supported referendum on independence came nearer. US military and political support was vital for the East Timor invasion and subsequent genocide—including use of US naval vessels (Lynch 2006). McGovern (1999) has explained that, as genocide re-erupted in 1999, Senator Tom Harkin (Iowa), Senator Jack Reed (Rhode Island), and he went on a fact-finding mission to East Timor. When they asked local leaders what they could do to help stop the violence, the response was, "Call off your dogs"—in other words, stop giving military and political support to the Suharto regime. This was what these Congressional leaders recommended to the Clinton administration (McGovern 1999). In September 1999, the United States stopped its military aid to Indonesia as a result of the human rights abuses in East Timor (Human Rights Watch 2010) and pushed for political change, which occurred when former Indonesian President Suharto's close political ally and successor B. J. Habibie decided in October 1999 not to run in the next presidential election (Associated Press 1999).

McGovern's work and analysis offer a crucial and all but ignored approach to genocide intervention. Almost without exception, intervention is assumed to mean external force (usually military) applied to the perpetrator group. But with Indonesia, it was *withdrawal* of military support, not military intervention, that stopped renewed genocide. Not only was this approach much more successful in preventing violence than a violent military intervention could have been (almost by definition), but it promoted an alternative, nonviolent approach crucial to a global cultural shift away from mass violence. If, subsequently, Indonesia has not been adequately transformed and the United States has not adequately supported real transformation, this is because the approach has not been carried through (Human Rights Watch 2010). Because of the global roles and impacts of powers such as the United States, China, Japan, Russia, France, and Britain, and their historical support for mass violence within their borders and in states over which they have influence, this approach has great potential for future intervention against mass violence. Indeed, according to Kovanda (2010), because of close relations between principal political leaders of the two countries and Rwanda's dependence on France for arms, France was in an optimal position to influence the Rwandan government prior to and during the 1994 genocide (200–201). Had France chosen to withdraw its support, it is very likely that the genocide would not have occurred or the ability of the government to carry it out would have been diminished. It would have likely made UN intervention with the resources that had already been committed much easier and more effective.

Crucial to following this kind of approach is breaking the hold of denial that allows outside powers to continue their support for violent regimes without international challenge and internal public outcries. Decisive responses to denial are thus important intervention and prevention tools, tools that do not depend on early warning mechanisms that are much more speculative and less proven. Unfortunately, as discussed in the previous section, there is a persistent political and journalistic culture of denial. One option for changing it is to leverage remorse over political and journalistic failures in the Rwandan and other cases in order to gain acceptance for programs that will train interested policy makers and journalists in the complex ways denial works and to ready them to recognize denialist fallacies and evidence falsifications as situations unfold, and to be able to respond convincingly to them. By educating journalists and policymakers about denial and stimulating better critical thinking, there is a chance that the lessons learned from the tragic consequences of successful contemporaneous denial can help prevent genocide in the future. With support from human rights-oriented political leaders, organizations such as the International Association of Genocide Scholars as well as university genocide studies programs should be pushing to be included, for instance, (a) as presenters in US Department of State training programs and (b) as speakers in workshops for journalists.

Better approaches to contemporaneous denial also depend on honest confrontations of the role of great powers in past genocides. For example, the Genocide Prevention Task Forces' (2008) *Preventing Genocide: A Blueprint for U.S. Policymakers* is riddled with historical assumptions about the US relationship to genocide that ignore the realities of US inaction about, complicity in, and even perpetration of genocide. If the US government is going to deal with future genocides effectively, it must acknowledge its own past relationship to genocide, identify and change the negative elements, and develop a better, honest approach for the future. This depends on overcoming the denialism obscuring the true historical US relationship to genocide.

Regarding consolidation, there are positive trends as well. In some academic circles, the issue of reparations for past genocides and related mass violence is an increasing focus of research. For instance, the 2011 9th Biennial Conference of the International Association of Genocide Scholars had as its focus "Truth, Memory, Justice, and Recovery," and addressed, in part, the role of reparative justice in postgenocide societies toward victim recovery. While reparations are still not central in genocide studies journals, in some disciplines such as philosophy, the topic has become a central area of research regarding genocide. For instance, Claudia Card and Armen T. Marsoobian's (2007) edited collection, *Genocide's Aftermath: Responsibility and Repair*, includes a range of articles analyzing both the harm done by genocide and the ethical requirements and bounds of repair. What is more, as movements for reparations for South African Apartheid, US slavery and Jim Crow, indigenous American genocides, the Armenian Genocide, the Herero Genocide, the Comfort Women system, and other cases of mass violence and oppression become more interlinked, a global movement for reparations is emerging. Successes of this movement can provide important challenges to consolidation of genocide. Reversing or ending consolidative processes of past genocides will change the calculation that would-be perpetrators make.

With this in mind, scholars, activists, and their organizations should make reparative justice a central component of genocide study and activism. Beyond ethically right support for victim groups' just claims, this is the key to ending the great attractiveness of genocide as lucrative and politically advantageous. If genocide stops having substantial benefits—better benefits than most alternatives—then genocide will be a much less attractive policy option.

Notes

1. One example is US President Bill Clinton's 1998 "apology" to victims of the Rwanda Genocide of 1994, in which he claimed not to have known at the time what was going on. The evidence is clear, however, that early on in the genocidal process the Clinton administration was well aware that genocide was happening (Bradshaw and Loeterman 1998).
2. Presumably, similar work can be done on Assyrian and Greek property in the 1914–1923 era.
3. Because of the diversity of peoples targeted for genocide, the expanse of time, and the variety of perpetrator groups committing genocide just in North America, it is possible to recognize many distinct Western Hemisphere genocides—of the Taino, of the Aztecs, of the Cherokee, of the Navaho, and so on. Yet, Ward Churchill (1997) argues that, given the cohesive nature of anti-Native exterminationist ideology and the overall demographic effect of these various exterminations, it makes sense to consider these part of one overall genocidal process. In this chapter, context determines which approach is used in a given passage.

References

Alvarez, Alex. 2011. "Reflections on the Mass Atrocity Response Operations Project." *Genocide Studies and Prevention: An International Journal* 6, no. 1: 70–76.

Associated Press. 2011. "Mladic Won't Enter Pleas to War Crimes Charges." *Los Angeles Times*, June 3. http://www.latimes.com/news/nationworld/world/la-fgw-mladic-court-20110604,0,7266570.story (accessed June 6, 2011).

———. 1999. "Habibie Resigns Candidacy," October 20. http://amarillo.com/stories/102099/usn_LA0876.001.shtml (accessed June 11, 2011).

BBC News. 2009. "Genocide Charge for Former Khmer Rouge Leader Khieu Samphan." December 18. http://news.bbc.co.uk/2/hi/8419789.stm (accessed May 31, 2011).

Beachler, Donald W. 2009. "Arguing about Cambodia: Genocide and Political Interest." *Holocaust and Genocide Studies* 23, no. 2: 214–38.

Bradshaw, Steve and Ben Loeterman. 1998. *The Triumph of Evil: How the West Ignored Warnings of the 1994 Rwanda Genocide and Turned Its Back on the Victims*. PBS Frontline. Sam Bailey, Andy Blackman, Loeterman, Mike Robinson, and Nick Vaughan-Barratt (Prods.). VHS. 60 minutes. Color.

Card, Claudia and Armen T. Marsoobian, eds. 2007. *Genocide's Aftermath: Responsibility and Repair*. Malden, MA: Blackwell.

Channel 4 News. 2011. "Ratko Mladic and the 'Genocide Defence,'" June 3. http://www.channel4.com/news/ratko-mladic-and-the-genocide-defence (accessed June 6, 2011).

Charny, Israel W. 1992. "A Contribution to the Psychology of Denial of Genocide." *Journal of Armenian Studies* 4, no. 1–2: 289–306.

Churchill, Ward. 1997. *A Little Matter of Genocide: Holocaust and Denial in the Americas 1492 to the Present*. San Francisco, CA: City Lights Publishers.

Delrio, Walter, Diana Lenton, Marcelo Musante, Mariano Nagy, Alexis Papazian, and Pilar Pérez. 2010. "Discussing Indigenous Genocide in Argentina: Past, Present, and Consequences of Argentinean State Policies toward Native Peoples." *Genocide Studies and Prevention: An International Journal* 5, no. 2: 138–59.

Demirer, Temel. 2010. Presentation. "1915 Within Its Pre- and Post-historical Periods: Denial and Confrontation" Symposium, Ankara, Turkey, April 25.

Des Pres, Terrence. 1986. "On Governing Narratives: The Turkish-Armenian Case." *Yale Review* 75, no. 4: 517–31.

Dunn, James. 2009. "Genocide in East Timor." In *Century of Genocide: Critical Essays and Eyewitness Accounts*, ed. Samuel Totten and William S. Parsons, 3rd ed., 265–95. New York: Routledge.

Genocide Prevention Task Force. 2008. *Preventing Genocide: A Blueprint for U.S. Policy Makers*. Madeleine K. Albright and William S. Cohen (Co-Chairs). Washington, DC: Genocide Prevention Task Force.

Grunberg, Slawomir. 2005. *The Legacy of Jedwabne*. VHS and DVD. 72 minutes. Color. Slawomir Grunberg (Prod.).

Hovannisian, Richard G. 1986. "The Armenian Genocide and Patterns of Denial." In *The Armenian Genocide in Perspective*, ed. Richard Hovannisian, 111–33. New Brunswick, NJ: Transaction Publishers.

Human Rights Watch. 2010. "Indonesia: US Resumes Military Assistance to Abusive Force—Obama Administration Lifts Ban Despite Military's Lack of Reform, Accountability," July 22. http://www.hrw.org/en/news/2010/07/22/indonesia-us-resumes-military-assistance-abusive-force (accessed June 11, 2011).

International Commission of Inquiry on Darfur. 2005. *Report of the International Commission of Inquiry on Darfur to the United Nations Secretary-General*. Geneva: United Nations.

Jardine, Matthew. 1996. *East Timor: Genocide in Paradise*. Monroe, ME: Odonian.

Kovanda, Karel. 2010. "The Czech Republic on the UN Security Council: The Rwandan Genocide." *Genocide Studies and Prevention: An International Journal* 5, no. 2: 192–218.

Lynch, Colum. 2006. "Report: U.S. Arms Helped Indonesia Attack East Timor." *The Washington Post*, January 25. http://www.washingtonpost.com/wp-dyn/content/article/2006/01/24/AR2006012401688.html (accessed June 11, 2011).

MacKinnon, Catharine A. 1994. "Turning Rape into Pornography: Postmodern Genocide." In *Mass Rape: The War against Women in Bosnia-Herzegovina*, ed. Alexandra Stiglmayer, 72–81. Lincoln, NE: University of Nebraska.

McCalpin, Jermaine O., Ara Papian, Alfred de Zayas, and Henry C. Theriault. 2010. *Resolution with Justice: Reparations for the Armenian Genocide—The Report of the Armenian Genocide Reparations Study Group*. Unpublished Draft, October 20.

McGovern, James P. 1999. "Human Rights Violations in East Timor: Prevention, Accountability, and US Policy." Lecture, Worcester State College, October 12.

Morgenthau, Henry. 2000. *Ambassador Morgenthau's Story*. Reprint. Princeton, NJ: Gomidas Institute.

———. 1918. *Ambassador Morgenthau's Story*. Garden City, NY: Doubleday.

Parry, Richard Lloyd. 2005. "Government Lied to Cover Up War Crimes in 1975 Invasion of Island." *The Times*, November 30. http://www.timesonline.co.uk/tol/news/world/asia/article598076.ece (accessed June 11, 2011).

Payaslian, Simon. 2003. "The United States Response to the Armenian Genocide." In *Looking Backward, Moving Forward: Confronting the Armenian Genocide*, ed. Richard G. Hovannisian, 51–80. New Brunswick, NJ: Transaction Publishers.

Power, Samantha. 2002. *"A Problem from Hell": America and the Age of Genocide*. New York: Basic Books.

Russell, John. 2005. "Terrorists, Bandits, Spooks and Thieves: Russian Demonization of the Chechens Before and Since 9/11." *Third World Quarterly* 26, no. 1: 101–16.

Russell, Steve. 2004. "The Jurisprudence of Colonialism." In *American Indian Thought: Philosophical Essays*, ed. Anne Waters, 217–28. Malden, MA: Blackwell.

Schabas, William. 2009. "Genocide and International Law: 60 Years after the Convention, Problems and Prospects." Presentation. Armenian Genocide and International Law Conference. Haigazian University, Beirut, Lebanon, September 3.

Simpson, Christopher. 1993. *The Splendid Blond Beast: Money, Law, and Genocide in the Twentieth Century*. New York: Grove Press.

Smith, Andrea. 2005. *Conquest: Sexual Violence and American Indian Genocide*. Cambridge, MA: South End Press.

Stanton, Gregory H. 2009. "The Rwandan Genocide: Why Early Warning Failed." *Journal of African Conflicts and Peace Studies* 1, no. 2: 6–25.

———. 1998. "The Eight Stages of Genocide." *Genocide Watch*. http://www.genocidewatch.org/aboutgenocide/8stagesofgenocide.html (accessed May 29, 2011).

Tatz, Colin.2011. "Genocide Studies: An Australian Perspective." *Genocide Studies and Prevention: An International Journal* 6, no. 3: 231–44.

Theriault, Hank [*sic*]. 2001. "Universal Social Theory and the Denial of Genocide: Norman Itzkowitz Revisited," *Journal of Genocide Research* 3, no. 2: 241–56.

Theriault, Henry C. 2011. "Reparations and the 'Last Stage of Genocide.'" Paper. International Association of Genocide Scholars 9th Biennial Conference, Center for Genocide Studies, Universidad Nacional de Tres Febrero, Buenos Aires, Argentina, July 20.

———. 2010. "Genocidal Mutation and the Challenge of Definition." *Metaphilosophy* 41, no. 4: 481–524.

———. 2009. "The Final Stage of Genocide: Consolidation." *The Armenian Weekly*, October 10, 4.

Totten, Samuel. 2009. "The UN International Commission of Inquiry on Darfur: New and Disturbing Findings." *Genocide Studies and Prevention: An International Journal* 4, no. 3: 354–78.

Üngör, Uğur Ümit, and Mehmet Polatel. 2011. *Confiscation and Destruction: The Young Turk Seizure of Armenian Property*. London: Continuum, 224.

VandeHei, Jim. 2005. "In Break with U.N., Bush Calls Sudan Killings Genocide." *Washington Post*, June 2. http://www.washingtonpost.com/wp-dyn/content/article/2005/06/01/AR2005060101725.html (accessed June 23, 2011).

Yoshiaki, Yoshimi. 2002. *Comfort Women: Sexual Slavery in the Japanese Military during World War II*. New York: Columbia University.
Yoshida, Takashi. 2000. "A Battle over History: The Nanjing Massacre in Japan." In *The Nanjing Massacre in History and Historiography*, ed. Joshua A. Fogel, 70–132. Berkeley, CA: University of California.

Annotated Bibliography

Publications

Beachler, Donald W. "Arguing about Cambodia: Genocide and Political Interest." *Holocaust and Genocide Studies* 23, no. 2 (2009): 214–38.

This article expands on Samantha Power's analysis in her *"A Problem from Hell": America and the Age of Genocide* concerning the role of external academic figures and journalists in downplaying or misconstruing the Cambodian Genocide as it occurred. The article is balanced and thoughtful, recognizing the legitimate concerns of left-leaning intellectuals that might have led them to be skeptical of apparently antileft information presented publicly about the Khmer Rouge while offering clear accounts of the problematic, Ptolemaic logic of figures such as Noam Chomsky in minimizing or misrepresenting the genocide by the Khmer Rouge. The article also offers an incisive analysis of the ways in which right-leaning political figures in the United States approached the Cambodian Genocide as confirmation of the "evils" of communism, but in some cases later downplayed the genocide out of political agendas that saw an advantage for the United States in "indirectly associate[ing] . . . with the Khmer Rouge."

The article also includes very useful accounts of the Cambodian Genocide as analyzed by a number of scholars. These accounts lay a groundwork of truth-seeking scholarship against which to measure the politically tainted denialist approaches to the genocide covered in this article.

Card, Claudia and Armen T. Marsoobian, eds. *Genocide's Aftermath: Responsibility and Repair*. Malden, MA: Blackwell, 2007, 278 pp.

While not explicitly addressing the concept of "genocide consolidation," this set of essays works through, in a serious and sustained way, and from various sophisticated philosophical angles, a number of challenging issues regarding the consolidation of genocide, including what is consolidated, how consolidation might be challenged materially and symbolically, and who is responsible for doing so.

Three chapters in the book—Karen Kovach's "Genocide and the Moral Agency of Ethnic Groups" (50–70), Marina A. L. Oshana's "Moral Taint" (71–93), and Marsoobian's "Epilogue: Reconciliation in the Aftermath of Genocide" (260–71)—treat the question of intergenerational responsibility for genocide that is central to the consolidation process. Each finds that there is intergenerational responsibility based on group membership, with Kovach arguing that if one chooses not to reject alignment with an ethnic group, one assumes some measure of responsibility for what the group is responsible for, while Oshana argues that the historical legacy of one's identity group creates an obligation to address past wrongdoing in some way. If Kovach's approach is dependent on a reductive concept of social groups as (ethnic) identity groups (a byproduct of atomic individualism) and Oshana's notion of "taint" is ultimately not made concrete, the discussions by each contain important ideas and challenges that advance discussion of intergenerational responsibility and thus consolidation. Marsoobian draws on both accounts and applies them to contemporary Turkish–Armenian relations as part of the legacy of the Armenian Genocide.

Four of the chapters—Rodney C. Roberts's "The Counterfactual Conception of Compensation" (132–46), Haig Khatchadourian's "Compensation and Reparation as Forms of Compensatory Justice" (147–65), Ernesto Verdeja's "A Normative Theory of Reparations in Transitional Democracies" (166–85), and William C. Bradford's "Acknowledging and Rectifying the Genocide of American Indians: 'Why Is It That They Carry Their Lives on Their Fingernails?'" (232–59)—deal with the issue of how to counter or prevent the consolidation of genocide and related mass violence through reparative measures. Of special interest are Khatchadourian's and Verdeja's articles, which focus on the central problem of denial and the need for truth-telling to stop the trajectory of denial.

Nir Eisikovits' "Rethinking the Legitimacy of Truth Commissions: 'I Am the Enemy You Killed, My Friend' " (206–31) is a different matter. The model Eisikovits develops treats perpetrator groups and victim groups as equivalents in a negotiative process, with victims just as responsible as perpetrators for repairing the damage done by mass violence. According to his way of thinking, each "side" should have sympathy for the other party's political positions and justify its own positions "by using the least controversial rationale available" (209). Of course, nearly every example of genocide and related mass violence and oppression shows that many members of a perpetrator group not only routinely deny the violence done by their group but also characterize the true accounts given by victims as extreme, illegitimate, and/or controversial positions. In this model, there is no recognition of the asymmetrical domination relation that is produced and/or exacerbated greatly by genocide and related mass violence and oppression. Elements of his treatment of the Israeli-Palestinian case are telling. He goes as far as equating the view of some Israelis that no "Palestinian" people legitimately exists with the reparative claim by some Palestinians that they have a right to return to the areas from which they were forcibly expelled by Israelis (which one can argue for or against, but which is an understandable position). Eisikovits' approach is inherently denialist, because it obscures the one-sided nature of genocide and related forms of mass violence. To the extent that this model becomes the norm for dealing with the aftermath of genocide, the message to would-be perpetrators is clear: you will not be held accountable for your actions.

Churchill, Ward. *A Little Matter of Genocide: Holocaust and Denial in the Americas 1492 to the Present.* San Francisco, CA: City Lights Publishers, 1997, 531 pp.

This work is an important account of the consolidation of genocide of Native Americans. One key aspect is Churchill's analysis of the various denialist arguments, especially those made in the twentieth century. Churchill's account of numerical denial is particularly important: by presenting a gross undercounting of the Native American population in what would become the continental United States, the Smithsonian Institution and individual deniers erase the true presence of Native Americans so that the survivor population at the end of the nineteenth century does not appear as dramatic a reduction from previous levels as it actually was. In this way, what was genocide can be presented as a milder demographic reduction plausibly due to such things as disease and (unfortunate) oppression. Another key aspect is examination of the way the dominance of the US government and civil society over Native American groups resulting from the overarching genocidal process has impacted Native Americans, for instance, through use of Native Americans to mine and mill uranium, which has resulted in horrific illnesses and premature death. Churchill's work is an attempt to challenge the denial and consolidation of the long-term aftermath of genocide of Native Americans.

Delrio, Walter, Diana Lenton, Marcelo Musante, Nagy Mariano, Alex Papazian, and Pilar Pérez. "Discussing Indigenous Genocide in Argentina: Past, Present, and Consequences of Argentinean State Policies toward Native Peoples." *Genocide Studies and Prevention: An International Journal* 5, no. 2 (2010):138–59.

This article exposes the centrality of denial regarding the true nature of Argentine and pre-Argentine destruction of native peoples in the territory of today's Argentina to contemporary Argentine national identity and the territorial form of Argentina. Denial of the fact of genocide allows consolidation of the land thefts and destruction of indigenous lives and cultures today without legal, political, or ethical qualms.

Des Pres, Terrence. "On Governing Narratives: The Turkish-Armenian Case." *Yale Review* 75, no. 4 (1986): 517–31.

This is one of the true classics in the literature on genocide denial. In it, Des Pres identifies the central cause of the tendency to give denial credence against true claims of genocide. This is a perversion of the legitimate principle of critical thinking that "there are two sides to every issue" (519). Historically, this principle functioned to legitimize alternative, critical viewpoints against hegemonic authority whose legitimacy was a function of power, not intellectual or scientific merit. Des Pres convincingly contends that, by the late twentieth century, this principle had been embraced by denialist perpetrator groups and their supporters to delegitimize historically true claims of victimization. Taking seriously the other side of the story was cynically perverted into a way of blocking the truth.

Des Pres identifies the cognitive framework we can see operating again and again in contexts of past and present genocides, as the false statements of powers who committed or are committing genocide are given just as much credence as the truth about what happened or is happening presented by victims and third-party observers.

Dunn, James. "Genocide in East Timor." In *Century of Genocide: Critical Essays and Eyewitness Accounts*, edited by Samuel Totten and William S. Parsons, 3rd ed., 265–95. New York: Routledge, 2009.

This chapter presents a comprehensive and clear account of the long process of genocide in East Timor and includes a good discussion of Indonesian and external denial efforts during the genocide.

Hovannisian, Richard G. "The Armenian Genocide and Patterns of Denial." In *The Armenian Genocide in Perspective*, edited by Richard Hovannisian, 111–33. New Brunswick, NJ: Transaction Publishers, 1986.

This chapter traces the evolution of Armenian Genocide denial from the execution phase through the short- and long-term aftermaths of this genocide.

It examines the political and geopolitical forces driving new developments and approaches by Turkish governmental and pro-Turkish deniers. By focusing attention on changes in denial methods (political, academic, mass media) and arguments that correspond to different stages in the overall genocidal process itself, including a nuanced treatment of the dynamic of long-term consolidation in the face of increasing Armenian and third-party calls for decisive recognition of the Armenian genocide, Hovannisian provides a template for relating different employments and effects of denial to different stages of genocide. This article also provides an important counterexample to the notion that denial is the final stage of genocide.

Jardine, Matthew. *East Timor: Genocide in Paradise*. Monroe, ME: Odonian Press, 1996, 95 pp.

Jardine provides a politically critical account of the genocide in East Timor, including a close examination of the geopolitical and economic factors. The book provides important details about US and other countries' contemporaneous denial efforts.

Kovanda, Karel. "The Czech Republic on the UN Security Council: The Rwandan Genocide." *Genocide Studies and Prevention: An International Journal* 5, no. 2 (2010): 192–218.

This is an exceptionally important article about the Rwandan Genocide by a member of the UN Security Council during that genocide. Kovanda provides a detailed history of the Security Council deliberations and the external and internal political forces and maneuvering that countenanced denial and allowed the genocide to proceed largely without intervention. The article is an invaluable resource of inside information on such things as then-French President Mitterrand's personal ties to rulers of Rwanda and the French military and economic relationship that resulted in French support of the genocidal regime. While much of what has come out of the United Nations and governments such as the United States has avoided a genuine engagement with the political and moral failures of each in the face of genocide, Kovanda offers an unflinching look into who did what and how their actions allowed genocide to happen.

MacKinnon, Catharine A. "Turning Rape into Pornography: Postmodern Genocide." In *Mass Rape: The War against Women in Bosnia-Herzegovina*, edited by Alexandra Stiglmayer, 72–81. Lincoln, NE: University of Nebraska Press, 1994.

MacKinnon's analysis of the function of rape in this genocide, which has important implications for other genocides, and the role of denial of rape, is part of the feminist work that has opened up a new and crucial dimension of genocide and human rights study. While this important aspect of genocide has not yet been given the full presence it should have in the literature, it is more and more being taken account of in discussions of genocide. Recognizing denial of rape as denial of genocide is an important step in challenging the effectiveness of denial. Because political leaders, journalists, and scholars often treat rape as a much less significant issue than killing, failure to take rape seriously and to respond to denial of mass rape is both a failure to protect female victims of genocide and a missed sign of genocide pursued by means other than killing. Not only do rapes and related gendered atrocities need to be taken very seriously in their own rights, but as Elisa von Joeden-Forgey has argued ("The Devil in the Details: 'Life Force Atrocities' and the Assault on the Family in Times of Conflict." *Genocide Studies and Prevention: An International Journal* 5, no. 1 [April 2010]: 1–19), they are important early warning signs of genocide in that responding to rape can be a mechanism of intervention against genocide as it occurs and the prevention of genocide as early violence escalates.

Power, Samantha. *"A Problem from Hell": America and the Age of Genocide*. New York: Basic Books, 2002, 620 pp.

This work is well known to genocide scholars and the broader human rights and political communities in the United States and elsewhere. It makes important contributions to our knowledge of contemporaneous denial by outside parties with various kinds of relationships to perpetrator groups and political agendas in relation to such cases as Cambodia, the Iraqi Kurds, Rwanda, and the former Yugoslavia. In this dimension, the work is highly useful.

At the same time, the book is also deeply problematic. It is an unabashed and un-self-reflective polemic in support of US military intervention in human rights problems globally. There is no critical examination of how US military power has historically abused human rights around the globe. Perhaps worse, it represents a form of consolidative denial. In more than 600 pages, Power mentions the "eradication of Native American tribes" in just two sentences on page 67, and that to dismiss the notion that Native Americans might have any claims against the United States under the UN Genocide Convention. Similarly, she mentions the 1965 Indonesian genocide against "communists" and the East Timor genocide in just one sentence on pages 146–47. Therein, she adopts a disingenuous critical attitude toward the United States for "look[ing] away" because Indonesia was our ally. She thus neglects the fact that the United States actively supported these genocides, including its providing military aid to Indonesia, for political and economic reasons. What is more, she does not mention Guatemala at all, a case in which the United States actively supported genocide in the 1980s. By ignoring US perpetration of and support for genocide, and thus the complex relationship of the United States to genocide, Power never gets to a level of analysis that explains *why* US leaders acted as they did regarding Bosnia, Rwanda, and other cases she treats. Furthermore, because her work has been so widely acclaimed as one of, if not *the*, book(s) on the US relationship to genocide, to the extent her narrative dominates, it displaces more factual, comprehensive analyses of that relationship and leaves intact the deeply held attitudes behind US genocidal activities and the many benefits of the genocides the United States has committed or supported. That the book appears to be critical of the United States' decision-making regarding genocide but de facto supports US genocidal activities by its crucial omissions and spin makes the book all the more effective for consolidation of the US Native American Genocide.

Russell, John. "Terrorists, Bandits, Spooks and Thieves: Russian Demonisation of the Chechens Before and Since 9/11." *Third World Quarterly* 26, no. 1 (2005): 101–16.

This article details the ways in which negative characterizations of Chechens and the generalization of Chechen violence served to delegitimize evidence of an overall pattern of Russian mass violence, possibly genocidal, against Chechens. Because the perpetrator in this case is a great power, the analysis offers important insight into another context of denial distinct from cases such as Cambodia, Rwanda, and Sudan, where the perpetrators were or are not major powers.

Simpson, Christopher. *The Splendid Blond Beast: Money, Law, and Genocide in the Twentieth Century*. New York: Grove Press, 1993, 399 pp.

Simpson's book offers insightful analysis and historical details of ways in which economic and political interests supported some individuals and corporations that participated or were culpably complicit in the Holocaust in escaping responsibility for and retaining benefits from their participation or complicity. This is an important aspect of the consolidation of genocide that is subtler and more difficult to perceive than more blatant forms, such as governmental expropriation of the land of victims.

Smith, Andrea. *Conquest: Sexual Violence and American Indian Genocide*. Cambridge, MA: South End Press, 2005, 245 pp.

This innovative book presents numerous aspects of the long-term consolidation of the genocide of Native Americans that are related concretely or that the author relates conceptually to male domination within a context of colonialism and racism.

Stanton, Greg. "Proving Genocide in Darfur: The Atrocities Documentation Project and Resistance to Its Findings." In *Genocide in Darfur: Investigating the Atrocities in Sudan*, edited by Samuel Totten and Eric Markusen, 181–88. New York: Routledge, 2006.

This chapter includes an important section outlining the motives and arguments of those denying genocide in Darfur, both inside the US government and beyond. While there might be some legitimate ways of debating whether the UN definition applies to Darfur, the denial arguments identified by Stanton depend on such incorrect assumptions or claims as denials of the intent of the perpetrators (which can be seen from the actions) and the false requirement that all members of the victim group be targeted for destruction, ignoring the "in part" element of the UN definition. This article provides insight into contemporaneous denial by outside parties, denial that is especially significant when considered in relation to contemporaneous denial of the Rwandan Genocide and subsequent apologetic commitments of "never again" to accept denial in the way the United Nations and others did regarding the genocide as it was ongoing.

Stanton, Greg. "The Rwandan Genocide: Why Early Warning Failed." *Journal of African Conflicts and Peace Studies* 1, no. 2 (2009): 6–25.

Stanton provides a useful account of various denial arguments and strategies pursued by powers outside of Rwanda, with a focus on the US government. Important for consideration of the role of denial as an impediment to intervention, the article links this denial effort to the failure of the United Nations and the United States to act against the Rwandan Genocide.

Theriault, Hank [*sic*]. "Universal Social Theory and the Denial of Genocide: Norman Itzkowitz Revisited." *Journal of Genocide Research* 3, no. 2 (2001): 241–56. Reprinted as Theriault, Hank [*sic*]. "Universal Social Theory and the Denial of Genocide: Norman Itzkowitz Revisited." In *Defining the Horrific: Readings on Genocide and Holocaust in the Twentieth Century*, edited by William L. Hewitt, 382–93. Upper Saddle River, NJ: Pearson-Prentice Hall, 2004.

This article develops the concept of a universal denialist conceptual framework, specifically an ideological or cognitive framework promoted by Itzkowitz and others that causes one-sided mass violence such as genocide to appear to be mutual violence or tension and thus not genocide and without one side being the perpetrator group and the other the victim group. Far beyond denial arguments made against the facts of a single genocide, this approach promotes a wide-ranging universal denial that applies to many genocides and other kinds of one-sided mass violence. To the extent that this framework has become more prevalent in recent years in academic, political, and journalistic circles, it has given contemporaneous and aftermath denial greater credibility than they otherwise would have had and undermines true claims about one-sided violence.

Theriault, Henry C. "Free Speech and Denial: The Case of the Armenian Genocide," In *Looking Backward, Moving Forward: Confronting the Armenian Genocide*, edited by Richard G. Hovannisian, 231–61. New Brunswick, NJ: Transaction Publishers, 2003.

This chapter extends Des Pres' work in order to develop the concept of "academic relativism" as a mentality in academia and beyond, according to which any position, including genocide denial, taken by any credentialed academic is considered automatically legitimate and as legitimate as any other position, including the truth about a genocide. Similar to abuse of "the other side of the story" principle, academic relativism suspends genuine critical evaluation and causes denial arguments to be much more appealing and accepted than they would be if judged on their actual merits.

Totten, Samuel. "The UN International Commission of Inquiry on Darfur: New and Disturbing Findings." *Genocide Studies and Prevention: An International Journal* 4, no. 3 (2009): 354–78.

This article provides a devastating critique of the 2005 UN report that found that genocide was not being committed in Darfur. The critique includes analysis of the contents of the report, the methodology of the research on which it was based, and the political forces and context affecting the report. Perhaps the central insight of Totten's critique is pointing out that the actual content of the report—the facts the commission determined to be the case in Sudan—support a finding of genocide that the authors refuse to make. Exposure of denial in the UN mechanisms that are supposed to protect populations against genocide is not only disturbing—as the article's title stresses—but highlights a consistency in UN treatment of genocide from Rwanda and the 1990s to Sudan and the 2000s, despite assurances after the UN's failure in Rwanda that it would get things right in the future.

Üngör, Uğur Ümit and Mehmet Polatel. *Confiscation and Destruction: The Young Turk Seizure of Armenian Property*. London: Continuum, 2011, 224 pp.

Through both sophisticated theoretical development and rich concrete local case studies, this book offers a detailed analysis of how Armenian property was expropriated, who the agents of expropriation were and who benefited in Turkish society, and the role of this expropriation in the development of the subsequent Turkish national economy and state more broadly. By looking at the "macro, meso, and micro" levels—that is, the political elites, local elites and state institutions, and the local populations, respectively—in their interconnections, the book argues that there was broad participation in and benefit from expropriation of Armenian property. This is an important point against those who would minimize the benefits accrued from the Armenian Genocide by contemporary Turkish society.

This analysis of the expropriation of Armenian property provides key insight into what is at stake regarding denial of the Armenian Genocide today. As calls for reparations for the Armenian Genocide mount, attempts to deny or obscure the Armenian Genocide support a final consolidation of these expropriations.

Waters, Anne, ed. *American Indian Thought: Philosophical Essays.* Malden, MA: Blackwell, 2004, 306 pp.

This collection of cutting-edge philosophical work from Native American scholars offers important insights into contemporary Native American philosophical methods and issues. By the very positioning of Native American scholars within the consolidative phase of the Native American Genocide, various articles deal with different aspects of the legacy of genocide as it impacts Native Americans today philosophically, politically, economically, culturally, and socially. Of particular relevance to the issue of genocide denial as an impediment to prevention and intervention are articles that consider aspects of the twentieth-century consolidation of the overarching process of the Native American Genocide. The fact that these tremendous benefits of genocide continue to accrue makes genocide quite attractive to some observers. Prevention of genocide, in part, depends on changing the calculation by stopping long-term consolidation of genocide of Native Americans and others.

In this collection, Leslie Nawagesic's "Phenomenology of a Mugwump Type of Life in an Autobiographical Snippet" (140–52) offers a firsthand account of among other things the process of forced assimilation of indigenous children in Canada.

In "Biocolonialism and the Commodification of Knowledge" (188–213), Laurie Anne Whitt discusses an important result of European domination of indigenous peoples of the Americas. Along with genocide, land theft, and destruction of indigenous ways of life, conquest also entailed the imposition of Western conceptual and legal apparatuses. The European notion of individual property that commodifies all elements of existence, including knowledge and natural matter such as plant types and uses, displaced indigenous notions of communal sharing of resources and knowledge and nonownership based on the view that such things were not created by would-be property owners and so cannot rightly be owned by individuals to the exclusion of others. Whitt describes how Euro-American corporations have claimed as intellectual property medicinal uses of various plant forms that were actually discovered by indigenous people, who willingly share them with any other people. She also discusses the desire to claim as intellectual property genetic analyses that might have medical benefits. As part of the consolidation of genocide, extensive indigenous knowledge is appropriated by the perpetrator groups for their own benefit, and to the exclusion of indigenous people.

In "The Jurisprudence of Colonialism" (217–28), Steve Russell details the policies, legal mechanisms, and extra-legal practices devised by the US government and private citizens to unfairly expropriate much of the land that remained in the hands of Native Americans in the twentieth century. An important technique was the parceling out of communally held and used land to individual owners. The result was a fragmentation of large land tracts into small, often unsustainable portions that could be easily swindled from their new "owners."

Films

Gibson, Dai Sil Kim. 1999. *Silence Broken*. VHS. 57 minutes. Color. Dai Sil Kim Gibson (Prod.). Sold by the Center for Asian American Media, 145 Ninth Street, Suite 350, San Francisco, CA 94104.

This documentary focuses on Comfort Women of Korea, from which probably the largest number of Comfort Women came. Specifically, it chronicles the horrific experiences of a set of former Comfort Women who in the early 1990s bravely came forward after more than four decades of virtual public silence vis-à-vis the issue to focus attention on the gross human rights violations to which they were subjected as sexual slaves of the Japanese military during the Pacific War. It combines interviews of numerous former Comfort Women, interviews of reputable scholars on the issue, interviews of deniers, period footage and photographs, and contemporary footage showing activism by the former Comfort Women.

While this was not a case of genocide, the systematic nature and impact of the slavery and violence (the high mortality rate of Comfort Women due to injury, disease, depression, forced drug use, and other factors), the crafty denial by academics and others in Japan, and the devastating long-term physical, economic, psychological, social, and cultural impact of the Comfort Women system on its victims make the case important in its own right and very instructive for the issue of consolidative denial.

After the issue exploded internationally in the early 1990s, the Japanese government refused to make an official apology, to recognize this mass crime against humanity for what it was, or to make official reparation. Individual court cases attempted by former Comfort Women were rarely accepted by Japanese courts, and those that were failed. By stalling for two decades, Japan has ensured that most of the former Comfort Women have died or will die without recognition, apology, or repair. Indeed, the desperate health conditions of former Comfort Women in their old age—the results of brutal physical abuse, crude surgeries, incessant rapes (sometimes reported to be thirty times per day), receipt of sexually transmitted diseases, psychological torment, and long-term trauma—required financing for medical care, especially because many Comfort Women, because of their experiences and physical and psychological damage, were poor and for various reasons (infertility, trauma, stigmatization by community, etc.) had little family and community support.

As in other cases, aggressive consolidative denial has meant that the perpetrator group has been able to harm, exploit, and benefit from what it did to victims without any final accountability. The lesson for would-be perpetrators is once more clear.

Grimm, Christopher (Wr.), Mandy Jacobson and Karmen Jelincic (Dirs.) 1996. *Calling the Ghosts: A Story about Rape, War and Women*. VHS and DVD. 63 minutes. Color. Julie Ormond (Exec. Producer). Purchase from Orders Department, Women Make Movies, 462 Broadway, Suite 500WS, New York, NY 10013.

Through incisive survivor narratives and analysis, this film offers an account of the rape camps used by the Serbs. A central element is a discussion of the relatively successful efforts by Serbs to cover up and deny the real nature of the camps from outsiders. Essentially, it captures the phenomenon of contemporaneous denial and its impact on victims.

Grunberg, Slawomir. 2005. *The Legacy of Jedwabne*. VHS and DVD. 72 minutes. Color. Slawomir Grunberg (Producers). Purchase from Log In Productions, LOGTV Ltd., 4 La Rue Road, Spencer, New York 14883.

This important film documents not only the Jedwabne pogrom of 1941 but also the denial by local Poles that it was Poles, not Germans, who carried out the massacre. In connection to denial, it exposes fears by some local Poles that victims will return to reclaim their property and thereby challenge permanent consolidation of the benefits that accrued to Jedwabne's Poles through their participation in the Holocaust.

4

The Wording and Interpretation of the UN Convention on the Prevention and Punishment of the Crime of Genocide: An Ongoing Impediment

Samuel Totten

Introduction

Ironic though it is, the UN Convention on the Prevention and Punishment of the Crime of Genocide (UNCG) has been an impediment—and in more ways than one—to the prevention and intervention of genocide. Time and again, the United Nations and individual states have either wavered over deeming certain atrocities to be genocidal in nature and/or totally avoided doing so, and that is due, at least in part, to the difficulty in ascertaining whether the perpetrators actually possess *the intent* (a key component of the UNCG) to commit genocide or not.[1]

Despite the fact that some genocide scholars are bound to groan at the focus of this chapter and think, "Not this worn out topic again," it is worthy of attention for at least five main reasons: (1) individual nations and the United Nations continue to be wary of asserting that certain mass atrocities constitute genocide—and while they waver, people in the tens and hundreds of thousands often, literally, lose their lives; (2) ad hoc criminal tribunals, national tribunals, and the International Criminal Court (ICC) continue to debate and battle over the interpretation of various words, phrases, and concepts in the UNCG; (3) relatively recent work by scholars, particularly specialists in international law, have raised critical questions in regard to how various aspects of the UNCG should be interpreted, which, ultimately, may impact case law; (4) varied interpretations of "intent" have been used in trials at the International Criminal Tribunal for the former Yugoslavia (ICTY) and the International Criminal Tribunal for Rwanda (ICTR), and this has resulted in removing some of the impediments once posed by the UNCG; and (5) a relatively recent finding at the International Court of Justice (ICJ) has altered the understanding of state responsibility in regard to preventing genocide. As one can readily ascertain, the interpretation and implementation of the UNCG continues to be a lively *and* timely issue.

Significantly, the version of the UNCG submitted for ratification resulted from a series of compromises.[2] Such compromises have had, and continue to have, an impact on ascertaining whether or not cases of mass violence constitute genocide (both while the atrocities are being perpetrated and as cases are being tried in tribunals and courts of law).

Among the thorniest issues vis-à-vis the UNCG are (1) the various concerns regarding the term and concept of "intent"; (2) the practical/actual meaning of the wording "in part"; (3) the fact that certain groups, most notably, political, are not listed as being protected under the UNCG[3]; and (4) how, in various crisis situations, to ascertain whether a victim group is actually protected under the UNCG (i.e., whether it is a racial group, an ethnic group, a national group, etc.).

Another major concern is that the UNCG primarily focuses on punishment versus *prevention*. As Kuper (1985) noted, "The convention . . . makes only two perfunctory references to prevention. [The UNCG] is essentially directed to punishment of the crimes, with the possibly deterrent effect of the threat of punishment as the main contribution to prevention" (11).[4] Schabas (2009) further notes, ". . . while the final Convention has much to say about punishment of genocide, there is little to suggest what prevention of genocide really means. Certainly, nothing in the debates about article 1 provides the slightest clue as to the scope of the obligation to prevent" (81).

By not addressing the issue of prevention head on (including that which constitutes prevention, and when and how the process is to be activated), those responsible for finalizing the wording of the

UNCG contributed to one of its main weaknesses. One has to wonder whether that was truly an oversight or whether the authors conspired to conveniently overlook the flaw. Unfortunately, the UNCG, by default, privileges punishment over prevention.[5]

In Real Time: The Perplexity of Ascertaining Atrocities Are Genocide

Just weeks into the 1994 Rwandan Genocide, officials of various states and international entities debated over what was taking place in Rwanda: whether it constituted a civil war, the outbreak of ancient enmities between the Hutu and Tutsi, crimes against humanity, or genocide. While the debates ensued, the killing (which, indeed, was genocide) continued unabated. Granted, some of the debates, such as those within the administration of President Bill Clinton in the United States, were disingenuous and engaged in for the express purpose of avoiding any and all responsibility to attempt to halt the genocide and protect the Tutsi and moderate Hutu from imminent slaughter. In fact, it is well documented that individuals in the State Department even commented on the need to avoid using the term "genocide" for if they did they feared it would obligate the United States, under the UNCG (and they mentioned the UNCG by name), to step into to prevent the atrocities.

That said, many of those involved in the guessing game—including journalists, scholars, and other governmental officials—were making honest attempts to piece together the bits and pieces of information that spluttered out of Rwanda, all in an ardent attempt to ascertain exactly what was taking place and why. In doing so, not a few referred to the UNCG in order to assist them to make such a judgment. Terrifyingly for the victims, as the debates continued apace the killing raged on unabated. Most, today, agree (though it does the dead absolutely no good) that the international community should not have wasted time debating whether the atrocities were one thing or another, and should have taken a proactive stance to halt the killing. The only way to prevent genocide is to quell a conflict before it reaches genocidal proportions.

Another classic example in regard to the difficulty governments and others have faced in their attempt to ascertain whether the perpetration of certain atrocities constitute genocide or not is the ongoing debate over what to deem the atrocities in Darfur, Sudan. While the United States, on September 9, 2004, declared that genocide had been perpetrated in Darfur by the Government of Sudan (GoS), the United Nations issued a report in late January 2005 that concluded that crimes against humanity but not genocide had been committed in Darfur by the GoS. Later still, following an in-depth investigation by the ICC into the crisis in Darfur, ICC Chief Prosecutor Luis Moreno-Ocampo requested a warrant (July 14, 2008) to arrest Sudanese President Omar al-Bashir on charges of genocide, but after examining the request, the majority of the ICC judges in Pre-Trial Chamber 1 chose to solely issue a warrant for crimes against humanity (March 4, 2009). One judge (Ms. Anita Usacka), though, wrote a separate and partly dissenting opinion in which she asserted that the court should have issued a warrant charging both genocide and crimes against humanity. On July 6, 2009, Moreno-Ocampo filed an appeal, arguing that the court's decision was wrong, and on February 3, 2010, the ICC Appeals Chamber rendered its decision, and in doing so reversed the majority's decision for requiring "an erroneous standard of proof." In turn, it ordered the judges in Pre-Trial Chamber 1 to reconsider its decision, taking note of its initial error. After reexamining the prosecutor's request for a warrant on charges of genocide, Pre-Trial Chamber 1 issued a warrant for the arrest of Omar al-Bashir on charges of genocide and crimes against humanity (July 12, 2010). To this day, various scholars continue to argue over whether the atrocities committed in Darfur constitute genocide or crimes against humanity.[6]

The Wording/Concept/Issue of Intent

Over the past two decades numerous scholars have called into question the sagacity of retaining the concept of "intent"[7] in the UNCG's definition of genocide, arguing that (a) the term is ambiguous; (b) without a record (written or oral) denoting intent, it is nearly impossible for potential interveners to know whether perpetrators intend to destroy a specific group in whole or in part, as such; and (c) intent is extremely difficult to prove in a court of law.[8]

A key question that prosecutors and courts have wrestled with is: If no written records (memoranda, directives, minutes of meetings, telegrams, etc.) are issued and no oral statements are made over television, radio, or other electronic means, how can intent be ascertained? Various prosecutors, judges, and scholars of international law have asserted that attempting to ascertain what a perpetrator was thinking while planning or carrying out atrocities is virtually impossible. In fact, during the Akayesu case at the ICTR, the judges admitted as much: "The Chamber considers that intent is a mental factor which is difficult, even impossible to determine" (ICTR 1998, supra note 98, para. 523).[9] (The issue of how to ascertain intent will be returned to later in the chapter.)

On a different but significant note, Kuper (1981) argued that "the requirement of 'intent' provides an easy means for evading responsibility. Its omission from a definition of genocide as quite simply the destruction of a human group might have been some contribution to the suppression and punishment of this crime" (35–36). A classic example of a government attempting to evade such responsibility took place in 1976 when Paraguay's Defense Minister replied as follows to accusations that Paraguay had committed genocide against the Guayaki Indians: "Although there are victims and victimizer, there is not the third element necessary to establish the crimes of genocide—that is, 'intent.' Therefore, as there is no 'intent,' one cannot speak of 'genocide'" (quoted in Lewis 1976).

Tellingly, Cherif Bassiouni (1993), a renowned expert on international law, believes that the authors of the UNCG should have, at least, provided an explanatory note as to what they meant by "intent" in relation to the crime of genocide. He also believes that the specific intent requirement of the UNCG is set too high (Bassiouni 1993, 233). In regard to the latter point, Bassiouni (1993) lambasted the International Law Commission (ILC) for neglecting "to progressively define Article 2 of the 1948 Convention in light of the clearly perceived need for it considering all of the quasi-genocidal conduct that have taken place since 1948" (233). In clarifying his position, Bassiouni (1993) asserted that "It is not difficult to think of a number of contemporary conflicts such as those in Cambodia and the former Yugoslavia, where there is obviously no paper trail and where the specific intent can only be shown by the cumulative effect of the objective conduct to which one necessarily has to add the inference of specific intent deriving from omission" (233).[10]

Both the ICTR and the ICTY have, in fact, resorted to using a less rigorous (or, put another way, a more lenient) intent requirement than that of *dolus specialis* (or specific intent), which most have regarded as mandated by the UNCG. More specifically, in cases where documents and/or oral statements have not been available (which is generally the case, as genocidaires are generally wily enough not to leave a paper or electronic trail of their thought processes vis-à-vis their plans, orders, and accomplishments), the prosecutors used, and the judges allowed, the presentation of facts about what took place on the ground and/or what the alleged perpetrators likely knew would be the results of their actions.[11]

For example, during the Akayesu case at the ICTR, the judges allowed a lower (or more lenient) level of intent to be used. In choosing to proceed with an intent requirement lower than *dolus specialis*, the judges stated (after noting, as previously mentioned, that "intent is a mental factor, which is difficult, even impossible, to determine") the following:

> [I]n the absence of a confession from the accused, his intent can be inferred from a certain number of presumptions of fact. The Chamber considers that it is possible to deduce the genocidal intent inherent in a particular act charged from the general context of the perpetration of other culpable acts systematically directed against that same group whether these acts were committed by the same offender or by others. Other factors, such as the scale of atrocities committed, their general nature, in a region or a country, or furthermore, the fact of deliberately and systematically targeting victims on account of their membership of a particular group, while excluding the members of other groups, can enable the Chamber to infer the genocidal intent of a particular act" (cited in ICTY, supra note 98, para. 523). Significantly, "the method adopted by the ICTR in this particular case was used as a benchmark in several other cases. (*Prosecutor v. Akayesu*, ICTR 1998, para. 523)

Concomitantly, the Trial Chamber I judges at the ICTY asserted that "the intent which is peculiar to the crime of genocide need not be clearly expressed . . .; in the Nikolic case, [the judges asserted that] the intent may be inferred from a certain number of facts such as the general political doctrine, which gave rise to the acts possibly covered by the definition in Article 4, or the repetition of destructive and discriminatory acts"[12] (Jones 2000, 101–2). Continuing, the judges asserted that "The intent may also be inferred from the perpetration of acts which violate, or which the perpetrators themselves consider to violate, the very foundation of the group—acts which are not in themselves covered by the list in Article 4(2) but which are committed as part of the same pattern of conduct" (Jones 2000, 101).

Finally, Goldsmith (2010) argues that, in actuality, the dolus specialis (or special intent) requirements "goes beyond what the [UNCG] intended and what Lemkin foresaw" (246). More specifically, she asserts that

> Otto Triffterer [an expert on international law] argues this point, adding that arguing *dolus specialis* 'would not only go beyond the wording, but would introduce a concept not precisely defined. . . . [or] . . . generally accepted in Common Law countries. And even in Civil Law countries the concept of specific or special intent in the sense of *dolus specialis* is highly disputed. . . . To include an intent requirement that is extremely difficult to provide after the fact, and which is a contested term in many civil law countries, renders the Genocide Convention both confusing and ineffective. (Goldsmith 2010, 246)

Wording of "in Whole or in Part"

To this day, both scholars and jurists continue to wrestle with exactly what "in part" means (or should mean) in the UNCG in relation to an actual case of genocide.[13] As Schabas (2009) notes, "The 1948 debates in the Sixth Committee [which was involved in pounding out the wording of the UNCG to be proposed to the international community for ratification], and for that matter, all of the preparatory work of the Convention, provide little guidance as to what the draftees meant by 'in part'" (275).

There are several reasons as to why it would not have made sense to have included a specific number (or, for that matter, a certain percentage) as constituting "in part" in the UNCG. First, if that had been done, genocidaires could have conveniently and purposely killed just under such a number or percentage. Second, different populations would be affected quite differently, and in some cases, radically, as a result of losing some arbitrary number or percentage of people. For example, a small indigenous group could be all but wiped out even if a relatively "small" number, say, 500 members were killed, whereas the murder of 500 Hindus residing in India would be horrific but not threaten the group's viability. So, to come up with a specific number or percentage would have made no sense at all.[14]

Be that as it may, as Schabas (2009) notes, "Even a small number of actual victims is enough to establish the material element. The quantity killed or injured remains a relevant material fact, but what is really germane to the debate is whether the author of the crimes *intended* to destroy the group 'in whole or in part'" (italics added) (276). Still, it is also true that debates continue unabated over whether "in part" means a substantive part and if so, what, exactly, substantive means in this regard.[15]

The following comments/observations by Schabas (2009) provide useful insights as to how the wording "in part" has been interpreted in various ways by both scholars and jurists in the courtroom:

> There are four different approaches to the scope of the term "in part." The first is the most narrow, and effectively insists that, while the result may only be partial destruction, the intent must be to destroy the entire group . . . The second approach adds the adjective "substantial" in order to modify "part." This is the interpretation that the United States eventually adopted when it ratified the Convention some forty years later. The United States formulated a declaration affirming that the meaning of article II is "in whole or in substantial part." In its own domestic legislation, the United States defines "substantial part" as "a part of a group of such numerical significance that the destruction or loss of that part would cause the destruction of the group as a viable entity within the nation of which such group is a part." The International Law Commission considered that "[i]t is not necessary to intend to achieve the complete annihilation of a group from every corner of the globe. None the less the crime of genocide by its very nature requires the intention to destroy at least a substantial part of a particular group . . . Similarly, the final draft statute of the Preparatory Committee of the International Criminal Court noted that "the reference to 'intent to destroy, in whole or in part . . . a group, as such' was understood to refer to the specific intention to destroy more than a small number of individuals who are members of a group." The International Criminal Tribunal for Rwanda, in [the cases of] Kayishema and Ruzindana, said, "that 'in part' requires the intention to destroy a 'very important part.'" In another judgment, the Tribunal referred to a "reasonably substantial" number relative to the group as a whole. The "substantial part" interpretation is well entrenched in the case law of the ad hoc tribunals. (277, 278)

What, though, constitutes "substantial." This is an issue that prosecutors, defenders, and judges have deliberated over and one that, at least for now, must finally be decided upon by the judges on a case-by-case basis. It is also an issue that continues to confound genocide scholars.

Continuing to issue the address the meaning of "in part," Schabas (2009) notes the following:

> . . . More helpful is the observation of a Trial Chamber of the International Criminal Tribunal for the former Yugoslavia to the effect that:
>
> . . . the intent to destroy a group, even if only in part, means seeking to destroy a distinct part of the group as opposed to an

> accumulation of isolated individuals within it. Although the perpetrators of genocide need not seek to destroy the entire group protected by the Convention, they must view the part of the group they wish to destroy as a distinct entity which must be eliminated as such. A campaign resulting in the killings, in different places spread over a broad geographical area, of a finite number of members of a protected group might not thus qualify as genocide, despite the high total number of casualties, because it would not show an intent by the perpetrators to target the very existence of the group as such. (280)

By "a distinct part of the group," the ICTY Trial Chamber seems to be suggesting such parts, for example, constitute one or more of the following: those who hold leadership positions; those who are educated (which could mean anyone with an education above, for example, fourth grade or so in areas where education of the populace is particularly limited, or it may be limited to those with a secondary level education); females of child-bearing age, etc.

Still addressing the issue of "in part," Schabas (2009) notes that:

> a third approach takes more of a qualitative than a quantitative perspective on the meaning of "in part," reading in the adjective "significant." . . . . [I]t treats viability not as if there is some critical mass of a group in a numeric sense below which it cannot survive, but rather in terms of irreparable impact upon a group's chances of survival when a stratum of its population, generally political, social or economic, is liquidated. (281)

This approach raises as many questions as it attempts to answer. For example, in this context what does "significant" mean? And who is to decide what constitutes "significant" versus "insignificant"? Furthermore, who is going to decide, and how, whether the attacks/violence have caused "irreparable impact upon a group's chances of survival"? Might that not only be accessed in the aftermath of the violence, and possibly many years afterward?

Schabas (2009) goes on to report the following:

> Citing the Whitaker report, the Commission of Experts, established by the [UN] Security Council in 1992 to investigate violations of international humanitarian law in the former Yugoslavia, held that "in part" had not only a quantitative but also a qualitative dimension. According to the chair of the Commission of Experts, Professor M. Cherif Bassiouni, it considered the definition in the Genocide Convention to be sufficiently pliable to encompass not

> only the target of an entire group, as stated in the Convention, but also the targeting of certain segments of a given group, such as the Muslim elite or Muslim women.
>
> This novel approach of the Commission of Experts was invoked by the Prosecutor of the International Criminal Tribunal for the former Yugoslavia in some indictments, and subsequently endorsed by the judges themselves (282–83). [See page 284 in the Schabas' article for a key quote from the *Krstic* judgment at the ICTY, which dealt with the Srebrenica case, in order to glean how the court addressed the issue of "significant part."]

Schabas (2009) concludes by observing the following:

> Finally, some interpretations[within the same Chamber at the ICTY] of "in whole or in part" focus on the groups in a geographic sense. Thus, destroying all members of a group within a continent, or a country, or an administrative region or even a town, might satisfy the "in part" requirement of article II . . . In Jelisic, another Trial Chamber of the same Tribunal, [it was] agreed that genocide could be committed in a "limited geographic zone." And in Krstic, the Trial Chamber held that "the physical destruction may target only a part of the geographically limited part of the larger group because the perpetrators of the genocide regarded the intended destruction as sufficient to annihilate the group as a distinct entity in the geographic area at issue." (285, 286)

As is readily apparent, the wording of the UNCG as it relates to the words "in part" leaves itself wide open to broad interpretation, which leads one to ponder how the authors of the UNCG understood the phrase.

Other Issues: The Distinction between "Complicity in Genocide" and "Aiding and Abetting" a Genocide

Article 3 of the UNCG lists the various acts that are punishable vis-à-vis the issue of genocide, and they are as follows: (a) genocide; (b) conspiracy to commit genocide; (c) direct and public incitement to commit genocide; (d) attempt to commit genocide; and (e) complicity in genocide. Like other terms/concepts in the UNCG, some of the aforementioned terms/phrases/acts have also led to confusion.

More specifically, in an article entitled "The Crime of Complicity in Genocide: How the International Criminal Tribunals for Rwanda and Yugoslavia Got It Wrong, and Why It Matters," Daniel M. Greenfield (2008) discusses the distinction between "complicity in genocide" and "aiding and abetting genocide," and how the ICTR and ICTY misinterpreted the meaning of the two concepts by assuming they were one and the same, and thus allowed alleged genocidaires from being held accountable for their crimes. More specifically, Greenfield (2008) asserts that

> Jurists at the International Criminal Tribunals for Yugoslavia and Rwanda have erroneously determined that "complicity in genocide" is identical to "aiding and abetting" genocide. Accordingly, they theorize that complicity in genocide is not a crime itself, but merely a misplaced and superfluous liability provision for the crime of genocide. In reality, the two crimes are distinct and designed to capture very different perpetrators. One guilty of aiding and abetting genocide had as his very purpose the facilitation of the commission of genocide. A perpetrator of the crime of complicity in genocide, in contrast, may not have had genocide as his purpose. Instead, genocide may merely have been the foreseeable result of his actions. As such, one found guilty of aiding and abetting genocide must have the heightened, and difficult to establish, *mens rea* of the genocidaire. . . . By comparison, one guilty of complicity in genocide need not have this heightened *mens rea*. Instead, a lesser *mens rea* such as malice or what I term the "specific intent without specific motive," should suffice to attach guilt. Failure to appreciate this difference creates a gaping loophole in international criminal law, providing unwarranted sanctuary to those who enable genocide." (951)

While this distinction is certainly significant, it needs to be noted that if the international community is eventually willing to move toward accepting a knowledge-based understanding/requirement of intent, then the concern over the issue of *mens rea* shall be moot.

Ascertaining Whether a Victim Group Is Protected under the UNCG

In regard to two relatively recent genocides—the 1994 Rwandan Genocide and the Darfur genocide in Sudan (2003 to present)—various scholars and jurists raised questions as to whether the victim groups—the Tutsi in Rwanda and the black Africans of Darfur—could be considered a protected group under the UNCG.

Larissa van den Herik (2007) addressed this very issue as cases concerning the Rwandan genocide were being tried at the ICTR:

> When the ICTR judges applied the legal definition to the situation of Rwanda they encountered another problem, namely the problem

> of how to define which classes of groups could be qualified as protected groups. After an initial failed attempt to provide some sort of objective, static definition for each of the four classes of groups [protected under the UNCG] on external factors, the ICTR Trial Chambers implicitly acknowledged that the concepts such as ethnicity and race were mainly social artifacts. Consequently, the Trial Chambers took the 'victims' and the 'perpetrators'[Hutus'] identification of the Tutsi as an ethnic group as a starting point. Hence, these subjective factors started to play a preponderant role in the process of determining whether the Tutsi as a whole were a protected group. . . . Ultimately, *[i]n the words of the Trial Chamber in the Semanza Judgment: "the determination of whether a group comes within the sphere of protection created by Article 2 of the Statute ought to be assessed in a case-by-case basis by reference to the objective particular of a given social or historical context and by the subjective perceptions of the perpetrators."* (italics added) (79–80)

The aforementioned issue and decision is bound to impact the ICC case against Omar al-Bashir and his cronies in regard to the Government of Sudan's and Janjaweed's attacks against the black Africans of Darfur. For years, various scholars, among others, have argued that the black Africans of Darfur and the Arabs who attacked them are one and the same as they have the same lineage, are all black, speak the same language, have the same religion (Islam), share the same culture, live in Africa, and so on. Other scholars, however, have argued that the perpetrators, who consider themselves to be Arab, perceive their victims to be "black" and not Arab. Concomitantly, these same scholars argue, the victims consider themselves to be "black" and their attackers "Arab."

The ICTY also wrestled over how to define a particular group and "displayed a willingness to interpret broadly." Like the ICTR, the ICTY "generally used the subjective approach complemented by the objective approach to determine whether the victim group was a group protected by the 1948 Genocide Convention" (van den Herik 2007, 86). More specifically, van den Herik (2007) notes that:

> In the Jelisic case, an ICTY Trial Chamber demonstrated that the groups mentioned in the Convention were originally supposed to be objectively defined. However, the Trial Chamber held that such an objective classification might not correspond to the perceived reality for the persons concerned. For that reason, the Trial Chamber opted for the subjective approach. In the case of Krstic, the Trial Chamber held that the relevant group could be identified *"by using as a*

criterion the stigmatization of the group, notably by the perpetrator of the crime, not the basis of its perceived national, ethnical, racial or religious characteristics." It thus emphasized that the subjective approach should prevail in identifying a group. However, the Trial Chamber also noted that "a group's cultural, religious, ethnical or national characteristics must be identified within the socio-historic context which it inhabits." The statement might reveal that objective criteria . . . should still play a complementary role. The Trial Chamber in the Blagojevic case also held: "The Trial Chamber finds that the correct determination of the relevant protected group has to be made on a case-by-case basis, consulting both objective and subjective criteria." (italics added) (86–87)

The UNCG and Its Interpretation at the ICTR and ICTY

As one can readily ascertain from the above discussion, decisions within the ICTR and ICTY have impacted the interpretation of the UNCG in numerous and significant ways. In certain cases, decisions have led to new and innovative interpretations (and applications) of key words and phrases in the UNCG. At one and the same time, different Chambers of *the same court* have interpreted the very same word or phrase in radically different ways.

Below is a sample of various decisions (some of which have already been touched upon or alluded to herein) that different ICTR and ICTY Chambers have made in regard to the interpretation of various concepts, words, and phrases in the UNCG[16]:

*Intent can be inferred from a certain number of facts, as concerns genocide, crimes against humanity and war crimes, for instance, from their *massive and/or systematic nature* (italics added) or their atrocity, to be considered *infra* in the judgment, in the Tribunal's findings on the law applicable to each of the three crimes which constitute its *ratione materiae* jurisdiction. (Tadic case, ICTY)

*Trial Chamber I of the International Criminal Tribunal for the former Yugoslavia stated that the specific intent of the crime of genocide "may be inferred from a number of facts such as *the general political doctrine which gave rise to the acts possibly covered by the definition in Article 4, or the repetition of destructive and discriminatory acts* (italics added). *The intent may also be inferred from the perpetration of acts which violate, or which the perpetrators themselves consider to violate, the very foundation of the group—acts which are not in themselves covered by the list in Article 4(2) but which are committed as part of the same pattern of conduct*" (italics added). Thus, in the matter brought before the International

Criminal Tribunal for the former Yugoslavia, the Trial Chamber, in its findings, found that "this intent derives from the combined effect of speeches or projects laying the groundwork for and justifying the acts, from the massive scale of their destructive effect and from their specific nature, which aims at undermining what is considered to be the foundation of the group." (Cited in Akayesu case, ICTR, Judgment, 134)

*For purposes of interpreting Article 2(2)(d) of the Statute, the Chamber holds that the measures intended to prevent births within the group should be construed as sexual mutilation, the practice of sterilization, forced birth control, separation of the sexes, and prohibition of marriages. In patriarchal societies, where membership of a group is determined by the identity of the father, an example of a measure intended to prevent births within a group is the case where, during rape, a woman of the said group is deliberately impregnated by a man of another group, with the intent to have her give birth to a child who will consequently not belong to its mother's group. (Akayesu case, Judgment, ICTR, 131)

*On the issue of determining the offender's specific intent, the Chamber considers that intent is a mental factor which is difficult, even impossible, to determine. This is the reason why, in the absence of a confession from the accused, his intent can be inferred from a certain number of presumptions of fact. The Chamber considers that it is possible to deduce the genocidal intent inherent in a particular act charged from the general context of the perpetration of other culpable acts systematically directed against that same group, whether these acts were committed by the same offender or by others. Other factors, such as the scale of atrocities committed, their general nature, in a region or a country, or furthermore, the fact of deliberately and systematically targeting victims on account of their membership of a particular group, while excluding the members of other groups, can enable the Chamber to infer the genocidal intent of a particular act. (Akayesu case, Judgment, ICTR, 133)

*In this connection, the Chamber recalls that, in its findings on the applicable law, it held that an accused is an accomplice to genocide if he or she knowingly and willfully aided or abetted or instigated another to commit a crime of genocide, while being aware of his genocidal plan, even where the accused had no specific intent to destroy, in whole or in part, a national, ethnical, racial, or religious group, as such. (Akayesu case, Judgment, ICTR, 175)

*In the case of Blagojevic, Trial Chamber 1 of the ICTY accepted that 'intent to destroy' means the physical or biological destruction of the group, but it also found that physical or biological destruction was the likely outcome of a forcible transfer if the group could no longer reconstitute itself.[17] (ICTY January 2005, para. 666)

> *A state, not just an individual, can be held under the UNCG for genocide, conspiracy to commit genocide, direct and public incitement to commit genocide, attempt to commit genocide, or of complicity in genocide. (*Bosnia v. Serbia*, The International Court of Justice February 2007)

> *The obligation on each contracting State to prevent genocide is both normative and compelling. It is not merged in the duty to punish, nor can it be regarded as simply a component of that duty. It has its own scope, which extends beyond the particular case envisaged in Article VIII, namely reference to the competent organs of the United Nations, for them to take such action as they deem appropriate. Even if and when these organs have been called upon, this does not mean that the State parties to the Convention are relieved of the obligation to take such action as they can to prevent genocide from occurring, while respecting the United Nations Charter and any decisions that may have been taken by its competent organs.[18] (International Court of Justice 2007, para. 427)

> *A State's obligation to prevent, and the corresponding duty to act, arise at the instant that the State learns of, or should normally have learned of, the existence of a serious risk that genocide will be committed. From that moment onward, if the State has available to it means likely to have a deterrent effect on those suspected of preparing genocide, or reasonably suspected of harbouring specific intent *(dolus specialis)*, it is under a duty to make such use of these means as the circumstances permit.[19] (International Court of Justice 2007, para. 431)

This last judgment (Case Concerning Application of the Convention on the Prevention and Punishment of the Crime of Genocide [*Bosnia and Herzegovina v. Serbia and Montenegro*, JUDGMENT OF 26 FEBRUARY 2007]) by the ICJ is what was referenced at the outset of this chapter. It virtually clears up the sixty-odd-year debate as to whether the UNCG obligates states that ratified the Convention to attempt to prevent genocide or not and whether that obligation is moral or legal. For years, legal scholars and others have argued that "obligation" was a moral but not a legal obligation. With the February 26, 2007, judgment by the ICJ, member states of the international community now understand that the obligation is, in fact, legal.

How this will play out, though, is the question that looms over the decision. That is, if states purposely avoid preventing genocide will there be a penalty for not doing so? And who will apply the penalty? It seems that while the decision is notable and could presage a sea change in international law, it is too early to be jubilant in regard to what it means vis-à-vis the actual prevention of genocide. Currently, it seems as if Scheffer's hope (i.e., "It is to be hoped that the ICJ's judgment will inspire national legal systems—and, ultimately, lead to future legislation and judicial decisions—to hold their own governments to the high standard of prevention and punishment now reflected in the ICJ's enforcement of the UNCG") may remain a hope and little more.

Alternative Concepts, Terms, and Approaches in Lieu of or in Addition to "Genocide"

Various individuals have suggested the need for the use of alternative concepts in lieu of and/or in addition to that of "genocide." Some of the more notable suggestions along this line are: politicide, crimes against humanity (see the discussion below concerning the Crimes against Humanity Initiative), atrocity crimes, precursors of genocide, and extremely violent societies. Among some of the many reasons such concepts/terms have been suggested are frustration with the definitional debates over that which constitutes genocide, the ambiguity of some of the wording in the UNCG and the problem that presents in ascertaining whether current atrocities constitute genocide or not, the difficulty of trying and winning cases of genocide in tribunals and courts of law, and the belief by some that the concept of genocide is now passé. Due to space constraints only two of the more recent ideas/innovations will be, even if only succinctly, outlined and commented upon here.

In 2008, the Crimes against Humanity Initiative was established by a group of international law specialists to "study the need for and to ultimately elaborate a comprehensive international convention on the prevention and punishment of crimes against humanity." In August 2010, the group completed its work on the development of its *Proposed International Convention for the Prevention and Punishment of Crimes Against Humanity*. Subsequent meetings were held with academics, diplomats, and members of civil society to discuss the proposed convention and seek support for it.

The proposed convention comprises "three core pillars": prevention, punishment, and effective capacity building to facilitate such prevention and punishment. Prevention, then, is purportedly an essential component of the proposed convention.[20]

Ostensibly, those who developed the proposed convention on crimes against humanity believe that it can replace the UNCG for, as some of them argue, it covers virtually the same crimes as the UNCG *and* would do away with the need to engage the thorny issue of "intent." That is, unlike the UNCG, where the intent of the perpetrators to destroy in whole or in part a particular group, as such, must be established in order for an act to be considered a case of "genocide," intent is not needed (or, put another way, not a factor) in determining whether one act or another constitutes a crime against humanity.[21]

Time and again in the recent past, both individual states and the UN sat and watched as mass atrocities unfolded. Reportedly, officials were either not sure (1) the actions constituted genocide versus civil war, ethnic cleansing, crimes against humanity, or something else altogether; and/or (2) whether the actual intent of the perpetrators was to destroy in whole or in part a particular group protected under the UNCG, as such. As a result, officials of individual states and the international community often insisted on waiting for additional evidence, even as tens and hundreds of thousands were slaughtered, before making a decision to intervene (in one way or another) or not. Essentially, officials seemed to be saying, "Well, if it is not a case of genocide then we do not have to act, and since genocide is so difficult to ascertain, if not prove, we'd better be absolutely sure before we make our final decision." A classic example of such wavering and dithering took place during the 1994 Rwandan Genocide. Not only did the UN fail to act, but the United States used its "confusion" and "lack of certainty" as a convenient excuse to do nothing. The fact is, the United States knew full well what was happening in Rwanda but wanted to avoid, at all costs, sending troops to intervene.

Essentially, those proposing the new convention seem to be saying that since crimes against humanity are easier to ascertain/establish than genocide, once the International Convention for the Prevention and Punishment of Crimes against Humanity goes into effect neither states nor the international community will be able to hem and haw, at least not legitimately, over what to call atrocities before choosing to intervene or not. Neither, of course, will they be handicapped by the need to establish the intent of the perpetrators.

If the proposed convention results in states, individually and/or collectively, actually becoming more proactive in addressing atrocity crimes and carrying out preventive and interventive efforts in a timely and effective manner, then that would certainly constitute a watershed event. *But that is a huge if.* Indeed, it seems as if *realpolitik* will come into play just as prominently and strongly as ever when, for example, the United Nations (here I am thinking of the UN Security Council, and particularly the Permanent Five, P5) is faced with a potential or actual outbreak of crimes against humanity or genocide.

The steering committee of the International Convention for the Prevention and Punishment of Crimes against Humanity and its supporters seem rather naïve vis-à-vis their belief in the projected efficacy of their proposed convention. After all, why would the international community suddenly lose its ostensible aversion to carrying out preventive and interventive efforts solely because of a new convention? And why would states suddenly succumb to *readily* carrying out preventive and interventive measures/missions that, as most seem to fear, could cost them dearly in a variety of ways: politically, at home *and* internationally, militarily, and monetarily? And why would countries all of a sudden be *more willing* to join preventive and interventive efforts when many already fear potential quagmires from which they might not be able to extricate themselves from for years?

It *is* understandable why the steering committee believes that it will be much easier to prosecute atrocities as crimes against humanity versus genocide, but prevention and intervention are something altogether different. The major point here, again, is that a tremendous amount of work needs to be done to overcome *realpolitik*, a lack of political will and a lack of caring. To not face this fact is sheer folly. Simply put, the introduction and ratification of a new convention and enactment of additional human rights law are highly unlikely to accomplish material change in global politics. To think otherwise is nothing short of naiviete.

On a different but somewhat similar note, David Scheffer (2008), a professor of international law at Northwestern University and a former US Ambassador at Large for War Crimes Issues, has proposed the development and use of two new terms, which he believes may facilitate the detection and intervention of genocide: "precursors to genocide" and "atrocity crimes," the latter of which he suggests as a "a unifying term" (111) for genocide, crimes against humanity, ethnic cleansing, and war crimes. Scheffer is not talking about doing away with the term or concept of genocide per se, but argues that the use of "precursors to genocide" and "atrocity crimes" could eliminate the debate over what to call mass killing *as it begins to be perpetrated.* He argues that the use of the terms could help to distinguish between the political and legal uses of the term/concept "genocide"; and in doing so, make the political application of genocide both broader (and more flexible), which, hypothetically, could expedite interventionary efforts as an intervention could be implemented as soon as any indicators of genocide were evident.

As one can imagine, there has been a fair amount of discussion and debate over the sagacity and value of introducing such terms into the mix. While many have complimented Schaffer for his ingenuity, others question whether the new terminology and concepts would truly result in making the international community anymore proactive in addressing genocide head on in a timely and effective manner. (For a detailed discussion of both the terms and a debate over them, see David Scheffer's "Genocide and Atrocity Crimes," in *Genocide Studies and Prevention: An International Journal* 1, no. 3 (2006): 229–50; and the special issue ["The Prevention of Genocide: Ideas from International Politics and a Symposium on International Law," in *Genocide Studies and Prevention: An International Journal* 2, no. 1 (Spring 2007).])

When it comes to Scheffer's proposition regarding the use of new terms, I tend to agree with Payam Akhavan's argument in his article entitled "Proliferation of Terminology and the Illusion of Progress":

> The arguments that the loaded term "genocide" intimidates states from responding effectively must be assessed against the fact that alternative categorizations have only marginal impact on meaningful action where there is a failure of political will. Are we to conclude, for instance, that US willingness to characterize the Darfur situation as "genocide" resulted in a more robust response compared to Rwanda where there was reluctance to use this term? Or, conversely, that if the term "atrocity crimes" had been used in an early-warning context, there would have been greater preventive engagement on the part of the United Nations prior to escalation into genocidal violence? (73)
>
> . . . The bottom line is that what we need most is not a conceptual or rhetorical magic bullet, but, rather, a greater focus on integrating and mainstreaming existing concepts and institutions into the daily habits and rituals of decision-makers, with a view to transforming an entrenched culture of reaction into a culture of prevention. (74)

Recommendation

Article 8 of the UNCG states that "Any Contracting Party may call upon the competent organs of the United Nations to take such action under the Charter of the United Nations as they consider appropriate for the prevention and suppression of acts of genocide or any of the other acts enumerated in Article 3." Since *realpolitik* generally plays a part in regard to whether a nation will call on the UN to take action to prevent and/or suppress acts of genocide (or the other acts enumerated in Article 3), and the likelihood of such happening is minimal, serious consideration by the United Nations should be given to revising Article 8 so that it allows nongovernmental organizations to report a situation that appears to be slouching toward genocide or has already broken out. In that way, potential and actual cases of genocide would have a better chance of being brought to the attention of the international community. That, in and of itself, could serve as a valuable means of early warning.

A classic case of where an NGO was more on top of a situation slouching toward genocide than, ostensibly, either the United Nations or individual nations, was Human Rights Watch's (HRW) repeated warnings throughout the early 1990s that massacres (actually, test massacres) were being carried out in Rwanda. If HRW had had the right to call upon the competent organs of the United Nations to take action under the Charter of the United Nations, perhaps some 500,000 to one million innocent people would have been saved from the savagery that engulfed them.

Providing an opportunity for more actors to report such situations would not obligate the United Nations to carry out an intervention, as that would ultimately be decided upon by the UN Security Council. Be that as it may, broadening the opportunity to report such situations would, at the least, draw attention to critical situations. Concomitantly, it would prevent individual nations, the Secretary General, and the Security Council from falsely claiming that they had not known about a crisis involving atrocity crimes, had somehow overlooked such a crisis, and/or had misinterpreted the events, etc.

Conclusion

As cases of genocide continue to be tried in international criminal tribunals and at the ICC, new interpretations and precedents are bound to be set vis-à-vis the meaning of key words and concepts in the UNCG. At one and the same time, what the future holds in regard to whether a knowledge-based approach will be more widely accepted, or not, will be interesting to see. The same is true in regard to the Crimes against Humanity Initiative and how, if at all, it impacts the prevention and intervention of genocide. No matter what, in the end all that really matters is that timely, strong, and effective action be taken to halt genocide in its tracks before it terminates tens and hundreds of thousands, if not millions, of innocent lives.

Notes

1. As Bartov (2003) has noted, such wavering, dithering, and inattention is also due, in part, to the fact that "the definition of genocide depends to a large extent on the political context within which it is discussed" (78).
2. For a thorough discussion of such compromises, see: Leo Kuper, *Genocide: Its Political Use in the Twentieth Century* (New Haven, CT: Yale University Press, 1981); William Schabas, *Genocide in International Law: The Crime of Crimes* (New York: Cambridge University Press, 2009). To ascertain the perspective of various genocide scholars about such compromises, see Samuel Totten and Steven Jacobs, eds., *Pioneers of Genocide Studies* (New Brunswick, NJ: Transaction Publishers, 2002).
3. The omission of the inclusion of various groups from protection under the UNCG shall not be discussed here. For detailed discussions of this issue, see Kuper (1981, 1985); Schabas (2009); Totten and Jacobs (2001); and Whitaker (1985).

   It is important to note that these, as well as other issues regarding the UNCG, can be addressed at any time by any Contracting Party. This is clearly stated in Article 16 of the UNCG: "A request for the revision of the present Convention may be made at any time by any Contracting Party by means of a notification in writing addressed to the Secretary-General." Once that is done, as stated in Article 16, "The General Assembly shall decide upon the steps, if any, to be taken in respect of such a request."
4. This, in turn, has, in its own way, contributed to a situation in which the UN Convention on the Prevention and Punishment of the Crime of Genocide has not lived up to its own name.
5. What is addressed in this chapter constitutes the proverbial tip of the iceberg. The issues addressed herein have been addressed in lengthy law journal articles, not to mention entire books. Readers are thus encouraged to seek out the titles mentioned in the narrative of the essay and listed in the accompanying Annotated Bibliography.
6. Tellingly, if the UN Commission of Inquiry into Darfur had adhered to the position delineated by the ICTY Trial Chamber I judges in the Nikolic case, it would have had no choice but to come to the determination that genocide, and not "simply," crimes against humanity, had been perpetrated by the Government of Sudan.
7. To prove genocide and, concomitantly, to obtain a conviction on genocide require the establishment of the "*intent* to destroy, in whole or in part, . . . [the protected] group, as such." In other words, to solely establish that deliberate unlawful killings of members of the group have occurred is not adequate. Not only must *intent* be proved but *the intent to destroy* must be proved. And not only must *the intent to destroy* be proved but *the intent to destroy in whole or in part a particular group (i.e., national, religious, racial and ethnical groups), as such*. Genocide, of course, is an act targeting a group, not "simply" individuals. Thus, for example, in the Akayesu case at the ICTR, the court proceedings indicated the following: "Genocide

is distinct from other crimes inasmuch as it embodies a special intent or *dolus specialis*. Special intent of a crime is the specific intention, required as a constitutive element of the crime, which demands that the perpetrator clearly seeks to produce the act charged. Thus, the special intent in the crime of genocide lies in 'the intent to destroy, in whole or in part, a national, ethnical, racial or religious group, as such'" (129).

As Northwestern University Professor of Law David Scheffer (2007) has noted, "A singular truth about the inference of intent is that clear and unambiguous statements of intent, including in any official statement of aims, likely will not be found . . . In order to properly analyze whether a government or any part thereof acted with the specified intent to commit genocide, the most plausible methodology is to establish the interference of specific intent by examining the evidence of a multiplicity and pattern of events and then understanding how such events can be explained by exposing direct and indirect linkages to the suspect government. A mystery tour through the psyches of political or military leaders is not essential to the task of dividing the requisite *mens rea* of inferential intent for state-sponsored genocide" (125, 126).

8. As Kuper (1991) noted, "The inclusion of intent in the definition of genocide introduces a subjective element, which would often prove difficult to establish. . . . In contemporary extra-judicial discussions of allegations of genocide, the question of intent has become a controversial issue, providing a ready basis for denial of guilt" (33).
9. Jean-Paul Akayesu was convicted of genocide in September 1998 by the ICTR. His conviction was the first international conviction of genocide.
10. Ultimately, in 1996, the ILC tackled the meaning of intent in the UNCG. It was the first official effort to do so. See The International Law Commission's (ILC) Draft Code of Crimes against the Peace and Security of Mankind (UN Doc. A/CN.4/L.532, 1996, 44, 17). Article 17 focuses on the crime of genocide.
11. In an article entitled "Rethinking Genocidal Intent: The Case for a Knowledge-Based Interpretation" in the *Columbia Law Review*, Alexander K. A. Greenawalt (1999) argued that an alternative approach needed to be considered and used in establishing "intent" in cases purported to be genocidal: "Relying on both the history of the Genocide Convention and on a substantive critique of the specific intent interpretation, in defined situations, principal culpability for genocide should extend to those who may personally lack a specific genocidal purpose, but who commit genocidal acts while understanding the destructive consequences of their actions" (2259).

Similarly, in an article entitled "The Permanent International Criminal Court," Bassiouni (2003) made the following argument: ". . . Article 6 (genocide) requires a specific intent that is a general intent 'to kill', for example, with the specific intent that it is done to 'destroy, in whole or in part' a protected group enumerated in the Statute. This confusion could have been resolved by requiring a lower standard for policy makers, a general intent up to and including knowledge, because of the ability of such persons to know or foresee the consequences of their acts due to their greater access to information and due to their ability to control the apparatus of the state.

For lower executors, specific intent or knowledge of the overall policy which they are acting in furtherance of should be required" (190).

Addressing the same issue, Abrams (2001), in an article entitled "Myths, Realities, and Prospects: The Atrocities in Cambodia and Kosovo: Observations on the Codification of Genocide," argued that "direct evidence of genocidal intent, such as official pronouncements of the need to eliminate a group, will not always be available or may be linked only to some perpetrators. This will force those attempting to make the determination of intent to examine the circumstantial evidence, such as the scale of the atrocities or efforts to destroy the group's unique characteristics of its leadership" (303–9). Similarly, Quenivet (2005) argued that "the underlying intent may be seen in the widespread or systematic occurrence of criminal acts or in the omission to prevent or punish the perpetrators" (167). Exactly how the distinction between, say, crimes against humanity and genocide, could be made is another question altogether. In that regard, Quenivet (2005) commented that "the ad hoc international criminal tribunals assert that one needs to look at the facts, at the repetition of such acts, at circumstantial evidence to prove that it was the intent of the perpetrators to destroy the particular groups" (167).

12. In explicating their point, the judges went on to state the following: "In this case, the plans of the SDS [Serbian Democratic Party] in Bosnia and Herzegovina contain elements which would lead to the destruction of the non-Serbian groups. The project of an ethnically homogeneous State formulated against a backdrop of mixed populations necessarily envisages the exclusion of any group not identified with the Serbian one. The concrete expressions of these plans by the SDS before the conflict would confirm the existence of an intent to exclude those groups by violence. The project does not exclude the use of force against civilian populations. Furthermore, it appears that a certain group, which had been targeted, could not, in accordance with the SDS plans, lay claim to any other specific territory. In this case, the massive deportations may be construed as the first step in a process of elimination. These elements, taken together, would confirm that the project which inspired the offences before the Trial Chamber, contemplates the destruction of the non-Serbian groups, and specifically the Bosnian Muslim group, as the ultimate step" (Jones 2000, 102).

13. Schabas (2009) asserted that "The term 'in whole or in part' refers to the intent of the perpetrators, not to the result" (277), which does not seem to be appreciated or agreed upon by various prognosticators or even official bodies. A classic example of the latter is the report issued by the UN Commission of Inquiry into Darfur.

14. In regard to the issue of numbers, Kuper (1981) commented as follows: "I assume that the charge of genocide would not be preferred unless there were a 'substantial' or an 'appreciable' number of victims" (32). Elsewhere, Kuper (1985) commented that "Presumably the Convention is intended to deal with acts against large numbers, relative to the size of the persecuted group, and it would rest with the courts to adjudicate on this issue" (12).

15. At various times over the past two decades, journalists, and, in some cases, even government officials have focused on an outbreak of mass killing and zeroed in on the numbers killed in an attempt to ascertain whether

genocide had been perpetrated or not. More than anything this speaks to their ignorance in regard to that which constitutes genocide. The point is, numbers are not the deciding factor as to whether a case of mass killing is genocide or not. Period. The key is whether the perpetrator had the intent to destroy in whole in part a specific group (protected under the UNCG), as such.

16. For a much more detailed discussion of these issues, see William Schabas, *Genocide in International Law*, 2nd ed.; Ralph Henham and Paul Behrens, eds., *The Criminal Law of Genocide: International, Comparative and Contextual Aspects* (Aldershot: Ashgate, 2007).

17. Behern (2007) notes that "Not everybody agrees with this [in the case of Blagojevic] assessment. The Trial Chamber in Stakic saw a clear difference between the 'mere dissolution' of a group and physical destruction. In this context, it went back to the *travaus preparatories* and pointed out that a proposal to include 'measures intended to oblige members of a group to abandon their homes [. . .]' had been rejected by the drafters of the Genocide Convention."

"... A co-existence of motives in this regard is perhaps not entirely inconceivable. If the perpetrators expel a protected group into a territory were [*sic*] death awaits its members—one may think of a desert—then it would appear entirely possible that genocidal intent and the intent of 'ethnic cleansing' share a place in the mind of the author of the act" (133).

18. "Secondly, it is clear that the obligation in question is one of conduct and not one of result, in the sense that a State cannot be under an obligation to succeed, whatever the circumstances, in preventing the commission of genocide: the obligation of State parties is rather to employ all means reasonably available to them, so as to prevent genocide so far as possible. A State does not incur responsibility simply because the desired result is not achieved; responsibility is however incurred if the State manifestly failed to take all measures to prevent genocide which were within its power, and which might have contributed to preventing the genocide. In this area the notion of 'due diligence,' which calls for an assessment *in concreto*, is of critical importance. Various parameters operate when assessing whether a State has duly discharged the obligation concerned. The first, which varies greatly from one State to another, is clearly the capacity to influence effectively the action of persons likely to commit, or already committing, genocide. This capacity itself depends, among other things, on the geographical distance of the State concerned from the scene of the events, and on the strength of the political links, as well as links of all other kinds, between the authorities of that State and the main actors in the events. . . . On the other hand, it is irrelevant whether the State whose responsibility is in issue claims, or even proves, that even if it had employed all means reasonably at its disposal, they would not have sufficed to prevent the commission of genocide. As well as being generally difficult to prove, this is irrelevant to the breach of the obligation of conduct in question, the more so since the possibility remains that the combined efforts of several States, each complying with its obligation to prevent, might have achieved the result—averting the commission of genocide—which the efforts of only one State were insufficient to produce." (International Court of Justice 2007, para. 430)

19. Continuing, the ICJ stated that "In view of their undeniable influence and of the information, voicing serious concern, in their possession, the Yugoslav federal authorities should, in the view of the Court, have made the best efforts within their power to try and prevent the tragic events then taking shape, whose scale, though it could not have been foreseen with certainty, might at least have been surmised. The FRY leadership, and President Miloševic, above all, were fully aware of the climate of deep-seated hatred which reigned between the Bosnian Serbs and the Muslims in the Srebrenica region. As the Court has noted in paragraph 423 above, it has not been shown that the decision to eliminate physically the whole of the adult male population of the Muslim community of Srebrenica was brought to the attention of the Belgrade authorities. Nevertheless, given all the international concern about what looked likely to happen at Srebrenica, given Miloševic's own observations to Mladic, which made it clear that the dangers were known and that these dangers seemed to be of an order that could suggest intent to commit genocide, unless brought under control, it must have been clear that there was a serious risk of genocide in Srebrenica. Yet the Respondent has not shown that it took any initiative to prevent what happened, or any action on its part to avert the atrocities which were committed. It must therefore be concluded that the organs of the Respondent did nothing to prevent the Srebrenica massacres, claiming that they were powerless to do so, which hardly tallies with their known influence over the VRS. As indicated above, for a State to be held responsible for breaching its obligation of prevention, it does not need to be proven that the State concerned definitely had the power to prevent the genocide; it is sufficient that it had the means to do so and that it manifestly refrained from using them." (International Court of Justice 2007, para. 438)

> APPLICATION OF GENOCIDE CONVENTION (JUDGMENT)
> Such is the case here. In view of the foregoing, the Court concludes that the Respondent violated its obligation to prevent the Srebrenica genocide in such a manner as to engage its international responsibility. (International Court of Justice, *Bosnia v. Serbia* 2007)

20. Article 2 (Object and Purposes of the Present Convention—Proposed International Convention on the Prevention and Punishment of Crimes Against Humanity) reads, in part: 1. "The States Parties to the present Convention undertake to prevent crimes against humanity and to investigate, prosecute, and punish those responsible for such crimes," and 2. "To these ends, each State Party agrees: (a) To cooperate, pursuant to the provisions of the present Convention, with other States Parties to prevent crimes against humanity; and (b) To investigate, prosecute and punish persons responsible for crimes against humanity fairly and effectively" (Whitney R. Harris World Law Institute 2010, 7).
21. In an article entitled "Genocide and the International Court of Justice: Finally, a Duty to Prevent the Crimes of Crimes," William Schabas writes: "Once crimes against humanity had been cured of its great shortcoming, the link with armed conflict, it quickly occupied the territory that had been reserved for genocide since 1948, namely attacks on minorities committed

during peacetime. Moreover, crimes against humanity also adequately covered all those atrocities that lie on the fringes of 'pure' genocide, such as ethnic cleansing. Thus, nobody saw any practical need for reform, and the Rome Conference's confirmation of the enduring nature of the 1948 genocide definition was little more than perfunctory. History helpfully explains why the distinction between genocide and crimes against humanity was once so important, and why it is no longer so" (117). (*Genocide Studies and Prevention* 2, no. 2 [Summer 2007]: 101–22.)

References

Abrams, J. 2001. "Universal Jurisdiction: Myths, Realities and Prospects: The Atrocities in Cambodia and Kosovo: Observations on the Codification of Genocide." *New England Law Review* 35, no. 2: 303–9.

Akhavan, Payam. April 2007. "Proliferation of Terminology and the Illusion of Progress." *Genocide Studies and Prevention: An International Journal* 2, no. 1: 73–80.

Bartov, Omer. 2003. "Seeking the Roots of Modern Genocide: On the Macro- and Microhistory of Mass Murder." In *The Specter of Genocide: Mass Murder in Historical Perspective*, ed. Robert Gellately and Ben Kiernan, 75–96. New York: Cambridge University Press.

Bassiouni, M. Cherif. 2003. "The Permanent International Criminal Court." In *Justice for Crimes against Humanity*, ed. Mark Lattimer and Philippe Sands, 173–211. Portland, OR: Hart Publishing.

———. 1993. "Commentary on the International Law Commission's 1991 Draft Code of Crimes Against the Peace and Security of Mankind." *Nouvelles etudes penales* 11.

Beherns, Paul. 2007. "A Moment of Kindness? Consistency and Genocidal Intent." In *The Criminal Law of Genocide International, Comparative and Contextual Aspects*, ed. Ralph Henham and Paul Behrens, 125–40. Aldershot, Hampshire, England: Ashgate Publishing.

Greenawalt, K. A. Alexander. 1999. "Rethinking Genocidal Intent: The Case for a Knowledge-Based Interpretation." *Columbia Law Review* 99, no. 8: 2259–94.

Greenfield, Daniel M. 2008. "The Crime of Complicity in Genocide: How the International Criminal Tribunals for Rwanda and Yugoslavia Got It Wrong, and Why It Matters." *The Journal of Criminal Law & Criminology* 98, no. 3: 921–52.

Goldsmith, Katherine. December 2010. "The Issue of Intent in the Genocide Convention and Its Effect on the Prevention and Punishment of the Crime of Genocide: Toward a Knowledge-Based Approach." *Genocide and Prevention: An International Journal* 5, no. 3: 238–57.

Hawk, David. 1987. "International Human Rights Law and Democratic Kampuchea." *International Journal of Politics* 16, no. 3: 3–38.

Henham, Ralph, and Paul Behrens. 2007. *The Criminal Law of Genocide: International, Comparative and Contextual Aspects*. Aldershot, Hampshire, England: Ashgate Publishing.

International Court of Justice, Reports of Judgments, Advisory Opinions and Orders. 2007. "Case Concerning Application of the Convention on the Prevention and Punishment of the Crime of Genocide (Bosnia and

Herzegovina v. Serbia and Montenegro) Judgment of 26 February 2007." The Hague: International Court of Justice, Reports of Judgments, Advisory Opinions and Orders.

Jones, John R. W. D. 2000. *The Practice of the International Criminal Tribunals for the Former Yugoslavia and Rwanda*. 2nd ed. Ardsley, NY: Transnational Publishers.

Kuper, Leo. 1985. *The Prevention of Genocide*. New Haven, CT: Yale University Press.

———. 1981. *Genocide: Its Political Use in the Twentieth Century*. New Haven, CT: Yale University Press.

Lewis, Norman. 1976. "The Camp at Cecilio Baez." In *Genocide in Paraguay*, ed. Richard Arens, 56–58. Philadelphia, PA: Temple University Press.

Quenivet, Noelle N. R. 2005. *Sexual Offenses in Armed Conflict and International Law*. Ardsley, NY: Transnational Publishers.

Schabas, William. 2009. *Genocide in International Law*. 2nd ed. New York: Cambridge University Press.

———. 2007. "Whither Genocide? The International Court of Justice Finally Pronounces." *Journal of Genocide Research* 9, no. 2: 183–92.

———. 2005. "Convention on the Prevention and Punishment of Genocide." In *Encyclopedia of Genocide and Crimes against Humanity*, ed. Dinah L. Shelton, 204–5. Farmington Hills, MI: Thompson Gale.

Scheffer, David. (January 1, 2008). "Atrocity Crimes Framing the Responsibility to Protect." (International Conference in Commemoration of the Sixtieth Anniversary of the Negotiation of the Genocide Convention)." *Case Western Reserve Journal of International Law* 40: 111–35.

Scheffer, David. 2007. "The Merits of Unifying Terms: 'Atrocity Crimes' and 'Atrocity Law.'" *Genocide Studies and Prevention: An International Journal* 2, no. 1: 91–95.

van den Herik, Larissa. 2007). "The Schism between the Legal and the Social Concept of Genocide in Light of the Responsibility to Protect." In *The Criminal Law of Genocide International, Comparative and Contextual Aspects*, ed. Ralph Henham and Paul Behrens, 75–95. Aldershot, Hampshire, England: Ashgate Publishing.

Whitaker, Ben. 1988. "Genocide: The Ultimate Crime." In *Human Rights*, ed. Peter Davies, 51–56. New York: Routledge.

Whitney R. Harris World Law Institute. 2010. *Proposed International Convention on the Prevention and Punishment of the Crimes Against Humanity*. St. Louis, MO: Washington University School of Law, Whitney R. Harris World Law Institute.

Annotated Bibliography

Alvarez, Alex. *Governments, Citizens, and Genocide: A Comparative and Interdisciplinary Approach*. Bloomington and Indianapolis: Indiana University Press, 2001, 224 pp.

Alvarez, a criminologist, includes a brief section in his book entitled "The United Nations Genocide Convention" in which he addresses the lack of protection for political groups under the UNCG and raises the issue of "the scale of killing." Some of his comments regarding these issues are thought-provoking.

Askin, Kelly Dawn. *War Crimes against Women: Prosecution in International War Crimes Tribunals*. The Hague: Martinus Nighoff Publishers, 1997, 455 pp.

Three short sections in this book address the issue of "genocidal rape" and "gender abuses as violations of the Genocide Convention under the ICTY Statute." Under "Terms and Definitions," the crime "genocidal rape" is defined as "an attempt to destroy, in whole or in part, a particular protected group through sexual assault, regardless of whether the destruction is physical or mental" (12). In the chapter entitled "Prosecuting Gender Crimes in the International Criminal Tribunal for the Former Yugoslavia (ICTY)," a short section (337–44) reviews the elements of genocide and then delineates "how gender abuses, including genocidal rape, can be prosecuted as genocide under Article 4 of the ICTY Statute" (337). Appendix A includes a section (III) entitled "Genocide (Genocidal Rape)" (392–93).

Bassiouni, M. Cherif. "'Crimes against Humanity': The Need for a Specialized Convention." *Columbia Journal of Transnational Law* 31, no. 3 (1994): 457–94.

Bassiouni, Professor of Law at DePaul University College of Law and Chairman of the Commission of Experts Established Pursuant to Security Council Resolution 780 (1992) to Investigate Violations of International Humanitarian Law in the Former Yugoslavia, "traces the origins and flaws of the early normative framework for 'Crimes Against Humanity' and identifies the reasons for the need to develop a specialized convention" (459). In part, Bassiouni notes that while the Genocide Convention of 1948 covers some "crimes against humanity," it does so "only with respect to certain specific acts, accompanied by specific intent, against specifically designated groups. Thus, it excludes all other acts and groups not specified in the Convention" (477).

Bassiouni, M. Cherif. "The Permanent International Criminal Court." In *Justice for Crimes against Humanity*, edited by Mark Lattimer and Philippe Sands, 173–211. Portland, OR: Hart Publishing, 2003.

In a section of this essay entitled "Ratione Materiae: The Crimes Within the Jurisdiction of the ICC," Bassiouni discusses the thorny issue of intent in relation to genocide.

Brugnola, Orlanda, Helen Fein, and Louise Spirer, eds. *Ever Again? Evaluating the United Nations Genocide Convention on Its 50th Anniversary and Proposals to Activate the Convention*. New York: Institute for the Study of Genocide, 1999, 99 pp.

The papers included herein were delivered at a conference ("Ever Again? Evaluating the United Nations Convention on Its 50th Anniversary and Proposals to Activate the Convention") sponsored by the Institute for the Study of Genocide (December 2–3, 1998). The conference was designed not only to review the critical issues of the prevention and punishment of genocide, but also to consider what could be done to reinforce the United Nations' actions under the UNCG. Among the questions and issues addressed at the conference were: "How do we identify, or recognize, a genocide under the U.N. Genocide Convention?"; "How do we stop a genocide in progress?"; "Who is responsible to intervene in a purported genocide?"; and "How is genocide made visible?" Among the contributors are Beth Van Schaack, John Fousek, Saul Mendlovitz, Sarah Sewell, Michael McClintock, Morton Winston, Samantha Power, and Roy Gutman.

Cassese, Antonio. *International Law*. Oxford: Oxford University Press, 2001, 469 pp.

Herein, Cassese, an Italian jurist and the first president of the ICTY, discusses, in part, the adoption, enforcement mechanism, and flaws of the UNCG.

Charny, Israel W. "The Study of Genocide." In *Genocide: A Critical Bibliographic Review*, edited by Israel W. Charny, 1–19. London: Mansell, 1988.

A section of this chapter is entitled "The Definition of Genocide." Therein Charny discusses how, and in some cases why, certain scholars have called for a broadening of the definition of genocide and/or proposed new terms/concepts to compensate for the weaknesses inherent in the UNCG definition of genocide.

Congressional Research Service. *CRS Report for Congress, RL32605: Genocide: Legal Precedent Surrounding the Definition of the Crime*. Washington, DC: Congressional Research Service, 2004, n.p.

The situation in Darfur, Sudan, in 2003–2004 and the debate over whether the Sudanese government's actions constituted genocide or ethnic cleansing provided the impetus for this report. The authors provide a succinct historical background of the UNCG, its ratification and implementation by the United States, and its incorporation into the Rome Statute that created the ICC. Decisions from the ICTY and ICTR are analyzed in order to determine when charges of genocide have been found to be legitimate.

Damrosch, Lori Fisher. "Genocide and Ethnic Conflict." In *International Law and Ethnic Conflict*, edited by David Wippman, 256–79. Ithaca, NY: Cornell University Press, 1998.

In her introduction, Damrosch, Professor of Law at Columbia University School of Law, states that "This chapter will consider the legal definition of genocide in situations of ethnic conflict as well as questions of implementation through the legal institutions available to address such conflicts. . . . Accordingly, Part I will consider conceptual problems in the definition of genocide in situations of ethnic conflicts, including problems having to do with the scope of protection afforded to ethnical (along with national, racial, and religious) groups as well as difficulties arising when an ethnic group becomes embroiled in an armed conflict" (257).

Dunne, Tim, and Daniela Kroslak. "Genocide: Knowing What It Is That We Want to Remember, or Forget, or Forgive." In *The Kosovo Tragedy: The Human Rights Dimension*, edited by Ken Booth, 27–46. London and Portland, OR: Frank Cass Publishers, 2001.

This essay comprises three parts: Part one discusses the evolution of the UN Convention on Genocide and the term "genocide"; Part two examines the 1990 Kosovo War through the prism of the UNCG and its concomitant parts; and in Part three, the authors consider the various ways in which the UNCG is being reinterpreted.

Fein, Helen. "Genocide: A Sociological Perspective." Special Issue of *Current Sociology* 34, no. 1 (1990).

Among some of the many issues Fein discusses are: the wording of the UNCG, including various ambiguities; "Lemkin's concept and the UNCG definition of genocide"; the effect of the UNCG; various definitions of genocide and how they compare and contrast with the definition found in the UNCG; and the issue of intent.

Goldsmith, Katherine. "The Issue of Intent in the Genocide Convention and Its Effect on the Prevention and Punishment of the Crime of Genocide: Toward a Knowledge-Based Approach." *Genocide and Prevention: An International Journal* 5, no. 3 (2010): 238–57.

A fascinating and thought-provoking article. Herein, Goldsmith observes and argues as follows: "It has been widely accepted that the meaning of 'intent,' within the Genocide Convention, refers to specific or special intent, *dolus specialis*. However, as more trials have taken place, creating more understanding of the crime of genocide, the linking of *dolus specialis* with the intent definition, that was so easily accepted at the first genocide trial (Akayesu at the International Criminal Tribunal for Rwanda [ICTR]), has been repeatedly put into question. The new approach being put forward as the most appropriate interpretation of 'intent' is the knowledge-based approach. The Vienna Convention on Treaties states that interpretations of laws should follow the treaty's original purpose and objective, and should do this by looking at the preparatory work and its circumstances. By looking at the Travaux Préparatoires of the Genocide Convention and Raphael Lemkin's original writings on the subject, this article will discuss which approach fits the original intentions of both the drafters of the Convention and Lemkin himself, to determine which interpretation should be used in the future when considering the crime of genocide."

Greenawalt, Alexander K. A. "Rethinking Genocidal Intent: The Case for a Knowledge-Based Interpretation." *Columbia Law Review* 99, no. 8 (1999): 2259–94.

The author argues that an alternative approach needs to be considered and used in establishing "intent" in cases purported to be genocidal: "Relying on both the history of the Genocide Convention and on a substantive critique of the specific intent interpretation, in defined situations, principal culpability for genocide should extend to those who may personally lack a specific genocidal purpose, but who commit genocidal acts while understanding the destructive consequences of their actions" (2259).

Hannum, Hurst. "International Law and Cambodian Genocide: The Sounds of Silence." *Human Rights Quarterly* (1989): 82–138.

Herein, Hannum, a highly respected human rights scholar, considers "the factual evidence of genocide in Cambodia, countering the view expressed by some that . . . the Khmer Rouge killings were not technically 'genocide.'" In doing so, he outlines the "elements of a successful application under the Genocide Convention, including questions of the Court's jurisdiction, the existence of a dispute between an applicant state and Democratic Kampuchea, and whether the killings of Cambodians themselves by the Khmer Rouge leadership constitute genocide against a 'national' group within the meaning of the Convention."

Healey, Sharon. "Prosecuting Rape under the Statute of the War Crimes Tribunal for the Former Yugoslavia." *Brooklyn Journal of International Law* XXI, no. 2 (1995): 327–83.

Healey examines the "legal precedent for prosecuting rape under each of the four charges set forth in the Statute of the ICTY."

Jones, John R. W. D. *The Practice of the International Criminal Tribunals for the Former Yugoslavia and Rwanda*. 2nd ed. Ardsley, NY: Transnational Publishers, 2000, 666 pp.

Several sections in this book address the UNCG and how various terms/concepts have been interpreted by judges and prosecutors at the ICTR and the ICTY. The sections that address the issue of intent are particularly interesting and thought-provoking.

Jorgensen, N. H. "The Definition of Genocide: Joining the Dots in the Light of Recent Practice." *International Criminal Law Review* 1, no. 3/4 (2001): 285–313.

Examines trials involving the alleged perpetration of genocide and how genocide was defined in each.

Karagiannakis, Magdalini. "The Definition of Rape and It Characterization as an Act of Genocide – A Review of the Jurisprudence of the International Criminal Tribunal for Rwanda and the Former Yugoslavia." *Leiden Journal of International Law* 12, no. 2 (1999): 479–90.

The author, a legal officer with the ICTY, reviews "the recent precedent-setting judgments of the international criminal tribunals for the Former Yugoslavia and Rwanda which have sought to define rape in international law using different approaches."

Kuper, Leo. *Genocide: Its Political Use in the Twentieth Century*. New Haven, CT: Yale University Press, 1981, 255 pp.

In a short section, Kuper discusses the ambiguity inherent in the definition of genocide found in the UNCG, the issue of the exclusion of politics groups as a protected group in the UNCG, and the "problem of intent."

Kuper, Leo. *The Prevention of Genocide*. New Haven, CT: Yale University Press, 1985, 286 pp.

Kuper addresses the following issues vis-à-vis the definition of genocide used in the UNCG: conflicts in the formulation of the UNCG, defects in the UNCG, the UNCG's emphasis on punishment (over that of prevention), and the exclusion of political groups as a protected group.

LeBlanc, Lawrence J. *The United States and the Genocide Convention*. Durham, NC: Duke University Press, 1991, 290 pp.

In this book, LeBlanc analyzes the nearly forty-year battle within the government corridors of the US government to ratify the United Nations Convention on the Prevention and Punishment of the Crime of Genocide.

Lippman, Matthew. "The Drafting of the 1948 Convention on the Prevention and Punishment of the Crime of Genocide." *Boston International Law Journal* 3, no. 1 (1985): 1–65.

An interesting and detailed piece on the drafting of the UNCG. The author also offers various suggestions for increasing the UNCG's potential efficacy in preventing and punishing the crime of genocide.

Lippman, Matthew. "A Road Map to the 1948 Convention on the Prevention and Punishment of the Crime Genocide." *Journal of Genocide Research* 4, no. 2 (2002): 177–95.

A somewhat updated version of the above article.

Morton, Jeffrey S., and Neil Vijay Singh. "The International Legal Regime on Genocide." *Journal of Genocide Research* 5, no. 1 (2003): 47–79.

The authors examine the contemporary legal status of the international regime on genocide, and in doing so they discuss the evolution of the regime and analyze, on an article-by-article basis, the provisions codified in the UNCG.

Neressian, David L. "The Razor's Edge: Defining and Protecting Human Groups Under the Genocide Convention." *Cornell International Law Journal* 36, no. 2 (2003): 293–327.

In part, Neressian, Adjunct Faculty at Boston School of Law and Candidate for Doctor of Philosophy in Law at Oxford University, "advocates a hybrid approach to defining groups that accounts for the subjective views of the perpetrators but requires some measure of baseline objective evidence linking the perpetrator's views to the groups' pre-genocidal existence." In the last section of the article, the author "analyzes how genocidal intent actually is manifested against the defined group in terms of the genocidist's efforts to achieve the group's destruction." Ultimately, "this Article makes the case for a broad conception of what it means to intend to destroy a group 'as such.' . . . It advocates the parallel recognition of a more flexible approach grounded principally in the intentions of the genocidist" (295–96).

Organization of African Unity. "International Panel of Eminent Personalities (IDEP): Report on the 1994 Genocide in Rwanda and Surrounding Events (Selected Sections)." *International Legal Materials* 40 (2001): 140–235.

In part, "The Panel called for a substantial re-examination of the 1948 Genocide Convention with attention to, inter alia: 1. The definition of genocide; 2. A mechanism to prevent genocide; and 3. The legal obligation of states when genocide is declared" (140).

Quenivet, Noelle N. R. *Sexual Offenses in Armed Conflict & International Law.* Ardsley, NY: Transnational Publishers, 2005, 210 pp.

Quenivet discusses the issue of "genocidal intent" in relation to rape and other sexual crimes (165–70). In doing so, she discusses how the ICTR and the ICTY have dealt with the issue of intent, how intent may be deduced, and closes with the assertion that "expressions such as 'genocidal rape' or 'gendercide' invented by feminist writers are not only superfluous but also misleading and, therefore, should be abandoned" (170).

Quigley, John B. *The Genocide Convention: An International Law Analysis.* London: Ashgate Publishing, 2006, 301 pp.

The author explores the question of whether the law, and genocide law, in particular, can prevent mass atrocities. He also discusses individual suits against states for genocide and explores the utility of genocide as a legal concept.

Ratner, Steven R., and Jason S. Abrams. *Accountability for Human Rights Atrocities in International Law: Beyond the Nuremberg Legacy.* New York: Oxford University Press, 1997, 368 pp.

Ratner and Abrams discuss numerous matters in regard to how the wording and the limitations of the UNCG complicate efforts to prevent genocide, including: the failure to delineate the attributes that define the groups protected under the UNCG, the confusion that has arisen over the term "intent," debate over the wording "in part," and the decision to exclude political, economic, and professional groups from protection under the UNCG.

Reid-Cunningham, Allison Ruby. "Rape as a Weapon of Genocide." *Genocide Studies and Prevention: An International Journal* 3, no. 3 (2008): 279–96.

Addresses, in part, the issue of intent vis-à-vis rape as it relates to genocide.

Ruhashyankiko, Nicodeme. *Report to the U.N. Sub-Commission Prevention on Discrimination and Protection of Minorities. Study of the Question of the Prevention and Punishment of the Crimes of Genocide.* E/CN.4/Sub.2/416, 4, July 1978, 186 pp.

"A major study of the UNCG undertaken by the UN. It was the first study of the UNCG since it was adopted in 1948. The rapporteur proposed significant improvements to the UNCG, such as universal jurisdiction for the prosecution of those who commit genocide. However, the report became widely known not for its significant contribution to the prevention of genocide but as a classic case of the cynical politicization within the corridors of the UN. After unceasing political efforts and threats, the Turkish Government succeeded in having the report revised so as not to acknowledge the Armenian genocide, an action that Leo Kuper referred to as casting the Armenian genocide 'down the memory hole.'" (Annotation by Israel W. Charny based on his essay "Intervention and Prevention of Genocide," in *Genocide a Critical Bibliographic Review.* New York: Facts on File, 1988, 36).

Schabas, William. *The Genocide Convention at Fifty.* Washington, DC: United States Institute of Peace, 1999, 8 pp.

Herein, Schabas, an international law specialist, discusses the following issues: the genesis of the UNCG; that which constitutes genocide; whether "ethnic cleansing" is a form of genocide; criminal prosecution of genocide; and how the attempt to prevent genocide constitutes the greatest failure of the UNCG. He concludes with a set of "Recommendations."

Schabas, William A. *Genocide in International Law: The Crime of Crimes.* New York: Cambridge University Press, 2009, 741 pp.

This book constitutes the most comprehensive examination to date of international law as it relates to the issue of genocide. In doing so, it presents a thorough discussion of the UNCG.

Scheffer, David. "The Merits of Unifying Terms: 'Atrocity Crimes' and 'Atrocity Law.'" *Genocide Studies and Prevention: An International Journal* 2, no. 1 (Spring 2007): 91–95.

An interesting proposal to adopt two new terms—"precursors to genocide" and "atrocity crimes"—in an effort to make key distinctions between the political and legal uses of the term "genocide" with an aim at broadening the political use, thus allowing for more rapid intervention when genocide appears on the horizon. (For a solid discussion of Scheffer's position/article, see the special issue "The Prevention of Genocide: Ideas from International Politics and a Symposium on International Law" of *Genocide Studies and Prevention: An International Journal* 2, no. 1 [Spring 2007].)

Schaack, Beth Van. "The Crime of Political Genocide: Repairing the Genocide Convention's Blind Spot." *The Yale Law Journal* 106, no. 7 (1997): 2259–91.

A thought-provoking piece in which Schaack argues that ". . . the Genocide Convention is not the sole authority on the crime of genocide. Rather, a higher law exists: the prohibition of genocide represents the paradigmatic *jus cogens* norm, a customary and preemptory norm of international law from which no derogation is permitted." Schaack's insights into the latter and the ramifications of such are powerful.

Continuing, she says, "The *jus cogens* prohibition of genocide, as expressed in a variety of sources, is broader than the Convention's prohibition as has been demonstrated with respect to the jurisdictional principle applied to acts of genocide. Notwithstanding that the framers of the Genocide Convention attempted to limit the prohibition of genocide by deliberately excluding political groups from Article II, the provision is without legal force to the extent that it is inconsistent with the *jus cogens* prohibition of genocide. Therefore, when faced with mass killings evidencing the intent to eradicate political groups in whole or in part, domestic and international adjudicatory bodies should apply the *jus cogens* prohibition of genocide and invoke the Genocide Convention vis-à-vis signatories only insofar as it provides practical procedures for enforcement and ratification." Ultimately, she goes on to "critique the political compromises that occurred during the drafting of the Genocide Convention."

Singleterry, Douglas. "'Ethnic Cleansing' and Genocidal Intent: A Failure of Judicial Interpretation?" *Genocide Studies and Prevention: An International Journal* 5, no. 1 (2010): 39–67.

This article discusses the similarities and distinctions between "ethnic cleansing" and genocide in the context of both Bosnia's and Croatia's genocide claims against Serbia brought before the International Court of Justice (ICJ). It examines the institutional role of the ICJ and the criticisms on how the Court handled *Bosnia and Herzegovina v. Serbia and Montenegro*. The legal definition and elements of genocide as contained in the UN Convention on the Prevention and Punishment of the Crime of Genocide (UNCG) are discussed, with a particular emphasis on the required intent to "destroy" a protected group. The article reviews case law from other international tribunals and argues that evidence of "ethnic cleansing" may demonstrate the intent to "destroy" a protected group and support a finding of genocide.

Totten, Samuel. *An Oral and Documentary History of the Darfur Genocide*. 2 vols. Santa Barbara, CA: Praeger International Security, 2010, 600 pp.

Volume one of this set comprises interviews with black Africans who were forced from their villages and homes in Darfur as a result of the genocidal assaults by the Government of Sudan. Volume Two contains key documents regarding the atrocities committed in Darfur issued by the US government, the United Nations, and the International Criminal Court. Throughout Volume Two, the interpretation and application of the UNCG are discussed.

Totten, Samuel, comp. and ed. *The Prevention and Intervention of Genocide: An Annotated Bibliography*. New York: Routledge, 2007, 1153 pp.

This massive annotated bibliography includes a chapter entitled "United Nations Convention on the Prevention and Punishment of Genocide (UNCG)" (83–102).

Totten, Samuel, and Eric Markusen, eds. *Genocide in Darfur: Investigating Atrocities in the Sudan*. New York: Routledge, 2006, 284 pp.

This book contains several chapters that highlight some of the many problems with the wording and limitations of the UNCG in relation to ascertaining whether atrocity crimes, while they are in the process of being perpetrated, constitute genocide or not.

Triffterer, Otto. "Genocide, Its Particular Intent to Destroy in Whole or in Part the Group as Such." *Leiden Journal of International Law* 14, no. 2 (2001): 399–408.

The abstract to this article by Triffterer, Professor of Law at the University of Salzburg, reads as follows:

> All crimes of genocide have a common structure. There must be an *actus reus*, a corresponding *mens rea* and, in addition, a second subjective element, "the intent to destroy in whole or in part, a . . . group as such." This so-called "genocidal intent" is characterized by the fact that responsibility for completed genocide does not depend on the result the perpetrator intended to achieve. The threshold of this intent is not higher than the *mens rea* described in Article 30 of the Rome Statue; in particular, no special quality of the volitive side of this intent is required. *Dolus eventualis*, therefore, is sufficient to commit the *actus reus* and to have, in addition, the particular "intent to destroy. . .," an inherent additional and independent, contextual criterion, as proposed in The Draft Elements of Crime, is neither admissible nor advisable to limit the punishability of genocide or the jurisdiction of the Court for such crimes." (399)

Whittaker, Ben. *Revised and Updated Report on the Question of the Prevention and Punishment of the Crime of Genocide*, 1985, 62 pp. (E/CN.4/Sub.2/1985/6, 2 July 1985).

In this major report, Whitaker, the UN Special Rapporteur on Genocide, calls for a revision of the definition of genocide found in the UNCG. He argues for such a revision on numerous grounds, including the fact that the exclusion of political and social groups was politically motivated and that such an exclusion was inherently wrong.

5

Data Limitations as an Impediment to Genocide Intervention

Cyanne E. Loyle and Christian Davenport

Introduction

There is possibly no greater ambition within the field of genocide studies than the goal of prevention and, forgoing that, effective intervention to halt genocide once it has begun. Over and above the promise of early warning systems, contemporary activists and scholars have sought to end ongoing genocide through humanitarian interventions. Tactics of intervention include economic sanctions, mediation and dispute resolution, and diplomatic as well as military intervention (both unilateral and multilateral); however, for the purpose of this chapter, we will focus exclusively on humanitarian *military* interventions.

Historically, though, there have been many impediments to military intervention, namely political will, enduring notions of state sovereignty, and availability of intervention resources (Bauer 2001). Insofar as we are able to overcome these limitations through political pressure and activist mobilization, genocide intervention remains hampered by a lack of reliable data on genocide violence once the violence is underway. Contemporary critiques of intervention have argued that most failures are the result of "too little, too late" (Lahneman 2004), yet evidence suggests that even under optimal political conditions (i.e., genuine political will, multilateral coalitions, and sufficient resources) intervention can be hampered by the lack of accurate and efficient information regarding events on the ground, what Kuperman (2001) calls the "physical impediments" to intervention (viii). This is not to say that accurate data are a substitute for any of the other aforementioned factors, but rather that without it efficient and effective intervention is impeded (Arts 2001). In this chapter we focus specifically on data limitations as an impediment to military intervention once genocide is ongoing and argue that before intervention of any type is possible it is first necessary to gather a minimum threshold of data on the actors and actions at work. This is particularly true of military interventions as they require extensive resources and risk additional lives.

Determining the presence of genocide and the patterns of violence unfolding around it is rarely as easy as we may hope. Confusion surrounding contemporaneous violence, deliberate misinformation campaigns by actors involved, and weak information infrastructure in given areas all prevent policymakers and scholars from determining actors and actions on the ground. This chapter focuses on the ways in which the reliability, or lack thereof, of conflict data (e.g., timely and accurate information on the where, when, and who of genocide violence) can be an impediment to military intervention. We explore these limitations within the case of Rwanda and discuss the ways in which data limitations complicated efforts toward rapid military intervention. In conclusion, we present a series of recommendations to help activists and policymakers attempt to overcome these limitations.

Data Needs for Genocide Intervention

In this chapter, we start with the basic contention that accurate data on violence are needed for a military intervention to halt genocide. We argue that these data are important for two reasons. First, in order to intervene to stop genocide it is first necessary to determine that genocide is taking place. In order to overcome norms of state sovereignty and to justify the legitimacy of a military intervention on foreign soil, it is necessary to ascertain that serious harm is being committed and that threats are "actual or imminent" (Evans 2008, 142). In other words, before proceeding with a military intervention to halt genocide it is first necessary to establish the what (i.e., which violent activities are taking place and classifying the relevant activity as genocidal in nature). Identifying if and how genocide is taking place (or that it is of greater likelihood) requires information on the types of actions involved, for example, separating civilian casualties from civilian targets as well as identifying deliberate intentions regarding perpetrators against a specific target group. This identification is complicated by contemporaneous violence that may not be genocidal in nature. Indeed, when multiple types of violence exist simultaneously it can be extremely difficult to correctly identify the actions of interest, not to mention the development of an intervention strategy to halt such actions. This point is not made to suggest that military intervention can or should not be used to stop other humanitarian disasters such as ethnic cleansing or other forms of state repression. Rather, we make this point to propose that if activists and scholars are interested in invoking claims of genocide and the legal responsibilities surrounding it, it is first necessary to identify how the violence in a given country is progressing.

Second, accurate data are important because they determine the characteristics of the intervention that is necessary. Even with the most sincere political will a military intervention requires establishing the main components of violent action, namely where it is taking place, when the violence began, and the actors involved in the violence. These components are necessary as they determine where an intervention will take place, when, and against whom. Each of these components is elaborated below.

Where?

In the presence of disparate forms of violence, it is not always possible to easily identify the location of genocide-related violence. Contemporaneous violence such as an ongoing civil war, predatory/opportunistic violence, and random activity that takes human life can make it very difficult to geographically separate genocide from other actions that are taking place. Likewise, it is often difficult to efficiently and accurately identify the appropriate location for intervention. Despite this challenge, correctly identifying the spatial location of genocidal violence is an essential component of intervention. Put simply, international actors must know where to intervene.

When?

Identifying when genocide has begun and how rapidly it is progressing is another necessary component for intervention. The pace and timing of genocide can be difficult to track in real time. This element is particularly problematic for genocides that progress rapidly. Often, much of the violence is committed before the international community is able to accurately identify the actions that are occurring. In Rwanda, for example, the majority of people killed throughout the genocide were killed during the first few weeks of violence and before human rights organizations identified the violence as genocide (Kuperman 2001), as we will discuss further below. It is also possible for violence to begin as civil conflict and then transition into genocide. The international community must be alert to this possibility. To the extent possible, identifying when genocide is taking place is a critical component for intervention, but one that is very difficult to determine.

Who?

The two main actors involved in genocide can be generally categorized as the "perpetrators" (and their collaborators) and the "victims." The perpetrators, of course, are those responsible for committing acts of genocide, while the victims are the group who are targeted by those acts. Despite the seeming simplicity of these categorizations, the reality of genocide is rarely this straightforward. Often perpetrators take part in multiple forms of violence, including conventional warfare targeting combatants and/or looting or violence not related to the conflict itself. While at times these groups are mutually exclusive, there may be individuals who move between tasks engaging in both conventional warfare and participating in genocide. At the same time, victims may be civilians who are targeted, but they may also be armed combatants who are members of the group being targeted. As a consequence, it may be difficult or impossible to separate perpetrators from victims, genocidal actions from nongenocidal actions, and to intervene in the genocide specifically and not a conflict more generally.

Data Limitations to Genocide Intervention

Data limitations have been and will continue to be a persistent problem within the study of violent conflict, and the study of genocide is no exception. Obtaining accurate information regarding periods of violence has never been an easy task (Ball 1996, 2005), even for data collection efforts that take place long after the conflict has ended (Humphreys and Weinstein 2007, 2008; Kalyvas 2006). Data collection with an aim toward genocide intervention, however, must happen in real time, thus further complicating the collection of accurate information. Efforts to identify genocidal violence are often limited by the same components that hamper our ability to collect conflict data more broadly, namely the confusion present during violence, deliberate incentives that actors may have to misrepresent information, and the lack of a well-developed intelligence infrastructure in a given area.

Confusion evolves from the data inaccuracies that result from an inability to separate multiple forms of action and actors ongoing across space and time. Conflicts are messy affairs. Even in the most straightforward violent confrontations it can be difficult to discern what is happening where and to whom. Genocide often takes place during periods of armed conflict (Harff 2003), making it even more difficult to identify genocide violence independent of other forms of violence. Confusion is the result of the potential simultaneous presence of armed conflict (inter- and intrastate), violence not directly related to the conflict (e.g., criminal as well as predatory vigilante action), internal displacement, and refugee movements along with genocide. In periods of great confusion it may be hard to come by reliable data or, for that matter, any data at all. Alternatively, as in the case of Rwanda, it may be that too much information is available making it difficult to separate out reliable sources from those less well founded (Kuperman 2001).

In addition to data inaccuracies caused by confusion, actors in the conflict may, as previously mentioned, have an incentive to deliberately misrepresent information. Misinformation results when actors in the conflict have a motivation to deny claims of genocide to the international press and observers as well as hamper investigations and intelligence gathering. For example, genocide perpetrators may be intent on covering their tracks, and thus they will do what they can to block the acquisition of information about their activities. This could involve destroying evidence of their involvement, eliminating witnesses, purging informants, restricting access to areas where violence is being committed, and/or legally restricting investigations. Under these conditions collecting accurate information may be almost impossible.

Finally, as noted above, weak intelligence infrastructure can be a further obstacle to data collection in that it complicates the ability to get accurate and reliable data in times of conflict. Weak intelligence infrastructure results when a country or its allies have not implemented proprietary information-gathering capabilities in a given area (e.g., local connections, embassy personnel, or military surveillance). This generally occurs when the area in conflict is of low strategic interest. Because intelligence systems were not previously in place, it is more difficult to collect and sort information once a conflict has begun. For example, at the time of the Rwandan Genocide, the United States only had a single intelligence person in central Africa—a defense attaché in Cameroon (Kuperman 2001).

Before we proceed further in our discussion, we would like to stress that we do not believe that military intervention is or should be the only method of genocide prevention. As we discuss below, military intervention is particularly susceptible to data limitations and is further complicated by generally being undertaken once a genocide has begun. Humanitarian action and genocide-prevention strategies have lower thresholds of data needs and therefore can be implemented before the components of the conflict are conclusively determined. It is possible, therefore, for more creative and rapid moving humanitarian interventions to be implemented without the data limitations outlined above.

Below we turn to the case of 1994 Rwanda and discuss the ways in which data limitations, particularly confusion and misinformation, contributed to the failure to accurately and efficiently identify the where, when, and who of genocide as well as the ability of the international community to effectively intervene.

Data Limitations during the Rwandan Genocide

The genocide perpetrated in Rwanda in 1994 is a telling case for discussions of data limitations as an impediment to intervention. In the decade following the violence, there has been an extensive debate concerning the role of the international community, particularly the United States, France, and the United Nations, and the failure of that community to identify and act to stop the genocide. This critique is strengthened by the fact that UN peacekeepers (the UNAMIR mission) were on the ground at the time when the genocide began, but did not act in any formal way to prevent the actions that unfolded. Existing literature argues that this failure to act was a product of the lack of political will and a general unwillingness to risk US or European lives in African conflicts (Khadiagala 2004; Power 2002). While we do not disagree that there was a general lack of will toward military intervention at the time, we further the debate on intervention in Rwanda by problematizing the actual information available on what was taking place. While we use the case of the Rwandan Genocide to further this investigation, the issues presented below are germane to all genocides that take place during the course of political violence and/or civil conflict.

Background

Important for our discussion here, the Rwandan Genocide unfolded in the midst of a contemporaneous civil war in a part of the world that was not well monitored by the international community. Following the

Rwandan Patriotic Front (RPF) invasion in 1990 and the subsequent ceasefire negotiated by the United Nations, a group of hard-line Hutu-ethnic extremists launched a massive campaign of violence against Tutsi civilians and Hutu political moderates. Ultimately, during the Rwandan Genocide, over 800,000 people were killed with estimates reaching upward of 1.2 million people (Commission Pour Le Memorial Du Genocide Et Des Massacres Au Rwanda 1996). Furthermore, these figures do not include the numerous people injured, displaced, and traumatized by the violence that racked the country over the course of one hundred days.

Concurrent with the genocide was a renewal of the civil war in Rwanda. On and around April 6, with the assassination of Rwandan President Habyarimana, the RPF moved out of its UN-assigned safe areas and resumed fighting against the Rwandan Army or FAR (Forces Armées Rwandaises). By all accounts this resembled a civil war. The RPF and FAR held territory, fought along battle lines, and employed traditional military tactics with conventional weapons. The civil war and the genocide ended when the RPF took control of the capital city, Kigali. At that time the FAR forces surrendered and/or fled to neighboring Zaire, Uganda, and Tanzania (Prunier 1995).

Limitations to Intervention in Rwanda

Many scholars and activists have argued that the genocide in Rwanda was preventable, specifically that there were clear and decisive early warning signs that should have prompted humanitarian action long before the violence of 1994 was underway (Stanton 2004). We do not challenge this point, but rather argue that once President Habyarimana was killed and the civil war had resumed, the access to reliable data on the violence was a major impediment to rapid military intervention. While much scholarship on the failure of the United States and the international community to act in Rwanda has been blamed on political will (Power 2002), the lack of access to reliable and timely data severely limited the ability of even the most willing actors to push for intervention.

This argument is consistent with existing research on intervention into the Rwandan genocide. In his 2001 analysis of the possibility of US intervention in Rwanda, Kuperman argues that intervention was hampered, in part, by the lack of accurate and efficient information. Kuperman (2001) convincingly demonstrates that intervention was delayed because the information regarding genocide in Rwanda was unclear until April 20. More specifically, he argues that initial information available through the media and human rights sources grossly misrepresented the facts on the ground. First, the violence was originally perceived as a two-sided civil war in which the Tutsi were winning. Second, early violence was depicted as waning as a result of media attention within the capital city that led to underestimated death counts. Third, he argues that no credible or knowledgeable observers raised the prospect that genocide was underway until the second week of violence (Kuperman 2001).

While Kuperman persuasively details the misinformation that was present at the time, he does not offer us an explanation as to how this information became distorted. Using data collected through the GenoDynamics project,[1] we illustrate the ways in which the confusion of the ongoing violence was sufficient enough to distort intelligence coming out of Rwanda and stymie the political message that could have led to a strong and early intervention to halt the violence.

Confusion across Actor, Space, and Time

The information collected by GenoDynamics problematizes our current understandings of violence in Rwanda from April through July 1994 in three important ways: (1) understanding the actions of actors involved, (2) locating battle lines, and (3) accounting for the rapid pace of killings. These three points highlight the limitations of collecting accurate data during genocide and demonstrate how the confusion surrounding the conflict complicated our understanding of what type of violence was taking place where, when, and by whom.

Regarding the first point, we find that there were two main actors involved in violence during 1994: (1) the then Hutu-extremist government (militarily represented by the FAR) and (2) the RPF. These actors fought with one another (i.e., they engaged in civil war) and also engaged in violent action behind the battle lines. The first is easy to understand; it was a civil war. The second is not. In our data collection we do our best to make the distinction between military actions and genocide, but this is not always possible. One way to accomplish this requires the identification of distinct zones: government, RPF, and government/RPF. In this way we can presume that violence behind government lines was genocidal in nature while in the latter case (i.e., violence behind the RPF front), the violence involved reprisal killing for suspected involvement in anti-RPF action as well as violence enacted to establish RPF control over territory. Yet, this pattern does not always hold. In the former case (i.e., the violence behind the government front), actions involved genocide but also nongenocidal violence (e.g., reprisal killing and random action disconnected from the larger conflict). Furthermore, genocide violence could have been taking place behind RPF lines where territory was not tightly secured. Separating the two types of action is impossible because for every single death one would need to identify perpetrators, victims, and motives. The difficulty of identifying who was in control of what territory further problematizes our ability to identify when and where genocide is being committed.

Tracking the battlefront is especially important for it reveals the relatively fast-paced nature of the violence, as Kuperman (2001) argues, as well as the quick routing of the Hutu-extremist government. Within two days of the assassination of the Rwandan president and renewed conflict (April 8), the RPF was in control of the northern part of the country. By April 22, the RPF controlled approximately half the country, pushing downward through the southeast. On May 25, there was a major push forward through and around Kigali and by July 15, the only remaining military force in the country aside from the RPF was the French, in the area surrounding Kamembe and Rwasero in the southwestern part of the country. This is where things stayed until the end of our study in July 31 (Davenport and Stam 2009).

The rapid movement also reveals that the pace of the killing was connected to the pace of the RPF advance. From the GenoDynamics data we find that the faster the RPF advanced, the faster people were killed in front of this invasion. The slower the invasion, the slower the kill rate. Changing rates of RPF advancement and genocide violence made it difficult to determine the patterns and pace of the genocide, further impeding the possibility of international military action (Davenport and Stam 2009).

As we demonstrated in the examples presented above, the GenoDynamics data complicate our understanding of who was committing violence when and where by demonstrating the ongoing confusion regarding genocidal events as they were taking place. With such complications, it becomes more difficult to assume that actors in Washington, DC, New York, Geneva, and on the ground in Rwanda were able to efficiently and accurately access the patterns of genocide that were unfolding around them. While we in no way challenge the presence of genocide in Rwanda and the severity and horror of those actions, we argue that the main indicators of violence necessary for intervention were complicated by the ongoing civil war and that it was difficult to parse different forms of violence at the time (and still to this day). The Rwanda case illustrates the difficulty with accurately and efficiently identifying genocide in time to intervene and the ultimately deadly outcomes data limitations can cause.

Critical Challenges Facing the Field

Through our brief discussion of the Rwanda case, we demonstrate that accurately and efficiently identifying the actors and actions taking place during conflict is a complicated enterprise. The critical challenge facing the field is to develop tools that allow us to more quickly and accurately separate between different actors and actions during political violence in order to identify the presence of genocide (or its early warnings) as soon as possible. This requires greater monitoring, better access to information, and ultimately developing greater skills at parsing the where, when, and who of political violence, particularly violence, which could be surrounding genocide.

This is a major challenge for political leaders. In order to construct more effective and ultimately more successful humanitarian military interventions, we must first develop greater information-gathering systems and better systems of monitoring. This involves the development of closer collaborations between those individuals who collect conflict data in real time (e.g., journalists, human rights activist, etc.) and those who are trained to analyze it (e.g., scholars and policymakers). Increasing partnerships between journalists, human rights reporters, intelligence officers, and conflict scholars promises to increase our ability to intake and process information that can then be quickly transmitted to leaders and activists. The challenge is to improve the accuracy of conflict data and the speed with which it is collected so that we can better implement and structure military interventions to stop genocide.

Yet, even if our intervention systems develop greater accuracy, that is still not a substitute for prevention. As Kuperman (2001) clearly states, "Rwanda and several other recent cases demonstrate that massive ethnic violence can be inflicted faster than the West can learn of it and deploy intervention forces to stop it" (viii). The data limitations that we present in this chapter are particularly relevant for military interventions, but the data threshold for prevention is significantly lower. For this reason, it is essential to support action surrounding early warning systems to provide political and humanitarian intervention before military intervention is needed. Here the challenge is for scholars to develop more creative solutions for preventative intervention (i.e., those types of nonmilitary intervention designed to prevent genocide before it begins).

Genocide prevention activism is already moving in this direction. For example, Greg Stanton (2004) describes a series of eight stages of genocide: classification, symbolization, dehumanization, organization, polarization, preparation, extermination, and denial. While intervention may be particularly complicated in the "extermination" stage, preceding stages offer potentially more straightforward opportunities for intervention that are not clouded by an ongoing conflict. Stanton provides corresponding intervention strategies for each step, such as blocking hate radio stations and preventing international travel for leaders who support dehumanizing policies. The challenge is for scholars to continue to develop these strategies as they require fewer resources, need not be state-sponsored, and ultimately require less reliable data than military interventions.

Probabilities of Progress in the Field

While the intervention and ultimately the eradication of genocide is an essential goal, the question remains as to whether or not it will ever be possible to accurately and efficiently address the main data components of genocide in a timely manner. Our effort to piece together these patterns in Rwanda through the GenoDynamics project required the collaboration of multiple institutions and individuals from around the world, hundreds of thousands of dollars, and approximately ten years to do so. Quite obviously, it is essential that we work to move faster but not lose the precision gained from such an effort. While the barriers to such research remain high, we continue to develop new techniques in the study of political violence that promise to further advance our ability to efficiently and accurately parse political violence and to take political and military action accordingly.

Despite these obstacles, the probability that we will develop strong tools of data collection to assist in military intervention remains high. New directions in human rights data collection, such as the increasing use of mobile phone technology to report human rights violations, suggest that scholars and activists are aware of data problems and increasingly working to address them. Such initiatives promise to provide an increased amount of timely data that can overcome the confusion and misinformation present in times of conflict. In addition, new directions within the subnational conflict studies movement suggest progress within the field of genocide studies. Sophisticated data-collection techniques including disaggregation and dyadic studies promise to move forward our understanding of violence and genocide; however, this work specializes in a systematic and nuanced collection of data, which is not quick. While we are hopeful, the probability of progress will remain directly linked to our ability to collect and process data expeditiously allowing policy makers and state leaders to make rapid intervention decisions.

Conclusion

Moving beyond the initial discussions of political will, legitimacy, and resources as necessary conditions for military intervention to halt genocide, in this chapter we demonstrate that it is often problematic and potentially impossible to identify the main components of genocide while the violence is progressing. Through the case of Rwanda, we demonstrate that these elements are particularly difficult to isolate during periods of contemporaneous conflict due to confusion, misinformation, and limited data-collection capacity. The sensitization to such data and information issues should assist those interested in intervention to develop the questions as well as the tools to prepare for such activities. When studying genocide it is necessary to identify what else is going on in the country at that time. When asking about military intervention it is essential to ask about how easily perpetrators of genocide can be identified relative to perpetrators of other forms of violence. When determining the logistics of intervention, it is important to understand the pace, severity, location, and timing of the violence. Only when these issues have been addressed will we have some ability to properly comprehend what is going on and take the appropriate military action.

Note

1. The GenoDynamics project collects disaggregated data on political violence in Rwanda from April through July 1994 (the period of genocidal violence). The data compilation and collection of GenoDynamics brings together a variety of sources of existing data in addition to other information-gathering efforts: (1) interviews (both structured and unstructured throughout all provinces in Rwanda); (2) focus groups in Kigali and Butare; (3) one randomly selected household survey in the prefecture/province of Butare; (4) information regarding the location of military units; (5) information on the location and strength of radio towers in Rwanda; (6) collection of census information, agricultural zones, forced migration (internal displacement

and refugees); (7) international media coverage about Rwanda and the conflict; and (8) numerous government and human rights reports.

References

Arts, Wiebe. 2011. "Preventing Genocide through Military Intervention: Peacekeeping Troops in the 'Responsibility to Protect' Era." In *Confronting Genocide*, ed. Rene Provost and Payam Akhavan, 117–30. New York: Springer.

Ball, Patrick. 2005. "On the Quantification of Horror: Field Notes on Statistical Analysis of Human Rights Violations." In *Repression and Mobilization*, ed. Christian Davenport, Hank Johnston, and Carol Mueller, 189–210. Minneapolis: University of Minnesota Press.

———. 1996. *Who Did What to Whom? Planning and Implementing a Large Scale Human Rights Data Project*. New York: American Association for the Advancement of Science.

Bauer, Yehuda. 2011. "Some Problems of Genocide Prevention." In *Confronting Genocide*, ed. Rene Provost and Payam Akhavan, 107–16. New York: Springer.

Commission Pour Le Memorial Du Genocide Et Des Massacres Au Rwanda. 1996. *Rapport Preliminaire D'Identification Des Sites Du Genocide et Des Massacres D'Avril-Juillet 1994 Au Rwanda* [Preliminary Report on the Identification of Sites of Genocide and Massacres from April to July 1994 in Rwanda]. Kigali, Rwanda: Ministere de L'Enseignement Superieur, De La Recherche Scientifique Et De La Culture.

Davenport, Christian, and Allan Stam. 2009. "What Really Happened in Rwanda?" *Miller-McCune* [an online journal]. http://www.miller-mccune.com/politics/what-really-happened-in-rwanda-3432/ (accessed July 22, 2012).

Davenport, Christian, and Patrick Ball. 2002. "Views to a Kill: Exploring the Implications of Source Selection in the Case of Guatemalan State Terror, 1977-1995." *Journal of Conflict Resolution* 46, no. 3: 427–50.

Evans, Gareth. 2008. *The Responsibility to Protect: Ending Mass Atrocity Crimes Once and For All*. Washington, DC: Brookings Institution Press.

Harff, Barbara. 2003. "No Lessons Learned from the Holocaust? Assessing Risks of Genocide and Political Mass Murder since 1955." *American Political Science Review* 97, no. 1: 67–68.

Humphreys, Macartan, and Jeremy M. Weinstein. 2008. "Who Fights? Determinants of Participation in Civil War." *American Journal of Political Science* 52, no. 2: 436–55.

———. 2007. "Demobilization and Reintegration." *Journal of Conflict Resolution* 51, no. 4: 531–67.

Kalyvas, Stathis. 2001. *The Logic of Violence during Civil War*. New York: Cambridge University Press.

Khadiagala, Gilbert M. 2004. "Intervention in Internal Conflict: The Case of Rwanda." In *Military Intervention: Cases in Context for the Twenty-First Century* ed. William J. Lahneman, 67–88. Lanham, MD: Rowan & Littlefield Publishers.

Kuperman, Alan J. 2001. *The Limits of Humanitarian Intervention: Genocide in Rwanda*. Washington, DC: Brookings Institution Press.

Lahneman, William J. 2004. "Military Interventions: Lessons for the Twenty-First Century." In *Military Intervention: Cases in Context for the Twenty-First*

Century, ed. William J. Lahneman, 165–200. Lanham, MD: Rowan & Littlefield Publishers.

Power, Samantha. 2002. *"A Problem from Hell": America and the Age of Genocide*. New York: Harper Collins.

Prunier, Gérard. 1995. *The Rwanda Crisis: History of a Genocide*. New York: Columbia University Press.

Stanton, G. 2004. "Could the Rwandan Genocide have been Prevented?" *Journal of Genocide Research* 6, no. 2: 211–28.

Annotated Bibliography

Arts, Wiebe. "Preventing Genocide through Military Intervention: Peacekeeping Troops in the 'Responsibility to Protect' Era." In *Confronting Genocide*, edited by Rene Provost, and Payam Akhavan, 117–30. New York: Springer, 2011.

In this chapter, Arts discusses some of the practical strategies for preparing peacekeeping forces to intervene in genocide. He cites the cases of Rwanda and Bosnia as examples where peacekeeping forces were on-the-ground and therefore should have been able to stop the violence. Arts argues that one of the limitations was the accurate flow of information, which resulted in limited resources and personnel when UN forces were needed.

Ball, Patrick. *Who Did What to Whom? Planning and Implementing a Large Scale Human Rights Data Project*. New York: American Association for the Advancement of Science, 1996, 83 pp.

In *Who Did What to Whom*? Ball provides us with a how-to manual for human right data collection and the development of an information management system for that data. He takes us through the four steps of management, namely collecting information, data processing and classification, database representation, and finally, reporting. For each of these four steps Ball elaborates the process and personnel needed to accomplish the task as well as potential questions that may arise along the way. He details data collection from interviews, documents, and investigations or physical evidence and then moves to a broader discussion of how this information can be converted into an analyzable form. In addition to presenting a model of best practices, Ball provides an overview of the problems and pitfalls with collecting data on human rights. For example, Ball describes the problems of data management systems, which only allow for one victim with one violation from one perpetrator. Ball demonstrates that conflict is rarely this straightforward and argues for the development of data management systems that are able to address this complexity.

Bauer, Yehuda. 2011. "Some Problems of Genocide Prevention." In *Confronting Genocide*, edited by Rene Provost and Payam Akhavan, 107–16. New York: Springer, 2011.

In this chapter, Bauer presents a series of problems afflicting the future of genocide prevention. Bauer champions public campaigns for stopping genocide such as Spielberg's refusal to organize the Olympic ceremonies in Beijing because of China's lack of action against the crisis in Darfur. Ultimately, he concludes that greater information and political pressure can sway international opinion.

Buhaug, Halvard, Lars-Erik Cederman, and Jan Ketil Rød. "Disaggregating Ethnonationalist Civil Wars: A Dyadic Test of Exclusion Theory." *International Organization* 62, no. 3 (2008): 531–51.

Advancing our understanding of patterns of ethnic conflict, Buhaug, Cederman, and Rød argue that actor-specific mechanisms are essential for understanding patterns of ethnic division and ultimately violence. This article uses geo-coded, center-periphery dyads in line with the suggestions of our essay herein to further our understanding of where in a country certain patterns of violence take place. Through this method the authors measure the balance of power between different ethnic groups and those groups in power in order to determine the likelihood and characteristics of future violence.

Cohen, Nissim, and Tamar Arieli. "Field Research in Conflict Environments: Methodological Challenges and Snowball Sampling." *Journal of Peace Research* 48, no. 4 (2011): 423–35.

Cohen and Arieli examine the difficulties of collecting research in conflict environments. They argue that because of issues such as distrust and suspicion, accurate data and representative samples of individuals can be hard to come by. They also discuss the potential limitations that arise for conducting research in contentious environments and advocate the use of snowball sampling to address these limitations.

Davenport, Christian, and Allan Stam. "What Really Happened in Rwanda?" *Miller-McCune* (2009) (an online journal, http://www.miller-mccune.com/politics/what-really-happened-in-rwanda-3432/ [accessed July 22, 2012]).

This work discusses the difficulties involving data collection on political violence in Rwanda for GenoDynamics. The work involved with such a case is both complex intellectually and somewhat difficult professionally, involving personal and institutional threats, resource issues, and extensive travel. This article presents an overview of the work undertaken to collect and analyze the data for the GenoDynamics project as well as a preliminary look at some of the more controversial findings.

Evans, Gareth. *The Responsibility to Protect: Ending Mass Atrocity Crimes Once and For All.* Washington, DC: Brookings Institution Press, 2008, 349 pp.

In this book, Gareth Evans provides a detailed and theoretical account of the concept of The Responsibility to Protect (R2P). As one of the cochairs of the International Commission on Intervention and State Sovereignty (ICISS), the Commission that first formulated R2P, Evans is in a unique position to lead this exchange. Evans begins with a discussion of the problem as he sees it, namely, the reoccurrence of mass atrocities in the twentieth and twenty-first centuries. He argues that the solution to that problem is a broader understanding of state sovereignty and a strengthening of the notions of the right to protect and the right to intervene when civilians are suffering from serious harm and the state in question has proven unwilling or unable to stop this suffering. He then spends the rest of the book operationalizing the tenants of R2P across different time points, specifically before, during, and after a humanitarian crisis. Evans concludes that if we, as an international community, are to adhere to this right then we must go further in developing the diplomatic capacity as well as civilian and military response capability. In closing, he argues that capability and capacity are still not a substitute for the mobilization of political will and leadership.

Galtung, Johan. "Violence, Peace and Peace Research." *Journal of Peace Research* 6, no. 3 (1969): 167–91.

In this keystone article, Galtung presents definitions for both peace and violence, and sets out a research agenda for theorizing and collecting data on these two concepts.

Grünfeld, Fred, and Wessel Vermeulen. "Failures to Prevent Genocide in Rwanda (1994), Srebrenica (1995), and Darfur (since 2003)." *Genocide Studies and Prevention* 4, no. 2 (2009): 221–37.

This article takes a comparative approach to try and understand the reason for intervention failures in Rwanda, Srebrenica, and Darfur. The authors conclude that while the resources for prevention were available, ultimately the failure to intervene was the result of leaders and decision makers being unable to perceive a change from a peace-settlement situation to an emerging genocide. In this way, lack of reliable and efficient information stymied the ability of decision makers to act.

Heidenrich, John G. *How to Prevent Genocide: A Guide to Policymakers, Scholars, and the Concerned Citizen*. Westport, CT: Praeger, 2001, 275 pp.

In *How to Prevent Genocide*, Heidenrich presents a conceptual overview of the means of genocide prevention, ranging from nonviolent pressure to military intervention with multinational forces. Across all of these conceptions of genocide prevention, Heidenrich offers the benefits and ultimately the limitations of each option with a case-thick description of similar techniques used in the past. Moving beyond some of the more discussed strategies in the genocide prevention lexicon, this book includes a discussion of covert action against genocide as well as possible psychological operations. Ultimately, Heidenrich concludes that activism and overcoming the lack of political will still remain some of the greatest challenges toward any type of action to prevent genocide in the future.

Honig, Jan Willem, and Norbert Both. *Srebrenica: Record of a War Crime*. New York: Penguin Books, 1997, 204 pp.

In *Srebrenica*, Honig and Both present a detailed account of the events leading up to and during the massacre at Srebrenica. More specifically, they discuss the failure of the United Nations to enforce their own safe areas and the ways in which the Serb military advance, denial, and misinformation led the UN and NATO forces to fail to act.

Kalyvas, Stathis. *The Logic of Violence during Civil War*. New York: Cambridge University Press, 2001, 508 pp.

Within this study of the Greek Civil War, Kalyvas attempts to show that civilian-oriented violence is tied to the complex dynamics of state–challenger interactions. In this study he distinguishes between selective violence and indiscriminate violence, arguing that selective violence is used by both political actors seeking information and individuals grabbing opportunities that the violence presents them. There are no simple macro explanations for the phenomenon (e.g., like the aggregate level of democracy). Rather, the degree of territorial control held by the different parties is viewed as the key factor, determined by the ability of distinct military units to hold territory at different parts of the day. Above all, Kalyvas demonstrates that the rationale behind conflict is complex and often produces surprising outcomes. Finally, this book displays the disjuncture between actions on the ground and narratives on the top, which is a persistent characteristic of civil conflict.

Kalyvas, Stathis N. "Promises and Pitfalls of an Emerging Research Program: The Microdynamics of Civil War." In *Order, Conflict, Violence*, edited by Stathis N. Kalyvas, Ian Shapiro, and Tarek Masoud, 1–14. New York: Cambridge University Press, 2008.

In this chapter, Kalyvas advocates for the use of disaggregated analysis for the study of civil war violence. To do this he critiques the findings of three articles on Nepal and demonstrates the existing problems of weak empirical proxy variables for theoretical concepts, observational equivalence, endogeneity, and omitted variable bias that are present in these studies. Kalyvas argues that these problems are the result of over-aggregation of the unit of analysis.

Kuperman, Alan J. *The Limits of Humanitarian Intervention: Genocide in Rwanda*. Washington, DC: Brookings Institution Press, 2001, 180 pp.

In *The Limits of Humanitarian Intervention*, Kuperman provides a detailed account of possible US intervention strategies for Rwanda as well as the likelihood of success for each of these proposals. Through an analysis of news sources, open source government documents, and previous military interventions, Kuperman argues that it would not have been possible for the United States to intervene in Rwanda prior to April 20, and that given the length of time necessary for troop deployment, an intervention would have done little to stop the bulk of the violence. Kuperman demonstrates that before April 20, there were five reporting trends that prevented intervention. First, violence in Rwanda was initially depicted as a two-sided civil war that the Tutsi were winning. Second, a few days after April 6, violence was reported as waning when it was really accelerating, a fact Kuperman blames on the exodus of international reporters. Third, most death counts by both the press and human rights organizations were gross underestimates. Fourth, initially all information sources were focused on violence in Kigali, which in turn minimized the destruction that was taking place outside the city. And fifth, no credible observers raised the prospect that a genocide was underway until the second week of violence. Given these gaps in information, Kuperman argues that a timely intervention would not have been possible, and that while a military intervention could have saved between 75,000 and 125,000 lives, the bulk of the genocide killing would have already been completed.

Lahneman, William J., ed. *Military Intervention: Cases in Context for the Twenty-First Century*. Lanham, MD: Rowan & Littlefield Publishers, 2004, 224 pp.

In this collection of essays on military intervention in the twenty-first century, authors grapple with the failures and successes of contemporary intervention efforts. This collection includes both theoretic overviews of civil violence and international intervention as well as detailed case studies of actual missions. The case studies include Somalia, Bosnia, Rwanda, Cambodia, Haiti, Sierra Leone, and East Timor. While not confined solely to a discussion of military interventions to prevent genocide, *Military Intervention* provides an in-depth analysis of lessons learned as well as lessons to be learned. In his closing essay, Lahneman provides an overview of the conclusions, which can be drawn across each intervention, and provides a detailed rubric for how to measure success and failure on humanitarian grounds.

Raleigh, Clionadh, Andrew Linke, Håvard Hegre, and Joakim Karlsen. "Introducing ACLED: An Armed Conflict Location and Event Dataset." *Journal of Peace Research* 47, no. 5 (2010): 651–60.

The ACLED dataset is an example of the ways in which innovative data collection methodology can be applied to outstanding questions in the study of political violence. Specifically, the ACLED disaggregates the location of armed violence so that local-level hypothesis can be tested. This article presents the data, discussing its structure and coding specifications.

Rohde, David. *Endgame: The Betrayal and Fall of Srebrenica, Europe's Worst Massacre Since World War II*. Boulder, CO: Westview Press, 1998, 450 pp.

In this Pulitzer Prize–winning book, Rohde provides a rich, descriptive account of the ten days surrounding the massacre of Srebrenica. This account pays particular attention to the inaction of the United Nations, highlighting issues of intelligence gathering, information transmission, and, ultimately, political will.

Schedler, Andreas. "The Measurer's Dilemma: Coordination Failures in Cross-National Political Data Collection." *Comparative Political Studies* 45, no. 2 (2012): 237–66.

There currently exists a major coordination failure across scholars who collect cross-national political data. In "The Measurer's Dilemma," Schedler argues that this lack of coordination has caused two larger collection problems: the systematic undersupply of data and the systematic inefficiency of data collection. Schedler concludes that this failure is the result of the majority of cross-national data being collected by private actors instead of a larger group effort to resolve many of the data issues outstanding in political science.

Snyder, Richard. "Scaling Down: The Subnational Comparative Method." *Studies in Comparative International Development* 36, no. 1 (2001): 93–110.

This article helps identify exactly why researchers interested in understanding diverse sociopolitical phenomenon, including conflict and violence, should disaggregate their investigations and consider subnational divisions. Such an approach not only increases the number of units the researcher is considering, but it allows better measurement of both concepts and relationships between variables of interest through the greater precision that it allows.

Spirer, Herbert F., and William Seltzer. "Obtaining Evidence for the International Criminal Court Using Data and Quantitative Analysis." In *Statistical Methods for Human Rights*, edited by Jana Asher, David Banks, and Fritz J. Scheuren, 195–226. New York: Springer, 2008.

In this chapter, Spirer and Seltzer discuss the benefits and weaknesses of using quantitative data as legal evidence for the International Criminal Court. Drawing on the experience of expert witnesses at the International Criminal Tribunal for Rwanda and the Former Yugoslavia, this chapter argues that the social chaos and physical destruction often present in times of genocide and massive human rights violations, complicates our ability to present methodologically rigorous quantitative data.

Weidmann, Nils B., and Michael D. Ward. "Predicting Conflict in Space and Time." *Journal of Conflict Resolution* 54, no. 6 (2010): 883–901.

In this article, Weidmann and Ward look at the ways in which geography can be used to predict the onset of violence. Using data from conflict events in Bosnia between March 1992 and October 1995, Weidmann and Ward demonstrate that both spatial and temporal dynamics were important predictors of the outbreak of violence in different locales across Bosnia.

Weinstein, Jeremy. *Inside Rebellion: The Politics of Insurgent Violence*. New York: Cambridge University Press, 2006, 430 pp.

In *Inside Rebellion,* Weinstein uses a disaggregated methodological approach like that advocated in this chapter to assess patterns of insurgent violence across Mozambique, Uganda, and Peru. Weinstein sets out to understand patterns of civilian targeting during insurgent violence and ultimately concludes that the targeting of civilians is often a product of the means by which rebels can extract resources to fight. When resources and financing are not readily available, rebel groups must appeal for local support and therefore will be less likely to target civilians during periods of violence. When resources are more readily available, such as through alluvial diamonds or timber, rebels are less likely to appeal for civilian support and therefore violence and civilian targeting is more likely. While dealing specifically with patterns of insurgency and not genocide, Weinstein demonstrates a methodologically sophisticated approach to understanding patterns of violence across time.

Weiss, Thomas G. *Humanitarian Intervention: Ideas in Action*. Malden, MA: Polity Press, 2007, 196 pp.

This monograph provides a detailed analysis of the theory and practice of humanitarian intervention as a modern concept. Weiss begins with what he calls the "conceptual building blocks" of humanitarian intervention. Here he discusses the norms of state sovereignty and nonintervention and how they clash with new norms of individual sovereignty and changes within the current international system. Drawing on information from ongoing humanitarian crises in the Democratic Republic of Congo, Uganda, and Darfur, Weiss argues that there is little evidence that new norms of intervention are being effectively put in place in a timely manner. From this observation, Weiss argues that we need new thinking on the responsibility to protect and offers policy options to overcome what he argues are the existing limitations to humanitarian intervention, namely the legacy of 9/11, the distraction of the world's major powers, and the domestic impediments to intervention, such as war economies, spoilers, and privatization of aid.

6

Aspects and Components of the United Nations That Constitute Impediments to the Prevention and Intervention of Genocide

Samuel Totten

Ironically, the United Nations, the one institution in the world whose primary mission is to maintain peace across the globe, contributes in significant ways to impeding the prevention and intervention of genocide.[1] While some of the ways are inadvertent, others are undoubtedly intended.

Among some of the many ways in which the United Nations impedes timely and effective efforts to prevent genocide (and short of that, the intervention of genocide) are as follows: ceaseless debates over whether a conflict is genocidal or not; the bureaucratic structure of the United Nations; the composition and operation of the Permanent Five (P5) of the UN Security Council; inadequate donations of personnel, vehicles, weapons systems, and other resources by member states for missions of prevention and intervention; naivety; and overshadowing everything, *realpolitik*.[2]

This is not to say that the United Nations has not tried to reform its handling of violent conflict. It is also not to claim, as some have, that the United Nations is absolutely useless and should be disbanded. In regard to its reform efforts, on January 31, 1991, for example, the UN Security Council requested that then Secretary-General Boutros Boutros-Ghali "prepare and circulate to the Members of the United Nations 'an analysis and recommendations on ways of strengthening and making more efficient within the framework and provisions of the UN Charter the capacity of the United Nations for preventive diplomacy, peacemaking and peace-keeping.'" That resulted in a report, replete with a set of recommendations, called "An Agenda for Peace."[3] Sadly, the decade proved to be anything but peaceful as, for example, the former Yugoslavia exploded with violence (both crimes against humanity and genocide), and Rwanda descended into genocide.

Boutros-Ghali's successor, UN Secretary-General Kofi Annan, also tried his hand at reforming the miserable state of UN peacekeeping missions. More specifically, the group he convened produced the *Report of the Panel on United Nations Peace Operations* (commonly known as the *Brahimi Report*, August 2000). According to the United Nations, the *Brahimi Report* constituted *the first systematic and comprehensive effort* to identify and address key problems within the United Nations' Department of Peacekeeping Operations. Its focus, in large part, was to create missions with mandates (e.g., Chapter VI or Chapter VII) that ostensibly complemented the situation on the ground, provide resources that complemented the mandates, and deploy such missions more selectively. Some, though, took the *Brahimi Report* to task for avoiding a discussion of the thorniest issues faced by such missions, including the ongoing lack of political will of many nations (particularly various members of the P5 in the UN Security Council) to carry out missions in a timely, efficient, and effective manner.[4]

Despite the criticism of the UN and its peace missions, in 2003, David Malone, President of the International Peace Academy in New York City, argued that due to the UN Security Council's decisions and efforts between 1993 and 2003, it "for good or ill, eroded the foundations of absolute conceptions of state sovereignty and fundamentally altered the way in which many of us see the relationship between state and citizen the world over. . . . Interpretations of what developments may constitute 'threats to the peace,' interpretations of the terms of Chapter VII of the Charter, and practice under Chapter VII all have evolved significantly in the post-Cold War era without Charter amendment or a clean break with earlier interpretations" (Malone 2003, 487). While that may have been so to a certain degree, Malone seemed to be looking at the situation through rose-colored glasses, for when all was said and done, the number of innocent people who lost their lives and/or had their lives ruined (meaning the survivors of various genocides and crimes against humanity) numbered in the millions.

Throughout 2004, 2005, and 2006, Annan continued to address the critical need to reform the United Nations, including the UN Security Council and the UN Secretariat. For example, in 2005, Annan presented a report ("In Larger Freedom") to the UN General Assembly and recommended that the membership of the permanent membership of the UN Security Council be expanded. In March 2006, he presented a report ("Investing in the United Nations, for a Stronger Organization Worldwide") in which he outlined a series of proposals for comprehensive reform of the UN Secretariat, many of which were focused on future missions to prevent mass atrocities. Only time will tell whether such recommendations will eventuate in anything significant.

Inspite of all of the aforementioned criticism, it is true that the United Nations had what could be described as moderate success in dealing with *some* humanitarian crises involving atrocity crimes. Two of the more notable cases were in Iraq in 1991 and East Timor in 1999, though each was late in coming. As for Iraq, Gunter (1994) made the following observation:

> The imperfect, but effective, UN collective security operation against Iraq following [Iraq's] conquest of Kuwait in August 1990 eventually led to an equally flawed, but still useful, peacekeeping operation to help save the Kurds from the further depredations of Saddam Hussein after their failed uprising in March 1991. The UN's response proved to be a unique peace-keeping operation because, in effect, it was taking the side of the Iraqi Kurds and the allies against Iraq. This situation patently contrasted with the criterion of impartiality previous peacekeeping operations had possessed." (106)[5]

As for East Timor, following a 1999 vote on whether to remain under Indonesia's rule or seek independence, the people of East Timor chose independence. In an immediate and violent backlash, Indonesia, using both its military troops and pro-Indonesian militia, retaliated by attacking and killing innocent people and virtually destroying the entire infrastructure (buildings, power lines, roads) of East Timor. In response, the United Nations authorized an international force to provide protection and security to the local people. The mission, led by an Australian commander and largely manned by Australian troops, brought peace and order back to East Timor, thus allowing the people to rebuild and carry on with their lives, free from the yoke of Indonesian oppression.

On a different but related note, the United Nations also created the International Criminal Tribunal for the former Yugoslavia (ICTY) and the International Criminal Tribunal for Rwanda (ICTR) in order to try alleged perpetrators of crimes against humanity and genocide during the crisis in the former Yugoslavia and the 1994 Rwandan genocide, respectively. Granted, the establishment of such tribunals seemed to be a way for the United Nations to cling to a shred of dignity in the face of its abysmal failure to first prevent and then to effectively intervene to halt the mass violence in both places. Still, both tribunals sent a loud and clear message that impunity, at least for "the big fish," was no longer acceptable and that at least some perpetrators of mass violence would be held accountable for their crimes.

Also, on July 17, 1998, the international community adopted the Rome Statute, which established the International Criminal Court (ICC). Subsequently, it came into force on July 1, 2002, after it was ratified by the sixtieth nation. According to its mandate, "The ICC is a court of last resort. It will not act if a case is investigated or prosecuted by a national judicial system unless the national proceedings are not genuine; for example, if formal proceedings were undertaken solely to shield a person from criminal responsibility then the ICC would step in and take over the case. In addition, the ICC only tries those accused of the gravest crimes." Among those crimes are genocide, crimes against humanity, and war crimes.

On a different note, in 2004, then Secretary-General Kofi Annan established a new position, Special Advisor on Genocide to the UN Secretary-General. The express purpose of the job, which was first held by Juan Méndez, (followed by Francis M. Deng, and, most recently, by Adam Dieng) is to "to fill critical gaps in the international system that allowed those tragedies to go unchecked." A key question that remains vis-à-vis the position is whether it is one in which the individual holding it can contribute in a substantive manner to the prevention of genocide or whether the post is more ceremonial in nature. To date, it appears as if the latter is more the case than the former.

Is It Genocide or Crimes against Humanity or. . . .? The Ongoing Difficulty of Ascertaining what Is and What Is Not Genocide under the UNCG

For decades, scholars have wrestled with and debated over the wording, concepts, and focus of the UN Convention on the Prevention and Punishment of the Crime of Genocide (UNCG). Such discussions have focused on the ambiguity of certain words/phrases (e.g., "intent," "in part," "mental harm"), the fact that various groups are not mentioned as groups protected under the UNCG (e.g., political and social groups) and that prevention is given short shrift in that it is barely mentioned.

As of late, some genocide scholars have scoffed at the ongoing discussions and debates over the wording and focus of the UNCG, inferring that such discussions are passé, if not inconsequential. If only that were true. What such scholars do not seem to appreciate is that the debates are even more serious today than they were a decade or two ago for today it is not simply scholars who are wrestling with the meaning of words, phrases, and the foci of the UNCG, but also those involved in cases dealing with alleged suspects of genocide and crimes against humanity. Indeed, prosecutors, defense attorneys, and judges at the ICTR, ICTY, and ICC have all engaged in various debates in an attempt to ascertain whether the alleged criminal acts of suspects constitute genocide, crimes against humanity, ethnic cleansing, or some other crime. The point is, the debates over such issues are timely and extremely pertinent.

The Darfur Crisis (2003–present) provides the latest example regarding the ongoing difficulty in coming to a consensus vis-à-vis certain terms and acts specified in the UNCG and how they should be interpreted and applied. For example, following a field investigation in refugee camps in Chad (the Atrocities Documentation Project) in which refugees from Darfur were interviewed about their experiences in Darfur, the US government declared on September 9, 2004, that genocide had been perpetrated and was possibly still being perpetrated by the Government of Sudan; however, following its own investigation in Darfur, Chad, and Khartoum in November and December 2004 and January 2005, the United Nations Commission Inquiry on Darfur found that the atrocities in Darfur did not amount to genocide but rather constituted crimes against humanity. The different findings led to a brouhaha of sorts between human rights activists, genocide scholars, and UN officials. Subsequently, following a multiyear and in-depth investigation by the ICC into the crisis in Darfur, ICC Chief Prosecutor Luis Moreno-Ocampo requested a warrant on July 14, 2008, to arrest Sudanese President Omar al-Bashir on charges of genocide, but after examining the request, the majority of the ICC judges in Pre-Trial Chamber 1 refused to issue a warrant charging genocide and, instead, issued a warrant, on March 4, 2009, for crimes against humanity. One judge (Ms. Anita Usacka), though, wrote a separate and partly dissenting opinion in which she stated that the court should have issued a warrant charging both genocide and crimes against humanity. On July 6, 2009, Moreno-Ocampo filed an appeal, arguing that the court's decision was wrong. On February 3, 2010, the ICC Appeals Chamber rendered its decision, and in doing so reversed the majority's decision for requiring "an erroneous standard of proof." In turn, it ordered the judges in Pre-Trial Chamber 1 to reconsider its decision, taking note of its initial error. After reexamining the prosecutor's request for a warrant on charges of genocide, on July 12, 2010, Pre-Trial Chamber 1 issued a warrant for the arrest of Omar al-Bashir on charges of genocide (along with the earlier charges of crimes against humanity).

Scholars, too, have debated whether the atrocities perpetrated in Darfur constitute genocide or not. Numerous scholars (most notably, William Schabas, Alex de Waal, and Mahomood Mamdani) have argued that the atrocities in Darfur do not constitute genocide, while a host of others (most notably, John Hagan, Stephen Kostas, Eric Markusen, Eric Reeves, Gregory Stanton, and Samuel Totten) have argued that they, in fact, do constitute genocide. The central issue in these debates has been whether the Government of Sudan had the requisite intent to destroy in whole or in part, the black Africans of Darfur, as such.

(Note: Since one of my other chapters in this book addresses the wording and concepts and the debates surrounding the UNCG, there is no need to address the issues/debates here. Thus, for an in-depth discussion as to how the definition of genocide in the UNCG constitutes an impediment to the prevention and intervention of genocide, see Chapter 4 in this volume.)

Finally, it should be noted that despite the fact that Article 16 of the UNCG clearly states that "A request for the revision of the present Convention may be made at any time by any Contracting Party by means of a notification in writing addressed to the Secretary-General," the international community has not, over the past sixty years or since the ratification of the UNCG, attempted to revise the Convention in order to address its many weaknesses that are now common knowledge.

UN Security Council (P5 and Veto Vote)

Over the past couple of decades many scholars, among others, have looked askance at both the make-up of the P5 of the UN Security

Council, and the power the P5 wields. The P5 of the UN Security Council constitutes an elite "club" of the United States, Great Britain, France, China, and the Federation of Russia. The two most notable aspects of the P5 are as follows: (1) those five nations/members are the only permanent members of the UN Security Council. All other members serve on a rotating basis[6] and (2) each of the aforementioned nations has veto power over votes on any and all matters considered by the Security Council. The latter means that if one member of the P5 vetoes, for example, a resolution, it is automatically defeated—no matter the issue or how ardent another member may be about it, or whether the vote was four in favor and one against.

Put a different way, if crimes against humanity and/or genocide break out somewhere in the world and a vote comes up in the Security Council concerning a potential intervention to halt the killing, a single veto by one of the members of the P5 quashes the effort to intervene. Thus, in a body composed of 192 nations, a single veto by a member of the P5 can and will prevent such an intervention. As the cliché goes, and as many commentators have noted, "there is something wrong with that picture!"[7]

For years, questions have arisen as to why those five countries should be privileged over all other countries with permanent membership on the Security Council, as well as an all-powerful veto. While they are certainly among the most powerful and richest nations in the world, some have argued that in this day and age other countries, which have gained a toehold on power, wealth, and influence internationally, should also be considered for potential membership in the elite club. For example, Germany, France, and India have all called for reform at the UN Security Council, including the expansion of permanent members on the UN Security Council. Since at least since 2007, German Chancellor Angela Merkel has campaigned for a German seat on the P5. Concomitantly, in November 2010, US President Barack Obama asserted that he believed that India should become a permanent member of the Security Council (Stolberg and Yardley 2010, n.p.). It was far from an altruistic gesture, though; in fact, it was ostensibly part and parcel of an effort to strengthen US ties with India and help create more commercial opportunities while also "attempting to check the influence of an increasingly assertive China" (Stolberg and Yardley 2010).

Others have argued that there should be more diversity represented among the permanent members, including, at the least, a nation from Africa and a nation from Central or South America. They argue that, perhaps, then, the Permanent Members of the Security Council might be more apt to listen to reason when it comes to crises in Third World nations. If only that were so, but the key problem, as discussed below, is that each member would still have the veto to squelch anything that a P5 member's government perceived as not in its or its allies' interest.

Some have even questioned the sagacity of allowing a select few to be accorded permanent membership, especially with veto power. Sooner or later, this issue is highly likely to erupt into a major issue, be it a decade, two decades, or more from now.

Adding grease to the fire, in dealing with cases of crimes against humanity and genocide in the past, the votes of the P5 were not guided by altruism but driven by *realpolitik*. Thus, in casting their votes, their primary concern was not based on the plight and fate of those facing genocide but rather on whether such an intervention was "good" for themselves or their allies. That is not surprising, of course. Disappointing, yes; but certainly not surprising. As it has been stated repeatedly, nation states do not have consciences.

Ineffective Missions to Prevent/Intervene in Case of Crimes against Humanity and/or Genocide

Another impediment to preventing, or halting, genocide is that more often than not, when the United Nations launches an operation dealing with crimes against humanity and/or genocide, it frequently sends a peacekeeping (Chapter VI) mission in place of what is really needed, a peace enforcement (Chapter VII) mission.[8] Time and again, peace operations with weak mandates—mandates in which troops are only allowed to protect themselves but not engage the perpetrators in battle in an effort to halt the killing—have been implemented in situations that call for the strongest mandates possible. The UN Security Council's reaction to the 1994 Rwandan genocide constitutes the classic example of such a situation cum fiasco. The UN Security Council's reactions to the crisis in Bosnia (in the 1990s) and Darfur (2003–present) come in a close second and third. More specifically,

> In Bosnia, Somalia, and Rwanda ... the international community ... demanded the UN "do something" even though Security Council members were not prepared to authorize a full-scale war

> to stamp out these crises. The result was a series of peacekeeping operations flawed by the contradictory mandates given the peacekeepers, who, without the weapons or troop strength necessary for the job, were expected to enforce "safe areas," "exclusion zones," and "no-fly areas," hunt down Somali warlords, and stop Hutus [from massacring Tutsis]—all the while trying to act impartially.
>
> [A key] lesson has been the difficulty of securing peacekeeping troops and equipment quickly enough. Although the U.N. now has a significant number of experienced officers as well as a "situation room" manned round the clock in New York, wired to its operations all over the world, the secretary-general likes to recall how not one of the nineteen countries which at that time had pledged 31,000 troops for future U.N. peacekeeping operations was prepared to send a single soldier to Rwanda. And the handful of African countries that finally offered troops had to hire American armored cars because they had nothing suitable themselves. (Lewis 1996, 39–40)

As mentioned above, another major impediment to the prevention and intervention of genocide results from the fact that, more times than not, there is a lack of vital support from member nations in relation to a donation of troops, equipment, and critical supplies to the mission. Such a lack of support results in missions being sorely undermanned, under-resourced, and outgunned, which certainly makes for a less than truly effective operation.

In the recent past, many countries have deployed ill-trained soldiers with rickety equipment or equipment that is not appropriate for the mission. Impoverished nations sometimes tend to send personnel for seemingly ulterior motives, that is, to benefit monetarily, to provide opportunities for their soldiers to gain critical field experience, and to allow their soldiers to work for the United Nations and thus earn a handsome wage, which they would not earn at home.

Whether a nation sends troops to serve on a mission or not, all member states are called upon to donate equipment and resources for keeping the mission in top operational shape. Many, however, simply ignore the call for weapons, four-wheeled vehicles, helicopters, spare parts for vehicles and aircraft, oil and petrol, and so on. The stories of such are legion. For example, in 2008, the UN/AU Hybrid Force was forced to rent a helicopter from a private firm due to the fact that nations had not been forthcoming with such equipment. That, bizarrely, resulted in an untenable situation for the mission's command. Because the helicopter was privately owned, the Government of Sudan placed constraints on when and where it could fly (not at night, and not into "hot" zones) thus preventing the force from traveling to areas that demanded their presence.

Lack of Effective Genocide Early Warning System

For decades, scholars and others have discussed the need for the development and implementation of a genocide early warning system. Some have even developed models and schemas for such (e.g., Israel W. Charny, Franklin Littell, and Barbara Harff).

The idea behind such a system, of course, is to track *any series of events* across the globe that have the potential to descend into gross human rights violations, including crimes against humanity and/or genocide. Essentially, such a system would need to track all types of human rights violations—including the threats of such—that have the potential to morph into massacres, crimes against humanity, ethnic cleansing, and so on, analyze the data, and then disseminate it as quickly as possible to key actors (e.g., various departments at the United Nations, the UN Security Council, the UN General Assembly, the European Union, various nations, and nongovernmental organizations).[9]

On a different but related note, for close to two decades both the United Nations and the United States have repeatedly reported that they are in the process of developing a genocide early warning system, and yet to this day, neither has put one into operation. The question is, why not? Among the many probable answers are: (1) the development and implementation of such a system is seemingly low on their list of priorities; (2) the development of such a system may be much more complicated than anyone had anticipated; (3) the cost of developing and implementing such a system may be inordinate; and/or (4) a change in officials/administrators may have resulted in such a system being placed, for whatever reason, on the backburner. No matter the reason, it is a shame that such a system has not at least been developed and implemented by the United Nations.

Why is an early warning system needed? At the least, it will prevent the United Nations and individual states from using the excuse that they did not know that a situation was dire and in need of immediate attention. Such a system would undercut any claim (cum mea culpa) such as the one US President Bill Clinton made in 1999 while visiting Rwanda: "All over the world, there were people like me sitting in offices, day after day after day, who did not fully appreciate the depth and the speed with which you were being engulfed by this unimaginable terror [the 1994 Rwandan genocide]" (quoted on Frontline, 1999).

On a more positive note, such a system would provide up-to-date information on crisis situations across the globe and, ideally, demarcate those that are most serious and possibly moving toward crimes against humanity and/or genocide. Such information could then be relayed to key actors with the aim that the latter would immediately set to work to ameliorate the situation(s) and prevent it/them from exploding into crimes against humanity and/or genocide.

Some genocide scholars mock the value of the development and implementation of such a system, arguing that it is not the vital mechanism that some make it out to be. Their basic argument is that in this day and age, the information age, the powers that be within the United Nations and individual governments certainly know when a situation is approaching crisis mode and yet, due to *realpolitik*, the lack of political will and/or simply a lack of care do not act to stanch the atrocities, and that any amount or type of information they might receive from any source would not necessarily make them any more proactive. Perhaps that is true, but there is no empirical evidence that corroborates such an assertion, and thus, even if there is only a slim hope that such a system could serve a positive purpose (meaning saving tens, and possibly hundredsof thousands of lives or more), then it would be worth implementing. Still, and this, in part, refers back to those who question the value of developing and implementing such an early warning system: when all said and done, if the international community or individual nations developed an elaborate system but neglected to address the warning signals in a timely and effective manner, then the system would be virtually useless. Michael Barnett (1996), a political scientist, corroborates the latter point when he notes the following:

> *an assumption of the search for early warning indicators and the proposal for a UN standing army for preventive deployment suggest that knowledge brings action. There is an unwritten belief that with knowledge the international community will act. Yet it was not the lack of knowledge that halted action in either Bosnia or Rwanda—it was politics. In both cases, states and UN officials knew of but chose to ignore the war crimes that were being committed. In both cases UN Forces were on the ground and were eyewitnesses to acts of ethnic cleansing and genocide, and in both cases the rules of engagement*

> *prevented UN forces from coming to the active aid of civilians. More technologies and capabilities are no elixir and no substitute for a politics of engagement.* (italics added) (156–57)

Lack of UN Rapid Action Force

Another major impediment to the prevention and intervention of genocide is the fact that when crimes against humanity and/or genocide break out and the international community actually does act, it takes a relatively long time to ramp up and deploy a mission to help stanch the killing. This is understandable as the logistics are many and complex, and not as streamlined as they could or should be. In some cases the entire process is slowed down due to cumbersome bureaucracies, including that of the United Nations. In others it is due to, as mentioned above, the fact that donor nations are not forthcoming with the requisite number of personnel, weapons systems, vehicles, helicopters, and other resources for such a mission.

Over the years, various scholars have suggested the need for some type of rapid reaction force that could be deployed in a fraction of the time that it takes a regular mission to be created and implemented. Currently, no such force exists for the express purpose of the prevention and intervention of crimes against humanity and/or genocide. This is an idea/approach that demands implementation.

Intervening versus Preventing the Outbreak of Genocide

Another impediment to the prevention of genocide is that the international community has a propensity for waiting until genocide is well under way before attempting to stanch it. Oftentimes, tens, if not hundreds, of thousands have been killed by the perpetrators before a mission is fully operational (for example, the Bangladesh Genocide, the 1994 Rwandan Genocide, the Darfur Genocide, and the current starvation that is claiming lives in the Nuba Mountains of Sudan).

It should be commonsense, but ostensibly it is not, that preventative efforts are not only capable of saving lives but preventing massive refugees' flows, the destruction of a region/country, and the expenditures of hundreds of millions of dollars in carrying out a military mission and then reconstructing an entire society from the ground up.

The time for the United Nations, and others who are truly interested in preventing genocide, to act is when comments/propaganda begin to circulate that malign and threaten a specific group of people.

If preventative action is not taken at the early stages of conflict, then the actions against the maligned group are likely to increase in frequency and in violence.

Bureaucratic Structure of the United Nations

In *Eyewitness to a Genocide: The United Nations and Rwanda*, Michael Barnett (2002) presents a series of extremely disturbing, and telling, insights into how the bureaucracy of the United Nations inadvertently created the conditions resulting in its anemic reaction to the 1994 genocide in Rwanda. Barnett, a noted political scientist, served as a political officer at the US Mission to the United Nations from 1993 to 1994 and witnessed up close the way in which various departments and sections worked—sometimes in a dither, sometimes blindly, many times at cross-purposes, and, ironically, in ways that purportedly were perceived as supporting the mission of the United Nations itself while, at one and the same time, minimizing the dire straits that the Tutsi faced in Rwanda. Shaped by, and steeped in, a UN culture that was cautious, fearful of taking missteps, and in which officials were expected to "play by the rules of the game" (and were working in such compartmentalized ways that the proverbial right hand knew little to nothing about what the proverbial left hand was doing), individuals made decisions accordingly (Barnett 2002, 19). All of this was impacted by another significant aspect of the culture at the United Nations, "an institutional ideology of impartiality even when confronted with attempted genocide" (Annan quoted in Barnett 2002, 158).

The point is this: if genocide scholars and human rights activists believe that the inept response to genocide by the United Nations is going to be solved solely as a result of a revamped UN Security Council, the implementation of a highly sophisticated genocide early warning system, and the development of a rapid reaction force, they are sorely mistaken and blind to the reality of how the United Nations works. In other words, if the bureaucracy of the United Nations is not somehow streamlined so that (1) all lines of communication are clear; (2) the different eyes, ears, mouths, and hands are well informed as to what the others are doing; and (3) a mechanism is put in place where a sole section/group oversees all communication sources, decisions, and has the power to speak directly and honestly with the UN Security Council and then is held accountable, the range of problems evidenced in its reaction to the 1994 Rwandan genocide will likely continue to be repeated time and again.[10] Is the issue intractable? No, but it does demand that the nation states that comprise the United Nations both desire and support such an operation. The likelihood of that, unfortunately, is dubious.

In his book, Barnett provides a much more detailed explanation of the aforementioned issues and also raises a host of other key concerns/issues vis-à-vis the bureaucracy of the United Nations and how it contributed to impeding the efforts to prevent and then intervene in the 1994 genocide in Rwanda. Space constraints preclude a discussion of each, but it is worth at least listing some of Barnett's more disturbing and significant insights and findings:

> The culture within the UN "contained orienting concepts such as neutrality, impartiality, and consent, which governed how peacekeepers were supposed to operate in the field" (xi). . . . These rules restricted the UN's scope of caring and operation; it was prepared to assist when it had the consent of the parties and there was stability on the ground, but it would shy away from humanitarian disasters. (13)
>
> As a collection of related units and subunits, the UN contains subcultures that have distinct interpretations of how the rules and standards of appropriateness can and should be applied. Hardly synchronized in their moments or thoughts, the Secretariat, the Council, and the field can have very different ideas about what is appropriate, how they should prioritize their commitments and responsibilities, and what constitutes an acceptable level of risk. These three UN elements disagree among themselves over the meaning of neutrality, impartiality, and consent—disagreements that have their roots in rival interpretations of recent history and present circumstances. (12)
>
> The culture within the UN "shaped how the UN came to know countries like Rwanda that were attempting to move from civil war to civil society. In brief, those working at the UN approached Rwanda not as individuals but rather as members of bureaucracies. They occupied roles that organizationally situated and defined their knowledge, and informed what they cared about, what behavior they considered appropriate and inappropriate, how they distinguished acceptable from unacceptable consequences, and how they determined right from wrong. Something about the culture at the UN could make *nonintervention* not merely pragmatic but also legitimate and proper—even in the face of crimes against humanity." (emphasis added) (xi)
>
> After sobering experiences in the field and a more realistic appraisal of the foundations of peacekeeping, New York [UN headquarters] developed a more precise and restricted set of rules to determine when peacekeeping was appropriate and how peacekeepers should

operate in the field. Peacekeeping was appropriate when there was a 'peace to keep.'" (10)[11]

Likelihood of Progress

As stated at the outset of this chapter, the United Nations has, time and again, attempted to reform various facets of its operational processes vis-à-vis violent conflict and humanitarian emergencies. Those, such as Kofi Annan, who challenged the organization to reform itself were serious, and many were sick over the millions who had perished through horrific deaths due to crimes against humanity and genocide over the past two decades in, for example, Rwanda, the former Yugoslavia, and Darfur.

But, of course, it is one thing to make changes and another to carry out those changes in the manner intended. Much of the evidence thus far—including the ongoing African Union/UN Hybrid Mission in Darfur and the reaction as of late (June 2011 through January 2012) to the Government of Sudan attack on the Nuba Mountains and the Blue Nile regions—suggests that changes made by the United Nations and their impact is more akin to the old saw about rearranging the deck chairs on the Titanic as it took on water.

In that regard, it is difficult to contest the following insights of David Shorr (2007):

> The root pathology of optimism at the UN is not idealistic naïveté, but self-deception. . . . The right course of action is always politically difficult and logistically formidable, and sometimes demands the investment of blood as well as treasure. Rather than facing up to these realities, UN staff and diplomats tailor their assessments, options, and recommendations to fit the will to act, instead of the other way around. The nonpurist staff. . . appear worn down by member states' resistance to taking action and a pervading skepticism that difficult steps by national governments are really required. The result is an utter mismatch between the tools and the real-world problems they are supposed to fix. The most persuasive diagnoses of the UN's weaknesses point toward a cultural pathology. [In this regard,] former Deputy Secretary General Mark Malloch-Brown [speaks about] "'a culture of political complicity' in which all parties conspired to evade accountability." The international body—whose purpose is to promote progress around the world—is too often a world unto itself.
>
> . . . The common theme of these symbolic debates is often the specter of outside intervention in nations' internal affairs and the

> erosion of their sovereignty. There are serious issues relating to the nature of sovereignty, with legitimate arguments on both sides. . . . But the vast majority of skirmishes over sovereignty in the UN have nothing to do with these complex and tricky issues. They are political sport, plain and simple. In the end (or, at least up to now), unfortunately, the UN continues to be "pushed and pulled between rigid principles and power realities, ground-level facts and diplomatic detachment, and most of all, history's greatest superpower and, well, everyone else." (Schorr 2007, n.p.)

Conclusion

What is delineated herein is not pleasant. In fact, after reading it one is bound to ask: Is there any hope at all that the world, the United Nations, individual states, anyone, for that matter, will ever be able to develop *a timely, efficient, and effective* regime against crimes against humanity/genocide. It is a fair question to ask. Right now, it seems as if the probability of such becoming a reality in the near future is extremely dim.

That said, it is also true that at no other time in the history of humanity has more attention, more thinking, more work, or more effort gone into developing ways to prevent genocide or, at the least, to halt it early on. True, the results thus far have been minimal and in many cases, absolutely miserable. Still, even a sliver of hope constitutes hope, meaning that if individuals, groups, organizations and nation states continue to focus on the prevention and intervention of genocide, who knows what the result might be. Be that as it may, even if the United Nations is streamlined, always lurking in the shadows are the Gordian Knots of *realpolitik*, the lack of political will, and a genuine lack of caring.

Notes

1. It is ironic, for according to the Charter of the United Nations among the UN's major purposes are the following:

> To maintain international peace and security, and to that end: to take effective collective measures for the prevention and removal of threats to the peace, and for the suppression of acts of aggression or other breaches of the peace, and to bring about by peaceful means, and in conformity with the principles of justice and international law, adjustment or settlement of international disputes or situations which might lead to a breach of the peace.

The UN Security Council has the power to establish missions to attempt to prevent genocide and implement interventions in actual genocidal situations. More recently, the UN established the position of The Special Advisor on the Prevention of Genocide, whose express purpose is "act as a catalyst to raise awareness of the causes and dynamics of genocide, to alert relevant actors where there is a risk of genocide and to advocate and mobilize for appropriate action."

2. It is also a fact, as Scheffer (1998) notes, that "The law and practice of the United Nations in [peacekeeping operations] have evolved at an accelerating pace during the 1990s and in ways that would have astonished the framers of the Charter in 1945. They would not have anticipated that ethnic conflicts of a largely internal character would necessitate U.N. engagement on so many fronts" (147).
3. Among some of the many reforms the United Nations attempted in the 1990s are as follows:

> *Extensive administrative restructuring involving the carving out of three new "action" departments—Political Affairs (DPA), Humanitarian Affairs (DHA), and Peacekeeping Operations (DPKO)—in order to rationalize both the division of labor as well as lines of authority and responsibility.
>
> *Formed a senior-level task force to develop co-ordination and procedural arrangements in order to improve inter-departmental communication and co-operation.
>
> *Assigned early warning responsibilities to DPA and, in humanitarian relief situations, to DHA.
>
> *Established a Situation Centre in DPKO, which maintains around-the-clock links with field operations.
>
> *Transferred the Field Operations Division (renamed the Field Administration and Logistic Division) from the Department of Administration and Management to DPKO to make it more responsive to mandated missions and answerable primarily to DPKO, its major client.
>
> *Initiated a program for more regular consultations on peacekeeping between Secretariat officials, the Security Council, troop-contributing nations, and other member states. . . .
>
> *Created a system of stand-by forces and capabilities which member states agree to maintain and make available for possible call-up when required for mandated peace operations.
>
> *Acquired a facility in Brindisi, Italy, to store and maintain excess equipment and the assembling of mission start-up kits. (Daniel and Hayes 1997, 114)

4. The abject response and results of the AU/UN Mission in Darfur, Sudan, speaks loudly to the fact that the *Brahimi* Report largely resulted in naught.
5. Notably, the United Nations had declared in Security Council 688 of April 5, 1991, that "the repression of the Iraqi civilian population, including most recently, Kurdish populated areas" could "threaten international peace and security." *In other words, the Council was saying that circumstances*

may arise in which extraordinary humanitarian needs would compel the world organization to intervene in the internal affairs of a sovereign state under the collective security provisions of UN Charter Chapter VII" (italics added).

As Gunter (1994) noted, "Previously, what a state did to its own minorities was of little or no concern to outsiders. Again, therefore, the UN peacekeeping operation in northern Iraq carried major implications for the future of international law and the organization" (106–7).

6. Ten nonpermanent members are elected to serve on the Security Council by the General Assembly for two-year terms. They are not eligible for immediate reelection. The number of nonpermanent members was increased from six to ten by an amendment of the UN Charter, which came into force in 1965.
7. A classic example that something is wrong with "that picture" was the United States' unconscionable actions during the 1994 Rwandan Genocide. More specifically, while many across the globe largely blamed the United Nations for its lame response to the genocide (and, in many ways, such blame was justified), it was the United States that pressured the United Nations to forego reconfiguring its mission (UN Assistance Mission in Rwanda) already on the ground in Rwanda in order to make it more robust. The result was that the mission was left without the means (a Chapter VII mandate, an adequate number of personnel, and requisite equipment/ resources) to halt the ongoing genocide. (For more details about this matter, see Samantha Power, *A Problem from Hell: America in the Age of Genocide* [New York: Harper, 2003].)
8. It is also a fact that when the UN Security Council actually chooses to act in the face of genocide, it is more apt to do so after genocide has broken out versus attempting to prevent it in the first place. That hardly honors the promise stated in Article 1 of the UNCG: "The Contracting Parties confirm that genocide, whether committed in time of peace or in time of war, is a crime under international law which they undertake to *prevent* and to punish" (italics added).
9. When one thinks about it, referring to such a system as a "genocide" early warning system is a misnomer and shortsighted. It would make much more sense to name such a system something along the lines of the following: Incremental and Gross Human Rights Violations Early Warning System, Human Rights Violations, Crimes against Humanity and Genocide Early Warning System or simply Crimes against Humanity and Genocide Early Warning System. Why? Because IF there is to be any chance to prevent genocide, the violations of human rights leading up to such a cataclysmic event need to be detected and ameliorated as early as possible, and such a system should reflect that fact.
10. In regard to these issues, Barnett (2002) notes the following: "Even if it can be shown that the UN's actions or omissions contributed to the genocide, the UN might have a valid excuse, some extenuating circumstances that interfered with its ability to act. . . . Many decision makers have claimed ignorance, insisting that the situation was highly uncertain. Others, notably those in the Secretariat, have cited pressures and the constraints imposed

by the Security Council. A striking feature of the form and content of these excuses is that they tend to implicate the 'UN.' Many of the participants have argued that their position in the bureaucracy gave them a partial view of Rwanda and therefore they were not fully informed. Others have insisted that they were immobilized by constraints imposed on them by others. The UN becomes either a veil of ignorance or a bureaucratic restraint" (19).

11. Barnett further states, "The reason for these rules was the recognition that the misapplication of peacekeeping was leading both to costly failures in the field and to fatal damage to the institution. But another consequence of these rules was the reduced likelihood that peacekeepers would be deployed during moments of mass human suffering" (10).

References

Barnett, Michael. 2002. *Eyewitness to a Genocide: The United Nations and Rwanda.* Ithaca, NY: Cornell University Press.

———. 1996. "The Politics of Indifference at the United Nations and Genocide in Rwanda and Burundi." In *This Time We Knew: Western Responses to Genocide in Bosnia,* ed. Thomas Cushman and Stejepan G. Mestrovic, 128–62. New York: New York University Press.

Daniel, Donald, C. F., and Bradd Hayes. 1997. "Securing Observance of UN Mandates Through the Employment of Military Force." In *The UN, Peace and Force,* ed. Michael Pugh, 105–25. London: Frank Cass Publishers.

Frontline. 1999. "The Triumph of Evil." (Air date: January 26, 1999.) http://www.pbs.org/wgbh//pages/frontline/////////shows/ . . . /script.html

Gunter, Michael M. 1994. "The Kurdish Peacekeeping Operation in Northern Iraq, 1991." In *Peacekeeping and the Challenge of Civil Conflict Resolution,* ed. David A. Charters, 97–110. New Brunswick, NJ: Centre for Conflict Studies, University of New Brunswick.

Lewis, Paul. 1996. "A Short History of United Nations Peacekeeping." In *Soldiers for Peace: Fifty Years of United Nations Peacekeeping,* ed. Barbara Benton, 25–41. New York: Facts on File.

Malone, David M. 2003. "The Security Council in the Post-Cold War Era: A Study in the Creative Interpretation of the U. N. Charter." *Journal of International Law and Politics* 35, no. 2: 487–517.

Scheffer, David J. 1998. "U.N. Engagement in Ethnic Conflict." In *International Law and Ethnic Conflict,* ed. David Wippman, 147–77. Ithaca, NY: Cornell University Press.

Shorr, David. 2007. "Dysfunction and Potential at the U.N.: A Review of James Traub's *The Best Intentions: Kofi Annan and the UN in the Era of American World Power* (Farrar, Straus and Giroux, 2006)." April 3. *Policy Review, No. 142,* n.p.

Stolberg, Sheryl Gay, and Jim Yardley. 2010. "Countering China, Obama Backs India for U.N. Council." *The New York Times,* November 8. http://www.nytimes.com/2010/11/09/world/ . . . /09prexy.html

United Nations. 2011. *Office of the Special Advisor on the Prevention of Genocide.* New York: United Nations.

———. 1948. *UN Convention on the Prevention and Punishment of the Crime of Genocide.* New York: United Nations.

Annotated Bibliography

General

Mayall, James, ed. *The New Interventionism: United Nations Experience in Cambodia, Former Yugoslavia, and Somalia*. New York: Cambridge University Press, 1996, 238 pp.

This is a valuable assessment of the three major UN interventions in the 1990s. In his introduction, Mayall cites the following as one of the major weaknesses of the "new interventionism": the UN peacekeeping bureaucracy's makeup itself interferes with its effectiveness in attempting to address complex political and military operations.

Price, Richard, and Mark Zacher. *The United Nations and Global Security*. New York: Palgrave Macmillan, 2004, 305 pp.

Herein, noted international scholars examine the role of the United Nations in preventing international and civil violence, deterring and reversing aggression, and addressing humanitarian crises. Among some of the many chapters in this volume are: "When Aspiration Exceeds Capability: The UN and Conflict Prevention" by Andrew Mack and Kathryn Furlong; "Can the UN Still Mediate?" by Fen Hampson; "Conundrums of International Power-Sharing: The Politics of Security Council Reform" by Mark W. Zacher; "The UN, Regional Organizations, and Regional Conflict: Is There a Viable Role for the UN?' by Brian L. Job; and "Human Security: An Opening for UN Reform" by Lloyd Axworthy.

Pugh, Michael, ed. *The UN, Peace, and Force*. London: Frank Cass, 1997, 209 pp.

Among some of the many chapters in this book are: "The United Nations and the Collective Use of Force: Whither or Whether?"; "Assessing the Success of UN Peacekeeping Operations"; "Securing Observance of UN Mandates Through the Employment of Military Force"; "Utopian or Pragmatic? A UN Permanent Military Volunteer Force"; and "From Mission Cringe to Mission Creep? Concluding Remarks."

Rieff, David. "The Illusions of Peacekeeping." *World Policy Journal* 11, no. 3 (Fall 1994):1–19.

A no-holds barred critique of the United Nations' "peacekeeping" efforts in Bosnia in the early to mid-1990s. Rieff, a Senior Fellow at the World Policy Institute, concludes with the following assertion: "The lesson of Bosnia is that the United Nations in general, and the Department of Peacekeeping Operations in particular, are still too committed to the norms of classical peacekeeping to play a central role in a more comprehensive system of international security" (18).

Schnabel, Albrecht, and Ramesh Thakur. "From *An Agenda for Peace* to the *Brahimi Report*: Towards a New Era of UN Peace Operations?" In *United Nations Peacekeeping Operations: Ad Hoc Missions, Permanent Engagement*, edited by Ramesh Thakur and Albrecht Schnabel, 238–55. Tokyo: United Nations University Press, 2001.

This chapter's focus is threefold. First, it succinctly discusses the failure of post–Cold War peacekeeping efforts from the period of the 1992 *Agenda for Peace* to the 2000 *Brahimi Report* on UN peace operations. Second, it discusses the lessons learned from post–Cold War peacekeeping practices as outlined in the *Brahimi Report.* Third, it examines that which constitutes "effective conflict prevention and the implementation, if needed, of humanitarian enforcement operations in failing and failed states to protect basic rights and security needs of individuals" (239).

Thakur, Ramesh, and Albrecht Schnabel, eds. *United Nations Peacekeeping Operations: Ad Hoc Missions, Permanent Engagement.* New York: United Nations Press, 2001, 267 pp.

This book comprises twelve chapters, including, for example, "The Role of the UN Secretariat in Organizing Peacekeeping" by Hisako Shimura; "Towards More Effective Peace Operations: Learning from the African 'Laboratory'?" by Mark Malan; "The Politics of UN Peacekeeping from Cambodia to Yugoslavia" by Yasushi Akashi; "Peacekeeping and the Changing Role of the United Nations: Four Dilemmas" by Margaret P. Karns and Karen A. Mingst; and "From *An Agenda for Peace* to the *Brahimi Report*: Towards a New Era of UN Peace Operations?" by Albrecht Schnabel and Ramesh Thakur.

Totten, Samuel, and Paul Bartrop. "The United Nations and Genocide: Prevention, Intervention, and Prosecution." In *Genocide at the Millennium. Genocide: A Critical Bibliographic Review,* edited by Samuel Totten, 113–46. New Brunswick, NJ: Transaction Publishers, 2005.

This essay by Totten (a genocide scholar based at the University of Arkansas, Fayetteville) and Bartrop (a historian based at Deakin University in Victoria, Australia) comprises the following sections: an overview of the UN's efforts vis-à-vis the prevention and intervention of genocide, the critical challenges, and the likelihood of progress in meeting such challenges, and an annotated bibliography of key works.

Traub, James. *The Best Intentions: Kofi Annan and the UN in the Era of American World Power.* New York: Farrar, Straus, and Giroux, 2006, 464 pp.

Traub delves into such questions as "Is this [the UN's] sixty-year-old experiment in global policing outlived its usefulness?" and "Do its failures arise from its own structure and culture, or from a clash with an American administration determined to go its own way in defiance of world opinion?"

Based on in-depth interviews with UN Secretary-General Kofi Annan and his top aides, Traub discusses, in part, the failed attempt to goad the Security Council to act decisively against state-sponsored ethnic cleansing in Sudan. He also recounts "Annan's effort to respond to criticism with sweeping reform—an effort which ultimately shattered on the resistance of U.S. Ambassador John Bolton. . . . Annan [is] a conscientious idealist given too little credit for advancing causes like humanitarian intervention and an honest broker crushed between American conservatives and Third World opponents—but also a UN careerist who has absorbed that culture and cannot, in the end, escape its limitations" (n.p.).

Williams, Michael C. "Civil-Military Relations and Peacekeeping." *Adelphi Paper 321.* New York: Oxford University Press, 1998, 93 pp.

In this monograph, Williams, Senior Consultant in the Office of the United Nations High Commissioner for Refugees (UNHCR), argues that peacekeeping operations in the 1990s were marked by insufficient military input at the strategic level, unclear mandates, and weak command and control by the United Nations. He also argues that in the field, missions were hampered by the culture clash between civilians and the military, by poor coordination of civilian and military tasks, by inadequate military training to meet specific demands of peacekeeping, and by differing approaches to human-rights issues and the media.

Reforming the United Nations

Müller, Joachim. *Reforming the United Nations*. Brill, The Netherlands: Martinus Nijhoff Publishers, 2010, 2006, 2001, 1997, 6,000 plus pages.

The six volumes of *Reforming the United Nations* "bring together a wealth of information and provide a comprehensive and in-depth presentation of UN reform initiatives, with over 6,000 pages of analysis, description and primary documents." The series is published by Martinus Nijhoff Publishers/Brill, The Netherlands, and edited by Joachim Müller. Among the volumes in the series are:

**Reforming the United Nations: The Challenge of Working Together (2010) presents the reform efforts of 2006–2009 associated with system-wide coherence, interagency coordination, management reform, and Security Council reform, 390 pp.*

**Reforming the United Nations: The Quiet Revolution (2001). The period from 1997 to 2002 is captured in the fourth volume, which presents, in particular, Secretary-General Kofi Annan's reform efforts, known as the Quiet Revolution, 968 pp.*

**Reforming the United Nations: New Initiatives and Past Efforts (1997) presents fifty reform initiatives and key reform documents originating during the period from 1950 to 1996 and was issued in three volumes, 3,464 pp.*

Schaefer, Brett D., ed. *ConUNdrum: The Limits of the United Nations and the Search for Alternatives*. Lanham, MD: Rowman & Littlefield, 2009, 400 pages.

Published in cooperation with the Heritage Foundation, this book, which is comprised of ten chapters, analyzes the weaknesses of the UN system and presents a series of potential solutions for reform. "They suggest ways to improve efforts to work within the U.N. framework to address critical international problems and ways to work outside of it when the U.N. proves to be a poor vehicle. In some cases, they propose alternative multilateral efforts to address problems for which the U.N. is uniquely unsuited."

Reforming the UN Security Council

Lund, Jakob Silas. *Pros and Cons of Security Council Reform*. New York: Center for UN Reform Education, n.p.

Through extensive interviews with experts as well as current and former ambassadors and diplomats who have been close to the UN Security Council reform process, this article outlines and analyzes the advantages and disadvantages of the components incorporated in the proposals currently on the table. Among the many issues Lund discusses are: expanding the size of the Security Council; categories of membership; extending the veto to new, semi permanent members; abolishing the veto for genocide and other crimes against humanity; extending the veto to semipermanent members conditionally; and completely abolishing the veto.

Realpolitik, a Lack of Will, Weak Mandates, and/or a Seeming Lack of Care by the United Nations

Dallaire, Roméo with Brent Beardsley. *Shake Hands With the Devil: The Failure of Humanity in Rwanda.* New York: Carroll and Graf Publishers, 2005, 562 pp.

In this book, Lt. General Dallaire, who served as the UN Force Commander of the UN Assistance Mission for Rwanda prior to during and following the 1994 genocide, and Major Brent Beardsley, Dallaire's aide in Rwanda, provide a detailed and harrowing view of the unfolding of the Rwandan Genocide. In part, the authors castigate the United Nations for its inept decisions and actions that exacerbated the crisis in Rwanda and left hundreds of thousands to be murdered in the most gruesome ways imaginable.

Lewis, Paul. "A Short History of United Nations Peacekeeping." In *Soldiers for Peace: Fifty Years of United Nations Peacekeeping*, edited by Barbara Benton, 25–41. New York: Facts on File, 1996.

Lewis, who served as the UN correspondent for *The New York Times* for eight years, provides a succinct but informative overview of the UN's peacekeeping efforts during the Cold War and the post–Cold War periods. In his discussion, Lewis briefly discusses, among many others issues, the crisis situations in the former Yugoslavia (early 1990s), Somalia (early 1990s), and Rwanda (1994).

MacInnis, John A. "Piecemeal Peacekeeping: The United Nation's Protection Force in the Former Yugoslavia." In *"The Savage Wars of Peace": Toward a New Paradigm of Peace Operations*, edited by John T. Fishel, 113–31. Boulder CO: Westview Press, 1998.

In this essay, MacInnis, who was the Deputy Force Commander of the United Nations Protection Force in the Former Yugoslavia from July 1993 to June 1994, examines the components of the United Nations Protection Force (UNPROFOR) missions in Croatia and Bosnia in the early to mid-1990s and the controversies in which they were mired and why—"and in particular why the UN effort in the former Yugoslavia left much to be desired and why the mission evolved as it did" (113).

Mays, Terry M. *The 1999 United Nations and 2000 Organization of African Unity Formal Inquiries: A Retrospective Examination of Peacekeeping and the Rwandan Crisis of 1994* (Paper Number 7 of the Pearson Papers). Clementsport, Nova Scotia: The Canadian Peacekeeping Press of the Pearson Peacekeeping Centre, 2002, 37 pp.

Several factors for the failure of the peacekeeping operation to prevent the 1994 genocide in Rwanda are highlighted within the UN and OAU investigations, and each is explored in this study. Also discussed is whether the 2,000-member UN peacekeeping operation in Rwanda could have halted the genocide had the political will at the United Nations existed to accomplish the task. Five options for the future are reviewed, and a postscript includes a brief discussion of the relationship between state sovereignty and humanitarian intervention as delineated by the International Commission on Intervention and State Sovereignty.

United Nations. *The Blue Helmets: A Review of United Nations Peace-Keeping*. New York: United Nations Department of Public Information, 1996, 808 pp.

Among some of the many issues discussed herein are the following: the United Nations Assistance Mission to Rwanda (UNAMIR), which, thanks to the constraints imposed by the United Nations, neglected to even attempt to prevent the 1994 Rwandan genocide; the United Nations Protection Force (UNPROFOR), February 1992–March 1995, which faced so-called "ethnic cleansing," summary executions, and rape in various areas, and the over-running of so-called "safe areas" (e.g., in Gorazde and Srebrenica); and the United Nations Operation in the former Yugoslavia after 1995, during which the Bosnian Serbs launched a full-scale assault against the "safe area" of Srebrenica and overran UNPROFOR positions.

United States Holocaust Memorial Museum. "A Good Man in Hell: General Roméo Dallaire and the Rwanda Genocide." (Note: This manuscript is available from the United States Holocaust Memorial Museum's Committee on Conscience, 100 Raoul Wallenberg Place SW, Washington, DC, 2002.)

In this interview of General Romeo Dallaire (the commander of a small UN peacekeeping force deployed in Rwanda in 1993 and who served in that position throughout the 1994 Rwandan genocide), Dallaire is brutally honest and withering in his attack regarding the weak mandate he was given by the United Nations once it became clear that a genocide was on the horizon. His bitter comments about the fact that he and his men were basically forced to watch as the 1994 Rwandan Genocide unfolded are wrenching. He asserts that he and his men could have likely contained and halted the genocide had his request to UN headquarters for several more battalions been provided. The interview was conducted by noted journalist Ted Koppel.

Vaccaro, J. Matthew. "The Politics of Genocide: Peacekeeping and Disaster Relief in Rwanda." In *UN Peacekeeping, American Politics, and the Uncivil Wars of the 1990s*, edited by William J. Durch, 367–407. New York: St. Martin's Press, 1996.

Vaccaro, a political–military planner in the Office of the US Deputy Secretary of Defense for Peacekeeping and Humanitarian Assistance, provides a detailed analysis of the peacekeeping mission in Rwanda before, during, and following the 1994 Rwandan genocide. He asserts that among the major shortcomings that hindered the peacekeepers' response to the crisis in Rwanda were "(1) the strategy adopted for UNAMIR I was too passive; and (2) the UN Security Council decision-making process was ill-informed" (339–440).

Weiss, Thomas G. "Collective Spinelessness: UN Actions in the Former Yugoslavia." In *The World and Yugoslavia's Wars*, edited by Richard H. Ullman, 59–96. New York: Council on Foreign Relations, 1996.

In his introduction, Weiss, a noted political scientist, notes that "This chapter details the painful dithering and ineffectiveness of UN actions from the beginning of the end of Yugoslavia on June 25, 1991, until the agreement on November 21, 1995, that partitioned Bosnia-Herzegovina into a Muslim-Croat federation and a Bosnia–Serb entity while reserving the fiction of a central government of a multiethnic state with its seat in Sarajevo" (59).

United Nations' Convention on the Prevention and Punishment of the Crime of Genocide (UNCG)

For annotations germane to this issue, see Chapter 4, "The Wording of the UN Convention on the Prevention and Punishment of the Crime of Genocide: An Ongoing Impediment," by Samuel Totten in this volume.

UN Bureaucracy

Barnett, Michael N. *Eyewitness to a Genocide: The United Nations and Rwanda.* Ithaca, NY: Cornell University Press, 2002, 215 pp.

Barnett, Professor of Political Science at the University of Wisconsin, Madison, presents an extremely detailed, highly informative, and thought-provoking discussion about how and why the United Nations reacted the way it did to the events on the ground in Rwanda prior to and during the 1994 Rwandan genocide. Having served as a political officer at the US Mission to the United Nations from 1993 to 1994 during which he handled issues related to Rwanda, he presents a unique and troubling perspective into the inner workings of the United Nations and its bureaucratic culture. His findings have profound ramifications vis-à-vis current and future efforts (or lack thereof) by the United Nations in the field of humanitarian diplomacy and humanitarian assistance during periods of potential and/or actual genocidal activity. *This is a must read.*

Barnett, Michael N. "The Politics of Indifference at the United Nations and Genocide in Rwanda and Burundi." In *This Time We Knew: Western Responses to Genocide in Bosnia*, edited by Thomas Cushman and Stejepan G. Mestrovic, 128–62. New York: New York University Press.

The author of this thought-provoking essay argues, in part, that the reason the United Nations did little to nothing to prevent the 1994 genocide in Rwanda was due to the fact that its member states did not care enough to act—either because they assumed their own citizens did not care about the situation and/or the belief that the effort to stop the genocide was not worth the attempt—especially in regard to the risk faced by its military personnel. That, though, Barnett further argues, constitutes only part of the story. The other part is that the UN's indifferent response was "shaped and filtered through the organizational culture and bureaucratic interests of the United Nations . . . . [Put another way,] from the UN's perspective, the United Nations had more to lose by taking action and being associated with another failure (e.g., along the lines of Somalia) than it did by not taking action and allowing the genocide in Rwanda to take its course. The choice was straightforward: genocide was acceptable if the alternative would harm the United Nations' future. [In other words,] the bureaucratization of peacekeeping contributed to the indifference to the suffering of the very people that it was mandated to assist" (129, 130).

UN Genocide Early Warning System

Adelman, Howard, and A. Surhke. *Early Warning and Conflict Management: Genocide in Rwanda.* Fontoft-Bergen, Norway: Chr. Michelsen Institute, Development Studies and Human Rights, 108 pp.

This report examines the effectiveness of international monitoring and management of the Rwanda conflict, which culminated in genocide of half a million to one million persons in the second quarter of 1994. The report has two distinct yet closely related foci: (i) the existence and effectiveness of early warning mechanisms anticipating escalations in violent conflict and mass murder; and, (ii) the nature and appropriateness of the responses of significant international actors toward the evolving conflict. Since the 1990 invasion marked the opening of the conflict cycle, which culminated in genocide, the study begins with the factors leading up to the invasion of October 1990 and ends in early 1995. Within this time frame, different phases of the conflict are identified and studied in varying degrees of depth. In the period after August 1994, consideration is only given to conflict management issues concerning internally displaced persons and refugees.

Duffy, Gavan, Ted Robert Gurr, Philip Schrodt, Gottfried Mayer-Cress, and Peter Brecke. "An Early Warning System for the United Nations: Internet or Not?" *Mershon International Studies Review* 39, no. 2 (1995): 315–26.

A fascinating forum examining and debating the prospects and problems of developing an Internet-based early warning system for the purpose of submitting early warnings directly to the United Nations concerning a variety of international crises.

Harff, Barbara. "An Early Warning System Is Needed." *The ISG* [Institute for the Study of Genocide]. *Newsletter* 11 (Fall 1993): 3–5,12.

Harff (Professor of Political Science at the U.S. Naval Academy) addresses, in part, the need for the development of an effective early warning system vis-à-vis humanitarian emergencies.

Harff, Barbara, and Ted Robert Gurr. "Systematic Early Warning of Humanitarian Emergencies." *Journal of Peace Research* 35, no. 5 (1998): 551–79.

"More than sixty communal minorities were victimized as a result of internal wars and state failures between 1980 and 1996. Two theoretical models provide the basis for systematic early warning of future victimization of communal and political groups. The potential for communal rebellion is said to be a joint function of group incentives, group capacity, and opportunities for collective action. Indicators of these concepts from the Minorities at Risk project are used to identify seventy-three groups at high risk of communal rebellion in the late 1990s. Genocide and politicide are attributed to background conditions (e.g., political upheaval), intervening conditions (e.g., elite fragmentation), and a short-term increase in theoretically prespecified accelerators. Monitoring of accelerators and deaccelerators in potential crisis situations provides a link between risk assessments based on structural models and early warnings of use to national and international policymakers. The approach is illustrated by an analysis of accelerators prior to the occurrence of the 1994 genocide in Rwanda."

Ramcharan, B. G. "Early Warning at the United Nations: The First Experiment." *International Journal of Refugee Law* 1, no. 3 (1989): 379–86.

This article recalls the Commission on Human Rights initiative on mass exoduses, and the powers of the Secretary-General under the UN Charter and in the exercise of "good offices." It describes how the UN Centre for Human Rights became the focal point in developing UN machinery for early-warning purposes, and the reporting and evaluation guidelines developed during an eighteen-month trial period. In March 1987, the Office for Research and the Collection of Information (ORCI) succeeded to these functions; it was responsible for the analysis and monitoring of potential threats to international peace and security, and also helped to implement the General Assembly's recommendations regarding international cooperation to avert new flows of refugees.

Woocher, Lawrence. *Developing a Strategy, Methods and Tools for Genocide Early Warning*. New York: Center for International Conflict Resolution, Columbia University, 2006, 46 pp.

This report, which was prepared for the Special Adviser to the UN Secretary-General on the Prevention of Genocide, addresses a host of critical issues, including but not limited to the following: The Special Adviser's Early Warning (EW) mandate and general approach to date, a conceptual framework for EW, key challenges to the Special Adviser's EW function, defining EW and its principal elements, alternative options, communicating EW concerns (to promote preventive action), and the role of outside supporters. Each section concludes with a set of recommendations.

Permanent Armed Force

Berdal, Mats R. "Whither UN Peacekeeping? An Analysis of the Changing Military Requirements of UN Peacekeeping with Proposals for Its Enhancement." *Adelphi Paper 381*, October. London: Brassey's Ltd. for the International Institute for Strategic Studies, 1993, 88 pp.

Chapter III, "Enhancing UN Peacekeeping Operations," includes a section entitled "Stand-by Forces and the Pre-Stocking of Equipment (Permanent versus Stand-By Forces)."

Morrison, Alex. "A Standing United Nations Military Force: Future Prospects." In *Peacekeeping and the Challenge of Civil Conflict Resolution*, edited by David A Charters, 185–204. New Brunswick, NJ: Centre for Conflict Studies, University of New Brunswick, 1994.

Morrison discusses the following: the reasons behind the inclusion of the standing military force concept in the UN Charter, the purposes for which it was intended, the factors that must be taken into consideration prior to implementation, and the alternative methods of achieving the same end (185).

Moxon-Browne, Edward. "A Future for Peacekeeping." In *A Future for Peacekeeping?* edited by Edward Moxon-Browne, 192–201. London: Macmillan Press, 1998.

Moxon-Browne discusses, in part, the concept of a permanent UN or "standing" force.

Pugh, Michael, ed. *The UN, Peace, and Force*. London: Frank Cass, 1997, 209 pp.

This volume includes a chapter entitled "Utopian or Pragmatic? A UN Permanent Military Volunteer Force."

Sohn, Louis B. "Authority of the United Nations to Establish and Maintain a Permanent United Nations Force." *American Journal of International Law* 52 (1958): 229–40.

Sohn, Professor of Law at Harvard University School of Law, examines the legal problems involved in the establishment of a permanent UN force—either on a full-time or standby basis—composed of either national contingents or volunteers.

Recommendations for Strengthening the Efforts of the UN vis-à-vis the Prevention and Intervention of Genocide

Alger, Chadwick F., ed. *The Future of the United Nations System: Potential for the Twenty-First Century*. Tokyo: United Nations University Press, 1998, 450 pp.

This book contains twelve chapters that address such issues as prevention of violence and creating economic and social structures that sustain human fulfillment. Included in the text are sixty-six recommendations for new institutions and programs on issues that include, among others, collaboration between UN peacekeepers and nongovernmental organizations. The recommendations are brought together in a concluding chapter and summarized in an appendix. A key recommendation is the establishment of a UN Institute for Mediation and Dispute Resolution.

Berdal, Mats R. "Whither UN Peacekeeping? An Analysis of the Changing Military Requirements of UN Peacekeeping with Proposals for Its Enhancement." *Adelphi Paper 381*, October. London: Brassey's Ltd. for the International Institute for Strategic Studies, 1993, 88 pp.

Key sections of Chapter III, "Enhancing UN Peacekeeping Operations," include the following: Reform of the [UN] Secretariat Structure; Stand-by Forces and the Pre-Stocking of Equipment (Permanent versus Stand-By Forces); UN Information-Gathering and Processing; UN Cooperation with Regional Organizations in Peacekeeping; NATO-NACC [North Atlantic Cooperation Council] Peacekeeping in Support of the United Nations; and Limits and Possibilities of NATO-NACC Support.

Chimni, B. S. "A New Humanitarian Council for Humanitarian Interventions?" *The International Journal of Human Rights* 6, no. 1 (Spring 2002):103–12.

In his introduction, Chimni calls for the establishment of what he deems a Humanitarian Council, whose express purpose would be to decide when a humanitarian intervention is needed and then to call for it.

Dallaire, Roméo. "The Rwandan Experience." In *The New Peacekeeping Partnership*, edited by Alex Morrison, 14–25. Clementspott, Nova Scotia: The Lester B. Pearson Canadian International Peacekeeping Training Centre, 1995.

Even though this article was published over a decade and a half ago, this is a must read for all of those interested in the issues pertaining to the intervention and prevention of genocide, for the author—Major-General Dallaire, Deputy Commander of the Canadian Army and the former Commander of the UN Mission in Rwanda (UNAMIR)—knows that of which he speaks. Having witnessed firsthand both the 1994 genocide in Rwanda and the impotence of the international community in effectively addressing the outbreak of violence, his insights regarding peace operations and the reforms needed at the United Nations in order to be able to address such situations as ethnic violence and genocide in a timely and effective manner are worthy of serious consideration.

In part, this essay includes the following sections: The Need to Reform the United Nations, and UN Reform Options ([a] A UN Multi-Disciplinary Senior Crisis Management Cell; [b] Reform of the UN Administration/Logistics

System; [c] A UN Contingency Fund; [d] UN Standby Military Forces and Equipment; [e] A UN Umbrella Humanitarian Agency; [f] A UN International Media Element; [g] A UN Information (Intelligence) Capability; and [h] UN Intervention for Humanitarian Reasons).

Daniel, Donald, C. F., and Bradd Hayes. "Securing Observance of UN Mandates Through the Employment of Military Force." 105–25. In *The UN, Peace and Force*, edited by Michael Pugh, 105–25. London: Frank Cass Publishers, 1997.

The authors (Director and Assistant Director, respectively, of the Strategic Research Department, Center for Naval Warfare Studies, U.S. Naval War College) discuss the complexities of post-1987 UN military operations and the conceptual confusion they resulted in; the distinctions between peacekeeping, inducement, and enforcement; and the ways in which the United Nations had begun to address some of the many problems plaguing military operations. They conclude by providing a series of recommendations for additional changes and reforms.

Eliasson, Jan. "Establishing Trust in the Healer: Preventive Diplomacy and the Future of the United Nations." In *Preventive Diplomacy: Stopping Wars Before They Start*, edited by Kevin M. Cahill, 215–39. New York: Routledge, 2000.

This chapter comprises the following sections and subsections: The Role of the UN in Conflict Prevention; Can the Healer Be Trusted?; and Beyond the Crisis: A Program for Preventive Action (Carry Out Financial and Structural Reform, Define a Rational Division of Labor with Regional and Other Organizations, Work Together with NGOs and Civil Society, Address the Root Causes of Conflict, Integrate Disarmament into Preventive Action, Reform the Security Council, Strengthen the Capacity of the Secretariat in Preventive Diplomacy, Make Better Use of Article 99, Develop the Instruments for Peaceful Settlement of Disputes, Keep Open the Possibility of Preventive Deployment of Peacekeepers, Develop Concrete Preventive Tasks for the General Assembly, and Mobilize All of the UN System).

Fisas, Vicenc. *Blue Geopolitics: The United Nations Reform and the Future of Blue Helmets*. East Haven, CT and London: Pluto Press with Transnational Institute, 1995, 184 pp.

Written by a disarmament researcher at the UNESCO Centre of Catalonia, the author examines ways in which the United Nations could be reformed in order to be more effective in the areas of conflict prevention, humanitarian intervention, and peacekeeping. For each issue he addresses, he presents a series of proposals for reform.

Hampson, Fen Osler. "Preventive Diplomacy at the United Nations and Beyond." In *From Reaction to Conflict Prevention: Opportunities for the UN System*, edited by Fen Osler Hampson and David M. Malone, 139–57. Boulder, CO: Lynne Rienner Publishers, 2002.

Various possibilities for strengthening the role of the United Nations in regard to preventive diplomacy are presented, including various recommendations for institutional reform and operational effectiveness.

Hillen, John. *Blue Helmets: The Strategy of UN. Military Operations*. Washington, DC: Brassey's, 1998, 312 pp.

Hillen basically argues that the United Nations' efforts are most efficacious when handling observation missions and traditional peacekeeping missions where military expertise is less significant than political or diplomatic concerns. Ultimately, Hillen concludes that the United Nations should not be asked or expected to conduct military operations that involve fighting, and that peacekeeping operations that could degenerate into fighting should be left to national armies and coalitions such as NATO. At the core of his argument is that the difficulty with military aspects of UN peacekeeping is, in part, the "absence of separate bilateral agreements between the United Nations and individual military powers as provided for in Article 43 of the United Nations Charter, along with the concomitant absence of a Military Staff Committee anticipated in Articles 46 and 47 . . . ." (9).

Kaysen, Carl, and George Rathjens. *Peace Operations by the United Nations: The Case for a Volunteer UN Military Force.* Cambridge, MA: Committee on International Security Studies, American Academy of Arts and Sciences, 1996, 64 pp.

The contents of this booklet comprise the following: "Peace Operations During the Cold War"; "The Changed Post-Cold War Environment for Peace Operations"; "The Challenges for the Future"; "The Question of a UN Military Force"; "Arguments for a Volunteer UN Force—Six Case Studies: The Congo, Yugoslavia, Somalia, Cambodia, Rwanda, Haiti"; "What Are the Lessons?"; "What Kind of UN Standing Force?"; "The Wider Context"; and "Appendix: Design for a Streamlined UN Legion."

Knight, Andy W., ed. *Adapting the United Nations to a Post Modern Era: Lessons Learned.* New York: Palgrave Macmillan, 2005, 272 pp.

This volume addresses a host of issues in regard to revamping the United Nations in order to more effectively deal with such activities as the following: collective security, early warning and global monitoring, preventative diplomacy, preventative deployment, peacekeeping, peacemaking, peace maintenance, and international legal, environmental, and trade regulation.

Kolodziej, Edward A. "The Great Powers and Genocide: Lessons from Rwanda." *Pacifica Review* 12, no. 2 (2000): 121–45.

While agreeing with some that there is little likelihood that a rapid action force under the auspices of the United Nations will come to fruition anytime soon, Kolodziej delineates what he perceives as being critical components of an anti-genocide regime. In part, he asserts that there is a critical need to clarify the criteria for applicable responses under Chapters VI and VII of the UN Charter, and strengthening the earmarking of military forces from national contingents for Chapters VI and VII security operations.

Langille, H. Peter. "Conflict Prevention: Options for Rapid Deployment and UN Standing Forces." In *Peacekeeping and Conflict Resolution*, edited by Tom Woodhouse and Oliver Ramsbotham, 219–53. London and Portland, OR: Frank Cass Publishers, 2000.

Langille, Professor of Foreign Policy and International Conflict Prevention and Management at the University of Western Ontario, addresses the following issues: the background regarding the establishment of a UN rapid reaction force; various national studies vis-à-vis the possibility of creating a rapid reaction force (e.g., from the Netherlands, Canada, Denmark); corresponding developments in the field; the UN Department for Peacekeeping Operations and the UN Secretariat; the United Nations Standby Arrangement System (UNSAS); the United Nations Rapidly Deployable Mission

Headquarters (RDMHQ); and Multinational Standby Forces High Readiness Brigade (SHIRBRIG).

Lee, John M., Robert von Pagenhardt, and Timothy W. Stanley. *To Unite Our Strength: Enhancing the United Nations Peace and Security System*. Lanham, MD: University Press of America, 1992, 166 pp.

A former Vice Admiral from the US Navy, a former Foreign Service Officer, and a former Defense Advisor and Minister at the US Mission to NATO discuss such concerns, among others, as "Military Forces for UN Operations" (Requirements for Force, The UN Legion, National Forces for United Nations Duty—including Quick Reaction Forces); "Reforming United Nations Machinery"; and, "Lessons from the Past" (Starting up the UN Legion).

Moxon-Browne, Edward. "A Future for Peacekeeping." In *A Future for Peacekeeping?* edited by Edward Moxon-Browne, 192–201. London: Macmillan Press, 1998.

Moxon-Browne discusses a host of issues, including but not limited to the following: the concept of a permanent UN or "standing" force; the need for a wider range of options and responses to differentiated conflict situations; and the role of NATO in peacekeeping operations.

Murphy, Sean D. *Humanitarian Intervention: The United Nations in an Evolving World Order*. Philadelphia: University of Pennsylvania Press, 1996, 427 pp.

The book includes a section entitled "Improvements for Future Interventions," which is composed of the following chapters: (7) "Regional Organizations and Humanitarian Intervention" ([A] Regional Arrangements under the Charter; [B] Applying Chapter VII to Humanitarian Intervention—[1] Practices, [2] Prospects); and (8) "Unilateral Humanitarian Intervention" ([A] Rules-Oriented Approach; [B] Policy-Oriented Approach; [C] Philosophy-Oriented Approach; [D] The Security Council as Authoritative Decisionmaker; and [E] Toward Criteria for the Conduct of Unilateral Humanitarian Intervention).

Peck, Connie. *The United Nations as a Dispute Settlement System: Improving Mechanisms for the Prevention and Resolution of Conflict*. Boston, MA: Kluwer Law International, 1996, 301 pp.

Peck discusses and examines the United Nations' work in the area of dispute resolution and makes suggestions regarding the reform and improvement of that role.

Pugh, Michael, ed. *The UN, Peace, and Force*. London: Frank Cass, 1997, 209 pp.

Addresses, in part "Weapons Control in Semi-Permissive Environments: A Case for Compellence" and "Utopian or Pragmatic? A UN Permanent Military Volunteer Force."

Ratner, Steven R. "The United Nations in Cambodia: A Model for Resolution of Internal Conflicts." In *Enforcing Restraint: Collective Intervention in Internal Conflicts*, edited by Lori Fisler Damrosch, 241–73. New York: Council on Foreign Relations, 1993.

In a section entitled "Beyond Cambodia: A New Paradigm for Responding to Internally Ravaged States?", Ratner suggests that "The establishment of UNTAC may point the way to expanded roles for the UN in restoring order to other states riven by violence, anarchy, and economic collapse" (259).

Rikhye, Indar Jit. *Strengthening UN Peacekeeping: New Challenges and Proposals*. Washington, DC: United States Institute of Peace, 1992, 48 pp.

The author suggests that the UN Security Council should devise and implement a program for preventive diplomacy that includes a preventive peacekeeping element. He also recommends the creation of a special standby force, available to the Security Council and the Secretary-General for rapid deployment (1–3).

Ruggie, John Gerard. "The United Nations and the Collective Use of Force: Whither or Whether?" In *The UN, Peace and Force*, edited by Michael Pugh, 1–20. London: Frank Cass, 1997.

In this essay, Ruggie, the John W. Burgess Professor of Political Science and International Affairs at Columbia University in New York City, argues that in the post–Cold War era, the United Nations has yet to devise a precise formulation of the specific strategic requirements needed to implement a "robust" peace operation. He goes on to argue for—and to outline—a "more systematic doctrinal approach" toward such operations, and also suggests changes regarding the organization of command functions at UN headquarters and at the field level.

Smith, Michael G. (with Moreen Dee). *Peacekeeping in East Timor: The Path to Independence.* Boulder, CO: Lynne Rienner Publishers, 2002, 213 pp.

Smith analyzes the successes and failures of the UN Transitional Administration in East Timor (UNTAET), which was designed to work in partnership with the East Timorese in guiding the country to independence following the 1999 vote to secede from Indonesia.

Smith (who retired from the Australian army as a major after thirty-four years of service, and served as deputy force commander of the UNTAET peacekeeping force from January 2000 through March 2001) highlights the urgent need for reforms within the United Nations. The absence of such reforms, he believes, will lead to more failed states, more refugees, more poverty, and more dead peacekeepers.

Tanner, Fred. "Weapons Control in Semi-Permissive Environments: A Case for Compellence." In *The UN, Peace and Force*, edited by Michael Pugh, 126–45. London: Frank Cass, 1997.

Tanner argues that the use of limited force by peace support units to achieve weapons control in "semi-permissive environments" is justified in light of the fact that the derailment of the weapons-control process jeopardizes the peace process as a whole.

United Nations. *Report of the Panel on United Nations Peace Operations.* New York: United Nations, 2001, n.p.

This is the report (also known as the *Brahimi Report*, named after the chair of the group that wrote the report) of the Panel convened by UN Secretary-General Kofi A. Annan to undertake a thorough review of the United Nations peace and security activities and to come up with a set of recommendations to improve such activities.

Among the many recommendations of the Panel are the following: the pivotal importance of clear, credible, and adequately resourced UN Security Council mandates; a focus by the UN system on conflict prevention and its early engagement, wherever possible; the need to have more effective collection and assessment of information at UN headquarters, including an enhanced conflict early warning system that can detect and recognize the threat or risk of conflict—including genocide; the need to build the UN's capacity to contribute to peace-building, both preventive and postconflict, in a genuinely integrated manner; and the necessity to provide field missions with high-quality leaders and managers who are granted greater flexibility and autonomy by UN headquarters, within clear mandate parameters, and with clear standards of accountability for both spending and results. (For the full report, see: http://www.un.org/peace/reports/peace_operations/docs/full_report.htm.)

7

The Impact of the Media on Genocide Intervention: A Prod, an Impediment, or Both?

Isabelle Macgregor

Introduction

The power and role of the media in relation to foreign policy are much debated. Some believe the media is capable of prompting policymakers to launch a military intervention in times of genocide, while others see it as being far less influential and believe that news coverage is more likely to have no significant effect. Still others accept the potency of the media but point out that it is vulnerable to manipulation by its own government or by foreign *genocidaires*. This chapter offers an overview of the general theory on the influence of the media vis-à-vis genocide. It also analyzes the genocidal events in Iraq, Rwanda, Bosnia, and Darfur, with particular focus on the extent and quality of the media coverage of each crisis, how the victim group and its attackers were portrayed, and whether there was a consensus among political powerbrokers regarding intervention policy.

This chapter's analysis is restricted mainly to Western democracies, primarily those that have engaged in an intervention in the last thirty years. It is, however, important to pay some attention to the media *within* a genocidal state, and this is also briefly explored in relation to the Rwandan Genocide.

The media has long been in a state of evolution. From the 1980s onward, however, changes became even more dramatic. "New media," or digital media, has radically changed the way news is reported

(Lister et al. 2009, 10). According to Flew (2008), a "combination of . . . computing and information technology (IT), communications networks, and digitized media and information content converged to form 'new media' " (2). As technology improves, so too does the media's ability to cover a story in greater detail. Visual images and live footage have become the primary means of coverage and these are arguably more emotionally powerful than the written word. Indeed, in his book *The Assault on Reason*, Al Gore (2007) points out that ". . . the visceral vividness portrayed on television has the capacity to trigger instinctual responses similar to those triggered by reality itself—and without being modulated by logic, reason, and reflective thought" (19).

The rapid change in the form, quality, and pervasiveness of the media has also meant a change in the relationship between it, national governments, and the general public. Numerous questions arise: Does the media now shape the value system and priorities of the people and the policy objectives of the government, or vice versa? Do journalists dictate to the public the ideas and values they believe are essential, or does the media only present what the public already wants to see and hear and already believes?

The Impact of Media vis-à-vis Genocide

Now, in regard to genocide, within the potentially *intervening* state, there exists a complex, and sometimes very subtle, relationship between the media, the government, and the public. This circular influence-based relationship structure is affected by information coming from the people and the media within the *genocidal* state, as well as from its government. On the other hand, the relationship between the media of the genocidal state, its people, and its government is very different and far less subtle. The genocidal government may be using the media as a political tool and there may be very little journalistic dissent. This may come about as a result of the power wielded by the government and/or because the media and the government are on the same side.

Two main theories exist regarding policy–media relations in Western democracies. They are defined by the perceived strength of a specific actor. First, there are some instances in which the media has only limited influence and can be manipulated into supporting government policy. This theory is entitled "Manufacturing Consent" (Herman and Chomsky,1988). The theory of *Manufacturing Consent* holds that the government is the stronger of the two, and thus able to manipulate the media. This theory predicts that the outcome of government–media interactions regarding genocide intervention will depend on how policymakers feel about intervention prior to news coverage.

Other analysts later observed that there were instances in which the media could influence government. This is entitled the "CNN effect" or "CNN factor." Coined during the 1991 Gulf War, it refers not only to CNN but the news media in general. In these cases, media coverage can significantly shape a nation's decision to intervene in a humanitarian crisis (Gilboa 2002, 733, Robinson 2002, 2). The thinking behind the *CNN effect* is that the media is perceived as the strongest player in certain situations, capable of influencing government decisions. Here, the result will be determined by the position of the journalists and the way in which they present the situation. The public is also influenced by these journalists and is able to mediate to a certain extent.

According to Robinson (2000), there are various factors that significantly affect the extent of the media's influence. Whether or not an administration possesses a preexisting policy regarding intervention is important. Robinson (2000) asserts that policy certainty exists when there are strong concerns regarding national interest. When this involves a policy of nonintervention, the media is powerless to persuade the government to intervene. The media can bring about an intervention only when there exists policy *uncertainty*—when there is no executive policy or when policymakers are divided as to the appropriate course of action—and when the media is clearly critical of the lack of action and obviously sympathizes with the suffering people. When the government is certain of its policy, it appears that not even critical and sympathetic media coverage can change its decision (Robinson 2000). When there is *no* policy, it is likely that policymakers will feel pressured to respond to critical media coverage or else face a public relations' crisis and a loss of voter confidence (Robinson 2002, 32). When a decision to intervene has already been made, it is likely that the executive will use its "substantial resources" to try to influence the media. The media may then *follow* the decision made by the executive. There may still be criticism of government policy, but this appears only to arise when there exists "elite dissensus over policy." When there is consensus among politicians, media coverage reflects this consensus in that news reports remain uncritical of government policy (Robinson 2000).

The manner in which a story is covered is also significant. Journalists can choose to write emotive reports, which focus on the plight of a specific group, presenting its members as individuals with whom the viewing public can identify. News coverage that empathizes with the suffering people and criticizes government inaction is defined by Robinson as being "critically framed." If policymakers have no clear intervention policy with which to counter this kind of media coverage, they may be forced to respond to "media driven public pressure or the fear of *potential* negative public reaction to government inaction" (Robinson 2000). Critically framed media coverage might thus prompt intervention. When it *can* change policy, Robinson believes that media coverage can generate aerial intervention but not the deployment of ground troops and that this was demonstrated in Bosnia (Robinson 2000).

Conversely, some kinds of news coverage can act as an intervention *deterrent*. A prime example is the situation in Somalia in 1993 and the resulting media coverage, which impacted the US attitude to intervention long after the crisis had ended. While attempting to capture the Somali warlord General Mohammed Aideed, two US helicopters were shot down. In the firefight that followed, eighteen Americans were killed. The body of one was dragged through the streets, an image which was broadcast repeatedly on American television. As Shawcross (2000) states, "the effects were momentous throughout the world" (101). Not only were US troops withdrawn from Somalia, the US administration, under President Bill Clinton, proceeded to withdraw from the concept of multilateralism, in general. It distanced itself from the United Nations and declared that US peacekeepers must never again be party to a conflict that did not directly impact the United States, in one way or another. Such an act became known as "crossing the Mogadishu line." Avoiding the crossing of this notional line anywhere in the world became the primary concern of the US presidential administrations of Bill Clinton and George W. Bush. Essentially, the United States returned to its 1984 principle of never entering a conflict unless doing so served its national interests and the conflict could be won (Shawcross 2000, 101–2). According to Badsey (1997), America's "sensitivity" to incurring casualties "is now such as to call into question the entire utility of the United States' massive armed forces (and those of some other NATO nations) other than for home defense or entirely symbolic purposes" (9).

Because of the potentially profound influence possessed by the media, a high level of journalistic accountability and responsibility is required. An optimal ethical code for journalists can be broadly outlined as striving for truth, avoiding bias, avoiding harm, serving the public, maintaining trust, escaping manipulation, inviting criticism and being accountable. Journalists are morally obliged to present the truth to the public. In essence, this means presenting all relevant facts and giving an objective and balanced account of those events covered (Klaidman and Beauchamp 1987, 30).

Iraq

There is a diversity of opinion regarding the role media played in relation to the US and British intervention policy in Iraq over the latter's killing of the Kurds residing in northern Iraq. While Samantha Power (2002) asserts that the media influenced governmental decisions, Piers Robinson (2002) and Nicholas Wheeler (2000) disagree.

Long before the 1991 military intervention in Iraq, news reports were broadcast by the Western media that highlighted and sympathized with the suffering of the Kurdish people. Immediately after the Halabja gas attack of 1988—the worst of the Iraqi chemical assaults, which killed an estimated 5,000 civilians—postgenocidal coverage of the carnage began to emerge. In March, it was a front cover story in both *The Washington Post* and the *Los Angeles Times* (Power 2003, 191). The word "genocide" was commonly used by journalists and editors to describe the event (Power 2003, 218).

Even so, Western governments had long dismissed the idea of forceful intervention in Iraq. In 1991, this decision was reversed within a matter of days (Shaw 1996, 156). There is disagreement over whether or not this was the result of new graphic images of Kurdish suffering in the north that appeared in the media.

The US Operation Provide Comfort, launched during the aftermath of the 1991 Gulf War, involved both air power and ground troops. The official reason for the deployment was to protect Iraqi Kurds in the north, hundreds of thousands of whom were fleeing the retribution of Iraqi authorities following armed Kurdish and Shi'ite uprisings. As there had been policy certainty *against* intervention during these uprisings, it is commonly held that it was the media coverage of the later Kurdish humanitarian crisis that led to US intervention and the establishment of "safe havens" (Robinson 2002, 63, 64). Many believe that "this position [of nonintervention] became untenable as the media—especially television—pinned moral responsibility on Western leaders for their abandonment of the Kurds after inciting them to rise up and overthrow Saddam Hussein" (Wheeler 2000, 165). It is believed that John Major and George Bush both realized that inaction would be viewed as unacceptable by the public and that their political standing would be threatened. According to this belief, intervention became politically expedient (Wheeler 2000, 165).

United States news coverage of the Kurdish crisis was intensive. Before US ground troops were deployed, *The New York Times* published over six articles a day, while *The Washington Post* published almost four a day. The situation constituted headline news almost every day on ABC, CBS, and NBC. This coverage emphasized the suffering of the Kurds and either explicitly or implicitly demanded action (Robinson 2002, 67, 68). According to Power (2003), Kurdish refugees "poured out their stories to journalists" and these eventually drew the attention of the US Secretary of State (201). Major claimed that it was his personal reaction to the images of Kurdish refugees that led him to choose the option of creating safe havens. It is supposed that Bush was then persuaded to overrule the Pentagon's advice and support the British and European Union safe haven initiative (Wheeler 2000, 165, 166).

Despite this common perception, neither Wheeler (2000) nor Robinson (2002) believe this to be a complete explanation. Military deployment was not the only response available to growing media pressure. Major could have chosen to "ride out the storm of media criticism" (Wheeler 2000, 165). The path of intervention was politically risky and the establishment of safe havens was very complex, both legally and operationally. According to Wheeler (2000), the intervention had more to do with the passing of Resolution 688, which provided "legitimating arguments" for the legal establishment of safe havens and no-fly zones (2000, 165, 166). Wheeler (2000) believes that without this resolution, intervention in Iraq would have been viewed as a violation of the UN Charter. Robinson (2002) is in agreement, claiming that media coverage served to *enable* policymakers, who had already decided to intervene for "non-media-related-reasons," by creating public support for the intervention (71). Given the unusual strength of force of the operation, this explanation seems likely. It appears to be primarily a case of "manufacturing consent." Indeed, Badsey (1997) states that "the American government, before it felt confident enough to employ military force against Iraq, had needed to create not just an international consensus but a suitable domestic environment by exploiting the media to influence public opinion" (12).

Rwanda 1994

Media coverage of the 1994 Rwandan Genocide was extensive. By the end of April, it had attracted significant and constant media coverage in the United States—although not blanket headline coverage. It featured several times as the front cover story of both *The New York Times* and *The Washington Post* and was mentioned many times on CNN, ABC, CBS, and NBC news bulletins (Robinson 2002, 71). Around this time, the first images began to emerge of thousands of mutilated bodies floating down the rivers of Rwanda. The UN force commander in Rwanda, Romeo Dallaire, recognized the importance of the media in prompting stronger intervention. He claimed that a "reporter with a line to the West was worth a battalion on the ground," and he actively encouraged and facilitated the filing of news reports (quoted in Power 2003, 355). So, why did Western intervention in Rwanda prove to be too slow and so inadequate?

The answer may lie in the fact that there existed a significant level of policy certainty regarding nonintervention, which helped to militate against any media influence. This was particularly strong in the United States as a result of the Somalia crisis (Robinson 2002, 111).

The lack of effective intervention may have also been a result of the way in which journalists portrayed the crisis. Many journalists believed the common myth—and the Rwandan government's official line—that the violence was caused by ancient tribal animosity, which implied that international intervention would be inappropriate or useless (Omaar and De Waal 1995, 251; Power 2003, 355). This type of news coverage is described by Robinson (2002) as "distance framing." Subsequently, the media failed to reveal the true nature of the killings, instead presenting them as part of "a breakdown in a ceasefire and/or as part of a regular round of tribal bloodletting" (Robinson 2002, 114). This "inhibited serious attention to the crisis from both policy-makers and the broader public" and "implicitly supported a policy of non-intervention" (Robinson 2002, 114, 115). Omaar and De Waal (1995) agreed that the inadequate political analysis presented by journalists had a detrimental effect regarding intervention (255).

Other journalistic pressures contributed to a lack of information. At the time of the genocide, the triumph of Nelson Mandela in South Africa was the main news story from Africa and the major newspapers and news corporations were unwilling to divert their journalists to focus on Rwanda. It was believed that most readers and viewers knew little or nothing about Rwanda and thus it would not make a profitable story. Initially, the international press focused mainly on the plight of foreigners. Journalists were only prepared to travel with international troops who were evacuating foreigners or interview evacuees arriving at European airports. Because of concerns about security and the problem of access, there were no journalists in the rural areas reporting on the massacres there. The regime managed to conceal the rural genocide from the outside world for almost three weeks. It was only when refugees started arriving in Burundi that the international media first began to realize the scale of the crisis (Omaar and De Waal 1995, 253, 254). Journalists also over relied on reports from certain foreign aid workers in the country who were seemingly not well-informed about the whole situation (Omaar and De Waal 1995, 252).

It is vital to also examine the *Rwandan* media and its impact on intervention. The government undertook a campaign involving the dissemination of murderous propaganda and the silencing of all dissent within the country. Undoubtedly, the killing of independent Rwandan journalists by the extremist Hutu regime affected the world's understanding of the situation and thus the likelihood of intervention. The aim was to create confusion so that neither the majority of Rwandans nor the foreigners knew what was happening. This, of course, prevented information about the extent of the killings becoming known, made any attempt at escape difficult, and prevented news of the genocide from reaching the outside world. In fact, this strategy proved highly successful (Omaar and De Waal 1995, 236).

Propaganda from two radio stations set the stage for and guided the genocide. Both Radio Rwanda and RTLM told listeners that the Tutsis planned to exterminate the Hutu population (Omaar and De Waal 1995, 236). During the genocide, RTLM was entirely devoted to maintaining the "war against the Tutsis" (Omaar and De Waal 1995, 161). Listeners were urged to arm themselves with any weapons at their disposal (Eltringham 2004, 67). Listeners were encouraged to call in and suggest places where Tutsis might be hiding. Radio Rwanda was equally focused on openly encouraging and maintaining the genocide (Eltringham 2004, 116, 164). Some of the journalists who were advocating genocide on RTLM and Radio Rwanda doubled as the local correspondents for the English BBC radio and informed them of "the state of affairs in the country," all of which were lies (Eltringham 2004, 165).

According to Robinson (2002), "the case of non-intervention in Rwanda is not indicative of the shallow and minimal impact of the media . . . but rather is suggestive of the minimal impact of a particular form of coverage, that of distance framing" (116). He also states, however, that even had coverage been "empathy framed," its influence on policy would still have been minimal due to the high level of uniform nonintervention policy certainty at the time (Robinson 2002, 116). There was a significant amount of media coverage of the Rwandan Genocide but much of it was ill-informed. Had it been more accurate from the outset, a more effective intervention may have been deployed sooner.

Bosnia 1994/1995

The media appears to have played a crucial role in prompting intervention in Bosnia. As Holbrooke (1999) stated, "The reason the West finally, belatedly, intervened was heavily related to news media coverage" (20). This coverage happened to operate in conjunction with policy *uncertainty* in the US executive branch (aka, the White House) as to whether or not to intervene (Robinson 2000). This appears to be why it was able to have an impact that was, ostensibly, so powerful.

The Bosnian Genocide stands out from many others because it was so highly visible. Cushman and Mestrovic (1996) claim that, "never has genocide been covered so much and so well" (9). Certainly that was, at least in part, due to the fact that there were many foreign journalists based in Sarajevo reporting the events as they occurred (Cushman and Mestrovic 1996). As a result, the policymakers of the West were aware of the atrocities that were unfolding.

Following the fall of the "safe area" of Srebrenica to the Bosnian Serb Army in July 1995, the United States intervened to defend the Gorazde "safe area" from the same fate. Between the fall of Srebrenica and the US threat to use force two weeks later, there were high levels of media coverage. The taking of Srebrenica featured many times in *The Washington Post* and *The New York Times* and was treated as a leading headline story by CBS (Robinson 2000). The news stories focused on the extreme suffering of civilians and were also critical of Western policy (Robinson 2002, 78). Because they both *emphasized* the failure of the West and *empathized* with the refugees, they encouraged action. This critical coverage coincided with policy uncertainty as to whether or not further violations of UN safe areas, particularly an attack on Gorazde, should justify the use of force. It appears, then, that a strong CNN effect was present, which influenced the decision to defend Gorazde (Robinson 2002, 82, 83).

There were, however, limits to this influence. Much of the media called for the deployment of ground troops in Bosnia in order to protect the safe areas. However, it was not successful in persuading Western governments to do so (Wheeler 2000, 300). According to Robinson, this indicates that the media has far greater influence over air power intervention—a form which is both economically and politically less costly—than ground troop intervention (Robinson 2002, 123).

The bombing of a Sarajevo market place in February 1994 is another example of where "critical and empathy-framed" media coverage coincided with policy uncertainty, and thus prompted a decision to threaten air strikes against the Bosnian Serbs. The footage of the aftermath of the bombing was extremely graphic, critical, and pervasive; and, within four days, the Clinton administration had presented the Bosnian Serbs with an ultimatum: stop shelling Sarajevo or face air strikes (Robinson 2002, 86, 90).

It has also been claimed that the UN forces in Bosnia were able to use the media to strengthen the peacekeeping mission. The British Army introduced an unofficial convoy system for journalists, which gave them a degree of military protection. This was because UN commanders found that they could use television footage taken of events such as local ceasefire agreements as a permanent record with which to deter violators. With the international community acting as witness to such agreements, signatories would be less likely to violate the terms and risk international condemnation. The threat of media exposure proved highly effective. As Major-General MacKenzie later stated, the media was "the only major weapon system that I had" (quoted in Badsey 1997, 19). Journalists took a proactive role during the Bosnian War. They often reported stories which they hoped would prompt Western policymakers to act. In 1992, images of starving Muslim men behind barbed wire "inflamed public outrage about the war" (Power 2003, 276). Producers of ITN news admitted to deliberately using footage, which would remind viewers of the Holocaust. In July of that year, it was recorded that 45 percent of Americans objected to US air strikes and 35 percent supported them. After the aforementioned footage was aired, and with no advice from their political leaders, these figures changed, with 53 percent approving and 33 percent disapproving. Approximately, the same percentage endorsed the contribution of

US troops to a "humanitarian or peacekeeping mission." The plight of Muslim prisoners was not previously unknown but, as Power (2003) points out, "popular interest and sympathy were aroused by pictures far more than they had been by words" (276). In the Netherlands, these same images caused a "morally based crusade" for military intervention (Ruigrok 2008, 293). The Holocaust analogy was repeated in newspapers across the United States. While some may have objected to this comparison (Power 2003, 277), it was an effective means of highlighting the severity of the situation.

According to Power, the Bosnia coverage raises the question as to whether or not atrocities are portrayed differently in the media according to their location and the ethnicity of the victim group. She claims that, "however disturbing viewers and readers found images from prior genocides, there was nothing quite like their discomfort that such horrors could occur again *in Europe*" (Power 2003, 277). The way in which journalists chose to portray the situation in Bosnia does indeed appear to differ markedly from their portrayal of the events in Rwanda, a crisis that undoubtedly constituted genocide but was reported as being the result of irreconcilable tribal differences. The coverage of the Darfur Genocide, however, demonstrates that news reports of an African crisis can be just as empathetic, as least as far as individual victims are concerned.

Darfur (2003–Present)

The case of Darfur is evidence that Western media has portrayed Black victims in a humane and personal way, to which white viewers and readers can relate. The news coverage of the Darfur Genocide was thorough and of a high quality but has tapered off dramatically since late 2005.

The foreign press has examined Darfur from many different angles. It has drawn its information from the reports of the United Nations and many different aid organizations, interviews with aid workers and refugees, the opinions and analyses of experts and academics as well as eyewitness accounts by the journalists themselves. Statements from the government in Khartoum and foreign governments such as that of the United States, Great Britain, and Australia have also been relied upon. In order to emphasize the severity of the situation, some articles have drawn comparisons between the mass murder in Darfur and that in Rwanda. They have also pointed out the similarities of the humanitarian crisis developing in the refugee camps and the situation in Somalia and Ethiopia a decade ago, and Darfur over the past eight years.

Journalism about Darfur often criticizes the lack of action on the part of governments and international organizations. This journalism is also highly critical of the general climate of impunity. It speculates as to what will happen if this inaction continues (Reeves 2005). In 2004, *Time Magazine* put the Darfur crisis on its cover because, as its editor claimed, "We saw a humanitarian disaster unfolding without sufficient public attention being paid to it. It's a story that has a lot of interesting questions larger than those raised by the conflict itself, such as how the United States defines and responds to genocide" (Ricchiardi 2005).

This investigative, empathy-framed journalism is largely the result of a few dedicated individuals who began reporting relatively early in the conflict. In October 2004, for example, a *New York Times* article by Nicholas D. Kristof focused on the traumatic experiences of several children and their families. The story was accompanied by graphic photos. Kristof had to secretly enter Sudan from neighboring Chad (Dart Center for Journalism and Trauma 2004). He was one of the first journalists to provide eyewitness accounts of the atrocities. Also in 2004, *The Washington Post* reporter, Emily Wax, risked her life by traveling across the Chad border into Sudan, hitching rides with rebel soldiers, hiking on foot, scavenging food, and sleeping on the ground for weeks at a time in order to reach remote territory and investigate the truth behind the crisis. Wax's stories were highly humanized, which was particularly true of her work about the rape of the black African girls and women in Darfur. It is commitment such as this that finally uncovered concrete evidence that the Sudanese government was bombing its own civilians, an act which it had publicly denied (Ricchiardi 2005).

Why did the Darfur coverage not lead to more effective intervention? Perhaps because there was strong policy certainty toward nonintervention on the part of foreign governments. In part, this may have been due to the Chinese presence within Sudan, which has strong commercial ties with Sudan. The Sudanese government allows China access to its oil and China, in turn, helps fund the genocidal militias (International Crisis Group 2008). Since 1996, Beijing has been Khartoum's leading supplier of weapons, military supplies, and weapons technology (Reeves 2007). China possesses the largest army in the world and a nuclear deterrent. These factors, combined with its position as a permanent member of the UN Security Council and its powerful economic influence across the globe, mean that it is easily capable of reinforcing a nonintervention policy.

The lack of effective intervention might also be due, at least in part, to the discrepancy between Western attitudes toward atrocities committed in Africa and those committed in Europe. If it is true that there is a level of global resignation concerning violence in Africa, then media comparisons between the Darfur crisis and the violent tragedies which have already occurred in Rwanda, Somalia, and Ethiopia will not encourage intervention but will only make the resignation and sense of hopelessness worse.

As noted above, media coverage waned as the crisis in Darfur continued. It has been many years since the atrocities caught the attention of the international community and it appears that both the media and the public have lost interest. The situation in Sudan is now rarely in the papers or on the television or radio news. One has to wonder: Has the public, and the media, simply grown tired of hearing about another violent African crisis in a seemingly distant and irrelevant country?

That said, there is still a certain amount of online journalism regarding the crisis. A prime example is that of Eric Reeves, academic and Sudan expert, who has established a website devoted to informing the public of the crisis and providing continuous updates (http://www.sudanreeves.org/). This kind of journalism is part of a new media phenomenon, the potential benefits and hazards of which are discussed below.

Critical Challenges Facing the Field

Journalism about genocide faces many difficulties. First, media bias is often at its most evident during times of genocide. Herman and Chomsky (1998) assert that the word "genocide" has often been used by the US media to describe the victimization of certain groups in enemy states but rarely, if ever, to refer to similar or worse cases of victimization led by the United States or its allies. Iraq and Turkey, for example, both engaged in brutal victimization of their Kurdish populations during the 1990s. The Iraqi regime, Herman and Chomsky argue, was a US enemy and so its treatment of the Kurds was categorized as "genocidal." Because Turkey was a US ally, its victimization of the Kurds, which was "in no way less murderous," was described merely as "repression" and was given minimal attention (Herman and Chomsky

1988, xx). Herman and Chomsky (1998) also maintain that there is a tendency for the media to focus on the inhumane treatment of "worthy victims," while downplaying or ignoring the abuse of "unworthy victims" (xxiii).

Journalists may "take sides" in certain conflicts and produce favorable reports of those they consider the victims, as opposed to the culprits. This is termed "journalism of attachment" by Ruigrok and is based on a framework of "good guys versus bad guys" and a firm idea of a preferred solution to the conflict—attached journalists may be factual and accurate but they are not neutral. To achieve their goal, these journalists either emphasize or downplay certain events or expert statements. They might also be selective in the sources they quote, taking advantage of "opportune witnesses" (Ruigrok 2008, 295–96). In Bosnia, for example, attached journalists reported on the conflict with a clear goal in mind: prodding Western powers to commit to military intervention in order to protect the victims of the war (Ruigrok 2008, 295). Some have also suggested that since the terrorist attacks of 9/11 against the United States, there has been a trend toward increased journalistic attachment. Journalists have "enthusiastically embraced" the new framework involving distinctly labeled "friends" and "enemies" (Ruigrok 2008, 221).

If an incident is prolonged, as genocides often are, news coverage eventually diminishes or will even cease altogether. This has clearly occurred in relation to the genocide in Darfur. When this is the case, it could either mean that the media has recognized the public's waning interest in the event and has turned its attention to another news story in order to retain viewers and readers, or that it has moved on of its own accord and the public has no choice but to move on with it. This again touches on the question as to whether the media shapes the value system and priorities of the public, or vice versa.

It has been suggested that news reports of crises are losing their emotional impact on audiences, and that this "compassion fatigue" is largely due to the way in which news is presented by the media. The public's knowledge of the world is limited by what the media chooses to disclose and, according to Moeller (1999), "editors and producers don't assign stories and correspondents don't cover events that they believe will not appeal to their readers and viewers" (2). Compassion fatigue means that it takes increasingly dramatic coverage to evoke the same level of sympathy in an audience as the last crisis. According to this theory or concept, at least some journalists reject stories that are not more dramatic or horrific than the ones that went before. Furthermore, new language or images will be used so that the new event at least *seems* more deadly than the last. This means that journalists are constantly searching for "ever more sensational tidbits in stories to retain the attention of their audience." Once the "range of possibilities of coverage" has been exhausted for a particular event, the media moves on to the next story so that the public does not become bored. This happens whether or not the situation in question has been resolved (Moeller 1999, 2). It is difficult for the media and its audience to sustain compassion and interest for the duration of a crisis, which might be months or even years. In the interim, other shorter and more decisive events capture public attention (Moeller 1999, 12).

Some news coverage of crises is "simplistic, formulaic" and compassion fatigue serves to reinforce this. To outline the relevance of a crisis, journalists often draw comparisons with other historical events. Journalists need to be confident that the audience understands the analogy, so only the most common references are used, for example, events of World War II. This often results in the gross oversimplification of the crisis in question (Moeller 1999, 16). If certain images have caught the public's attention in the past, then similar images may likely be used during coverage of the next crisis. When news stories start to look the same the public may stop caring (Moeller 1999, 2).

Compassion fatigue can also occur when a crisis seems too remote and not sufficiently connected to the lives of the audience (Moeller 1999, 12). Badsey (1997) points out that while the media has become more international in reach, the news media of the United States, in particular, remains parochial (9). Unless Americans are involved in a crisis, or it affects their country in some other way, various events may not receive attention, from either the media or the public (Moeller 1999, 12).

Journalists who cover crimes against humanity and genocide often face physical danger. Violent regimes feel threatened by vigilant media. As technology and the possibility of better coverage grows, there is greater exposure of violent crises and some combatant groups show a greater level of hostility toward journalists when they think they are being covered in a way that makes them appear unworthy of support. Media crews on the ground often run a risk of being actively targeted by those who would rather keep their criminal actions private. As the risk to journalists' lives increases, it is possible that fewer and fewer journalists will be willing to risk their lives covering dangerous stories.

At the very least, it is likely to mean a change in journalistic practices. If, for example, in order to stay safe, journalists pool together and work closely with the military during an operation, this might mean a decrease in high quality, unbiased reporting. This may also result in a phenomenon known as "pack journalism" (Ruigrok 2008, 296) in which journalists tend to write about the same stories in the same way. This may particularly be the case in a pool system.

On a different note, the truth can become clouded due to the current proliferation of new forms of information gathering and dissemination. A greater number of individuals are now capable of broadcasting information. While this enables greater exposure for those suffering in humanitarian crises, these information gatherers may be amateurs with little knowledge of the principles of good journalism. Many are likely to produce low-cost, low-tech recordings and distribute them in real, or near-real, time (this is particularly true today in regard to the ongoing crisis in Syria and it is also true, though in a much more limited fashion, in regard to the ongoing crisis in the Nuba Mountains in Sudan). Because this form of information gathering and distribution is fast, it is able to dominate during an emergency, circumventing the traditional media. This form of information distribution can also be manipulated and used by combatant groups. Authorizing the sources of the information being disseminated becomes much harder. This was demonstrated in Rwanda when genocidaires were acting as "reporters" as they fed information to the BBC. It is also possible that, in times of financial crisis, news organizations may tend to rely more heavily on less reliable sources of information as news organizations receive less funding and as cost-cutting increases.

Badsey (1997) argues that the United Nations does not respond effectively to anti-peacekeeper propaganda, particularly that "promulgated by political authorities in target countries" (7). Such countries are able to exploit the international media for propaganda purposes in order to gain political advantage or subvert a UN peacekeeping operation. In nondemocratic countries, the authorities that control the national media use it to extend their power. Through the images of his enemies being dragged through the streets of Mogadishu, General Aideed demonstrated to his own people the power he had over the United Nations and the United States. This was at least as important as the effect of these pictures back in the United States (Badsey 1997, 17).

What Are the Real Probabilities of Progress in This Field?

There are two different areas in which progress can be made. The first of these involves our understanding of the influence of media on foreign policy. We must also improve the accuracy and investigative nature of the journalism itself.

A major restriction when assessing the degree of media influence on policy makers is that such influence is very hard to detect. Also, measuring policy "certainty" or "uncertainty" regarding intervention may not always be entirely accurate. Reliance on press briefings, for example, may give an incorrect impression of policy certainty. Public support is vital in crisis situations and policymakers are, more often than not, unwilling to show any signs of uncertainty (Robinson 2002, 135).

According to Robinson (2002), one way to identify the level of policy certainty may be to conduct interview-based research that involves asking policymakers directly for their assessment of the media's importance (126). This, however, might be difficult due to security restrictions and the fact that politicians might not be willing to admit that their decisions were strongly influenced by media reports.

Another option is case study research. More specifically, further analysis needs to be conducted regarding the different degrees of CNN effect: when it has a personal effect on policymakers or influences them via public opinion, when it enables intervention, and when it presents an impediment to action. Research also needs to focus on other factors that might influence intervention decisions, not just that of the media (Robinson 2002, 126–28).

The second area in which progress can be made involves the improvement of journalistic practices in times of genocide and mass atrocity. A major problem is that conflict sells, conflict resolution does not. The media, therefore, tends to focus on extremist positions and the irreconcilable differences of the parties involved. The media generally only cover the conflict during phases of dramatic escalation of violence. Reporting that focuses on conflict prevention is often too abstract to attract or hold the public's attention (Havermans 1998). Focusing on only the most violent phases of a conflict, as well as the impossibility of reconciliation between ethnic groups, is likely to discourage any foreign intervention.

According to Havermans (1998), journalists should be "promoters of peace" rather than reporters of violence who promote hopelessness and irreconcilable differences simply because this appears to sell news stories. This role of promoting peace should not be seen as "taking sides," but rather as a recognition of the degree to which journalists are already parties in the conflict they are covering. It is argued that there are various ways in which journalists can help bring warring parties closer to the negotiating table. The Australian NGO, Conflict Resolution Network (CRN), suggests that journalists "avoid simplistic representations of baddies and goodies" and that they "report areas of agreement as well as disagreement" as this "encourages the problem-solving process to continue" (Havermans 1998, 4). Similarly, Shiras (1996) suggests, journalists should "focus not only on the conflict, but also on an array of . . . strategies for dealing with the conflict" (111–12).

It is possible that knowledge of media relations by the intervening force could lead to fewer casualties in future military interventions. Media manipulation is starting to be included in U.S. military thinking. A concept known as "command and control warfare" (C2W) is a method of preemptive defense in which a strike is made, either electronically or physically, at the enemy's communications systems, potentially paralyzing its military capabilities without causing mass loss of life.

A furthering of this concept is "Information Warfare" or INFOWAR. This idea includes propaganda, computer virus attacks through the Internet, and media manipulation to coerce or destabilize an enemy. The issue of state sovereignty, however, is a significant problem here, particularly when these actions are seen as part of UN peacekeeping. Also, this approach would be ineffective against some forms of propaganda such as newsprint or video—the latter being a common way in which politicized sermons are distributed in some Muslim countries (Badsey 1997, 13–14).

Conclusion

The media's impact on foreign policy during times of genocide is a complex subject. Two forms of influence may come into play: (1) the government may "manufacture the consent" of the media and use it to gain support for its actions and (2) through the "CNN effect," the media may persuade the government of the necessity for intervention, or simply force its hand by making the intervention politically expedient.

The media is sometimes able to take an idea already present within society and give it direction. The trust a society places in the media means its advocacy of a particular cause gives that cause legitimacy in the eyes of the people. Arguably, the media is also sometimes shaped by a preexisting feeling within society. This may include a preexisting empathy for, or prejudice against, the people within the genocidal state. It might also include a rough sense of the public's "compassion fatigue" in relation to certain regions or conflicts.

In either case, the press carries a great responsibility. It is capable of selecting which of the many crises occurring around the world at any one time is to receive attention from the public. As Lipstadt (1991) points out, if an event is not covered, or is presented in a way that is not easily believed by the readers, it is as if it never took place (116). Intervention in genocide is more likely when the press has roused the public to push government to intervene in an ongoing crisis. The responsibility of the press is not only a question of whether or not it reveals information, but also how that information is presented to the people. The attitude and tone taken by a journalist will convey to the public how important that story is and how it is to be interpreted.

At one and the same time, there are also limits to the media's influence. It should not be assumed that journalists always have the power to change a situation. The government may fail to act in a genocide even though it has been well reported. When there is policy certainty as to whether or not to intervene, it appears that media coverage is unable to change this, no matter how critical it is of the policy or how empathetic of the suffering. It is suggested that, even at its most influential, media coverage can prompt the use of air power but not the deployment of ground troops (Robinson 2000). As Wheeler (2000) points out, if the media was as powerful an influence as many believe it to be, Western governments would have been pushed into a greater number of far more risky interventions (165).

The media can be a central element of genocide intervention—either as a motivator and facilitator, or as an impediment. It is a constantly evolving element of society and in recent years it has changed dramatically. For these reasons, continuing analysis is crucial if we are to truly understand the relationship between it, the government and the public.

Tellingly, the United Nations does not appear to recognize the value of the media and does not incorporate it into its peacekeeping doctrine.

According to Badsey (1997, 10), it is critical that academic theory now integrate the role of the media with other aspects of international relations. Without further analysis, discussion, debate, and evaluation, there can be no improvement of journalistic practices during times of genocide, a failure that could, literally, have fatal consequences.

References

Badsey, S. 1997. "The Media and UN 'Peacekeeping' Since the Gulf War." *The Journal of Conflict Studies* 17, no. 1: 7–27.

Cushman, T., and S. G. Mestrovic. 1996 *This Time We Knew: Western Responses to Genocide in Bosnia.* New York: New York University Press.

Dart Center for Journalism and Trauma. 2004. *Faces From Darfur: Nicholas Kristof Shows Us a Picture of Terrorism in Sudan.* October 26. http://www.dartcentre.org/articles/oped/2004_10_26.html (accessed April 13, 2005).

Eltringham, N. 2004. *Accounting for Horror: Post Genocide Debates in Rwanda.* London: Pluto Press.

Flew, T. 2008. *New Media, an Introduction: Third Edition.* New York: Oxford University Press.

Gilboa, E. 2002. "Global Communication and Foreign Policy." *Journal of Communication* 52, no. 4: 731–48.

Gore, A. 2007 *The Assault on Reason.* New York: The Penguin Press.

Havermans, Jos. 1998. "Better Media, Less Conflict." *Conflict Prevention Newsletter. European Platform for Conflict Prevention and Transformation* 1, no. 2: 4–5.

Herman, E.S., and N. Chomsky. 1988. *Manufacturing Consent: The Political Economy of the Mass Media.* New York: Pantheon Books.

Holbrooke, R. 1999. "No Media – No War." *Index on Censorship* 28, no. 3: 20–21.

International Crisis Group. 2008. *China's Thirst for Oil.* http://www.crisisgroup.org/home/index.cfm?l=1&id=5478 (accessed April 15, 2009).

Klaidman, S., and T. L. Beauchamp. 1987. *The Virtuous Journalist.* New York: Oxford University Press.

LeBor, A. 2006. *"Complicity with Evil": The United Nations in the Age of Modern Genocide.* New Haven, CT: Yale University Press.

Lipstadt, D. E. 1991. "Through the Looking Glass: Press Responses to Genocide." In Special Issue ("Teaching about Genocide" edited by Samuel Totten and William S. Parsons) of *Social Education, February* 55, no. 2: 116–20.

Lister, M., J. Dovey, S. Giddings, I. Grant, and K. Kelly. 2009. *New Media, a Critical Introduction: Second Edition.* London: Routledge.

Moeller, S. D. 1999. *Compassion Fatigue: How the Media Sell Disease, Famine, War and Death.* New York: Routledge.

Omaar, R., and A. De Waal. 1995. *Rwanda: Death, Despair and Defiance.* London: African Rights Publications.

Power, S. 2003. *A Problem from Hell: America and the Age of Genocide.* London: Harper Collins.

Reeves, E. 2007. *Partners in Genocide: A Comprehensive Guide to China's Role in Darfur.* http://www.sudanreeves.org/Article197.html (accessed April 15, 2009).

——. 2005. *Darfur Mortality Update: March 11, 2005.* http://www.sudantribune.com/article.php3?id_article=8505 (accessed April 13, 2005).
Ricchiardi, S. 2005. *Déjà vu.* March 30. http://platform.blogs.com/passionofthepresent/2005/03/dj_vu.html (accessed April 13, 2005).
Robinson, P. 2002. *The CNN Effect: The Myth of News, Foreign Policy and Intervention.* London: Routledge.
——. 2000. The News Media and Intervention: Critical Media Coverage, Policy Uncertainty and Air Power Intervention during Humanitarian Crisis. Paper presented at the Political Studies Association-UK 50th Annual Conference, April 10–13, 2000, London. http://ics.leeds.ac.uk/papers/pmt/exhibits/820/robinson.pdf (accessed January 22,, 2009).
Ruigrok, N. 2008. "Journalism of Attachment: Dutch Newspapers During the Bosnian War." *Media, War and Conflict* 1, no. 3: 293–313.
Shaw, M. 1996. *Civil Society and Media in Global Crises: Representing Distant Violence.* London: Pinter.
Shawcross, W. 2000. *Deliver Us From Evil: Warlords and Peacekeepers in a World of Endless Conflict.* London: Bloomsbury.
Shiras, P. 1996. "Big Problems, Small Print: A Guide to the Complexity of Humanitarian Emergencies and the Media." In *From Massacres to Genocide: The Media, Public Policy, and Humanitarian Crisis,* ed. R. I. Rotberg and T. G. Weiss, 93–114. Washington, DC: The Brookings Institution.
Sudan Watch. 2005. *Sudan: Darfur Mortality 380,000+15,000 Deaths Per Month. March 13.* http://sudanwatch.blogspot.com/2005/03/sudan-darfur-mortality-380000-15000.html (accessed April 13, 2005).
Wheeler, N. J. 2000. *Saving Strangers: Humanitarian Intervention in International Society.* New York: Oxford University Press.

Annotated Bibliography

Government–Media Relations

Allen, Tim, and Jean Seaton, eds. *The Media of Conflict: War Reporting and Representations of Ethnic Violence.* New York: Zed Books, 1999, 256 pp.

The authors in this collection examine the role of the media in times of conflict. In doing so, they consider the media's ability to sensationalize "war" and the negative impact of this. They basically seek to uncover the truth behind the sensationalism. They also examine the roles that the media seem to create for ethnic groups, which the public often internalizes. The question is asked, "Do reports document ethnicity, or produce it?" Nine case studies are examined in order to explore these issues.

Badsey, Stephen. "The Media and UN 'Peacekeeping' Since the Gulf War." *The Journal of Conflict Studies* 17, no. 1 (Spring 1997): 7–27.0020

Badsey argues that the changes in United Nations (UN) "peacekeeping" operations between 1992 and 1997 were dramatic and multifaceted. This article attempts to show that the media (particularly those of the United States, which are dominant within and may, under most circumstances, be taken as virtually identical to the international media) were critical elements in determining the success or failure of the various operations. It points to three principal areas of current practice regarding the media that contributed to the failure or partial failure of recent UN "peacekeeping" missions. One of these was a failure of an understanding of the media exhibited by the government and military forces of the United States, which was the result of doctrine established before the end of the Cold War. Another was the failure of the United Nations and its constituent members to respond effectively to anti-peacekeeper propaganda, especially that promulgated by political authorities in the countries targeted for "peacekeeping," including their ability to exploit the international media for propaganda purposes. The third was the failure of the United Nations to develop "peacekeeping" doctrine that took the value of the media into account. The article calls for advances in international relations theory in this field as an aid to further understanding.

Bahador, Babak. "Did the Global War on Terror End the CNN Effect?" *Media, War and Conflict* 4, no. 1 (April 2011): 37–54.

This article examines the question as to whether independent media coverage of foreign policy was eradicated by the events of 9/11 and the subsequent War on Terror. Bahador ultimately challenges the argument that foreign policy coverage has become subservient to the state.

Beschloss, Michael, R. *Presidents, Television and Foreign Crisis*. Washington DC: The Annenberg Washington Program in Communications Policy Studies of North Western University, 1993, 34 pp.

This work examines how US television coverage of news and world affairs has changed, and the effects of this new kind of coverage on presidential decision making in foreign crises.

Entman, Robert M. *Projections of Power: Framing News, Public Opinion and US Foreign Policy*. Chicago, IL: The University of Chicago Press, 2004, 240 pp.

Entman examines the ways in which policymakers sell their ideas through the media to diverse audiences across the United States and around the world. The central analysis of the book is the relationship between the US government's preferred version of foreign issues and events, and the way they are actually framed in the media. While not focused on genocide, the case studies are all informative and instructive: the Korean Airline and Iran Air tragedies; the US military operations in Grenada, Libya, and Panama in the 1980s; and the 1990–1991 war in Iraq.

Gowing, Nik *Real-time Television Coverage of Armed Conflicts and Diplomatic Crisis: Does it Pressure or Distort Foreign Policy Decisions? Harvard Working Paper*. Cambridge, MA: The Joan Shorenstein Barone Center on the Press, Politics and Public Policy at Harvard University, 1994, 84 pp.

This working paper challenges the belief that real-time television coverage drives foreign policy. Gowing claims that while this coverage can prompt the provision of humanitarian aid, it has little or no influence on intervention to end a conflict.

Hawkins, Virgil. "Selectivity and the Other Side of the CNN Effect: The Consequences of Not Paying Attention to Conflict." *Media, War and Conflict* 4, no. 1 (April 2011): 55–68.

Hawkins points out that many conflicts around the world go unreported by the media. He examines the selectivity and disproportionality of media coverage and the consequences of such a lack of attention.

Herman, Edward, S. "The Media's Role in US Foreign Policy." *Journal of International Affairs* 47, no. 1 (1993): 23–45.

Herman argues that in foreign affairs reporting a number of factors contribute to making the mainstream media supportive of government policy and vulnerable to government manipulation.

Herman, Edward S., and Noam Chomsky. *Manufacturing Consent: The Political Economy of the Mass Media*. New York: Pantheon Books, 1988, 412 pp.

Herman and Chomsky argue that the media serve and promote the interests of the powerful societal forces that control and finance them. In this light, the book examines the concept of "worthy and unworthy victims"; elections in El Salvador, Guatemala, and Nicaragua; free-market disinformation; and the Indochina Wars.

Hoge, James, F. "Media Pervasiveness." *Foreign Affairs* 73, no. 4 (July/August, 1994): 136–44.

Hoge argues that while the media has advanced technologically in recent years and has become an effective tool of diplomacy, it has also become a disruptive and unpredictable force in the shaping of foreign policy.

Jakobsen, Peter Viggo. "Counter Point: Focus on the CNN Effect Misses the Point: The Real Media Impact on Conflict Management is Invisible and Indirect." *Journal of Peace Research* 37, no. 2 (March 2000): 131–43.

Jakobsen argues that media coverage is not determined by humanitarian need. He further asserts that as a result of the fact that in the 1990s media attention focused on only a few conflicts, resources were transferred from cost-effective, long-term conflict-prevention measures to short-term emergency relief. He concludes that this indirect impact on conflict management is stronger than the direct impact of the "CNN effect."

Moeller, Susan D. *Compassion Fatigue: How the Media Sell Disease, Famine, War and Death*. New York: Routledge, 1999, 390 pp.

Moeller claims that it is getting harder for viewers to feel compassion for the subjects of horrific news reports. She believes this is because of formulaic media coverage, sensationalized language, and overly Americanized metaphors. Modern media is thus threatening the public's ability to understand world events. Through case studies of disease, famine, death, and war, Moeller examines media coverage of international crises between 1980 and 2000, and thus explains why journalists covered them in the way that they did. Further, she reveals that the media was increasingly being run like other large profit-seeking businesses, and notes that in doing so, it abdicated its special responsibility to the public, thus creating compassion fatigue.

Neuman, Johanna. *Lights, Camera, War: Is Media Technology Driving International Politics?* New York: St. Martin's Press, 1996, 327 pp.

Neuman argues that the evolution in media technology has had a minimal impact on international relations, changing little more than "the outer garments of international affairs." She further argues that instead of influencing the decisions of leaders, new communications technology can be used by skilled policy makers for their own ends.

Paletz, David L., and Robert M. Entman. *Media, Power, Politics*. New York: The Free Press, 1981, 308 pp.

Paletz and Entman explore the ways in which the news media affects power in the United States. They argue that the media can unintentionally influence the thinking and behavior of both those who possess power and the general public. The authors also examine how the media can be manipulated, especially by presidential candidates, presidents, members of Congress, Supreme Court justices, and interest groups, among others. Ultimately, the book demonstrates how public opinion on domestic and foreign policy is influenced by the media and those who manipulate it.

Parenti, Michael. *Inventing Reality: The Politics of the Mass Media.* New York: St. Martin's Press, 1986, 258 pp.

Parenti argues that the majority of the population gains their information and beliefs through the media, but that the news media often intentionally misrepresents this information. The book examines *how* the media distorts information and *why*. In doing so, he examines various biases, concentrating primarily on "national and international politico-economic class issues."

Price, Monroe, E. *Media and Sovereignty: The Global Information Revolution and its Challenge to State Power.* Cambridge, MA: The MIT Press, 2002, 352 pp.

Price argues that globalization is fundamentally altering media practices, institutions, and content. Among the many issues he addresses are: emerging foreign policies that govern media, and how the state, in the face of institutional or technological change, controls the information reaching the public. International case studies are used to explore the ways in which the media is regulated to political ends, including "self-regulation," media regulation in conflict zones, control of harmful and illegal content, and use of foreign aid to alter media in target societies.

Robinson, Piers. *The CNN Effect: The Myth of News, Foreign Policy and Intervention.* London: Routledge, 2002, 177 pp.

Robinson examines the relationship between the media and the state. He defines the "CNN effect," assesses the influence of news media on intervention decisions, and develops a "policy-media interaction model." Case studies include Somalia, Iraq, Bosnia, Kosovo, and Rwanda.

Robinson, Piers. "The News Media and Intervention: Triggering the Use of Air Power during Humanitarian Crisis." *European Journal of Communication* 15, no. 3 (2000): 405–14.

Robinson claims that media coverage can drive intervention policy when there is policy uncertainty and critical and empathetic media coverage. When there is policy certainty, he argues that not even this kind of coverage can change policy.

Robinson, Piers. "The Policy-Media Interaction Model: Measuring Media Power during Humanitarian Crisis." *Journal of Peace Research* 37, no. 5 (2000): 625–45.

A discussion of a model whose purpose is to predict the influence of the media, depending on the level of policy certainty that exists. Robinson explores two case studies: the US intervention in Bosnia to defend the Gorazde "safe area" and Operation Allied Force in Kosovo.

Robinson, Piers. "Theorizing the Influence of Media on World Politics: Models of Media Influence on Foreign Policy." *European Journal of Communication* 16, no. 4 (2000): 523–44.

Robinson highlights the "theoretical and empirical shortcomings" of the theory of "manufacturing consent." In doing so, he seeks to reconcile the contrasting claims regarding the power of the news media.

Robinson, Piers. "World Politics and Media Power: Problems of Research and Design." *Media, Culture and Society* 22, no. 2 (2000): 227–32.

Robinson examines major works on the subject and highlights problems with media-centric and world politics-centric research. In doing so, he explores the ways in which different research strategies have resulted in different conclusions regarding the power of the media. The article suggests new ways of researching the relationship between the media and world politics.

Rotberg, Robert I., and Thomas G. Weiss, eds. *From Massacres to Genocide: The Media, Public Policy, and Humanitarian Crisis*. Cambridge, MA: The World Peace Foundation, 1996, 203 pp.

A number of leading academics and journalists contributed chapters to this book, which is divided into three parts: "Capitalizing on Technology and Sustaining Media Attention"; "Building Greater Humanitarian Capacity"; and "Improving US Policy." The various chapters examine interactions and tensions between the media, policymakers, and humanitarians. The central hypothesis is that major crises, such as that which occurred in Bosnia, Rwanda, and Somalia in the 1990s, can be avoided or relieved, and that the media can make a significant contribution beyond the "CNN effect." Essentially, the book seeks new ways of improving interactions between the media, policymakers, and humanitarian organizations in an effort to prevent or halt genocidal situations.

Journalism: Different Forms and Practices

Ammon, Royce J. *Global Television and the Shaping of World Politics: CNN, Telediplomacy and Foreign Policy*. Jefferson, NC: McFarland, 2001, 197 pp.

Ammon examines the interconnectedness of communications and diplomacy. He analyzes the CNN coverage of the Persian Gulf War in 1991, claiming that aid was provided to the Iraqi Kurds because their plight was televised. This is in contrast to the case of the Shiite Muslims who were forced to flee because they received no television coverage and thus no Western aid. Ammon also looks at conditions that can weaken the impact of television and its potential to bring about intervention. To explore this issue, he analyzes the Rwandan Genocide.

Aday, Sean, Henry Farrell, Marc Lynch, John Sides, John Kelly, and Ethan Zukerman. *Blogs and Bullets: Evaluating the Impact of New Media on Conflict*. Washington, DC: The United States Center of Innovation for Science, Technology, and Peacebuilding, 2010.

This report points out that "new media" (e.g., blogs, Twitter, Facebook, and YouTube) have played a major role at times of contentious political upheaval. The authors argue that this role is nuanced and critically assess both the "cyberutopian" and "cyberskeptic" approaches to this issue. They believe that the impact of new media on political movements is best understood through a consideration of five levels of analysis: individual transformations, intergroup relations, collective action, regime policies, and external attention.

Paul, Christopher, and James J. Kim. *Reporters on the Battlefield: The Embedded Press System in Historical Context*. Santa Monica, CA: RAND, 2004 150 pp.

The authors argue that since Vietnam, an intense distrust and antagonism has developed between the military and the press. This tension has led to a number of different manifestations of the press–military relationship. Of these, the "embedded press system"—in which journalists travel with military units—appears to be the best at balancing the needs of the press, the military, and the public. The book examines this system in detail, including its strengths, weaknesses, and possible improvements.

Philo, Greg. *Seeing and Believing: The Influence of Television*. London: Routledge, 1990, 244 pp.

This book examines television as the main source of information for the majority of Western populations. Philo poses the question, "Do we believe what we see?" and builds on earlier studies to analyze the ways in which the media can influence public consciousness and "establish the priorities for public discussion." He also examines its ability to dictate the *meaning* of events.

Pilger, John, ed. *Tell Me No Lies: Investigative Journalism and its Triumphs*. New York: Avalon, 2005, 655 pp.

Edited by the well-known Australian journalist John Pilger, this is a wide-ranging collection of investigations of cover-ups of atrocities by investigative journalists who challenged the limitations of their profession and "broke" the stories. The reports include the liberation of the Dachau concentration camp, the US massacre of Vietnamese at My Lai during the Vietnam War, the Russia–Chechnya war, and massacres in Iraq.

Kerbel, Matthew R. *If It Bleeds, It Leads: An Anatomy of Television News*. Boulder, CO: Westview Press, 2001, 149 pp.

This book is an examination of what goes into television news. The reader is taken through two-and-a-half hours of syndicated, local and network information programming to uncover what exactly is being presented as "news" in an attempt to keep viewers watching.

The History of Conflict Journalism

Allan, Stuart, and Barbie Zelizer, eds. *Reporting War: Journalism in Wartime*. New York: Routledge, 2004, 374 pp.

This is a collection of chapters by many different authors, examining the role of journalists during war: their powers and responsibilities. Topics covered include information warfare, terrorism, US and British media, the Gulf Wars, the Balkans, the portrayal of African conflicts, and online reporting.

Hudson, Miles, and John Stanier. *War and the Media: A Random Searchlight*. New York: New York University Press, 1998, 339 pp.

A broad examination of the Western media during various major wars and violent crises in a 150-year period. The book examines the Crimean War, World War I, World War II, Korea, Vietnam, Suez, the violence in Ireland, the Falklands War, US military operations from 1980 to 1989, Iraq 1991, Somalia, and the Balkan Wars. The authors explore propaganda, the tensions between the military and the press, and the commercial nature of the media and journalists' bias. The authors believe that the media, particularly that of television, set the international agenda in many, if not most, of the crises.

Knightley, Phillip. *The First Casualty: The War Correspondent as Hero and Myth-maker from the Crimea to Iraq*. Baltimore, MA: The John Hopkins University Press, 2004, 574 pp.

This book examines the history of the reporting of war. Knightley looks at the ways in which journalists have omitted or twisted the truth, their role in promoting war, and the responsibility they bear in determining the outcome.

Power, S. *A Problem From Hell: America and the Age of Genocide*. London: Harper Collins, 2003, 620 pp.

Power examines genocide and its history in international criminal law. She focuses on the role played by the United States during the atrocities perpetrated in Armenia, during the Holocaust, and in Cambodia, Iraq, Bosnia, Rwanda, and Kosovo—part of which involves the actions of the American media.

Taylor, Philip M. *Global Communications, International Affairs and the Media Since 1945*. London: Routledge, 1997, 248 pp.

This is a broad examination of the role of the media and journalists during wars in recent history. It emphasizes their power to influence policy and events, as well as to misinform. Among some of the many issues Taylor analyzes are the so-called "Vietnam Syndrome," Operation Desert Storm, information warfare, and psychological operations.

Publications on Specific Crises

Hammond, Philip, and Edward S. Herman, eds. *Degraded Capability: The Media and the Kosovo Crisis*. London: Pluto Press, 2000, 222 pp.

The central argument of this book is that during the NATO bombing campaign against the Federal Republic of Yugoslavia, Western journalists were generally uncritical of NATO's actions and, in fact, framed their reports with the claim that NATO was trying to help. Hammond and Herman challenge this view, critically analyzing both the war and the resulting media coverage around the world.

Hawkins, Virgil. "National Interest or Business Interest: Coverage of Conflict in the Democratic Republic of Congo in *The Australian* Newspaper." *Media, War and Conflict* 2, no. 1 (April 2009): 67–84.

Despite the conflict in the DRC being one of the "deadliest" in the world today, it has been largely ignored by the media. This article examines coverage of this conflict in *The Australian* and compares this to the coverage of the Israel–Palestine, Darfur, and Zimbabwe conflicts. Hawkins points to the narrow perceptions of "national interest" and a focus on news that sells as the explanation of this marginalization.

Kurspahic, Kemal. *Prime Time Crime: Balkan Media in War and Peace*. Washington, DC: United States Institute for Peace, 2003, 261 pp.

This book examines the connection between nationalism, ethnic strife, and the media during the Balkan Wars of the 1990s. Of particular concern is the media manipulation that occurred in Serbia, Croatia, and Bosnia from Slobodan Milosevic's rise to power in 1987 to his fall in 2000. Kurspahic views the media as a kind of "midwife to the birth" of the Milosevic regime and outlines what he sees as the three main lessons for the international community. First, the role of the media in both conflict and keeping of the peace should not be underestimated. Second, the media can be a powerful tool for both "balkanization" and reconciliation. Third, the audience for good journalism transcends ethnic boundaries—support must be given to independent news organizations that seek to reach beyond ethno-political lines.

Mamdani, Mahmood. *Saviors and Survivors: Darfur, Politics, and the War on Terror*. New York: Pantheon, 2009, 416 pp.

The introduction to this book examines the "CNN effect" in relation to the violence in Darfur and the ways in which it influenced the "Save Darfur" movement. Mamdani argues that as a result of relying solely on pictures and interviews, the movement sought to respond early on to what it has been told is genocide, and only seek to understand the real context of events later. Mamdani argues that the movement "over-racialized" the conflict, thus delaying reconciliation.

Ruigrok, Nel. "Journalism of Attachment: Dutch Newspapers During the Bosnian War." *Media, War and Conflict* 1, no. 3 (2008): 293–313.

Ruiogrok argues that journalists practicing "journalism of attachment" tend to frame conflicts in terms of "good guys" and "bad guys," and have a tendency to report with a clear idea as to how the conflict should be resolved. Ruigrok argues that this type of journalism was demonstrated during the Bosnian War in that it took on moral overtones and actively pushed for military intervention. Ultimately, this study outlines the extent to which, and the ways in which, journalism of attachment was reflected in Dutch newspapers during the Bosnian War. It also looks at the consequences in relation to the impact on the objectivity and credibility of the news.

Sobel, Richard, and Eric Shiraev, eds. *International Public Opinion and the Bosnia Crisis.* Lanham, MD: Lexington Books, 2003, 366 pp.

Sobel and Shiraev examine the ways in which public opinion impacted various democratic governments' responses to the Bosnian War from 1991 to 1997. Case studies are used to provide an overview of the national media coverage and public reaction to the war, as well as the links between public opinion and political and military intervention.

Thompson, Allan, ed. *The Media and the Rwanda Genocide.* London: Pluto Press, 2007, 463 pp.

The contributors examine the role of radio and print media propaganda within Rwanda prior to and during the 1994 genocide, the international media coverage of the genocide, the task of prosecuting Rwandan media figures for the crime of incitement to genocide, and the role of the media in postgenocide Rwanda. It includes contributions from many leading scholars of the Rwandan genocide, a brief foreword by then-UN Secretary-General Kofi Annan, and a chapter by the former UN Force Commander in Rwanda Romeo Dallaire.

8

The International Arms Trade and the Prevention of Genocide: The Law and Practice of Arming Genocidal Governments

Hannibal Travis

Nam, qui non prohibet, cum prohibere possit, jubet.
For he who forbids not, when he may, consents.
—A maxim of Roman justice

—Tyler 1819, 110

Introduction

Genocides may be grouped into two broad categories: economic and political. Helen Fein (1984) calls the former "developmental genocides" and the latter "retributive genocides," while subdividing retributive genocides into those motivated by (a) a single despot's self-preservation, (b) victory in war or counter-insurgency, (c) an ethnic or religious group's perpetuation of its supremacy, and (d) the purgation of ideological monsters, demons, or generalized "Others" (11, 18). One may, of course, deconstruct these categories to reveal the presence of each category in the others, as, for example, when one analyzes the economic aims and ethnic distinctions of ideological zealots like the Nazis, Soviet, or Maoist communists, or the Khmer Rouge (Kiernan 2007, 23, 379–437, 486–500, 529–59). Nevertheless, genocide scholarship describes a trend whereby an early, colonial period of developmental genocides seems to have given way to a modern, nationalist period of politicized genocides, only to be followed in the late 1990s and 2000s with renewed developmental or "resource curse" genocides. At each stage, the traffic in arms from mercantile centers and imperial capitals to peripheral, colonial, and client states facilitated the commission of genocide, and often thwarted efforts at resistance to the crime. The Cold War period aggravated these trends as aircraft, tanks, howitzers, automatic weapons, and chemical and nuclear weapons proliferated to dictatorships around the world.

Most scholars and historians agree that the genocides in Bosnia, Rwanda, and Kosovo took place within States whose governments and/or rebel movements were armed by the great powers, including members of the UN Security Council. It is less well known but nevertheless true that foreign involvement, including substantial shipments of arms, preceded genocides against minorities and indigenous peoples in the Ottoman Empire, Afghanistan, Cambodia, the Democratic Republic of the Congo,[1] Guatemala, Ethiopia,[2] Indonesia, Iraq,[3] Sudan, and Tibet.[4] In nearly all of these cases, and particularly in Bosnia and Iraq, arms flows from member States of the Security Council to dictatorial regimes facilitated genocidal campaigns. This was also true of the Holocaust, which occurred in part due to the arming of Adolf Hitler and his National Socialist party by German and American bankers and industrialists. During the Cold War, China, France, the Soviet Union, the United Kingdom, and the United States consistently armed and financed genocidal regimes and movements, including Maoist China and the Khmer Rouge; dictators in Ethiopia, Guatemala, Indonesia, Iraq, Nigeria, and Pakistan (Bangladesh); and fundamentalist rebels in Afghanistan.[5] These arms were put to use in massacring minorities and indigenous peoples, including Assyrians, Bangladeshis, Buddhists, Catholics, Chinese, East Timorese, Hazaras, Ibos, Kurds, Mayans, Muslims, Tibetans, and Vietnamese (in Cambodia).

Since the end of the Cold War, States flouting arms embargoes have stymied UN initiatives to prevent the flow of arms and other support to genocidal governments.[6] Several permanent members of the UN Security Council have broken arms embargoes against genocidal regimes, which they either supported or did not veto. Germany and several Muslim countries armed the Bosnian and Croatian rebels against the Federal Republic of Yugoslavia, and the Soviet Union and then the Russian Federation lavishly equipped the Yugoslav military and Serbian militias. This traffic, on all sides, involved the violation of UN arms embargoes after September 25, 1991 (Goshko 1991, A1, A26). China and France exported small arms, ammunition, and machetes to the Rwandan army and militias in the months leading up to the anti-Tutsi genocide. China continued the pattern during Sudan's Darfur genocide.

The Role of Arms Disparities and the Arms Trade in Genocide

World War I

German imperialism proved to be more destructive in absolute terms than anything seen since the Spanish and Portuguese Empires. German armies caused between three and seven million military and civilian deaths in the Russian Empire during World War I, including deaths from disease (Rummel 1998, 195–98). The German occupation of Belgium involved widespread massacres and burnings of homes and villages (*New York Times* 1915, 6). In Raphael Lemkin's view, German colonization of present-day Namibia "decimated" the Herero people of that area through gunfire, slavery, hunger, and the prevention of births (Gewald 2004, 61–62; Schaller 2005, 534). One Herero is recorded as having said, "[our chief] knew . . . we would be crushed in battle, as our people were nearly all unarmed. . . . [But we] were driven to desperation by the cruelty and injustice of the Germans" (Bridgman 2009, 39–40).

The German Empire funded the Ottomans' entry into World War I with an initial payment worth two million Turkish lira. After the gold bullion arrived, the Ottoman Navy attacked the Russian Empire, and crossed the Russian frontier. The Ottoman Empire received over five billion marks by the end of the war, as well as arms and ammunition (McMurray 2001, 114). After engaging in repeated massacres of Armenian, Greek, and Assyrian civilians, the Ottomans encountered resistance by these populations and condemnations from the British, French, and Russian Empires, after which the Ottomans rushed to exterminate their remaining Ottoman Christian inhabitants behind the frontlines, using artillery, guns, blades, and exposure. Ottoman Christian cities and villages were shelled and burned, adults and children alike were massacred and raped, and thousands perished from disease and hunger (Dadrian 1994, 100–24; Lepsius 1919, 295–96; *The New York Times* 1919; Surma 2000, 203–18; Travis 2006, 332–38).

World War II

After the Allied victory in World War I, the Versailles Treaty and Covenant of the League of Nations sought to outlaw war, entrust the League to control the trade in arms and ammunitions, limit the size of the German army and navy, prohibit German air forces, and monitor the payment of war reparations (Treaty of Versailles 1919, Articles 1, 8, 159–210). The scheme devastated steel and weapons magnates like Fritz Thyssen and Gustav Krupp, who financed the rise of right-wing German veterans of World War I to power in the 1930s, in the form of the Nazi Party, which repudiated Germany's League of Nations obligations (Fear 2005, 445; Levin 2001, 162; Nicholls 2000, 149). The Nazi government, in the five-year period after 1933, spent nearly as much on arms as the United States, the United Kingdom, and France, combined (Dunn 1995, 21). Bankers at Brown Brothers Harriman and the Union Banking Corporation in New York "bought and shipped millions of dollars of gold, fuel, steel, coal and US treasury bonds to Germany, both feeding and financing Hitler's build-up to war" (Aris and Campbell 2004, n.p.). Executives at US multinational corporations Ford and General Motors publicly defended Hitler and supplied large numbers of vehicles to the regime (Warsh 2008, 42–147). Many "key financiers and industrialists" committed war crimes "because they had made German rearmament possible, with knowledge that Hitler intended to use his military machine for aggression against his neighbors," and utilized the slave labor of camp inmates (Meltzer 1995, 505–10).

As the Germans advanced into Poland and the Soviet Union, local forces wilted at first under superior firepower. As Panzer Divisions raced toward Moscow at an unprecedented pace, German tanks and machine guns cut down Russian riflemen (Stolfi 1993, 132). At Stalingrad, unarmed Slavs went into battle against the Germans, whose fighter-bombers ruled the skies. They were ferried across the Volga to pick up rifles from their dead fellow Slavs (Radetsky 2007, 124). The Germans deported over one million Jews from across Europe to Auschwitz for extermination, sometimes preceded by slave labor, along with 15,000 Soviet prisoners, 21,000 Roma people, and 75,000 Poles (Thomas 2007, 697). After the war, the owner of the chemical firm Tesch and Stabenow was tried and convicted for knowingly supplying crystallized hydrogen cyanide gas (Zyklon B) to the Auschwitz death camp (The Zyklon B Case 1946, 94).

Soviet Communism

German intelligence decided in 1915 to support and finance the rise of the Bolsheviks with fifty million gold marks (Brackman 2001, 143; Crowdy 2006, 298). In power, the Bolsheviks executed millions of their ethnic and political opponents and deported millions of people from their traditional homelands, including Poles, Ukrainians, Chechens, Circassians, Armenians, Assyrians, Jews, Greeks, Central Asians, Catholics, Germans, Koreans, Mongolians, and other peoples (Arnold 2007; Conquest 1991; Geraci 2008, 346; Rummel 1999, 64). About ten million deaths resulted from Soviet policies from 1927 to 1939, including Ukrainian famine victims (Mace 2009, 95–126; Serbyn 2005a, 628–30; Serbyn 2005b, 1055–961), victims of executions by the security services, and deportees to Siberia who were starved, worked to death, or exposed to the frigid elements (Conquest 1991; Wheatcroft and Davies 1994, 2–77). Stalin and his agents deported hundreds of thousands of ethnic minorities to Siberia, where they died of murder, torture, starvation, exposure, overwork, and disease. The deportation to Siberia or to the Kazakh steppe of other peoples accustomed to a temperate climate, such as the Germans, Chechens, Crimean Tatars, Estonians, Latvians, Koreans, Ingushes, Kalmyks, Greeks, Kurds, Armenians, and Assyrians also served to destroy more than 500,000 members of these non-Russian peoples, including many formerly intact ethnic communities (Mälksoo 2001, 757–80; Rywkin 1994, 67). Raphael Lemkin regarded Soviet starvation and persecution of ethnic minorities such as the Ukrainians and Kazakhs as a genocidal policy.

Cold War Era

During the Cold War era, countries often debated whether to continue supplying arms to governments engaged in massacring their minority populations. Be that as it may, British Prime Minister Harold Wilson and Soviet Premier Leonid Brezhnev supplied the Federal Republic of Nigeria with abundant weaponry to blockade, massacre, and starve over a million majority Christian Igbo people prior to and during the Nigerian-Biafran War (Bangura 2006, 178, 183–84). Questioned about the extent of British aid by Parliament, the Secretary of State for Foreign and Commonwealth Affairs reported "that it is untrue that there is any widespread starvation" in Biafra, despite a BBC Panorama documentary showing precisely that (Parliamentary Debates 1970, 727). Similarly, in 1971, the British Secretary of State for Foreign and Commonwealth shrugged off efforts in Parliament to act in unison with the United States to withhold arms from Pakistan, whose dictator Yahya Khan directed massacres of Hindus and secessionist Muslims during the independence struggle in Bangladesh (Kiernan 2007, 572–77; Parliamentary Debates 1971, 1056).

The United States and Britain initially blocked trade with the Chinese communists who threatened Tibet, but Britain relaxed its embargo under pressure from local business, even as the Maoists stepped up their campaign to destroy the Tibetan culture (Fauber 1957, 1; Reuters 1956, 2).The United States armed the Indonesian fascist dictator Suharto, who consolidated his power with massacres of 500,000 people (many of Chinese origin) in the 1960s (Cribb 2009, 234–62), invaded East Timor in 1975 and displaced or killed many Timorese, and misappropriated about $15 billion by 2008 (AP-Reuters 1971, 4; Associated Press 1983; Blum 2003, 197–98; Dunn 2009, 264–95; Leow and Moestafa 2008).

In the 1970s and 1980s, a pattern of alliances emerged with China, the Cambodian Khmer Rouge, and the United States on one side, and the Soviet Union and Vietnam on the other (Kiernan 1999; Morris 1999). The US and Chinese sided politically and materially aided the Khmer Rouge, for example, with $100 million in Chinese arms per year in the 1980s, despite the movement's extermination of Vietnamese and Buddhists in the 1970s (Kiernan 2004, xxix; Kiernan 2009). Also in the 1980s, US President Ronald Reagan armed and praised Guatemalan dictators (Jonas 2009, 388–89) and Afghan fundamentalists who massacred thousands of minorities and indigenous people (Blum 2003, 238–39, 338–52; Mousavi 1997, 189–201; Rashid 2002, 55–81, 250; Valentino 2004, 196–233).

The Soviet Union was even more culpable in genocidal conflicts during the Cold War.[7] It supplied Mao's communists with the arms to take over China and begin executing millions of peasants and "rightists." At the same time, China subjected tens of millions to famine as it exported grain to the Soviet Union and its allies in exchange for Soviet nuclear weapons technology (Becker 1997, 56–62, 155–70; Valentino 2004, 75, 93, 125–33, 1430). Ethiopian dictator Mengistu Haile Mariam, armed with billions in Soviet aid and thousands of Soviet advisers, prosecuted wars, deportations, and scorched-earth tactics that together claimed 1–1.5 million lives (De Waal 1991, 16, 76, 181–82, 190–91, 238–39).

About 5,000 Soviet advisers and thousands of advanced Soviet tanks and helicopters were dispatched to Iraq, where they were used to massacre Kurds, Assyrians, and Shi'a Arabs (Allawi 2007, 132; Simons 1996, 267). During the Anfal campaign, the Iraqi army and pro-government Kurdish militia (the Jash) bombed and shelled Kurdish, Yezidi, and Assyrian villages, executed thousands and dumped them in mass graves, destroyed all homes and foodstuffs in "prohibited areas," and used chemical weapons (Leezenberg 2009, 461–81; Middle East Watch 1993, 1, 7–12, 14, 18, 280–317).

The Post–Cold War Era

About a year after imposing a similar arms embargo on Iraq due to its invasion of Kuwait, the UN Security Council enacted Resolution 713, imposing "a general and complete embargo on all deliveries of weapons and military equipment to Yugoslavia" (U.N. Security Council 1991, paragraph 6). Nevertheless, German businessmen supplied weapons to the Croatian rebels within Yugoslavia, which the rebels used to massacre and deport Serbian civilians, and loot their homes and property (Djilas 1995, 60; Mennecke 2008, 424). For its part, Russia reportedly armed the Yugoslav federal government, which supported autonomous Serb-led zones within the breakaway provinces of Croatia and Bosnia (Associated Press 1993a, 3). Turkey, Iran, and Sudan armed the Bosnian Muslims through Croatia and Germany (Pomfrey and Ottaway 1996; Wiebes 2003, 195–96). The result was numerous massacres, the largest of which was perpetrated in Srebrenica (Associated Press 1993b, 4; U.N. Secretary-General 1999).

The forgotten lead-up to the Rwandan Genocide was the October 1991 attack on Rwanda by the rebel Tutsi army (the Rwandan Patriotic Front or RPF) based in Uganda. In 1994, Human Rights Watch reported that in February 1993, the RPF violated a cease-fire with the Rwandan government, leading to "[h]undreds" of civilian deaths and the flight of 650,000 from their homes. During the offensive, "the RPF extrajudicially executed at least 100 civilians in and near Ruhengeri in northwestern Rwanda" (4), and Catholic parishes in Gahanga and other communities near Ruhengeri reported "that up to 200 civilians were extrajudicially executed by the RPF in their areas alone" (4). Human Rights Watch (1994) also commented that "throughout the war, . . . both the Rwandan army and the RPF engaged in frequent incidents of indiscriminate attacks in known civilian areas as well as direct attacks on civilians" (6).

The Security Council considered but rejected a proposed condemnation of the Rwandan genocide in April 1994. Then, on May 17, 1994, the UN Security Council, noting that armed individuals operated with impunity in Rwanda, a humanitarian and refugee crisis existed, and entire ethnic groups were being destroyed in whole or in part, directed all UN member States to prevent the sale or supply of arms to Rwanda from their territories, or using their ships or aircraft (U.N. Security Council 1994). However, that very May, British corporations arranged arms supplies to the Rwandan regime through Albania and Israel. Concomitantly, French firms, which had supplied Rwandan armed forces with weapons between 1990 and 1993, shipped additional weapons, clearly in violation of the UN arms embargo, to the Rwandan government in May and June 1994 (Dallaire and Manocha 2007, 61–64, 70–71).

In the fifteen months prior to the genocide, China had shipped double the usual number of machetes and related farm implements to Rwanda, nearly 600,000 in all or an estimated one for every three Rwandan men (Semelin 2009, 173, 409).

After the fall of the Hutu nationalist government of Rwanda and the flight of many of its leaders to the Democratic Republic of the Congo (DRC), the Tutsi-led government of Rwanda supported operations that led to excess deaths in DRC that were estimated to equal five Rwandan genocides (Egeland 2008, 13; Ray 2000). Rebels in the DRC, aided by Rwanda and Uganda, massacred and systematically raped many members of indigenous peoples of the DRC, such as the Bambuti or "Pygmies" (BBC 2004; Penketh 2004).

According to Human Rights Watch (1997), a Rwandan officer was "in charge of troops at several massacres sites in Congo," and a large militia in the Congo backed by Rwanda and staffed by Rwandans and ethnic Tutsis "carried out large scale killings of civilians, predominantly refugees as well as some Congolese," while blocking humanitarian aid to civilians to such an extent that "thousands of additional deaths" likely occurred. "Like others in Europe, the U.S. knew from the start that Rwanda and Uganda had each sent at least 1,000 troops to support [a Congolese rebel faction blamed for massacres and other crimes], but for months it maintained the position that the [faction] was a purely Congolese force." In March 1997, "a high-ranking State Department official confirmed to Human Rights Watch/FIDH that Rwandan troops were playing an important part in Congo conflict." One of the Rwandan-backed rebels, Major "Jackson" Nkurunziza, was known to Congolese aid workers as "the exterminator" due to his involvement in massacres of Hutu in the Congo (whom he called ex-FAR and Interahamwe apparently without conducting any trials) (Human Rights Watch 1997, 4, 15, 34, 39).

In the Darfur region of Sudan, the Government of Sudan responded to an insurgency by mobilizing forces known to Darfurians and many in the international community as the *Janjaweed* and by "overlook[ing] minor offences by the mujahedeen against civilians who [were] suspected members of the rebellion" (Human Rights Watch 2005, n.p.).[8] In fact, on July 30, 2004, the UN Security Council found that the Janjaweed's campaign of murder, rapes, and forced displacement of ethnic minorities placed the lives of hundreds of thousands at risk, and imposed an embargo against arms sales to all "nongovernmental" organizations in Darfur, even though it was well known that the government backed the Janjaweed (U.N. Security Council 2004). On March 27, 2005, the Security Council expanded the arms embargo to the Government of Sudan, by which time about 300,000 had already died (Prunier 2008, 151–52; U.N. Security Council 2005). Despite the embargo, China continued to supply Sudan with fighter-bombers, tank factories, artillery, and automatic weapons, and the means to build tank factories. While the bombers, tanks and artillery were used by Government of Sudan troops in its attacks on Darfur, the automatic weapons were delivered to the Janjaweed (Amnesty Int'l 2007, Prunier 2008, 231; Small Arms Survey 2007, 5).

Finally, in post-2003 Iraq enormous massacres of Iraqi civilians were financed, organized, and supported politically by nationals of Saudi Arabia and other Gulf Arab States (Allawi 2007, 234–36, 302–3, 368; Boucek 2006). The US Treasury Department tracked Saudi financing to Sunni terror groups that had killed as many as 500 people at a time in Iraq and destroyed many cultural and religious sites, as well as other civilian targets essential to life in Iraq such as oil, electrical, and medical infrastructures, and concluded that Saudi Arabia was the top source of terrorist financing (Center for Systemic Peace 2009, 3–10; Meyer 2008). Between 2003 and July 2006, an estimated 600,000 excess violent deaths occurred in Iraq (Burnham et al. 2006, 2). The attackers were often unknown, but a third of attacks were by car bombs and other explosions, about half by gunfire, and one in eight by coalition air strikes (Burnham et al. 2006, 8–9). The death toll may have topped one million by 2008 (Opinion Research Bureau 2008).

Obstacles to Genocide Prevention through Limitations of Arms Traffic: Impunity for Crimes and Paralysis of International Institutions

Half-Hearted Efforts to Outlaw War and Crimes against Humanity

Inadequate penalties for the individuals and corporations who provide the means for dictators to massacre entire local populations have dimmed the prospect for restricting and shutting off the various aspects of the trade, including financing, transporting, and the weapons, themselves. The opportunity to punish the perpetrators of the Ottoman Christian genocide, along with the Germans (starting with the German emperor) who armed the Ottoman war machine, was allowed to slip away after World War I. Although the Ottoman wartime leaders were condemned to death *in absentia* for the Armenian and Assyrian massacres and deportations, they were spirited out of Turkey by Germans and then welcomed in Germany, and the German emperor enjoyed safe haven in the Netherlands where he schemed with Hermann Göring and praised Hitler's occupation of France before passing away quietly in 1941 (Cecil 1996, 32, 331, 337–52; Dadrian 1991, 552, 570; *New York Times* 1919). After World War II, although the Zyklon B case resulted in the conviction of one of the worst industrialist supporters of the Nazis, the Farben, Krupp, and Thyssen conspirators with Hitler were not consistently prosecuted, leading to cries of a historical "whitewash" (Kaufman 1948, 7). Even the Nazi Minister of the Economy (later the "War Economy"), who solicited millions of marks from the I.G. Farben Trust and others to propel the Nazis to their electoral victory in 1933, was acquitted of conspiracy to wage aggressive war and crimes against humanity (International Military Tribunal 1946). Alfried Krupp, an early Hitler supporter in the prewar period, then slave overlord and supplier of arms to the Nazis for world conquest, enjoyed an early release from custody after a few years, as well as restoration to his industrial empire (Ferencz 2002, 69–76). Japanese industrialists were similarly spared, along with the Japanese emperor, despite using slave labor and conspiring in massive crimes against humanity throughout East Asia (*Chicago Daily Tribune* 1947, 1–10).

The Genocide Convention and Its Evasion

Reservations to the Genocide Convention represent a further formidable challenge to efforts to enforce international law against complicity in, conspiracy to aid, or attempt to commit genocide.

Articles III and IX of the Genocide Convention establish the international responsibility of States for conspiracy or attempt to commit, or complicity in, genocide, and the power of the International Court of Justice (ICJ) to prevent such acts (Quigley, 2006, 56, 130–32, 236). The principal contributors[9] to the trade in arms to genocidal governments, however, did not accept Article IX of the Genocide Convention, relating to the prevention and remediation of genocide by the ICJ. The Soviet Union issued a reservation to Article IX in 1954, which it withdrew in 1989, but the United States attached a similar reservation when it ratified the Convention in 1988 and has never withdrawn it. The United States also utilized the reservation to dismiss a genocide claim by Yugoslavia before the ICJ during the Clinton administration (LeBlanc 1991, 2, 145–48, 201–14; Quigley 2006, 217–21). China ratified the Genocide Convention very late in the Cold War, in 1983, and similarly attached a reservation excluding the ICJ from exercising jurisdiction (Schindler and Toman 1988, 239–41).

Human Rights and International Law versus Security Cooperation and Realpolitik

The description of post–Cold War genocides above should make clear that arms embargoes are widely flouted even when mandated by the UN Security Council to prevent genocide or other mass killings. Domestic and international pressure to suspend arms exports to genocidal governments is often beat back by considerations of *realpolitik.*

In the United States, groups pushed President Richard Nixon to stop supporting the government of Nigerian dictator Yakubu Gowon, but his administration continued with a pro-Nigeria, anti-Ibo policy (Campbell 1987; Shalom 1992, 118–19).

Questioned before the US Congress in 1979 as to why the United States was supplying arms to the Indonesian regime of Suharto that was engaged in saturation bombing of civilian areas, causing widespread refugee flight and starvation that the Red Cross compared to the genocide in Khmer Rouge Cambodia, the Ford administration blamed inefficient native agricultural practices and praised Suharto for "moving the villages near much better land" (Hovey 1979, A3).

During the 1980s, a measure in the US Congress that was even entitled the "Prevention of Genocide Act," aiming at cutting off the flow of arms and money to Saddam Hussein's regime during the Anfal campaign in northern Iraq, which included the gassing of civilians, was defeated by the Reagan administration, then tilting toward Iraq as a means of weakening Iran (Wright 1990, 1).

Although military aid to genocidal dictators and the proliferation of weapons of mass destruction was often justified by considerations of Cold War advantage, the five permanent members of the UN Security Council (United States, Great Britain, Russia, China, and France) continued in these practices during the post–Cold War era. China, the main supplier of weapons to genocide-era Rwanda and Sudan since 2004, has opposed the condemnation of genocide in these countries by the UN Security Council (van den Herik 2005, 279).

What Are the Prospects of Restricting Arms Flows to Genocidal Regimes?

Secondary Liability for Genocide

The Rome Statute of the International Criminal Court establishes criminal liability for complicity in genocide, joint criminal enterprise, and conspiracy to commit genocide. This would seem to support indictments and convictions of arms suppliers who knew of and condoned genocidal campaigns, as in the Zyklon B case or the case of a Dutch national charged with aiding and abetting war crimes by supplying chemical weapons components to Iraq during the Anfal campaign (van der Wilt 2008, 557–59). In addition, judges in the United States, sitting on a court with federal appellate jurisdiction over New York State, among other places, applied the principles of the Zyklon B case to find corporations who supplied oil and revenue to the government of apartheid-era South Africa potentially liable to the victims of crimes against humanity in that country (United States Court of Appeals for the Second Circuit 2007, 258–60, 276, 290–94). These principles would seem to provide new hope for preventing the flow of arms to genocidal regimes.

Enforcement Problems

Arms dealers and other firms frequently use third countries as transit points for the flow of arms to regimes and movements suspected of engaging in mass killings. The arms traffic to Bosnia and Croatia, for example, was often routed through other destinations using misleading end-user certificates (Schmetzer 1995, 1). In order to plug all the holes in sanctions regimes, the United Nations would need to impose a common system of arms exports registration and verification (e.g., end user certificates) on arms-exporting countries, develop superior intelligence and interdiction capabilities, and coordinate multilateral efforts by member States to secure arms stockpiles and cut off dictatorships (Klare 1997, 62–63).

Unintended Consequences

One argument against arms embargoes is that they violate the Genocide Convention by leaving the victims of genocide defenseless under the pretext of creating formal equality between rebel groups and governments despite existing disparities in power and weaponry (Kopel, Gallant and Eisen 2006, 158). Critics of arms embargoes propose that potential victims of genocide be guaranteed their human right of self-defense against genocide by lifting UN arms embargoes (Kopel, Gallant and Eisen 2006, 158). The difficulty with this well-intentioned proposal is that it will not level inequalities in regard to the ability to *pay* for arms. For example, Rwanda's massive imports of machetes and small arms appear to have been financed in large part by diverted World Bank loans (Semelin 2009, 409). Likewise, in Sudan, the government budget doubled from about $5 billion in 2004 to $10 billion in 2008, fueled by oil exports of about 500,000 barrels per day and loans of about $8 billion from the International Monetary Fund and other sources between 2000 and 2008, meaning that in an arms race, Darfur's displaced people could never win (IMF 2008, 33–34).

Conclusion

Yet there is hope, as the lawless era of World War II and the Cold War slowly give way to efforts to contain the economic and political conflicts of a multipolar world. The Security Council has, to varying degrees of success, attempted to cut off arms exports to a few of the many countries that have experienced mass killings and other gross human rights violations since 1989. In other instances, as in Iraq and Sudan, permanent members of the Security Council have been complicit in the flow of weapons to dictators and criminal apparatuses of allied States (Amnesty International, 2008). Even so, the awareness is growing that international law criminalizes such behavior by States and arms dealers, and may guarantee civil compensation to victims and their families.

Notes

1. In the Congo, the Batwa and Bambuti peoples, known as Pygmies in the West, are facing extinction due to frequent violence, displacement from the forests they know how to survive in, and sexual assault. (See Adrien Sinafasi Makelo's "Garden Furniture for Europeans, *The New Internationalist*, April 1, 2008 http://www.newint.org/features/special/2008/04/01/congoart; Fergal Keane's "GPS Helps Pygmies Defend Forest," *BBC NEWS*, January 30, 2008, http://news.bbc.co.uk/1/hi/world/africa/7218078.stm; CTV's (CANADA) "Africa's Pygmies Facing a Terrible Future," April 8, 2007, http://www.ctv.ca/servlet/ArticleNews/story/CTVNews/20070422/pygmies_070422/20070422?hub=TopStories; Jeff Lule's "Population of Batwa People Reduces." *New Vision* (Uganda), December 14, 2008, http://www.newvision.co.ug/D/8/18/664591; Internal Displacement Monitoring Centre's "Batwa 'Pygmy' Population Has Been Displaced and Marginalized." August12, 2003, http://www.internaldisplacement.org/idmc/website/countries.nsf/(httpEnvelopes)/A9B47DC22230A0CC802570B8005A71E8?OpenDocument; and Refugees International's "Forgotten People: The Batwa 'Pygmy' of the Great Lakes Region of Africa," August 12, 2003, http://www.reliefweb.int/rw/rwb.nsf/AllDocsByUNID/a84e5cbac3ac8c2885256d800079aaba.
2. In Ethiopia, the communist dictator Mengistu Haile Mariam bombed ethnic Tigrayan villages and created one of the worst famines of the late twentieth century, in what numerous scholars regard as a genocidal campaign. (See: Jennifer Balint's "Law Responds to the Holocaust and Genocide: Redress and Perpetration," in *Encyclopedia of Genocide*, ed. Israel W. Charny (Santa Barbara, CA: ABC-CLIO, 1999), 389–94; Alex De Waal's *Famine Crimes: Politics and the Disaster Relief Industry in Africa* (Bloomington: Indiana University Press, 1997), 115; Edward Kissi and Eric Markusen, "Ethiopia, Genocide," in *Encyclopedia of Genocide*, 214; Edward Kissi, *Revolution and Genocide in Ethiopia and Cambodia* (Lexington, MA: Lexington Books, 2006); Stephanie Kleine-Ahlbrandt's "Ethiopia," in *Encyclopedia of Genocide and Crimes Against Humanity*, ed. Dinah Shelton, vol. 1 (Farmington Hills, MI: Thomson Gale, 2005), 164, 604; and Kristin Urbach's "Famine as a Human Rights Violation: The Case of Ethiopia and the Great Famine of the 1980s," *Interdisciplinary Journal of Human Rights* 1, no. 1 (2006): 27–42.)
3. In Iraq, the Ba'athist regime of Saddam Hussein massacred thousands of Kurds, Assyrians, and Yezidis during the late 1980s, destroyed thousands of villages belonging to these communities in the 1970s and 1980s, and deported thousands of members of these communities in the 1990s in order to replace them with Arabs. (See: "Iraq," *Human Rights Watch World Report*, New York, 1989. http://www.hrw.org/legacy/reports/1989/WR89/Iraq.htm; Kanan Makiya's *Republic of Fear* (Berkeley: University of California Press, 1989), 20–30; Middle East Watch, *Genocide in Iraq: The Anfal Campaign Against the Kurds* (New York: Human Rights Watch, 1993), 5–15, 62–68, 113–281, 312–17).

   Starting in 2003, al Qaeda and other terrorist organizations targeted Iraqi religious minorities in Iraq with mass-casualty bombings and threats to destroy the Christian, Yezidi, Mandaean, and pro-Western Muslim cultures in Iraq. An estimated one million excess deaths occurred between 2003 and 2007, due largely to shootings and bombings (See Gilbert Burnham et al.'s "Mortality after the 2003 Invasion of Iraq: A Cross-sectional Cluster Sample Survey," *The Lancet*, October 11, 2006, 1–8; Massimo Calabresi's "Is Iraq Headed for Genocide?" *Time Magazine*, November 29, 2006, http://www.time.com/time/world/article/0,8599,1564270,00.html; Ben Kiernan's *Blood and Soil: a World History of Genocide and Extermination from Sparta to Darfur* (New Haven, CT: Yale University Press, 2007), 598–605; Iraq Body Count's "Large Bombings Claim Ever More Lives," October 4, 2007, http://www.iraqbodycount.org/analysis/numbers/biggest-bombs; and Opinion Research Business's "More than 1,000,000 Iraqis Murdered," September 2007, http://www.opinion.co.uk/Newsroom_details.aspx?NewsId=78.)

4. In Tibet, China killed more than one million Buddhists and other Tibetans, and destroyed thousands of Tibetan Buddhist shrines and monasteries (See Samuel Totten and Paul Bartrop's "China, Genocide," in *Dictionary of Genocide*, ed. Samuel Totten and Paul R. Bartrop (Westport, CT: Greenwood Publishing Group), 69; and John *Heidenrich's How to Prevent Genocide: A Guide for Policymakers, Scholars, and the Public* (Westport, CT: Greenwood Publishing Group, 2001), 87–88; R. J. *Rummel's China's Bloody Century: Genocide and Mass Murder Since 1900* (New Brunswick, NJ: Transaction Publishers, 2007), 272–73; and Robert Thurman's "Statement on U.S. Policy Considerations on the 40th Anniversary of the Tibetan Uprising & the Dalai Lama's Flight into Exile." Hearing Before the U.S. House of Representatives, Committee on International Relations, 106th Cong., 1st sess., March 11, 1999, 10.)
5. More than one thousand Hazaras and other Shi'a Afghans may have been massacred by rampaging mujahideen in Kabul in 1992. The Taliban killed another 20,000 Hazaras during their assault on the Hazara areas of Bamiyan, Mazar-i-Sharif, and Kabul from 1994 to 2001. (See David Filipov's "Reconstruction: Hazaras Hold Key Role after Taliban Destruction," *Boston Globe*, February 14, 2002, http://www.afgha.com/?af=article&sid=12366; Christina Lamb's *The Sewing Circles of Herat: A Personal Journey Through Afghanistan* (London: HarperCollins, 2002), 20; and Ahmed Rashid's *Taliban* (New Haven, CT: Yale University Press, 2000), 58–76, 138.)
6. Some initiatives have aimed to block arms flows without declaring a genocide to be underway, while the UN Security Council has on at least two occasions referred to predicate acts under the Genocide Convention in issuing arms embargoes against the former Yugoslavia and Rwanda, and made a referral to an international commission of inquiry and eventually to the International Criminal Court with respect to the Darfur region of Sudan.
7. It was owed $146 billion in arms credits by 1993 (Erlanger 1993).
8. Those that Khartoum referred to as "mujahedeen" were known by their victims and the UN Security Council as Janjaweed.
9. Between 2002 and 2007, it was the United States (31%), Russia (25%), Germany 10%), France (9%), Britain (4%), and others (21%). Most of the arms exports from these countries were not delivered to countries engaged in genocide, due in part to various laws restricting exports to gross human-rights abusers.

References

Akçam, Taner. 2004. *From Empire to Republic: Turkish Nationalism and the Armenian Genocide.* London: Zed Books.

Amnesty International. 2007. *Sudan: Arms Continuing to Fuel Serious Human Rights Violations in Darfur.* May 8, http://www.amnesty.org/en/library/asset/AFR54/019/2007/en/c464853c-d396-11dd-a329-2f46302a8cc6/afr540192007en.html.

Amnesty International. 2007a. "Time Is Running Out to Protect the People of Darfur." AI Index No. AFR 54/016/2007. http://www.amnesty.org/en/library/info/AFR54/016/2007/en.

Aris, Ben, and Duncan Campbell. 2004. "How Bush's Grandfather Helped Hitler's Rise to Power." *The Guardian*, September 25, http://www.guardian.co.uk/world/2004/sep/25/usa.secondworldwar.

Arnold, Chloe. 2007. "Russia: Cobblers Face the Boot in Moscow." *Radio Free Europe/Radio Liberty*, October 14. http://www.rferl.org/content/article/1078944.html.

Associated Press. 2009. "Sudan Leader, UN Chief Face Off at Summit." *ABC News*, March 30. http://abcnews.go.com/International/wireStory?id=7205623.

Associated Press. 1993a. "Russia May Supply More Arms to Serbs." *Pittsburgh Post-Gazette*, March 1, 3.

Associated Press. 1993b. "Serbs Grieve for Victims of Massacre." *Chicago Tribune*, May 18, 4.

Associated Press. 1983. "Amnesty International Condemns Governments that Kill." *The Ledger (Florida)*, March 23, 9A.

Associated Press-Reuters. 1971. "U.S. Doubles Arms Aid to Indonesia." *The Age*, July 14, 4.

Bangura, Abdul Karim. 2006. "Multifaceted Ethnic Conflicts and Conflict Resolution in Nigeria." In *Perspectives on Contemporary Ethnic Conflict: Primal Violence or the Politics of Conviction?* ed. Santosh C. Saha, 173–96. Lanham, MD: Lexington Books.

BBC. 2004. "DR Congo Pygmies 'Exterminated.'" *BBC News*, July 6. http://news.bbc.co.uk/2/hi/africa/3869489.stm.

Becker, Jasper. 1997. *Hungry Ghosts: Mao's Secret Famine.* New York: Free Press.

Blum, William. 2003. *Killing Hope: US Military and CIA Interventions Since World War II.* 2nd ed. London: Zed Books.

Boucek, Christopher. 2006. "The Presence of Saudi Nationals in the Iraqi Insurgency." *Terrorism Monitor* 4, 8. http://www.jamestown.org/single/?no_cache=1&tx_ttnews%5Btt_news%5D=744.

Brackman, Roman. 2001. *The Secret File of Joseph Stalin.* London: Routledge.

Bridgman, Jon and Leslie J. Worley. 2009. "Genocide of the Hereros." In *Century of Genocide: Critical Essays and Eyewitness Accounts*, ed. Samuel Totten and William S. Parsons, 39–40. New York: Routledge.

Burnham, Gilbert et al. 2006. *The Human Cost of the War in Iraq: A Mortality Study, 2002-2006.* Baltimore, MD: Johns Hopkins University. http://web.mit.edu/humancostiraq.

Campbell, Colin. 1987. "Starvation Was the Policy." *The New York Times*, March 29. http://www.nytimes.com/1987/03/29/books/starvation-was-the-policy.html?pagewanted=all.

Cecil, Lamar. 1996. *Wilhelm II: Emperor and Exile, 1900-1941.* Durham: University of North Carolina Press.
Center for Systemic Peace. 2009. "High Casualty Terrorist Bombings (15 deaths): September 11, 1995 – March 10, 2009." http://www.systemicpeace.org/inscr/HCTBMar09.pdf.
Chicago Daily Tribune. 1947. "Turning Away from Nuernberg." *The Chicago Daily Tribune,* September 27, 1–10.
Conquest, Robert. 1991. *Stalin: The Breaker of Nations.* New York: Viking.
Cribb, Robert. 2009. "The Indonesian Massacres." In *Century of Genocide: Critical Essays and Eyewitness Accounts,* ed. Samuel Totten and William S. Parsons, 234–62. New York: Routledge.
Crowdy, Terry (2006). *The Enemy Within: A History of Espionage.* Oxford: Osprey Publishing.
Dadrian, Vahakn. 1994. "Documentation of the Armenian Genocide in German and Austrian Sources." In *The Widening Circle of Genocide; Genocide: A Critical Bibliographic Review,* ed. Israel W. Charny, 77–125. New Brunswick, NJ: Transaction Books.
Dallaire, Roméo, and Kishan Manocha. 2007. "The Major Powers and the Genocide in Rwanda." In *The Criminal Law of Genocide: International, Comparative, and Contextual Aspects,* ed. Ralph Henham and Paul Behrens, 61–74. Hampshire, England, UK: Ashgate.
Davies, Robert William, and S. G. Wheatcroft. 1994. *The Economic Transformation of the Soviet Union, 1913-1945.* New York: Cambridge University Press.
Democratic Republic of the Congo. 1999. *Case Concerning Armed Activities on the Territory of the Congo (Democratic Republic of the Congo v. Rwanda), Application Instituting Proceedings,* June 23. http://www.icj-cij.org/icjwww/idocket/icorw/icorwapplication/icorw_iapplication_19990623.pdf
Djilas, Aleksa. 1995. "Germany's Policy Towards the Disintegration of Yugoslavia," In Stephen *Can Europe Work? Germany and the Reconstruction of Postcommunist Societies,* ed. E. Hanson and Willfried Spohn, 151–67. Seattle: University of Washington Press.
Dunn, James. 2009. "Genocide in East Timor." In *Century of Genocide: Critical Essays and Eyewitness Accounts,* ed. Samuel Totten and William S. Parsons, 265–95. New York: Routledge.
Dunn, Walter Scott. 1995. *The Soviet Economy and the Red Army, 1930-1945.* Westport, CT: Greenwood Publishing Group.
Egeland, Jan. 2008. "Affluent Baltic Region Must Increase Its Assistance." *Baltic Rim Economies, Bimonthly Review,* February 29. http://www.tse.fi/FI/yksikot/erillislaitokset/pei/Documents/bre2008/BRE_1_2008.pdf.
Erlanger, Steven. 1993. "Moscow Insists It Must Sell the Instruments of War to Pay the Costs of Peace." *The New York Times,* February 3. http://www.nytimes.com/1993/02/03/world/moscow-insists-it-must-sell-the-instruments-of-war-to-pay-the-costs-of-peace.html.
Fauber, Fernand. 1957. "British Controls on Trade with Red China Eased in Break with Policy of U.S." *Toledo Blade,* May 31, 1.
Fear, Jeffrey R. 2005. *Organizing Control: August Thyssen and the Construction of German Corporate Management.* Cambridge, MA: Harvard University Press.

Fein, Helen. 1984. "Scenarios of Genocide: Models of Genocide and Critical Responses." In *Toward the Understanding and Prevention of Genocide*, ed. Israel Charny, 3–31. Boulder, CO: Westview Press.
Ferencz, Benjamin B. 2002. *Less than Slaves: Jewish Forced Labor and the Quest for Compensation.* Bloomington and Indianapolis: Indiana University Press.
Gewald, Jan-Bart. 2004. Imperial Germany and the Herero of Southern Africa: Genocide and the Quest for Recompense." In *Genocide, War Crimes, and the West: History and Complicity*, ed. Adam Jones, 59–77. London: Zed Books.
Gibbs, David N. 1991. *The Political Economy of Third World Intervention: Mines, Money, and U.S. Policy in the Congo Crisis*. Chicago, IL: University of Chicago Press.
Goshko, John M. 1991. "U.N. Imposes Arms Embargo on Yugoslavia." *The Washington Post*, September 26, A1 and A26.
Gunn, Geoffrey C. 1997. *East Timor and the United Nations: The Case for Intervention*. Patchogue, NY: Red Sea Press.
Hansard Parliamentary Debates. 1971. *Official Report, House of Lords*, July 12, col. 1056.
———. 1970. *Official Report, House of Lords*, July 16, col. 728.
Horowitz, Irving Louis. 2001. *Taking Lives: Genocide and State Power*. New Brunswick, NJ: Transaction Books.
Hovey, Graham. 1979. "House Panel Hears of Starvation in East Asian Area of East Timor." *The New York Times*, December 5, A3.
Human Rights Watch. 2005. *Darfur: Militia Leader Implicates Khartoum*. New York: Human Rights Watch. http://www.hrw.org/fr/news/2005/03/02/darfur-militia-leader-implicates-khartoum.
———. 1997. *Democratic Republic of the Congo: What Kabila Is Hiding, Civilian Killings and Impunity in Congo*. New York: Human Rights Watch.
———. 1994. *Arming Rwanda: The Arms Trade and Human Rights Abuses in the Rwandan War*. New York: Human Rights Watch. http://www/hrw/organ/reports/1994/01/01/arming-rwanda
International Court of Justice. 2007. *Case Concerning the Application of the Convention on the Prevention and Punishment of the Crime of Genocide (Bosnia and Herzegovina v. Serbia and Montenegro), Judgment of 26 February 2007.* 2007 I.C.J. 140. http://www.icj-cij.org/icjwww/idocket/ibhy/ibhyjudgment/ibhy_ijudgment_20070226_frame.htm.
International Monetary Fund. 2008. *Sudan: First Review of Performance Under the 2007-08 Staff-Monitored Program*. IMF Country Report No. 08/174, June. http://www.imf.org.
Jonas, Susanne. 2009. "Guatemala: Acts of Genocide and Scorched-Earth Counterinsurgency War." In *Century of Genocide: Critical Essays and Eyewitness Accounts. Third Edition*, ed. Samuel Totten and William S. Parsons, 376–411. New York: Routledge.
Kaufman, Joseph. 1948. "Krupp, Farben Cases Held No 'Whitewash'" *The New York Times*, August 1, 7.
Kiernan, Ben. 2007. *Blood and Soil: A World History of Genocide and Extermination from Sparta to Darfur*. New Haven, CT: Yale University Press.
———. 2004. *How Pol Pot Came to Power: Colonialism, Nationalism, and Communism in Cambodia, 1930-1975*. 2nd ed. New Haven, CT: Yale University Press.

Klare, Michael T. 1997. "The Subterranean Arms Trade: Black-Market Sales, Covert Arms, and Ethnic Warfare." In *Cascade of Arms: Managing Conventional Weapons Proliferation*, ed. Andrew J. Pierre, 43–74. Washington, DC: Brookings Institution Press.

Kopel, David B., Paul Gallant, and Joanne D. Eisen. 2006. "Is Resisting Genocide a Human Right?" *Notre Dame Law Review* 81, no. 4: 101–69.

LeBlanc Lawrence J. 1991. *The United States and the Genocide Convention*. Durham, NC: Duke University Press.

Leow, Claire, and Bernie Moestafa. 2008. "Suharto, Indonesian Dictator for 32 Years, Dies at 86 (Update 3)." *Bloomberg News*, January 27. http://www.bloomberg.com/apps/news?pid=20601087&sid=aDW_5EnP5Eb8&refer=home.

Lepsius, Johannes. 1919. *Deutschland und Armenien: Sammlung diplomatischer Aktenstücke.* Potsdam: Tempelverlag.

Levin, Itamar. 2001. *His Majesty's Enemies: Great Britain's War against Holocaust Victims and Survivors.* Westport, CT: Greenwood Publishing Group.

Levy, Adrian, and Catherine Scott-Clark. 2007. *Deception: Pakistan, the United States, and the Secret Trade in Nuclear Weapons.* New York: Walker.

Mace, James E. 2009. "Soviet Man-Made Famine in Ukraine." In *Century of Genocide: Critical Essays and Eyewitness Accounts*, ed. Samuel Totten and William S. Parsons, 3rd ed., 95–126. New York: Routledge.

MacKinnon, Elaine. 2005. "Stalin, Joseph." In *Encyclopedia of Genocide and Crimes Against Humanity*, ed. Dinah Shelton, 996–98, vol. 3. Farmington Hills, MI: Thomson Gale.

Mälksoo, Lauri. 2001. "Soviet Genocide? Communist Mass Deportations in the Baltic States and International Law." *Leiden Journal of International Law* 14, no. 4: 757–87.

Matosyan, Tigran. 2007. "Comparative Aspects of the Armenian and Jewish Cases of Genocide." In *The Armenian Genocide: Cultural and Ethical Legacies*, ed. Richard Hovannisian, 291–302. New Brunswick, NJ: Transaction Publishers.

McMurray, Jonathan S. 2001. *Distant Ties: Germany, the Ottoman Empire, and the Construction of the Baghdad Railway.* Westport, CT: Greenwood Publishing Group.

Meltzer, Bernard. 1995. "Telford Taylor Panel: Critical Perspectives on the Nuremberg Trials (Panel I of Symposium: 1945-1995: Critical Perspectives on the Nuremberg Trials and State Accountability)." *New York Law School Journal of Human Rights* 12, no. 1: 453–544.

Mennecke, Martin 2009. "Genocidal Violence in the Former Yugoslavia: Bosnia Herzegovina and Kosovo." In *A Century of Genocide: Critical Essays and Eyewitness Accounts*, ed. Samuel Totten and William S. Parsons, 3rd ed., 507–52. *New York: Routledge.*

Meyer, Josh. 2008. "Saudi Arabia Is Prime Source of Terror Funds, U.S. Says." *The Los Angeles Times*, April 2. http://articles.latimes.com/2008/apr/02/nation/na-terror2s.

Middle East Watch. 1993. *Genocide in Iraq: The Anfal Campaign against the Kurds*. Washington, DC: Middle East Watch.

Moran, Daniel. *Wars of National Liberation.* New York: HarperCollins.

Morris, Stephen J. 1999. *The Soviet-Chinese-Vietnamese Triangle in the 1970s: The View from Moscow.* Washington, DC: Cold War International History

Project, Paul H. Nitze School of Advanced International Studies, Johns Hopkins University, Working Paper No. 25.
Mousavi, Sayed. 1997. *The Hazaras of Afghanistan: An Historical, Cultural, Economic and Political Study.* New York: St. Martin's Press.
The New York Times. 1919. Turkey Condemns Its War Leaders: Court-Martial Gives Death Sentence to Enver Pasha, Tallat Bey, and Djemal Pasha. *The New York Times,* July 13. http://www.cilicia.com/armo10c-nyt19190713.html.
Nicholls, David. 2000. *Adolf Hitler: A Biographical Companion.* Santa Barbara, CA: ABC-CLIO.
Opinion Research Bureau. 2008. *More Than 1,000,000 Iraqis Murdered, ORB Report.* London: Opinion Research Bureau. http://www.opinion.co.uk/Newsroom_details.aspx?NewsId=78.
Otman, Waniss A. and Erling Karlberg. *The Libyan Economy: Economic Diversification and International Repositioning.* Dordrecht: Springer, 474 pp.
Penketh, Anne. 2004. "Extermination of the Pygmies." *The Independent,* July 7. http://www.globalpolicy.org/component/content/article/164-icc/28466.pdf.
Pomfret, John, and David B. Ottaway. 1996. "U.S. Allies Fed Pipeline of Covert Arms to Bosnia." *The Washington Post,* May 12. http://www.highbeam.com/doc/1P2-784643.html
Prunier, Gérard. 2008. *Darfur: A Twenty-First Century Genocide.* 3rd ed. Ithaca, NY: Cornell University Press.
———. 1998. *The Rwanda Crisis: History of a Genocide.* New York: Columbia University Press.
Quigley, John. 2006. *The Genocide Convention: An International Law Analysis.* London: Ashgate Publishing.
Radetsky, Peter. 2007. *The Soviet Image: A Hundred Years of Photographs from Inside the TASS Archives.* San Francisco, CA: Chronicle Books.
Rashid, Ahmed. 2002. *Taliban: Islam, Oil and the New Great Game in Central Asia.* New Haven, CT: Yale University Press.
Ray, Ellen. 2000. "U.S. Military and Corporate Recolonization of the Congo." *Covert Action Quarterly,* Spring/Summer. http://www.thirdworldtraveler.com/Africa/US_Recolonization_Congo.html.
Reuters. 1956. "Uprising in East Tibet Reported; Chinese Losses Termed Heavy; Reds Said to Raze Several Monasteries." *The New York Times,* June 30, 2.
Rohde, David, and Carlotta Gall. 2007. "US Sees Waste in Aid Given to Pakistan: Billions Went to Military." *The Boston Globe,* December 24. http://www.boston.com/news/world/ articles/2007/12/24/us_sees_waste_in_aid_given_to_pakistan/.
Rome Statute of the International Criminal Court. 1998. *U.N. Doc. A/CONF. 183/9.* July 17. http://www.un.org/icc.
Rummel, R. J. 1999. "Soviet Union, Genocide in." In *Encyclopedia of Genocide,* ed. Israel Charny, 520. Santa Barbara, CA: ABC-CLIO.
Rywkin, Michael. 1994. *Moscow's Lost Empire.* Armonk, NY: M.E. Sharpe.
Schindler, Dietrich, and Jiří Toman. 1988. *The Laws of Armed Conflicts.* 3rd ed. Leiden, The Netherlands and Boston, MA: Brill.
Schmetzer, Uli. 1995. "How West Let Croatia Sneak Arms." *Chicago Tribune,* August 20, 1.
Semelin, Jacques. 2009. *Purify and Destroy: The Political Uses of Massacre and Genocide.* New York: Columbia University Press.

Serbyn, Roman. 2005a. "Kulaks." In *Encyclopedia of Genocide and Crimes against Humanity*, vol. 2, ed. Dinah Shelton, 628–30. Farmington Hills, MI: Thomson Gale.

———. 2005b. "Ukraine (Famine)." In *Encyclopedia of Genocide and Crimes against Humanity*, vol. 3, ed. Dinah Shelton, 1055–961. Farmington Hills, MI: Thomson Gale.

Shalom, Stephen. 1992. *Imperial Alibis: Rationalizing U.S. Intervention after the Cold War.* Boston, MA: South End Press.

Simons, Geoffrey Leslie. 1996. *Iraq: From Sumer to Saddam.* New York: Palgrave Macmillan.

Small Arms Survey. 2007. *Arms, Oil, and Darfur.* July 7. http://64.233.169.104/search?q=cache:zcVjwucTnd8J:www.smallarmssurvey.org/ files/portal/spotlight/sudan/Sudan_pdf/SIB%25207%2520Arms.pdf.

Squassoni, Sharon. 2005. *Nuclear Threat Reduction Measures for India and Pakistan. Congressional Research Service Report No. RL31589.* http://digital.library.unt.edu/govdocs/crs/permalink/meta-crs-6185:1.

Stolfi, R. H. S. 1993. *Hitler's Panzers East: World War II Reinterpreted.* Norman: University of Oklahoma Press.

Surma, Khanim. 2000. "Refugees from Hakkiari." In *The Treatment of Armenians in the Ottoman Empire, 1915-1916*, ed. Ara Sarafian, Viscount James Bryce, and Arnold Toynbee, 206–10. London: Taderon Press.

Thomas Jr., Donald E. 2007. "The Holocaust." In *Encyclopedia of World War II: A Political, Social, and Military History, Volume 2*, ed. Spencer C. Tucker, n.p. Santa Barbara, CA: ABC-CLIO.

Totten, Samuel, and Paul R. Bartrop. 2008. *Dictionary of Genocide.* Westport, CT: Greenwood Publishing Group.

Totten, Samuel and William S. Parsons, eds. 2009. *Century of Genocide: Critical Essays and Eyewitness Accounts. Third Edition.* New York: Routledge.

Travis, Hannibal. 2006. "'Native Christians Massacred': The Ottoman Genocide of the Assyrians during World War I." *Genocide Studies & Prevention: An International Journal* 1, no. 3: 327–71.

Tyler, Thomas. 1819. *A Law Glossary of the Latin, Greek, Norman, French, and Other Languages.* London: W. Clarke and Sons

U.N. Secretary-General. 1999. *The Fall of Srebrenica.* U.N. Doc. A/54/549, November 15. http://www.un.org/peace/srebrenica.pdf.

U.N. Security Council. 2005. Resolution 1591 on the Situation in Sudan. March 27. http://en.wikisource.org/wiki/United_Nations_Security_Council_Resolution_1591.

U.N. Security Council. 2004. *Resolution 1556 on the Situation in Sudan.* July 30. http://en.wikisource.org/wiki/United_Nations_Security_Council_Resolution_1556.

U.N. Security Council. 1994. *Resolution 918 on the Situation in Rwanda.* May 17. http://www.undemocracy.com/S-RES-918(1994).

U.N. Security Council. 1991. *Resolution 713 on the Situation in Yugoslavia.* September 25. http://www.undemocracy.com/S-RES-713(1991).

United States Court of Appeals for the Second Circuit. 2007. *Khulumani v. Barclay National Bank Ltd., 504 F.3d 254. Per curiam.* http://caselaw.findlaw.com/data2/circs/2nd/052141p.pdf.

Van den Herik, Larissa. 2005. *The Contribution of the Rwanda Tribunal to the Development of International Law.* Leiden, The Netherlands and Boston, MA: Martinus Nijhoff Publishers.

Van der Wilt, Harmen. 2008. "Genocide v. War Crimes in the *Van Anraat* Appeal." *Journal of International Criminal Justice* 6, no. 3: 557–67.

Warsh, Daniel. 2008. *The Silent Partner: How the Ford Motor Company Became an Arsenal of Nazism.* Philadelphia: University of Pennsylvania History Department. http://repository.upenn.edu/hist honors/17.

Wiebes, Cees. 2003. *Intelligence and the War in Bosnia, 1992-1995.* Munster: LIT Verlag.

Wright, Robin. 1990. "White House Ignored Iraq Rights Abuses for Years." *The Los Angeles Times*, August 30, 1.

The Zyklon B Case. 1946. (Trial of Bruno Tesch and Two Others). *Law Reports of Trials of War Criminals* 1, 93. Hamburg: British Military Court.

Annotated Bibliography

Amnesty International. *Blood at the Crossroads: Making the Case for a Global Arms Trade Treaty.* New York: Amnesty International, 2008, 136 pp.

Part 7 describes how in post-2003 Iraq, the "easy availability of small arms and lack of accountability has contributed to sectarian killings by armed groups, as well as torture and other ill-treatment and sectarian extra-judicial executions by Iraqi government forces and the continuing arbitrary detention of thousands of suspects by Iraqi soldiers backed by US armed forces since 2003." It names, as one cause of the "massive proliferation and misuse of weapons in Iraq," the "failure of invading US-led forces to . . . prevent human rights abuses, control stockpiles, disarm Iraqi soldiers when the armed forces were disbanded, and safeguard against arms surpluses and imports getting into the hands of militias working as death squads or insurgents." It estimates that over one million additional small arms such as automatic rifles would arrive in Iraq from 2003 to 2009, despite the presence of fifteen million assault rifles and other weapons in the country prior to 2003. China, Russia, the United Kingdom, and the United States are the key suppliers of these weapons. This report describes in Part 10 how Chinese suppliers have armed Sudan's *Janjaweed* militia, including one group of over 20,000 men in control of southern Darfur, with a "considerable arsenal" of assault rifles, machine guns, sniper rifles, mortars, rocket launchers, and antiaircraft guns. China and the Russian Federation supplied the Sudan Air Force with advanced fighter-bombers and attack helicopters used to indiscriminately massacre civilians on the ground.

Amnesty International, International Action Network on Small Arms, and Oxfam. *Guns or Growth? Assessing the Impact of Arms Sales on Sustainable Development.* New York: Amnesty International, International Action Network on Small Arms, and Oxfam, 2004, 100 pp.

This report outlines the need for and terms of a proposed Arms Trade Treaty or Framework Convention on International Arms Transfers that would codify customary and treaty-based international humanitarian law to the effect that States must not become complicit in or otherwise participate in the internationally wrongful acts of another State. Specifically, under the proposed codification, States would be obligated not to transfer arms to another State where they know the arms will be used for genocide, crimes against humanity, torture, aggression, serious violations of human rights, or diverted for use in such acts.

Anthony, Ian. "Patterns and Trends in Arms Transfers and Prospective Developments." In *Cascade of Arms: Managing Conventional Weapons Proliferation*, edited by Andrew J. Pierre, 13–42. Washington, DC: Brookings Institution Press, 1994. 486 pp. .

This chapter estimates the Soviet share of global deliveries of major conventional weapons at 39 percent of the total in 1989, compared to 28 percent for the United States. By 1995, with the end of the Cold War, dissolution and economic collapse of the Soviet Union, and proliferation of new nations and rebel movements, the US share had risen to 42 percent, compared to 18 percent for Russia. The author also documents efforts within France and the United Kingdom to conceal the nature and scale of their weapons exports to Iraq during the rule of Saddam Hussein, who was prosecuted for genocide after the fall of his regime and his subsequent capture in 2003.

Bahala, Father Jean-Bosco, Diocesan Media Director, Archdiocese of Bukavu, Democratic Republic of the Congo. "Suffering and Despair: Humanitarian Crisis in the Congo." Prepared Statement to U.S. House of Representatives, Committee on International Relations, Subcommittee on International Operations and Human Rights. May 17, 2001, 23–52. http://commdocs.house.gov/committees/intlrel/hfa72638.000/hfa72638_0f.htm.

In his congressional testimony, Father Bahala describes US aid to Rwanda and Uganda, and the US' backing of militias in the Congo blamed for massacres and related deaths from hunger, disease, and displacement, resulting in an estimated 2.5 million excess deaths from 1998 through 2001. He states that the United States "provided Rwandan authorities with firm political support throughout its military campaign in Congo," and "that the American army has been training and assisting the Rwandan Patriotic Army (RPA) on Congolese territory."

Connor, Steve. "Outcry over Creation of New Smallpox Virus." *The Independent (U.K.)*, January 22, 2005. http://www.religiousconsultation.org/ . . . /outcry_over_creation_of_new_smallpox_virus.htm.

This article exposes plans by the World Health Organization (WHO) to genetically engineer a new version of the smallpox virus to aid in preparation for potential bioterrorism. Professor Donald Henderson, of the Centre for Biosecurity at the University of Pittsburgh, warned that the manipulation of the smallpox virus was a dangerous and unnecessary enterprise. The article implies that Russian and US laboratories remain in possession of the smallpox virus, states that Australian researchers created a vaccine-resistant strain of the mousepox virus through genetic engineering, and notes that smallpox killed 300 million people before being eradicated in 1977.

Cushman Jr., John. "Inside the Arsenals." *The New York Times*, September 16, 1990, SM52.

This article identifies Austria and South Africa as the source of Iraq's advanced high-explosive and/or mine-scattering howitzers, as well as smaller artillery, "which massacred waves of Iranian troops in the 1980s." It also describes its purchase of $600 million in howitzers from France.

Gesellschaft für Bedrohte Völker [Society for Threatened Peoples]. *Germany and Genocide in Iraq: Persecution and Extermination of Kurds and Assyrian Christians—1968-1990. Threatened Peoples, Report No. 4.* Gottingen, Germany: Gesellschaft für Bedrohte Völker, 1991, 52 pp.

This report indicates that German firms sold chemical weapons components and facilities to Iraq, which were then used to gas Kurdish and Assyrian civilians in a campaign of genocide.

Human Rights Watch Arms Project. *Arming Rwanda: The Arms Trade and Human Rights Abuses in the Rwandan War.* New York: Human Rights Watch, 1994, 39 pp.

This important report describes how Rwanda was flooded with weapons in the period leading up to the Rwandan genocide, with large numbers of heavily armed rebels invading Rwandan territory from bases in Uganda, acting in collaboration with the Ugandan military. Massacres of Hutu and other Rwandan civilians may have contributed to a climate of fear and repression stoked by the Rwandan government and its propaganda. Automatic rifles and heavy weapons manufactured by Belgian, French, German, Chinese, Egyptian, and South African entities supplied the Rwandan government, which received training and diplomatic support from the United States through 1992.

Human Rights Watch and Federation Internationale des Droits de l'Homme. *What Kabila Is Hiding: Civilian Killings and Impunity in Congo.* New York: Human Rights Watch, 1997, 60 pp.

This report describes how the Alliance of Democratic Forces for the Liberation of Congo-Zaire (ADFL), with support from Rwanda, Uganda, and other neighboring States, "carried out massive killings of civilian refugees and other violations of basic principles of international humanitarian law during attacks on refugee camps in the former Zaire (now the Democratic Republic of Congo) that began in late 1996, and in the ensuing seven months as war spread across the country." The ADFL, which included Rwandan and Ugandan soldiers, "slaughtered the refugees," and "untold thousands died of hunger or disease because ADFL and Zairian authorities denied humanitarian agencies permission to enter their zones to deliver assistance. . . ."

Hutchens, Kristen. "International Law in the American Courts—*Khulumani v. Barclay National Bank, Ltd.*: The Decision Heard 'Round the Corporate World." *German Law Journal* 9, no. 5 (2008): 639–82.

This article describes the decision of the United States Court of Appeals for the Second Circuit, a court one level below the US Supreme Court in the federal judiciary, that multinational corporations may be liable to suits by victims for compensation in US courts for aiding and abetting crimes against humanity abroad. The author notes that the wrongfulness of complicity in genocide, torture, and other crimes is well established by international treaties and court decisions.

International Court of Justice. *Application of the Convention on the Prevention and Punishment of the Crime of Genocide (Bosnia and Herzegovina v. Serbia and Montenegro), Further Requests for Indication of Provisional Measures, General List No. 91 of September 13, 1993.* 1993 I.C.J. 325.

In this case, Bosnia and Herzegovina sought provisional measures before the World Court to stop the Federal Republic of Yugoslavia (Serbia and Montenegro) from committing acts of genocide or "providing, directly or indirectly, any type of support—including training, weapons, arms, ammunition, supplies, assistance, finances, direction or any other form of support—to any nation, group, organization, movement, militia or individual engaged in or planning to engage in military or paramilitary activities in or against the People, State and Government of Bosnia and Herzegovina." Yugoslavia requested, for its part, that the court direct the Bosnian authorities "to allow, without delay, the Serb residents to leave safely Tuzla, Zenica, Sarajevo and other places in the 'Republic of Bosnia and Herzegovina,' where . . . they may suffer the same fate as the Serbs in eastern Bosnia, which was the site of the killing and massacres of a few thousand Serb civilians." The court reiterated its previous order that Yugoslavia take "all measures within its power to prevent commission of the crime of genocide," and "in particular ensure that any military, paramilitary or irregular armed units which may be directed or supported by it, as well as any organizations and persons which may be subject to its control, direction or influence, do not commit any acts of genocide, conspiracy to commit genocide, . . . or of complicity in genocide, whether directed against the Muslim population of Bosnia and Herzegovina or against any other national, ethnical, racial or religious group." It did not act on Yugoslavia's request.

International Court of Justice. Application of the Convention on the Prevention and Punishment of the Crime of Genocide (*Bosnia-Herzegovina v. Yugoslavia*), Judgment of July 11, 1996 on Preliminary Objections. 1996 ICJ 595.

In an important ruling in 1996, the World Court stated that Article IX of the Genocide Convention confers jurisdiction upon the court to prevent acts of genocide by adjudicating interstate disputes regarding the interpretation and application of the Convention. Bosnia and Herzegovina cited sources from the US State Department who stated that Yugoslavia was supporting and equipping Bosnian Serb army units and irregulars, and that General Ratko Mladic was appointed by Yugoslavia to command troops formerly with the Yugoslav army, who retained their Yugoslav equipment. Two judges argued that the court lacked jurisdiction, while two others argued that the Convention creates individual, not state, responsibility.

International Court of Justice. *Case Concerning Armed Activities on the Territory of the Congo (Democratic Republic of the Congo v. Uganda), Judgment of December 19, 2005*, 2005 ICJ LEXIS 1. cij.org/docket/index.php?p1=3&p2=3&k=51&case=116&code=co&p3=4.

In this opinion, the World Court found that Uganda violated the laws of war and of belligerent occupation in the DRC, destroyed homes and villages, breached human rights and international humanitarian law, and must pay compensation to the DRC for the damage. The court further declared that under customary international law, every State has the duty to refrain from tolerating or supporting any armed activities directed toward committing acts of rebellion or terrorism against another State, and not to permit any organized activities within its territory directed toward fomenting or maintaining civil war or internal strife in another State. The Congo alleged that Uganda had armed rebel groups operating in Congolese territory, including members of the Congolese Rally for Democracy and the Congo Liberation Movement, which had committed massacres of civilians. The court found that the Congo had provided persuasive evidence that Uganda had, among other things, incited ethnic conflicts between Congolese of Ugandan and non-Ugandan national origin, and had contributed to 10,000 deaths and the displacement of some 50,000 Congolese.

International Court of Justice. *Application of the Convention on the Prevention and Punishment of the Crime of Genocide (Bosnia and Herzegovina v. Serbia and Montenegro), Judgment.* 2007 I.C.J. 140, February 26, 2007, http://www.icj-cij.org/icjwww/idocket/ibhy/ibhyjudgment/ibhy judgment_20070226_frame.htm.

In this case, the court applied the principles of state responsibility for internationally wrongful acts that it articulated in the Nicaraguan contras case to conclude that although the political, military, and logistical relationships between Yugoslavia and its army and the Republika Srpska and its army had been close for a period of years, the Republika Srpska and its army were nevertheless autonomous entities, independent from Yugoslavia. Dissenting Judge Al-Khasawneh, by contrast, credited evidence that the Republika Srpska officials perceived themselves to be working for Yugoslavia, and that Yugoslavia claimed at least one of the Republika Srpska units as its own. Bosnia and Herzegovina argued that Yugoslavia (or Serbia and Montenegro) violated the Genocide Convention by controlling, being complicit with, and/or aiding and abetting acts of genocide within Bosnia and Herzegovina. The army of Yugoslavia, the allegation was, left its equipment and many of its members of Bosnian Serb origin behind when it withdrew in May 1992. Yugoslavia also allegedly financed part of Republika Srpska's budget.

The Netherlands Institute for War Documentation. *Srebrenica—A 'Safe' Area: Reconstruction, Background, Consequences and Analyses of the Fall of a Safe Area.* Amsterdam: The Netherlands Institute for War Documentation, 2002, 3 vols. 3,500 pp. n.p.

In a summary for the press, The Netherlands Institute for War Documentation describes the efforts and failure of a Dutch Air Battalion, under UN command, to protect the Srebrenica safe haven in mid-1990s. The Dutch encountered a difficult situation created by the militarization of the safe haven, a Bosnian Serb Army blockade of the area, and army of Bosnia and Herzegovina attacks on the Serbs, which were followed by Bosnian forces taking cover with the Dutch, placing the latter at risk. As a contributing factor to the genocide of male Bosnian Muslims carried out by Bosnian Serb forces in the area starting in July, the report identified UN rules of engagement restricting the Dutch troops to self-defense, the killing of a Dutch soldier by a Bosnian Muslim, the absence of requested armed force or NATO air support in response, and the "background support ('logistical patronage') [of] the Americans [who] were very closely involved in secret supplies of arms to the Croats and Bosnian Muslims (which were illicit in light of the arms embargo in force at the time)." The Bosnian Serbs sought to use attacks from within the Srebrenica enclave by armed Muslims as an excuse to occupy it. The report states that these arms shipments "took the form of covert operations conducted through third party countries such as Iran and Turkey: the so-called 'Croatian Pipeline' and the 'Black Flights' to Tuzla," which resulted from calls within the US Congress, US media, and the Arab world for support for the Muslims. Appendix II describes violations of the UN arms embargo between 1992 and 1995 by Germany, Iran, Turkey, Saudi Arabia, and the United States.

Small Arms Survey. *Frequently Asked Questions.* Geneva, Switzerland: Small Arms Survey, 2009, 6 pp. http://web.archive.org/web/20090415231202/http://www.smallarmssurvey.org/files/sas/home/FAQ.html.

The Small Arms Survey estimates that small arms and light weapons, including military-issue and commercial firearms, account for between 60 and 90 percent of direct conflict deaths, presumably not including hunger and disease. It says that the top exporters of small arms and light weapons in 2003 were, in descending order, the Russian Federation, the United States, Italy, Germany, Brazil, and China. They each exported more than $100 million worth of such weapons.

Van der Wilt, Hermann. "Genocide v. War Crimes in the Van Anratt Appeal." *Journal of International Criminal Justice* 6, no. 3 (2007): 557–67.

This report of a case decided by the Hague Court of Appeal against a Dutch businessman involved the charge that the defendant violated Article 1 of the Genocide Convention Implementation Act (the Netherlands) by selling at least 1,100 tons of a compound useful in the production of chemical weapons to Iraq between 1985 and 1988, despite reports of the use of such weapons on Iranian troops and "parts of the Kurdish population suspected of collaborating with Iran." There was evidence that thousands of civilians died from the weapons, and that others suffered permanent and severe illnesses. The defendant was acquitted of genocide due to the absence of evidence of intent, but convicted of complicity in war crimes against Iran by being an accessory, and complicity in war crimes against the Iraqi civilian population as a method of systematic terror. The victims' claims for compensation from the defendant were dismissed as being overly complex.

9

Do Criminal Trials Prevent Genocide? A Critical Analysis

Maureen S. Hiebert

Introduction

In the quest to prevent the "old scourge" of genocide, scholars, policymakers, and activists have looked to a number of different strategies to give real force and effect to the oft-repeated expression "never again." International criminal law, and criminal trials specifically, became part of this discussion beginning with the International Military Tribunals (Nuremberg and Tokyo Trials) in the aftermath of World War II and after a decade-long hiatus during the Cold War with the creation of The International Criminal Tribunal for the former Yugoslavia (ICTY) and The International Criminal Tribunal for Rwanda (ICTR), various domestic and hybrid tribunals (e.g., Extraordinary Chambers in the Courts of Cambodia, the Special Chambers for Sierra Leone), and even more recently the permanent International Criminal Court (ICC). Criminal trials for atrocity crimes like genocide are believed by some observers to prevent genocide through deterrence. Trials are said to deter further acts of genocide by unequivocally demonstrating that top civilian and military commanders who initiate and order genocidal policies and subordinates who execute them are engaging in actions that the international community considers morally wrong and that they and anyone else who perpetrates such outrages will be punished for their crimes. The thinking behind this argument is that the costs of committing genocide will be calculated by the perpetrators to be too high, thus successfully dissuading would-be *genocidaires* from adopting genocidal policies in the first place. Critics of this position argue that there is little evidence to suggest that deterrence works due to a lack of capacity by international actors to effectively support trials and/or the failure of genocidal perpetrators to act according to the expectations of deterrence theory.

This chapter critically analyzes both of these positions. The first section of the analysis deals with the case for deterrence, beginning with a brief discussion of what sociologists call "general deterrence," followed by an analysis of the prodeterrence position. The next section presents the case against trials leading to effective genocide prevention through deterrence by examining prima facie empirical evidence that seems to suggest that trials do not lead to deterrence, that the international community lacks the capacity to effectively support the trial process, that problems with legal procedures and sentencing undermine the requirements of deterrence, and that perpetrators either behave irrationally or behave according to a skewed rationality such that the threat of punishment at trial is neutralized. The chapter concludes with a brief assessment of what critical challenges face the role of trials in wider genocide prevention strategies and the probability of progress toward effective genocide prevention through deterrence as a result of criminal trials.

The Case for Deterrence through Trials

Deterrence is one of the many functions of law in society. Certain kinds of law, particularly criminal law and to a lesser extent tort law, exist to set out what kinds of activities society has determined are unacceptable and, are therefore, prohibited. By prohibiting certain activities and attaching sanctions to them if they are committed, society sends a signal to specific offenders and members of society alike that there will be unambiguously negative consequences for breaking the law. As such, the law and the legal process of assessing individual responsibility and the meting out of punishment through criminal trials serve as a mechanism of social control. There are two forms of deterrence. The first is specific deterrence, which is designed to prevent those who have already offended from committing crimes in the future by punishing the individual through some sort of sanction (e.g., fines, imprisonment, hard labor, death). In the case of those who receive prison sentences, the offender may also be removed from society not just as a form of punishment but in order to protect society from the individual. This process is called incapacitation. The second form of deterrence, general deterrence, is intended to prevent all members of society from committing criminal acts by demonstrating that there will be serious costs for breaking the law. Both forms of deterrence are believed to rest on a Benthamite utilitarian model that individuals will naturally try to conduct their lives in such a way as to maximize pleasure and avoid pain. More recent rational choice formulations of this thesis suggest that with respect to the law and deterrence individuals will follow the law, and are deterred from committing crimes, when the cost of breaking a law is considered to be so high that it outweighs the benefit of breaking a law (Miller, Schreck, and Tewksbury 2006).

Unlike in the domestic context, the debate over whether trials can lead to effective genocide prevention through deterrence does not deal with the specific deterrence of those already judged responsible for human rights abuses. This is so largely because the individuals who commit atrocity crimes more often than not have no prior criminal record and commit their offenses under extraordinary conditions that are unlikely to be repeated locally (see, e.g., *Prosecutor v Dragljub Kunarac, Radomir Kovac, and Zoran Vukovic*, IT-96-23/I, Trial Chamber Judgement, February 22, 2001, at para. 840). Instead, the debate over whether trials can lead to genocide prevention focuses on the issue of general deterrence, namely whether the demonstration effect of the trial and punishment of individuals who have already committed atrocity crimes will prevent other leaders from perpetrating genocide somewhere else sometime in the future.

Those who argue that trials do help prevent future atrocities essentially accept the rational choice argument that trials act as a credible deterrent by making real the threat of punishment for committing genocide and other human rights abuses. In a passionate and eloquent article ("Beyond Impunity: Can International Criminal Justice Prevent Future Atrocities?") evaluating the positive deterrent effect of the International Criminal Tribunals for Yugoslavia and Rwanda (ICTY and ICTR) on genocide prevention, legal scholar and former ICTY legal advisor Payam Akhavan (2001) forcefully sets out the claims of the prodeterrence position. Akhavan gives several internally consistent, logically coherent, but ultimately speculative verging on normative arguments about why trials should lead to deterrence. Key to Akhavan's (2001) position is the notion that ending impunity through trials will give rise to a "culture" of criminal accountability in international relations, which in turn will send the message that committing atrocity crimes is politically unacceptable (8–9). Atrocities will also come to be seen as politically unpalatable because trials attach a stigma to criminal conduct (Akhavan 2001, 7). In making this argument, the author explicitly adopts the logic of the rational choice deterrence model, arguing that the deterrent effect of trials works on elite decision makers because of their "conscious and unconscious responses to punishment," specifically that "threats of punishment can increase the cost of a policy that is criminal under international law" (Akhavan 2001, 7). Taking an approach consistent with liberal internationalist international relations theory, Akhavan suggests that even though would-be perpetrators may be motivated by the perceived short-term gains of repressing or eliminating certain groups, these gains may be overshadowed by the long-term costs of "downfall and humiliation" in an increasingly globalized world in which leaders are unlikely to risk their international prestige (Akhavan 2001, 12). Akhavan (2001) acknowledges that the demonstration effect of trials, in general, and the ICTY/R, in particular, on the rational calculations and subsequent behaviors of decision makers is "subtle" since trials deter future atrocities by "publicly vindicating human rights norms" and "morally ostracizing criminal leaders," which sets a "powerful moral example to transform behaviour" (Akhavan 2001, 10). In other words, the deterrent effect of trials indirectly alters elite behavior by changing the norms that underpin elites' strategic calculations.

Turning to what he identifies as a "constructivists possibility," Akhavan reinforces the indirect effect of trials by offering that trials may prevent the "aberrant contexts" within which genocide and other atrocities take place by "instilling 'unconscious inhibitions against crime' or 'a condition of habitual lawfulness in society'" (Johannes Andenaes 1966, quoted in Akhavan 2001, 12–13). Lastly, Akhavan (2001) argues that, from a pragmatic point of view, trials remove and discredit abusive elites from power, thus taking out of the political equation key actors who often oppose the very peace deals that are necessary for ending atrocities in the short run (7).

While Akhavan's arguments have an internally consistent logic to them, most of the arguments he provides are speculative (they are frequently preceded by the word "may") and are not supported with empirical evidence that proves how elite decision makers are influenced by trials. The evidence that he does use to illustrate the impact of the ICTY/R deal more with peacemaking in the Balkans and Rwanda, not deterrence of future atrocities in other locations. Similarly, when he does provide evidence of deterrence, he refers to the arrest, prosecution, and incarceration of specific individuals and the effect this has had on the immediate situation. As such, Akhavan's evidence deals with either the specific deterrence of individual perpetrators, not general deterrence, or the effects of incapacitation, which is also a separate process from general deterrence. To be fair, we should not be too critical of Akhavan and other supporters of prevention through deterrence on the issue of proving whether deterrence through trials works or not given the methodological difficulties associated with proving definitively why something *did not* happen. Critics of deterrence theory have, however, challenged the underlying logic of the prodeterrence position.

The Case against Effective Deterrence through Trials

Criminologists and sociolegal scholars have spent decades testing whether the threat of punishment deters crime at the domestic level. Their research results suggest that the potential for effective deterrence is mixed at best. Sociologist William Chambliss' seminal research in the late 1960s showed that deterrence is more likely to be effective against individuals who commit what Chambliss called "instrumental" offenses committed for economic or material gain, which typically involve a high degree of prior planning such as robbery, burglary, or auto theft. Conversely, deterrence is less effective for "expressive" violent offenses, including homicide and assault, which are committed for emotional reasons and are spontaneous rather than planned. Since instrumental crimes involve prior planning, Chambliss argued that individuals were more likely to be deterred by the threat of punishment from committing these sorts of crimes by virtue of the fact that the would-be perpetrator has time to weigh the costs and benefits of his or her actions. Expressive crimes, on the other hand, are less deterrable because of the lack of prior planning and the emotionally driven nature of the crime.

On this score alone, Chambliss' research does not provide a clear guide for assessing whether deterrence will work against would-be *genocidaires* since genocide is, by definition, a carefully planned and systematic crime but one that is hugely violent and seemingly driven by powerful emotions.[1] However, Chambliss argued further that deterrence works best on individuals who exhibit a low level of commitment to criminal behavior and less effectively on those who are highly committed to criminal activity such as "professional criminals" (highly skilled burglars, gang members, or organized criminals) and addicts. The latter group "places great importance on their criminal behaviour and thus are less likely to be deterred by the threat of legal sanctions" (Barkan 2009, 139). Chambliss also contended that perpetrators who commit expressive violent crimes are less deterrable because of their strong emotional commitment to the perpetration of their crimes even though such crimes do not usually involve prior planning. Given the planned, violent, and emotionally or ideologically driven nature of genocide, elite perpetrators (if not low-level perpetrators) fit squarely into the category of committed hard-to-deter criminals who both plan their crimes and are emotionally committed to perpetrating them.

More recent research goes beyond Chambliss' approach to call the value of both rational choice and deterrence theory into question. Contrary to Cambliss' thesis that instrumental criminals are more easily deterred, research shows that these kinds of offenders, even if they know they may face legal sanctions for their actions, calculate that they will not get caught because they carefully plan their crimes, or they simply give little thought to their chances of being apprehended (Tunnell 2006; Walker 2006; Wilson and Abrahamse 1992; Wright et al. 2004).

Other research into the efficacy of deterrence deals with two specific aspects of the criminal justice system that are hypothesized to lead to greater deterrence: the certainty and severity of punishment. The former refers to the likelihood of being arrested (calculated by the number of arrests for a given kind of crime divided by the number of offenses for that type of crime), while the latter refers to the harshness of sentencing at trial. Early research in the 1960s found what appeared to be a positive relationship between the certainty of arrest and low crime rates, and a weaker, but still positive relationship between the severity of punishment and low crime rates (Gibbs 1968, 515–30; Tittle 1969, 409–23). But more recent investigations suggest that the relationship between certainty, severity, and deterrence may be more complicated and ultimately driven by the capacity of the justice system to control crime. The causal relationship between certainty and severity of punishment and low crime rates may in fact actually be reversed in that neighborhoods with low crime rates may produce greater certainty of arrest because local police forces are not overburdened and understaffed and are thus available to detect criminal behavior. Meanwhile, areas with high crime rates have fewer police resources available on the streets relative to the number of actual and potential perpetrators. The imbalance between perpetrators and law enforcement produces fewer arrests while at the same time jails and prisons may be overcrowded to such a degree that penalties handed down for wrongdoing may be reduced jail time or sanctions other than prison sentences (Barkan 2009, 143. See also Decker and Kohfeld 1985, 437–50; Nagin 1978; Pontell and Henry 1984). The limited capacity of the domestic criminal justice system to punish crime with certainty is striking. Steven Barkan calculates that in the previous decade only eight out of ten serious crimes ended in arrest in the United States, and that of these, only four out of one hundred were prosecuted, with only one out of one hundred resulting in incarceration. Barkan (2009) concludes that "in the United States, serious street crime is thus such a low-risk event (in terms of arrest and punishment) for offenders that it would be surprising if law did have a strong deterrent effect" (142).

The sobering empirical evidence concerning the lack of efficacy of deterrence drawn principally from advanced industrial democracies with highly developed policing systems, court procedures, and penal institutions does not bode well for the prospects of deterrence in what is now only a nascent criminal justice system in the international sphere. A quick glance at the frequency with which genocide and other atrocity crimes have been committed since the IMT following World War II seems to suggest on the face of it that trials do not act as a deterrent to future atrocities. Barbara Harff has calculated that from 1955 to the early 2000s there were fully thirty-six cases of genocide and politically motivated mass killing (Harff 2003, 67–68). To be sure, we do not know how many additional atrocities might have been committed without the demonstration effect of the IMT at Nuremberg and Tokyo but the fact that so many cases have occurred suggests that the influence of the IMT, the ICTY and the ICTR, and various domestic trials has, at the very most, been modest in terms of deterrence. Indeed, we can see that the creation of the ICTY in 1993, which was in part specifically created to stop the atrocities being committed in the Balkans in the early 1990s, failed to prevent some of the worst atrocities of the war, including the seige of Sarajevo and the genocide targeting Muslim men in Srebrenica in 1995, and certainly did not have a wider deterrent effect on the Hutu Power regime in Rwanda in 1994. Similarly, the example of the ICTR has not apparently dissuaded the Sudanese leadership from perpetrating what some call genocide in Darfur.

Why is this the case? One explanation is that the international community lacks sufficient enforcement capabilities. Although the international community has developed an increasingly robust set of laws and procedures for trying individuals accused of atrocity crimes, it still lacks the means to enforce indictments against those wanted by international tribunals and courts. Chapter VI of the UN Charter mandates UN peacekeeping forces and Chapter VII mandates collective security and "peace enforcement" forces, both of which are only constituted on an ad hoc case-by-case basis while regional security organizations such as NATO and the African Union operate across only limited territorial boundaries (although NATO's operations in Afghanistan expanded the reach of NATO forces beyond Europe). Despite the fact that UN forces and regional security organizations can and have been deployed to enforce indictments for the ICTY and the ICTR and the new ICC, these forces can only operate with a UN mandate on the territory of another state if the host state consents to the presence of an international force, something genocidal and abusive regimes are unlikely to do. Even when UN and regional forces are allowed to operate in countries where individuals are under indictment for war crimes, international forces may not receive the cooperation they need or they may be so over-stretched by the many facets of what are often highly complicated missions that they are unable to free up resources to execute arrest warrants. NATO's experience in Bosnia and the UN/AU tenure in Sudan are cases in point.

Failing a UN mandate, international forces can only enforce arrest warrants by forcibly violating the sovereignty of a state. There are no examples of this having happened although nation-states have sent their forces clandestinely into other states to apprehend wanted persons as in the case of the Israeli abduction of Adolf Eichmann in Argentina and the US extraction of General Manuel Noriega from Panama. Given the lack of enthusiasm with which the international community has acted to save lives when genocide and other atrocities are actively being committed, it seems unlikely that a new zeal will be found for transgressing the principle of state sovereignty, not to mention risking lives and resources in far-flung places, to arrest the very people the international community was too timid to stop in the first place. The alternative is to rely on national security and police forces. This strategy is mostly likely to work in states where atrocities have not actually been committed but to which indictees have fled. It is least likely to work where it is potentially needed most: in states where the regime itself is the perpetrator and continues in power after the killing has ended.

The overall lack of enforcement capability delays (as in the cases of Radovan Karadzic and Radko Mladic) or does not lead to (as in the case of Omar Al-Bashir) the arrest of indicted war criminals, thus reducing the certainty of arrest and possible punishment. To paraphrase Barkan (2009), the lack of certainty of arrest for atrocity crimes makes the perpetration of such outrages a "low-risk event." This is particularly true in genocide where the perpetrators are legion and the courts, domestic or international, cannot possibly try all those responsible for the perpetration of the crime.

Another explanation for why trials may not lead to genocide prevention through general deterrence is the nature of the trials themselves. The question here is, does the manner in which trials are conducted and the kinds of sentences that are meted out produce general deterrence? Again, critics of deterrence through trials argue no. In the first instance, international and, in many places, national, trials for atrocity crimes have been and continue to be based on a Western legal model that emphasizes individual criminal responsibility and that proceed according to established procedures of *habeas corpus*, the presumption of innocence, and due process. From Nuremberg onward, the drive to employ established Western legal procedures to affix criminal liability to individuals through trials has been motivated by the dual goals of enhancing the rule of law,[2] and diverting blame for atrocities away from whole groups in order to stop continuous cycles of vengeance aimed at the many by the many, to justice aimed at a few specific individuals (Ball 1999). These are laudable goals that quite possibly have been realized in certain circumstances such as the former Yugoslavia. But the fixation on process and the accountability of the individual may also inadvertently undermine the effectiveness of deterrence given the collective nature of the crimes involved.

Criticism of the adoption of Western legal procedures to try what one critic calls "extraordinary international crimes" rests on the wholesale adoption of legal liberalism with its liberal focus on the individual to determine criminal liability at trial (Drumbl 2007). While not a problem in the domestic context and the trying of ordinary crimes, the focus on individual responsibility is problematic at the international level when prosecuting those responsible for what are essentially collective crimes in which large numbers of people, from elite decision makers, to midlevel commanders and civilian officials, to low-level killers, are all involved in a coordinated project of mass destruction. Mark Drumbl (2007) argues that ordinary criminal law is based on the understanding of criminal activity as "deviant" acts committed by individuals. Atrocity crimes, on the other hand, are communal acts that are committed under extraordinary circumstances in which individuals lack the personal autonomy that underpins liberal legal assumptions of criminal liability (8). Moreover, individual criminal acts under such circumstances are likely not to be seen as deviant by either the perpetrator or by others on the ground (save the victims of course) since they are motivated by gratification (the desire to belong to violent groups that provide "comfort and solidarity") and/or self-preservation (Drumbl 2007, 171–72).

While we can question Drumbl's assertion that we should not try to affix individual responsibility for crimes that involve many actors, it is important to note that if perpetrators feel that they are acting collectively and that their actions are perceived to be in accord with an altered societal norm, the threat of punishment at trial is likely to be ineffective. Similarly the lack of legal mechanisms for assessing bystander liability leaves bystander populations unaccountable and, therefore, undeterred from allowing genocide to unfold through their passive acceptance, or at the very least, lack of resistance, to genocidal policies (Drumbl 2007, 122). The additional lack of accomplice liability that goes beyond direct perpetrators and accomplices with a significant level of knowledge of the crime to other individuals, states, and organizations that indirectly support the perpetration of genocide and other atrocities (Clapham 2003) also hampers deterrence.

Next, there is the issue of sentencing as a deterrent. Rational deterrence theory argues that the severity and consistency of sentencing both have a positive effect on deterrence, that is, the more severe the punishment and consistent the sentencing practices across similar cases, the more actors will be deterred from criminal behavior. Research done in the United States suggests, however, that crime rates have not declined since the mid-1990s in states with strict "three strikes" sentencing policies (Austin et al. 1999; Kovandzic, Sloan, and Vieraitis 2004), nor has the death penalty reduced homicide rates in US states with the death penalty to a greater degree than states that do not impose capital punishment (Levitt and Miles 2006, 147–64).

There is little reason to think that the severity of punishment handed down to perpetrators of atrocity crimes would have any different effect internationally. As for consistency, critics of the ICTY and ICTR have argued that the tribunals are myopically focused on the legal procedures of the trial phase of the process while leaving sentencing as an after thought. The statutes for both the ICTY and the ICTR say little by way of specifics in terms of sentencing, thus leaving trial and appellate judges wide latitude to hand out sentences. While the tribunals have generally adhered to the principle that the more serious crimes are to be punished more severely and that those who are most responsible are to receive more severe sanctions than those who bear less responsibility (Meernik and King 2003), there have been a few notable high-profile cases in which sentencing practices have been inconsistent, particularly when charge and plea bargaining in exchange for guilty pleas and testimony against other witnesses have been involved (Drumbl 2009, 120; Overly 2003, 8–12).

Finally, there is the issue of perpetrator rationality and whether actors who contemplate committing genocide are susceptible to the threat of punishment at trial. As noted above, rational deterrence theory rests on the assumption that perpetrators or, rather, would-be perpetrators of crime are rational and that as such they will not commit crimes if the cost of doing so is calculated to outweigh the benefits of committing a crime. Scholars such as Martha Minow (1990), however, argue that "individuals who commit atrocities on the scale of genocide are unlikely to behave as 'rational actors' deterred by the risk of punishment" (50). The alleged lack of perpetrator rationality is either implied from the outrageous nature of the crime itself—a crime so abhorrent its perpetrators exhibit an "evil that exceeds the bounds of instrumental rationality that seeks no objective beyond itself" such that "calculations about the likelihood of future punishment do not enter the picture" (Koskenniemi 2002, 1245–48)—or is attributed to an equally irrational extremist ideology or extraordinary conditions. Drumbl (2009), for example, is skeptical that "genocidal fanatics" who construct "industrialized . . . well-oiled machineries of death make cost-benefit analyses prior to beginning work" (171), while Federic Megret (2002) contends that "it beggars belief to suggest that the average crazed nationalist purifier or abused child soldier . . . will be deterred by the prospect of facing trial" (203). Added to the irrationality argument is the idea that the perpetrators of genocide evince an altered morality in which extermination is not only "normal" (i.e., not deviant) but is the highest expression of the good (Koskenniemi 2002, 1245).

Even if we assume that genocidal decision makers are rational actors who engage in cost–benefit analyses, deterrence through trials may still not work. Genocide, although evil and seemingly irrational, is, as Helen Fein suggests, a "rational choice"—a "goal-oriented act [that] is rationally instrumental" to elite perpetrators' ends (Fein 1979, 7–8).[3]

Genocide is a rational choice not because of the ideas or perceptions upon which it is based, but because of the decision-making process that leads to its perpetration. But to understand why elites make the choice to commit genocide, and why the way in which this choice is framed may immunize elite actors against the threat of punishment, we need to inquire into how elite decision makers frame their preferences and the "problems" they believe need solving.

Lebow and Stein (1989) argue in a different context that because rational deterrence theory does not inquire into how leaders form their preferences in the first place, the theory incorrectly assumes that preferences and choice options are only exogenously given. They argue that if we want to know how preferences are formed, and, therefore, under what circumstances deterrence is likely to work (i.e., when the costs of performing an action are calculated to outweigh the benefits of not doing it), we must look at how actors define and construct the problem to be decided (Lebow and Stein 1989, 214). For Lebow and Stein (1989) this construction includes perceptions of the domestic political context and not just calculations of possible responses by external actors (in our case, the threat of trial and punishment).

Following Lebow and Stein (1989) we can further argue that the construction of problems also involves perceptions of group identity and the meaning of group interaction in society. If we want to understand how it is that elites come to choose genocide as a policy option and in turn why they are likely not deterred by the threat of trials, we need to concentrate on how genocidal elites construct the identities of their victims. Precisely how elites construct the identities of groups in society determines whether genocide or some other form of repression or violence becomes the policy of the state and whether the threat of trials is perceived to be greater or lesser than the threat believed to be posed by the victim group. When elite decision makers come to conceptualize the victim group as a powerful and dangerous "enemy within," whose overwhelming power is believed to be derived from their physical existence, then the threat of trials is overwhelmed by the perception of the victim group as an even greater existential threat that must be destroyed. In genocide the victims are constructed by the perpetrators as (i) outside or foreign to the political community, (ii) an almost superhumanly powerful dangerous "enemy within" whose continued existence threatens the very survival of the political community, and (iii) as subhuman who, from a moral and psychological point of view, can be easily exterminated (Hiebert 2008).

The threat of trials is unlikely to trump this powerful conception of the victim group for three reasons. First, once elite decision makers come to adopt these three conceptions of the victim group the perpetrators are operating in a fundamentally altered and perverted moral universe. By their moral standards the perpetrators believe that they are acting morally by adopting genocidal policies designed to protect the political community not just from nonmembers but nonhumans who pose a fundamental mortal threat to the community's very survival. Second, because political elites do not, in their view, confront a powerless group of men, women, and children, but an overwhelmingly powerful adversary whose power is perceived to rest with the members' continued physical existence, and not power capabilities that can be removed without killing the victims, genocide becomes the only "rational" policy option. Third, once elites come to see their victims as the one true threat from a strategic point of view against which all other threats, internal and external, pale, it then becomes a logical strategic choice to ignore the threat of trials and punishment in favor of fighting the "real" enemy that poses an existential mortal threat to the very future of the state and society.

Critical Challenges to the Field

In light of the very real barriers that exist to effective genocide prevention through criminal trials, the question is not so much how to make trials more effective in terms of prevention, but to acknowledge that trials do not play a central role in genocide prevention. As in domestic law the role of criminal trials for atrocity crimes is to assess moral blameworthiness by establishing both the harm (*actus reus*) and the fault elements (*mens rea*) of the crime and to assign a specific punishment to those found guilty of wrongdoing. As such, trials are judicial processes that are concerned with the adjudication of allegations of international criminal activity and the meting out of justice after an atrocity crime has been committed. For scholars and practitioners of international criminal law and genocide prevention, the task is to recognize that we cannot rely on ad hoc tribunals, domestic trials, or the ICC to function as an iron-clad deterrent to future atrocities. The task of genocide prevention lies elsewhere with other actors, institutions, and processes, many of which are reviewed in this volume. To do otherwise is to put our faith in a process that we would *like* to be effective but which in reality is not. Part of figuring out how to prevent genocide is to critically assess all possible strategies and to disregard those that are likely to fail.

Similarly, states, intergovernmental organizations, nongovernmental organizations, and other actors should not substitute ex post trials of those who have already committed genocide and other atrocities for the heavy lifting of implementing strategies that can prevent genocide or interrupt the killing if it has already begun. Trials, in other words, are not a substitute for long-term early prevention strategies or short-term interventions to stop genocidal violence. The international community must not abdicate its responsibilities for genocide prevention to tribunals and courts and instead needs to assume a central role in genocide prevention while leaving international criminal law and trials to assess criminal responsibility for those who commit such terrible crimes.

Another challenge for analysts is to carefully fashion an analytical jurisprudential foundation for assessing collective accountability without assigning the same level of moral blameworthiness reserved for specific perpetrators to whole national, ethnic, religious, racial, political, or other groups. This issue is important as Drumbl notes, because genocide is not a crime committed solely by discreet individuals. Genocide cannot succeed without the acquiescence of bystander populations, yet there are no mechanisms for acknowledging the liability of those who do not engage in the killing themselves but nonetheless allow it to happen by facilitating acts of omission or commission.

Real Probabilities of Progress in the Field

The probability that analysts will find a strong theoretical or empirical foundation to show that trials can lead to genocide prevention through general deterrence is low. As we have seen, decades of criminological and sociolegal research into the lack of connection between criminal law and deterrence at the domestic level is unlikely to be refuted when it comes to the perpetration of atrocity crimes like genocide. There is no reason to believe that perpetrators of atrocity crimes will be any more swayed by the threat of being caught, or being punished at trial, or forced to bear the stigma of being publicly judged a murderer than perpetrators of ordinary crimes. In fact, the commitment with which elite-level perpetrators plan their crimes, their emotional attachment to executing their crimes, and the way in which they conceptualize their victims as mortal threats that trump all other threats, would seem to suggest that *genocidaires* are the least likely perpetrators to be deterred by the demonstration effect of the law and trials.

While trials may not lead to deterrence, this does not mean that we can stop thinking about ways to ensure that those who perpetrate atrocity crimes are brought to justice. To ensure that justice is done, serious thought and action needs to be put into how to boost the enforcement capabilities of the international community so that warrants can be executed in a timely fashion. Doing so will ensure that punishment will be swift and certain for those who commit the worst of the worst crimes. To be sure, the changes needed to enhance enforcement are far reaching, are likely to prove to be extremely difficult to effect, and may, therefore, constitute theoretical rather than realistic possibilities. These possibilities include: the creation of a standing UN force that could be used to execute arrest warrants; fostering a greater willingness by existing UN and regional security forces to serve warrants; and the robust transition of the Responsibility to Protect (R2P) doctrine from a morally attractive doctrine that states like to embrace rhetorically to an operational doctrine that states, intergovernmental organizations, security organizations, militaries, and so on, employ to ensure that killing ceases and that those who are responsible are quickly brought to justice.

Scholars, policymakers, and activists must also continue to construct the analytical and philosophical foundations for what some scholars have identified as an emerging anti-genocide norm. Partly a product of the accretion of successful genocide trials, the status of genocide as illegal in treaty and customary international law, and as a principle of *jus cogens* (a fundamental principle of international law that cannot be violated under any circumstances), this anti-genocide norm is becoming and should become a centerpiece of genocide prevention. Although this norm is unlikely to restrain leaders and followers bent on extermination for the reasons discussed above, it can, and should, serve as a foundation for the R2P doctrine. The anti-genocide norm, reinforced through trials, can act as a forceful reminder to the international community of its obligation to prevent genocide through long-term prevention strategies and to intervene diplomatically, economically, and even militarily if need be to stop genocide once it has begun. The real targets of trials with respect to bolstering an anti-genocide norm are actors who do not intend to commit such acts but who have a responsibility to prevent and stop such acts.

Conclusion

On the face of it, criminal trials for atrocity crimes would seem to be an important piece of the genocide prevention puzzle. Putting perpetrators on public trial either domestically or internationally, adjudicating their guilt or innocence through recognized fair and impartial legal procedures, and punishing those found guilty with lengthy prison sentences would appear to send a strong signal to others thinking of perpetrating genocide to think again. But no matter how much we would like this scenario to be the case, it likely is not. Empirical evidence at both the international and domestic levels seriously undermine the rational deterrence thesis that trials lead to genocide prevention through general deterrence. If we are serious about genocide prevention we must look elsewhere rather than counting on trials to serve a function they do not perform or at the very least do not seem to perform well. Trials and legal institutions like the ICC are not a panacea, they cannot both judge wrongdoing and prevent it and they cannot relieve the international community of its responsibility to fashion and implement workable prevention strategies. Trials perform a valuable function—the meting out of justice and punishment in the aftermath of atrocity. That trials do not prevent genocide is not a failure but an admission that trials and the law can only do so much: to adjudicate disputes, to assess criminal liability, to prescribe punishments that fit the crime, to write a version of the history of a particular case of genocide or other atrocity crime, and to provide some sort of justice if not solace to the victims. These are sufficiently weighty tasks for trials and the international criminal justice system to bear.

Notes

1. For the role fear plays in motivating genocidal violence see: Daniel Chirot and Clark McCauley, *Why Not Kill Them All? The Logic and Prevention of Mass Murder* (Princeton, NJ: Princeton University Press, 2006), 20–44.
2. See Telford Taylor's *Anatomy of the Nuremberg Trials* (Boston, MA: Little, Brown, 1992, 36–42) regarding Henry Stimson's view that an international tribunal would not only serve to outlaw the use of force as a foreign policy tool but also that trials would help bring the rule of law to Germany. See, also, Resolution for the International Criminal Tribunal for the Former Yugoslavia, United Nations Security Council Resolution 1503, Adopted on August 28, 2003, S/RES/1503; Resolution for the Special Court of Sierra Leone, United Nations Security Council Resolution 1315, adopted on August 14, 2000, S/RES/1313; Resolution for the Extraordinary Chambers of

Cambodia, United Nations General Assembly Resolution, GA/52/135 and GA 57/228B, adopted on February 27, 1998, A/RES/52/135.

3. For other scholars who understand genocide as a rational choice made by elites, see *Genocide: The Psychology of Mass Murder* by Peter du Preez (London: Boyars/Bowerdean, 1994), 3; and "State, Power, and Genocidal Intent: On the Uses of Genocide in the Twentieth Century" by Roger Smith, in *Studies in Comparative Genocide*, ed. Levon Chorbajian and George Shirinian (New York: St. Martin's Press, 1999), 3–14.

References

Akhavan, Payam. 2001. "Beyond Impunity: Can International Criminal Justice Prevent Future Atrocities?" *The American Journal of International Law* 95, no. 7: 8–9.

Austin, James; John Clark, Patricia Hardyman, and D. Alan Henry. 1999. *Three Strikes and You're Out: The Implementation and Impact of Strike Laws.* Washington, DC: National Institute of Justice, U.S. Department of Justice.

Ball, Howard. 1999. *Prosecuting War Crimes and Genocide: The Twentieth-Century Experience.* Lawrence: University of Kansas.

Barkan, Steven E. 2009. *Law and Society: An Introduction.* Upper Saddle River, NJ: Pearson Prentice Hall.

Clapham, Andrew. 2003. "Issues of Complexity, Complicity, and Complementarity: From the Nuremberg Trials to the Dawn of the New International Criminal Court." In *From Nuremberg to The Hague: The Future of International Criminal Justice*, ed. Philippe Sands, 50–60. New York: Cambridge University Press.

Drumbl, Mark A. 2007. *Atrocity, Punishment, and International Law.* New York: Cambridge University Press.

Gibbs, Jack P. 1968. "Crime, Punishment, and Deterrence." *Southwestern Social Sciences Quarterly* 48: 515–30.

Harff, Barbara. 2003. "No Lessons Learned from the Holocaust?: Assessing Risks of Genocide and Political Mass Murder Since 1955." *American Political Science Review* 97, no. 1: 67–68.

Hiebert, Maureen. 2008. "The Three 'Switches' of Identity Construction in Genocide: The Nazi Solution and the Cambodian Killing Fields." *Genocide Studies and Prevention* 3, no. 1: 5–32.

Koskenniemi, Martti. 2002. "Between Impunity and Show Trials." *Max Planck Yearbook of United Nations Law* 6, no. 1. Reprinted in *International Human Rights in Context*, ed. Henry J. Steiner, Philip Alston, and Ryan Goodman, 1245–48. New York: Oxford University Press, 2008.

Kovandzic, Tomislav V., John J. Sloan, and Lynn M. Vieraitis. 2004. "'Striking Out' at Crime Reduction Policy: The Impact of 'Three Strikes' Laws on Crime Rates in U.S. Cities." *Justice Quarterly* 21, no. 2: 207–39.

Lebow, Richard Ned, and Janice Gross Stein. 1989. "Rational Deterrence Theory: I Think Therefore I Deter." *World Politics* 41, no. 2: 214.

Levitt, Steven D., and Thomas J. Miles. 2006. "Economic Contributions to the Understanding of Crimes." *Annual Review of Law and Social Science* 2:147–64.

Meernik, James, and Kimi King. 2003. "The Sentencing Determinants of the International Criminal Tribunal for the Former Yugoslavia: An Empirical and Doctrinal Analysis." *Leiden Journal of International Law* 16, no. 4: 717–50.

Megret, Frederic. 2002. "Three Dangers for the International Criminal Court: A Critical Look at a Consensual Project." *Finnish Yearbook of International Law* 12: 203.

Miller, Mitchell J., Christopher J. Schreck, and Richard Tewksbury. 2006. *Criminological Theory: A Brief Introduction.* Boston, MA: Allyn and Bacon.

Minow, Martha. 1990. *Between Vengeance and Forgiveness: Facing History after Genocide and Mass Violence.* Boston, MA: Beacon Press Books.

Overly, Richard. 2003. "The Nuremberg Trials: International Law in the Making." In *From Nuremberg to The Hague: The Future of International Criminal Justice,* ed. Philippe Sands, 8–12. New York: Cambridge University Press.

Prosecutor v Dragljub Kunarac, Radomir Kovac, and Zoran Vukovic, IT-96-23/I, Trial Chamber Judgement, February 22, 2001, at para. 840.

Tittle, Charles R. 1969. "Crime Rates and Legal Sanctions." *Social Problems* 16: 409–23.

Tunnell, Kenneth D. 2006. *Living Off Crime.* Lanham, MD: Rowman & Littlefield.

Walker, Samuel. 2006. *Sense and Nonsense about Crime and Drugs: A Policy Guide.* 6th ed. Belmont, CA: Wadsworth Publishing.

Wilson, James Q., and Allan Abrahamse. 1992. "Does Crime Pay?" *Justice Quarterly* 9, no. 3: 359–77.

Wright, Bradley R. E., Avshalom Caspik, Terrie E. Moffitt, and Ray Paternoster. 2004. "Does the Perceived Risk of Punishment Deter Criminally Prone Individuals? Rational Choice, Self-Control, and Crimes." *Journal of Research in Crime and Delinquency* 41, no. 2: 180–213.

Annotated Bibliography

Akhavan, Payam. "Beyond Impunity: Can International Criminal Justice Prevent Future Atrocities?" *American Journal of International Law* 95, no. 7 (2001): 7–31.

A passionate defense of the prodeterrence position, Akhavan's article argues that trials will lead to both deterrence of future atrocities and enhance peace processes in postconflict situations. By implicitly adopting a rational deterrence model, Akhavan contends that trials will end impunity by raising the costs of pursuing policies, which the international community has criminalized. Trials will not only hold those who have already committed atrocities accountable, they will deter others by signaling that atrocity crimes are politically unacceptable. Trials will directly alter the calculations, and thus behavior, of would-be perpetrators through their "conscious and unconscious responses to punishment," specifically that they will suffer both legal sanctions for perpetrating legally prohibited actions and the stigma of being labeled a murderer. Trials will also lead to genocide and atrocity prevention, in Akhavan's view, by creating and reinforcing an anti-genocide, pro-human rights norm that has the capacity to transform behavior in general.

As noted in the essay in this chapter, Akhavan's argument, while forcefully argued and appealing on a normative and emotional level, is not substantiated by the empirical evidence he uses to prove his case. He concentrates primarily on the effect trials have had on the peace process in the Balkans, particularly the removal of problematic elites who had stymied efforts to end the conflict until their indictment (or subsequent movement underground) or arrest. This, however, is a different process than deterrence as it deals with the incapacitation of specific individuals either from positions of power in the state or from society, which ends their ability to continue to perpetrate atrocities or to obstruct the peace process. At best, Akhavan is talking about the specific deterrence of individuals who have already committed atrocities, not the general deterrence of would-be *genocidaires* elsewhere. Absent the kind of empirical evidence needed to show that trials really do deter elites thinking of committing atrocity crimes, Akhavan's argument stands as an example of the hope that trials will deter genocide, rather than proof that they actually do.

Clapham, Andrew. "Issues of Complexity, Complicity, and Complementarity: From the Nuremberg Trials to the Dawn of the New International Criminal Court." In *From Nuremberg to The Hague: The Future of International Criminal Justice*, edited by Philippe Sands, 30–67. New York: Cambridge University Press, 2003.

In this chapter, Clapham, drawing on Schabas, explores the principle of accomplice liability and the effect this might have on deterring atrocities were it to be operationalized at the International Criminal Court (ICC). He argues that the principle of accomplice liability could help deter atrocities by serving notice that not only will principal perpetrators be held legally accountable at the ICC but that all who aid and abet atrocity crimes from bystanders on the ground to the international community at large will be held accountable for their actions and inactions. With respect to the ICC, Clapham optimistically notes, irrespective of the nonexistence of accomplice liability, that the "real story of the new Court may actually be the crimes which never take place" since the existence of the ICC "serves to put us all on notice that we all have responsibilities not only towards those we see around us but also those who suffer due to our actions, our inactions, and our silence" (67).

Drumbl, Mark A. *Atrocity, Punishment, and International Law*. New York: Cambridge University Press, 2007, 318 pp.

A relatively slim but comprehensive volume that points out in unequivocal terms the paucity of analytical jurisprudence underpinning one of the cornerstones of international criminal justice: punishment (i.e., sentencing) for those found guilty of what the author calls "extraordinary crimes." Drumbl criticizes international criminal tribunals and courts, as well as some international legal scholars and practitioners, for their seemingly unquestioning transposition of the domestic criminal court model for the adjudication of ordinary violent criminal offenses to the national and international stage for the trying of atrocity crimes. In the first chapters of the book, Drumbl questions the utility of the use of "legal liberalism" to adjudicate crimes that are committed by large numbers of people in a context in which the crimes committed (genocide, war crimes, crimes against humanity) are unlikely to be seen as deviant acts by the perpetrators or society at large. Here, Drumbl also criticizes the lack of available legal means to adjudicate the responsibility of bystander populations for the perpetration of atrocities. In subsequent sections of the book, Drumbl engages in a detailed qualitative analysis of sentencing practices at the International Criminal Tribunal for the former Yugoslavia (ICTY) and the International Criminal Tribunal for Rwanda (ICTR) and national and local legal institutions in postconflict societies such as Rwanda and the former Yugoslavia. Based largely on an analysis of statutory requirements for punishment as well as the legal reasoning provided in judgments for sentencing, Drumbl argues that criminal trials for extraordinary crimes have become overly focused on the trial process itself while leaving sentencing, and, more importantly, the legal principles that underpin sentencing, as an afterthought. As result, Drumbl suggests that sentencing is inconsistent and incoherent. As for prevention, Drumbl rejects that rational deterrence model, arguing that perpetrators of atrocity crimes are not likely to be deterred by the example of trials because those who commit such crimes are fundamentally irrational actors.

Lebow, Richard Ned, and Stein Janice Gross. "Rational Deterrence Theory: I think Therefore I deter." *World Politics* 41, no. 2 (1989): 208–24.

A classic in the military deterrence literature, Lebow and Stein forcefully challenge the assumptions of both classical military deterrence theory and rational choice theory. By looking at the beginning of a number of conventional military conflicts in the twentieth century, Lebow and Stein challenge a number of assumptions found in what they call rational deterrence theory, namely that elite decision makers will always rationally calculate costs correctly, that elites will be dissuaded from using force even when they calculate costs correctly, and that elite actors' calculations are only driven by exogenous factors rather than domestic political considerations. Lebow and Stein suggest that if we really want to know how and why elite decision makers make the choices they do, we need to take a more constructivist approach by looking specifically at how decision makers frame the threats that confront them and the influence of domestic political considerations on this process. The authors' observations are relevant to attempts to understand whether atrocity crimes can be deterred through the trials as they warn us that political elites do not always engage in simple cost/benefit analyses based only on an actor's correct calculation of utility. Rather, elite decision making, including whether to engage in domestic acts of violence like genocide or not in the face of the example of trials for human rights abuses, is likely a complex process based on international and domestic influences and the manner in which elite actors construct the "problems" or threats that they face.

Mayerfeld, Jamie. "Who Shall Be Judge? The United States, The International Criminal Court, and The Global Enforcement of Human Rights." *Human Rights Quarterly* 25 (2003): 93–129.

Although mostly focused on the relationship between the United States and the ICC, Mayerfeld suggests that the ICC can play a role in deterring future atrocities. More specifically, Mayerfeld contends that "the ICC is intended, above all, to block the exemption from punishment that genocide, war crimes, and crimes against humanity may otherwise be destined to enjoy. It seeks thereby to prevent their adoption as policy in the first place" (98). For Mayerfeld, the obligation to deter atrocities constitutes the core rationale for punishing human rights violations. This obligation rests on a conception of rights, specifically the right to physical integrity backed up by a credible threat, presumably in the case of trials through the loss of personal liberty. The ICC can, therefore, result in both effective deterrence and the restoration of human rights. While coming down mostly on the prodeterrence rational choice side of the equation, Mayerfeld acknowledges that "tyrants" who commit atrocities may not stop for fear of punishment, but he continues that the fear of punishment may also give tyrants "a reason to cut their losses by halting or reducing the violation of human rights." As such, trials remain for Mayerfeld "a useful deterrent to the initiation of violations of other potential tyrants" (102). The author does not cite any empirical evidence to support his claims.

Meernik, James. "Victor's Justice or the Law? Judging and Punishing at the International Criminal Tribunal for the former Yugoslavia." *Journal of Conflict Resolution* 47, no. 2 (2003): 140–61.

In this article Meernik confronts the criticism that the ICTY is not a tribunal that employs fair and impartial legal criteria but rather a forum for "victor's justice" aimed primarily at Serbian defendants. Employing both quantitative and qualitative analysis of ICTY verdicts and sentencing Meernik concludes that judges follow what the author labels a "legal model" rather than a "political model" for adjudicating cases and imposing sentences in which verdicts and punishments are not influenced by political considerations or legal bias (differences in legal experience, ethnicity of the defendants, judges' powers and the presumption of innocence, NATO bias, and Stabilization force influence) but rather impartial legal criteria (seriousness of the offense, level of responsibility, and plea bargaining). Although Meernik's article does not deal directly with the effectiveness of deterrence through trials, his findings refute the argument of some authors that sentencing practices at the ICTY (and by extension other tribunals) have been inconsistent, which, such critics argue undermines rational deterrence theory's requirement that sentences must be consistent as well as rationally and proportionally related to the severity of the offense in order for deterrence to be successful.

Meernik, James, and Kimi King. "The Sentencing Determinants of the International Criminal Tribunal for the former Yugoslavia: An Empirical and Doctrinal Analysis." *Leiden Journal of International Law* 16 (2003): 717–50.

Exploring the determinants of sentencing, Meernik and King analyze sentencing practices at the International Criminal Tribunal for the former Yugoslavia (ICTY), both doctrinally and empirically, arriving at the conclusion that sentencing practices at the tribunal are largely fair and are based on sound legal criteria, namely the ICTY statutes governing sentencing and the tribunal's own Rules of Procedure and Evidence.

Megret, Frederic. "Three Dangers for the International Criminal Court: A Critical Look at a Consensual Project." *Finnish Yearbook of International Law* 12 (2002): 193–247.

In this at times withering critique of international criminal legal scholarship on the International Criminal Court (ICC), Megret focuses on three "dangers," or perhaps more aptly put, "mistakes," the author thinks legal scholars are making concerning the creation and operation of the ICC. One of these dangers is seeing the ICC as an "anti-political" institution that can deftly deploy impartial international criminal justice to manage international affairs. Megret contends that politics cannot be successfully severed from the ICC and that the law cannot and will not supplant politics among nations. As for deterrence, Megret argues that deterrence through international criminal justice is more of a wish than a reality although he stops short of suggesting that deterrence does not work at all. For Megret, the threat of "fair trials" is unlikely to work on the "average crazed nationalist" or "child soldier" because the "[c]ontext of extreme societal violence [is] precisely where liberal rhetoric is at its weakest because it is there that the ideal of the rational risk-averse, pareto-optimizer individual . . . is at its most fragile" (203).

Minow, Martha. *Between Vengeance and Forgiveness: Facing History after Genocide and Mass Atrocity*. Boston, MA: Beacon Press, 1998, 224 pp.

A now classic philosophical work on postatrocity justice and reconciliation, Minow's chapter on criminal trials calls into question whether trials, particularly the IMT/IMTE, were truly fair and impartial and therefore useful in repairing the damage done by conflicts and atrocity crimes. Minow argues that the IMT was marred by three key problems: "victor's justice" in which the Allies were prepared to judge the actions of the vanquished as wrong but not their own morally and legally suspect conduct (e.g., fire bombing of Dresden, the dropping of atomic bombs on Hiroshima and Nagasaki); the politicization of the legal process, particularly the choice of who to indict; and retroactivity in which defendants were tried under laws that did not exist when the offenses were committed. In questioning the utility of trials, Minow dismisses their deterrent effect by eschewing the suggestion that perpetrators of atrocity crimes are rational actors. Since perpetrators are not rational in Minow's view, they will not be swayed by the threat of punishment at trial.

Overy, Richard. "The Nuremberg Trials: International Law in the Making." In *From Nuremberg to The Hague: The Future of International Criminal Justice*, edited by Phillpe Sands, 1–29. New York: Cambridge University Press, 2003.

A brief chapter that recounts the problems of selectivity, the disconnect between command responsibility and those who were indicted, and the legally "dubious" practice of choosing indictees to represent certain groups at the Nuremberg trials.

Prosecutor v. Dragoljub Kunarac et al., Case nos. IT-96-23 and IT-96-23/1, para. 840 (February 22, 2001).

In their judgment in *Dragoljub Kunarac et al.*, the Appeals Chamber downplayed the role of general deterrence in sentencing despite the fact that the UN Security Council resolution that created the International Criminal Tribunal for the former Yugoslavia (ICTY) stated that deterrence of future atrocities was one of the main reasons for the creation of the tribunal. Hewing closely to a strict liberal legal understanding of the function of judgment and punishment, the Appeal Chambers argued that sentencing must only be concerned with the criminal liability of the individual and must be proportional to the crime found to have been committed. In doing so, the Chamber rejected the notion that stricter sentences than warranted by the crime should be meted out solely on the belief that tougher sentences will deter others.

Prosecutor v. Rutaganda, Case no .ICTR-96-3-T, para. 456 (ICTR Trial Chamber, December 6, 1999) aff'd on appeal Prosecutor v. Rutaganda, Case No. ICTR-96-3-A (ICTR Appeals Chamber, May 26, 2003).

The *Rutaganda* decision at the International Criminal Tribunal for Rwanda (ICTR) stands in marked contrast to the International Criminal Tribunal for the former Yugoslavia's Appeals Chamber's judicial reasoning in *Dragoljub Kunarac et al.* with respect to the relationship between sentencing and deterrence. For the ICTR Trial Chamber in Rutaganda the purpose of international criminal trials is to "dissuade forever others who may be tempted in the future to perpetrate such atrocities. . . ."

Roper, Steven D., and Lilian A. Barria. *Designing Criminal Tribunals: Sovereignty and International Concerns in the Protection of Human Rights.* Hampshire (England): Ashgate Publishing, 2006, 189 pp.

A slim but informative volume that traces the evolution of international humanitarian and international criminal law and the function of the International Criminal Tribunal for the Former Yugoslavia (ICTY) and the International Criminal Tribunal for Rwanda (ICTR), hybrid tribunals in Sierra Leone and Cambodia, and domestic tribunals. The authors identify four main functions of international humanitarian/criminal law and tribunals: (1) criminal accountability brings victims closure and a sense of justice; (2) facilitation of national reconciliation; (3) deterrence of future atrocities through the example of punishment, the promotion of justice, legal reform, and the rule of law; and (4) rehabilitation of the offender. Throughout the volume the authors insist that there is an intimate relationship between international law, tribunals, and politics and that politics directly influences the form, function, effectiveness, and financing of domestic and international tribunals.

Sands, Philippe, ed. *From Nuremberg to The Hague: The Future of International Criminal Justice.* New York: Cambridge University Press, 2003, 206 pp.

A brief edited work containing some chapters (included in this bibliography) that deal with the issue of prevention through trials, as either a goal that likely cannot be reached due to the shortcomings of trials thus far or an outcome that may be enhanced by changes in international criminal law (e.g., accomplice liability, aiding, and abetting) and the advent of the International Criminal Court.

Schabas, William A. 2007. "Genocide and the International Court of Justice: Finally, a Duty to Prevent the Crime of Crimes." *Genocide Studies and Prevention* 2, no. 2 (2007): 101–22.

A detailed and careful analysis of the 2007 International Court of Justice decision in the case *Bosnia and Herzegovina v. Serbia and Montenegro.* In the article, Schabas deals only indirectly with the issue of trials and prevention by suggesting that the verdict provides a legal foundation for the R2P doctrine. While the ICJ decision was in Schabas' view flawed in certain respects, it nonetheless established that the United Nations' Convention on the Prevention and Punishment of the Crime of Genocide does impose a general duty on states to prevent the crime.

10

"Paved with Good Intentions": Attempts to Design Mechanisms to Prevent Genocide in the Twenty-First Century and Why They Have Not Succeeded

Herbert Hirsch

Introduction

As the twenty-first century rolls on, it is important to reexamine the attempts to prevent genocide. From the Armenian Genocide, through the Holocaust to the Cambodian (Khmer Rouge) Genocide and all the way to the Former Yugoslavia, Rwanda, and Darfur, lessons concerning prevention have been learned and are quite clear. If the human community, such as it is, wants to save lives and prevent genocide and human rights atrocities, specified actions are required. These, in fact, have been spelled out in research, in conferences, and recently in a series of government and university and NGO-sponsored publications. Yet, twelve years into the twenty-first century, and ninety-six years after the events of 1915, while such lessons may be clear, the actual implementation of programs derived from these lessons so seriously lag behind the academic discussion and means that slogans such as "never again" reverberate with a ring of insincerity.

Within the last ten years, at least five major international and national prescriptions have appeared that attempt to outline the mechanisms necessary to prevent genocide in the new century. This chapter sets out to analyze the strengths, weaknesses, and relative effectiveness of these in light of the continued atrocities perpetrated thus far in this century.

In order to set the stage and provide a context, an explication of what happened in the last century will be presented, and that will then be followed by examination of the recent attempts to provide a formula to prevent genocide. Throughout this chapter, it will become increasingly evident that the good intentions of those devoting so much energy to devising means to prevent genocide often come to naught as they only pay lip service to the lessons learned and thus never really overcome the primary impediments and obstacles to the prevention of genocide.

Failure to Prevent Genocide in the Twentieth Century

In order to understand the various means that have been proposed to prevent genocide, we must begin with a brief overview of key issues germane to the international state system. Elementary though it is, it is absolutely essential.

Beginning with the Peace of Westphalia in 1648, the nation-state system grew and evolved in such a fashion that the modern nation-state continues to be guided in its behavior by two broad concepts: sovereignty and national interest. As much as we would like to believe that this has changed over the many years that international politics has been dominated by the international system of nation-states, it remains true. In fact, many of the present-day conflicts involve not only failed or failing states, but a desire on the part of one entity or another to have a state of its own based on ethnic, religious, or some other identity.

This became particularly important at the end of the Cold War in the late 1990s, when the world was confronted by a change in the dominant paradigm of international politics. From 1945 until that time, international politics had been dominated by the bipolar balance of power and the contest for dominance between the United States and the Soviet Union. When the Soviet Union suddenly collapsed, and along with it the former colonies of Eastern Europe, the world was cast into a much more complicated situation. Instead of two dominant super powers checking and balancing each other and overseeing proxy wars, but avoiding, or at least attempting to avoid, direct confrontation, due to the fear of possible escalation to all out nuclear destruction, the world now was, in one sense, cast adrift.

All the former colonies previously held together by threat or force of Soviet intervention suddenly desired to invoke their sovereignty and to create new ethnic, religious, or some other-based nation-state. In many cases this led to massive violations of human rights and genocide. This was particularly true in the former Yugoslavia.

As the twentieth century drew to a close, therefore, the examples of genocide, in particular in Rwanda and the former Yugoslavia, brought about renewed interest in how genocide might be prevented. Scholars and diplomats began to turn out articles and book, sponsor conferences and discussions, and to form organizations, such as the International Association of Genocide Scholars. Some of the proposals included, for example, the following:

1. Creating an Early Warning System that would alert the public and exert pressure on nations or groups to stop atrocities. It would consider the indicators of genocide as identified by numerous scholars.
2. Creating a UN Rapid Reaction Force.
3. Creating ad hoc judicial tribunals. (Special tribunals have limited jurisdiction and do not have the power to try crimes committed anywhere but in their area of jurisdiction.) At first there were two tribunals: The International Criminal Tribunal for the Former Yugoslavia (ICTY), created in May 1993, and The International Criminal Tribunal for Rwanda (ICTR), created in 1994.

In addition, The United Nations also created Special Courts for East Timor, Sierra Leone, and Cambodia, and there have also been trials in Iraq, the latter of which resulted in authorities questioning their legitimacy.

Such ad hoc tribunals, however, did not provide a permanent mechanism to deal with genocide or human rights violations. To remedy that, on July 1, 2002, the International Criminal Court (ICC) was created when the Rome Statute entered force after being ratified by sixty states.

Other positive signs toward prevention included the indictments of Augusto Pinochet and Slobodan Milosevic, and the February 2001 conviction for rape and sexual enslavement of three former members of the Bosnian Serb armed force who were found guilty of crimes against humanity and violating the laws of war. This was noteworthy because it was the first time that sexual enslavement and rape were punished as crimes against humanity.

Two events, however, side-tracked this progress toward genocide prevention: (1) the election of George W. Bush as president of the United States in the disputed election of 2000 and (2) the terrorist attacks against the United States on September 11, 2001, which largely shifted the world's and the US focus from genocide to terrorism. In spite of the overwhelming attention addressed toward terrorism, certain nations remained concerned about genocide. Consequently, in January 2004, the Government of Sweden attempted to refocus the nations of the world on preventing genocide by convening the Fourth International Stockholm Forum on the Prevention of Genocide. As a result of that forum, on April 7, 2004, UN Secretary-General Kofi Annan announced his plan to appoint a Special Advisor on Genocide and undertake the development of an action plan to prevent genocide. The plan involved five points:

1. Preventing armed conflict.
2. Protecting civilians in armed conflict.
3. Ending impunity through judicial action in both national and international courts.
4. Information gathering and early warning through a UN Special Advisor for genocide prevention.
5. Swift and decisive action along a continuum of steps, including possible military action.

These, in fact, constitute excellent summaries of the lessons derived from studying the genocide of the last century. The question that remained was how to implement them. The answer or at least the theoretical answer to this question was provided by four publications that have appeared in the last several years. The first, and most often discussed, is entitled *The Responsibility to Protect.*

The Responsibility to Protect

The attempt to find a method to get around the purported sanctity of sovereignty, which had stymied interventions in Bosnia and Rwanda, was further highlighted by the situation in Kosovo in 1999. The divided UN Security Council appeared to be prepared to stop the advancing ethnic cleansing pursued by the forces of Serbia and, in desperation, Secretary-General Kofi Annan "made compelling pleas to the international community to try to find, once and for all, a new consensus on how to approach these issues to 'forge unity' around the basic questions of the principle and process involved" (International Commission on Intervention and State Sovereignty 2001, vii). According to the introduction to The Responsibility to Protect (R2P), Annan posed the question directly: "... if humanitarian intervention is, indeed, an unacceptable assault on sovereignty, how should we respond to Rwanda, to a Srebrenica—to gross and systematic violations of human rights that affect every precept of our common humanity?" (International Commission on Intervention and State Sovereignty 2001, vii).

In response to Annan's challenge, the Canadian government, along with several major foundations, established the International Commission on Intervention and State Sovereignty in September 2000, which resulted in the now famous doctrine, the Responsibility to Protect. As noted in the introduction, the basic idea of the Responsibility to Protect is that "sovereign states have a responsibility to protect their own citizens from avoidable catastrophe—from mass murder and rape, from starvation—but that when they are unwilling or able to do so, that responsibility must be borne by the broader community of states" (International Commission on Intervention and State Sovereignty 2001, viii).

The report proceeds to note that

> The responsibility to protect embraces three specific responsibilities:
>
> A. The responsibility to prevent: to address both the root causes and direct causes of internal conflict and other man-made crises putting populations at risk.
>
> B. The responsibility to react: to respond to situations of compelling human need with appropriate measures, which may include coercive measures like sanctions and international prosecution, and in extreme cases military intervention.
>
> C. The responsibility to rebuild: to provide, particularly after a military intervention, full assistance with recovery, reconstruction and reconciliation, addressing the causes of the harm the intervention was designed to halt or avert. (International Commission on Intervention and State Sovereignty 2001, Section 8.28, n.p.)

When the responsibility is not exercised, a number of options are potentially triggered. The basic idea is that "Prevention is the single most important dimension of the responsibility to protect" (International Commission on Intervention and State Sovereignty 2001, xi) and should "always be exhausted before intervention is contemplated..."

(International Commission on Intervention and State Sovereignty 2001, xi).

The report also makes a series of recommendations to the United Nations. Among them are:

> 8.28 The Commission recommends to the General Assembly:
>
> That the General Assembly adopt a draft declaratory resolution embodying the basic principles of the responsibility to protect, and containing four basic elements:
>
> [1] an affirmation of the idea of sovereignty as responsibility;
>
> [2] an assertion of the threefold responsibility of the international community of states—to prevent, to react and to rebuild—when faced with human protection claims in states that are either unable or unwilling to discharge their responsibility to protect;
>
> [3] a definition of the threshold (large-scale loss of life or ethnic cleansing, actual or apprehended) which human protection claims must meet if they are to justify military intervention; and
>
> [4] an articulation of the precautionary principles (right intention, last resort, proportional means and reasonable prospects) that must be observed when military force is used for human protection purposes (International Commission on Intervention and State Sovereignty, 2001, n.p.).
>
> 8.29 The Commission recommends to the Security Council:
>
> (1) That the members of the Security Council should consider and seek to reach agreement on a set of guidelines, embracing the "Principles for Military Intervention" summarized in the Synopsis, to govern their responses to claims for military intervention for human protection purposes.
>
> (2) That the Permanent Five members of the Security Council should consider and seek to reach agreement not to apply their veto power in matters where their vital state interests are not involved, to obstruct the passage of resolutions authorizing military intervention for human protection purposes for which there is otherwise majority support (International Commission on Intervention and State Sovereignty, 2001, n.p.).
>
> 8.30 The Commission recommends to the Secretary-General:
>
> That the Secretary-General give consideration, and consult as appropriate with the President of the Security Council and the President of the General Assembly, as to how the substance and action recommendations of this report can best be advanced

> in those two bodies, and by his own further action. (International Commission on Intervention and State Sovereignty 2001, n.p.)

The attempt to implement the responsibility to protect has run into numerous obstacles. Foremost among them is the basic idea that sovereignty may be overcome when nations fail to protect their citizens from atrocity remains, even to this day, controversial, and thus an impediment to making solid progress in regard to the prevention and the intervention of genocide.

Along with sovereignty, three other factors cause nation-states to hesitate to undertake actions to prevent genocide. First, perceptions of national or states' interest. Often states believe, not always correctly, that their interests are best protected by not taking action to stop genocide. One telling example involves natural resources such as oil. If a state decides that it is more important to have oil to fuel its development, it will not take action or will even veto action to stop genocide. An example is China in Darfur. Two additional factors are national and international politics. Politics within a nation-state often determine foreign policy. For example, the United Sates maintains a hostile attitude toward Cuba largely because of the importance of the Cuban vote in Florida. As for international politics, nation-states may decide that it is more important to carry on negotiations with a perpetrator than it is to take action against that perpetrator, and this is one of the reasons for US hesitancy to take action to stop the atrocities in the Nuba Mountains. Part of this rationalization also involves the justification that the perpetrator, in this case President Omar al-Bashir of Sudan, is helping to fight terrorism.

Yet, in spite of the obstacles, this basic construct was expanded upon and was further elaborated and reinforced by three even more recent attempts to create mechanisms to prevent genocide. Even though they add little to the original, they have received some attention largely because of when and by whom they were promulgated.

The Genocide Prevention Task Force

The Genocide Prevention Task Force is largely a product of the US government and might be viewed as an attempt to recover from some of the embarrassment stemming from the lack of action on the part of the United States to do anything about preventing or halting the atrocities perpetrated in the 1990s. It was officially launched in November 2007 by a consortium of nongovernmental agencies—The US Holocaust

Memorial Museum, The American Academy of Diplomacy, and The US Institute of Peace—under the joint chairmanship of Madeline Albright and William Cohen. Albright served as US Ambassador to the United Nations and then Secretary of State during the Clinton administration. Cohen was Secretary of Defense during Clinton's second term. Participants in the Task Force, including consultants, comprised over fifty individuals with international, diplomatic, political, government, military, academic, humanitarian, and other relevant experience.

The Genocide Prevention Task Force's (2008) mandate is set out in the title of its official report, *Preventing Genocide: A Blueprint for U.S. Policymakers.*[1] In their foreword, Albright and Cohen state the following: "This report provides a blueprint that can enable the United States to take preventive action, along with international partners, to forestall the specter of future cases of genocide and mass atrocities. The world agrees that genocide is unacceptable and yet genocide and mass killings continue. Our challenge is to match words to deeds and stop allowing the unacceptable."[2]

The "Blueprint" has turned out to have had virtually no impact on the Obama administration. When his administration took office, they were confronted with what appeared to be more salient issues, actually crises, including a global economic recession, climate change, two ongoing wars, nuclear disarmament, and the control of so-called loose nukes. Not only has the "Blueprint" faded into insignificance, but it manifested even greater weaknesses than R2P. In particular:

1. It is poorly written and filled with bureaucratic jargon.
2. It is historically inaccurate and in certain cases almost revisionist. Due to the weak analysis of the recent history of genocide, the report cannot offer a foundation for adequate policy.
3. The report is written and edited by individuals who participated in past policy failures (meaning, their attempts to prevent genocide either failed or were not undertaken). This is part of a "recycling" process in Washington, DC, whereby policy makers never achieve a new perspective because former members of previous administrations are recalled when a new administration enters office. Therefore, it is difficult for new and/or different views to be represented.
4. Reports by commissions, such as this one, often do not change policy. Sometimes they do not even influence policy. Often in government, the presence of a report is pointed to as the equivalent of policy. This is a form of cooptation, since in the place of action, policy makers focus on the report.

5. The report is characterized by the "clashing cultures" of the academy and the policy makers, which contributes to different perspectives, with academics taking a more analytic and critical view, and policy makers arguing they are more "practical."

These critical weaknesses, along with various crises confronted by the new administration, moved, not only this report, but even the consideration of genocide prevention, away from the central consciousness of the US government.

As the attention of the world was drawn away from genocide, two additional reports on prevention found their way to publication. The Montreal Institute for Genocide and Human Rights published *Mobilizing the Will to Intervene: Leadership and Action to Prevent Mass Atrocities,*[3] and the United States Council on Foreign Relations issued a Special Report written by Matthew C. Waxman called *Intervention to Stop Genocide and Mass Atrocities.*[4]

The most recent attempt to design policies to prevent genocide and mass atrocities is the result of collaboration between the Carr Center for Human Rights Policy and the US Army Peacekeeping and Stability Operations Institute, *MARO: Mass Atrocity Response Operations: A Military Handbook.*

Mass Atrocity Response Operations, MARO: A Military Planning Handbook

MARO grew out of the US military *Quadrennial Defense Review,* which contained a statement noting that the US military needed to focus on "preventing human suffering due to mass atrocities or large-scale natural disasters abroad."[5] Ultimately, the Carr Center for Human Rights Policy at the Harvard Kennedy School and the US Army Peacekeeping and Stability Operations Institute collaborated in writing the MARO's handbook.

MARO is the second attempt of late by the United States or related organizations to design policies to prevent genocide and to protect civilian populations. MARO, along with *Preventing Genocide: A Blueprint for U.S. Policymakers,*[6] is what I deem a "semi-official" US government document. "Semi-official" because they are actually sponsored and published by universities or other organizations outside of the sphere of government, and thus are not official policy pronouncements. Rather, they constitute recommendations and have not been incorporated into the decision-making apparatus of the government or the military. In common with virtually all such exercises, MARO, as its predecessor, suffers from an excess of bureaucratic jargon, acronyms, and diagrams that look as though they were designed by sixth-graders after playing video games and referents that often bear little or no relationship to reality—in this case the reality of genocide and mass atrocities. They also often ignore or rewrite history, or perhaps create their own version of history that fits with their policy recommendations.[7]

The immediate background of MARO is most likely the failure to stop the massive human rights violations in the former Yugoslavia and Rwanda in the 1990s. Embarrassed and determined to justify US policy, which allowed those atrocities to occur virtually unimpeded.

In March 2007, the US Army War College sponsored a conference on "The National Security Implications of Climate Change," and as a result attention began to shift to the possible importance it held for military operations and how it would affect human rights around the globe. As the two wars in Afghanistan and Iraq began to slowly recede from public consciousness, the military saw the importance of a new mission in the new environment. This is referred to by Dyer (2010) in his daring new book *Climate Wars: the Fight for Survival as the World Overheats* as "selling a mission" (10).[8] As he describes it:

> The next mission of the U.S. armed forces is going to be the long struggle to maintain stability as climate change continually undermines it. The "war on terror" has more or less had its day and, besides, climate change is a real, full-spectrum challenge that may require everything, from Special Forces to aircraft carriers. So it's time to jolt the rank and file of the officer corps out of their complacency—orient them towards the new threat and get them moving." (10)

Of course, this also guarantees continued funding for the military, for those corporations that depend on military funding, and for the congressional districts, which contain such installations. It also means that when the missions in Afghanistan and Iraq end, the military will have a new mission. It is the answer to the debate started by Eisenhower's military–industrial complex speech and the answer to the questions, which have been raised since the end of the Cold War.

In fact, as the Cold War faded into an historical anachronism in the 1990s, it became clear that the "mission" was ambiguous. What would replace the Cold War? The War on Drugs was not only inadequate, but it was a war that the ongoing demand for drugs in the United States defeated. Until September 11, 2001, there was nothing to sell in regard to the need for a new mission, to mobilize the fear of the public, and/or to unite the country behind the military. Climate change and protecting human rights is perfect. Not only does it serve the purpose but it is also a response to a very real threat. A threat, incidentally, that the liberal, humanitarian left has supported for years, and lo and behold, now the military suddenly picks up that thread that has been woven ever since the atrocities in the former Yugoslavia and Rwanda in the 1990s.

This is where MARO fits and it is hard to criticize the apparently good intentions behind the new mission. As the authors of MARO argue

> The Mass Atrocity Response Operations (MARO) Project seeks to enable the United States and the international community to stop genocide and mass atrocity as part of a broader integrated strategy by explaining key relevant military concepts and planning considerations. The MARO Project is based on the insight that the failure to act in the face of mass killings of civilians is not simply a function of political will or legal authority; the failure also reflects a lack of thinking about *how* military forces might respond. States and regional and international organizations must better understand and prepare for the unique operational and moral challenges that military forces would face in a MARO. (5)

Accordingly, the project states that it

> addresses the concrete and practical challenges of using military forces to halt ongoing mass atrocities through a MARO. The Project has developed operational concepts, a tailored planning guide, tabletop exercises, and other tools for military institutions and political actors. While military force will not always be required to halt mass atrocity, the MARO Project helps make credible, effective options more likely and it better prepares intervening forces in the event that they are directed to act. In this respect, the Project can help shift the policy debate from "whether" to "how" to intervene to stop widespread violence against civilians. (5)

It all sounds very honorable. That is, if MARO is ever adopted and instituted as an official policy response, the US military will hence be dedicated to humanitarian intervention and to the protection of civilian populations. This, though, is highly unlikely.

A key problem is that the report begins with faulty premises. While it is true that the "failure to act in the face of mass killings of civilians is not simply a function of political will or legal authority" (5), it is an oversimplification to argue, as MARO does, that "the failure also reflects a lack of thinking about *how* military forces might respond" (5). In fact, the US military was reluctant to act in the face of atrocities in both the former Yugoslavia and Rwanda. The so-called Powell doctrine, which was a response to the Vietnam Syndrome coupled with the fiasco in Somali in 1993, argued that any response must include a massive infusion of US force along with an exit strategy. Throughout the course of the atrocities in the former Yugoslavia, the US military and its political allies in the Clinton administration argued against intervention on the basis that the long-standing ethnic and religious hostilities responsible for the ongoing slaughters were an intractable force not amenable to a military solution. Similar arguments were made concerning any possible intervention in Rwanda. The real lesson here is not that there was not "a lack of thinking about *how* military forces might respond," but that there were political reasons why the United States did not wish to intervene and those sources in support of an intervention were not politically influential. Neither Bosnia nor Rwanda had sufficient oil reserves to justify action similar to that taken in the Persian Gulf and no national or international movement to apply pressure on the government to intervene. As for Darfur, even with a strong Save Darfur movement supported by students, film stars, NGOs, and others, the atrocities continued unabated. The fact is, there is a reluctance to intervene and there remain strong political forces militating against any interventionary action. Those are the impediments to reach action, and not a lack of planning as claimed by MARO.

The authors of MARO also argue that "The Project has developed operational concepts, a tailored planning guide, tabletop exercises, and other tools for military institutions and political actors" (5–6). "In this respect," the authors state, "the Project can help shift the policy debate from "whether" to "how" to intervene to stop widespread violence against civilians" (6). The problem is that answering the question of "whether" to intervene must come before any discussion of "how" to intervene. Here, once again, political factors play a major role as an impediment to intervention.

Furthermore, since every crisis/case is different, it does not seem logical to lay out a one-size-fits-all plan. The Pentagon has done this repeatedly, much to its detriment. For example, in the aftermath of World War II, planning for war on the plains of Europe did not lead to successful prosecution of successive wars in Korea or Vietnam. In fact, the opposite was the case, as US strategy was self-defeating and undermined by an absence of understanding of the cultural and political situation of both of those conflicts. Therefore, body counts as the measure of success in Vietnam led to atrocities on the part of US troops as any Vietnamese was counted as an enemy casualty. Concomitantly, the policy of free fire zones led to mass killing of civilians. Ultimately, what is much more important is an in-depth understanding of each situation so that planning may be pursued in order to develop a successful strategy to meet each exigency.

In an attempt to respond to these factors, MARO seemingly intends to overcome the reluctance to intervene by advocating that it is in the national interest of a nation such as the United States to protect human rights. In that regard, the authors state that "Some argue that it is unlikely that, despite advocacy and education to the contrary, the United States will ever decide that it is within its national strategic interest to launch an intervention to stop a mass atrocity, and therefore that planning for this eventuality is not a priority. Such a position is not only ahistorical; it represents an abdication of responsibility to prepare for contingencies" (14). Yes, contingencies must be anticipated, but what is ahistorical is to interpret US past foreign policy as one aimed at intervening to protect human rights. To be sure, that does not mean planning should not occur, but it does mean it would be a new and unusual step for the United States to undertake such intervention. Actually, and in contradiction to their aforementioned statement, the MARO's authors recognize this to some extent when they comment as follows:

> A Mass Atrocity Response Operation (MARO) describes a contingency operation to halt the widespread and systematic use of violence by state or non-state armed groups against non-combatants. The term MARO is not yet enshrined in military doctrine—but it should be. The United States does not currently recognize mass atrocities as a unique operational challenge, and there is no operational concept or doctrine that might help commanders understand the dynamics and demands of responding to mass atrocities. (17)

Problems with R2P and Genocide Prevention

The R2P doctrine is the most widely discussed of all of the new approaches, and has often been referred to in the UN discussions of several cases of genocide, and especially in the case of the genocide in Darfur.

Unfortunately, there are numerous problems with the concept of "the responsibility to protect." If I have this correct, a simplified view of how prevention is now supposed to work is that a "genocide early warning system" triggers a warning, which in turn sets off policies outlined in R2P. These may include, but are not limited to

1. sanctions;
2. humanitarian intervention;
3. apprehension, trials, and punishment of perpetrators;
4. reconciliation and rebuilding of the destroyed society.

Ultimately, if none of this occurs, the reason is a "failure of will."

As with so many attempts to overcome sovereignty and to prevent genocide there is nothing, in general, to argue with these manifestations of good intentions, but there are major problems in conceptualization and implementation. In particular, there are (1) major weaknesses in the conceptualization and operationalizing of early warning systems and R2P, (2) there are major problems with sanctions and humanitarian intervention, and (3) the overall explanation for why nothing is done begs the question and misses the reality of domestic and international politics. In fact, these are my main criticisms of most of the literature, scholarly and prescriptive, in the area of genocide studies, namely, that it does not provide operational definitions necessary or sufficient to allow for implementation.

Of course, words and good intentions may have a profound impact, and language carries thought and may motivate action, but the lack of specificity and the absence of clear and realistic descriptions and explanations allow the level of generality to persist and generally means that action is not forthcoming.

R2P in the "Real" World

That R2P has become the new panacea is made clear by the attention it has received in recent conferences and in continued attempts to invoke it to deal with present genocidal situations in places such as Darfur and recently with the Libyan targeting of civilians in the ongoing civil war. Critiques of the failure to implement R2P have appeared throughout the period and yet have hardly corrected the lacunae in R2P.

For example, in February 2008, John Prendergast and Lisa Rogoff distributed their "R2P, The ICC, and Stopping Atrocities in the Real World."[9] Prendergast and Rogoff argue that the R2P doctrine is "real only on paper" because it has essentially failed in Darfur, Congo, and Uganda. "R2P's and the ICC's potential for confronting real cases of genocide and crimes against humanity remains largely unfulfilled" (n.p.). They proceed to examine the three cases in terms of what they call the "3Ps of crisis response: Peacemaking, Protection, and Punishment." They conclude that in Uganda there had been no protection or peacekeeping. There has been some attempt at punishment. Similarly in Congo and Darfur there have been real problems in providing protection, bringing about peace or even meting out punishment. Their lament could not have been more timely, and yet their recommendations for action and their account of why none of these is implemented reflects the same old bromides that simply reinforce my present criticisms.

For example, Prendergast and Rogoff recommend multilateral action, with increased participation and leadership by the United States, and contend that "It is only with significantly increased political will—generated by the growing anti-genocide movement—that this doctrine can help create a world in which R2P is the standard and the United Nations instinctively turns to this doctrine whenever it faces even the possibility of genocide or mass atrocity crimes" (n.p.). And how do they say this is to be implemented? Change brought about by the voters "demanding that R2P becomes more than just a wonderful intention or bumper sticker slogan" (n.p.).

While the conceptualization of R2P is relatively new, and the ideals are slowly seeping into international law and international and national politics, we do not have to trace the attempts over the years to know that utopian thoughts often are not translated into action. Of course, our reach should exceed our grasp, but we also want to be able to grasp and hold on to some result.

My view is that the model of R2P, the explanation for the lack of action, failure of will, and the three magic bullets intended to prevent genocide and save lives—early warning systems, humanitarian intervention, and trials and punishment—are based on the traditional models of genocide derived from study of the Armenian Genocide and the Holocaust, and to a lesser extent, the massacres in the former Yugoslavia and the genocide in Rwanda, and that they may no longer be the most salient models in the present century. While the 1948

United Nations' Convention on the Prevention and Punishment of the Crime of Genocide, which defines genocide in international law, is based upon these models, and fit very nicely the atrocities of the last century, the new century has brought new or altered paradigms.

Confronted with the reawakening of ethnic, tribal, and religious conflict used in the service of political ends, the world appears to be much more complex than the bimodal balance of power that dominated the fifty or so odd years from World War II to 1999 (which presented their own set of grievously difficult problems for those who wished to prevent the rising tide of war crimes, crimes against humanity, and genocide across the globe). We are once again witness to a shifting set of paradigms, and as a result our long-held conceptualization of genocide may no longer provide an adequate description of the real world of international and national politics. And yet, most of our attempts to prevent or stop genocide, including R2P, are based on these increasingly outdated examples.

What is left out of R2P, and this is a major weakness, is that the new paradigm of genocide in the new century appears to involve large states, such as the US action in Iraq, Russia in Chechnya, and nonstate actors, sometimes supported by states, such as China in Darfur and the many complications in the Congo. While the traditional definition of genocide remains valid for the last century, it does not really fit the newer manifestations of genocide.

R2P is designed to protect against small states, or small nonstate affiliated groups, committing large crimes, but not against large states committing large crimes. If this is, in fact true, R2P neglects a huge chunk of human rights violations. Here it is important to point out that I am not arguing that implementing R2P and successfully dealing with Darfur, Congo, or other examples is not important. I am arguing that our conceptualization of R2P and genocide ignores a major problem that reflects and helps explain why we are not able to deal with these large crimes committed by large states—of course, that the world has also not been successful in dealing with large crimes committed by smaller states or groups is also true. Be that as it may, imagine attempting to apply R2P to the United States or, for that matter, Russia or China.

Empirically it is most likely true that, in the twentieth and twenty-first centuries, as many innocents were killed by war crimes and crimes against humanity, if not genocide, committed by the United States as have been killed by the examples, such as Darfur, upon which the international community tends to focus. Just take the most obvious: Vietnam, Guatemala, El Salvador, Nicaragua, Chile, Argentina, Persian Gulf, Iraq, and Afghanistan.

R2P makes little or no impact in this regard and, in fact, the document recognizes its relative impotence when faced by violations by the large states in sections 4.41 and 4.42 (37). It states, for example:

> Application of this precautionary principle would, on purely utilitarian grounds, be likely to preclude military action against any of the five permanent members of the Security Council even if all the other conditions for intervention described here were met. . . . The same is true of other major powers who are not permanent members of Security Council. This raises again the question of double standards—but the commission's position here, as elsewhere, is simply this: the reality of interventions may not be able to be mounted in every case where there is justification for doing so is no reason for them not to be mounted in any case. (37)

In spite of the attempted rationalization, the case remains that the R2P has not been successfully implemented in cases for which the authors have held out the highest of hopes, small states or nonstate actors committing large crimes. This is perhaps most obvious with the ongoing atrocities in Darfur and the recent explosion of violence in the Nuba Mountains, also in Sudan.

The explanation often provided for this failure of implementation is the "failure of will" on the part of the large powers or the international and national political institutions.

Failure to Prevent: Lack of Political Will

As a result of the widespread human rights atrocities of the last century, a new field of academic endeavor was created. Loosely called "genocide studies," this new focus of inquiry produced a virtual explosion of scholarship on the causes, history, and prevention of genocide. Scholars from many disciplines, as well as activists, diplomats, and international lawyers, all contributed to the explosion of research that helped bring the topic to greater public consciousness than ever before. As noted above, the genocides in Bosnia and Rwanda, and more recently the situation in Darfur, made explicit the relevance of this issue for the contemporary world. The unchecked violence over nearly a decade (2003–present) in the Darfur region of the Sudan continued to reveal the difficulty experienced by the international community in intervening to prevent genocides and similar kinds of human rights abuses.

Despite the apparent increase in attention and interest that genocide has elicited in recent years, modern states consistently appear unable or unwilling to prevent or effectively intervene to stop the loss of life when massive crimes against humanity and/or genocide break out. Rising to grasp the hope represented by the widespread public attention and the publication of the *Responsibility to Protect,* this failure on the part of the international community to act has become an important focus for many interested scholars and activists as they rush to attempt to explain the ongoing failure of international politics. Many attributed the lack of action to a "failure of will" on the part of political leaders and governmental institutions. These arguments, however, as popular and as appealing as they may be, dramatically oversimplify the situation.

In the conclusion to her prize-winning book, *"A Problem from Hell": America and the Age of Genocide,* Samantha Power (2002) lays out a plan to prevent genocide. Couching it in the context of US foreign policy, she asserts that "What is most shocking is that U.S. policy makers did almost nothing to deter the crime [of genocide]" (504).[10] The United States, according to Power, did "not give genocide the moral attention it warranted" (504). Finally, Power comes to what has become the widely circulated notion that any genocide in the past could have been prevented if the political will to act had been present. This is an idea propounded by not only Samantha Power, but others as well. Power argues forcefully that "the real reason the United States did not do what it could and should have done to stop genocide was not a lack of knowledge or influence but a lack of will" (508).[11] It is my contention, however, that this widespread belief about the failure of political will is partial but far from a sufficient explanation for the absence of action to stop genocide. Power, in relying on the notion of the failure of political will, in fact begs the question. "Why is there an absence of 'will'?" The reality is as old as the nation-state system and as recent as the creation of R2P and the attempt to overcome sovereignty.

We may define political will as the motivation and determination to act; in other words, it is a result of perceived needs and pressures in both national and international politics. It is not the other way around. That means that states in the international system act to protect what they perceive as their interests, not the interests of some vague, to them, notion of morality. Nations are not likely, as we have seen repeatedly, to act unless their perceived interests are affected.

Asserting that there is a lack of political will and leaving it at that begs the question: Why does the will not exist? It also begs the question: Why is there no common perception of an international common good?[12] Put yet another way, arguments about political will tend to ignore the psychological, political, cultural, and institutional reasons that make preventing genocide, war crimes, or other forms of human violence very difficult. Unfortunately, good words or a worthy cause do not necessarily translate into meaningful action, and political leaders often allow other concerns to trump humanitarian ones. In fact, acknowledging that genocide is taking place may in fact be a political tactic to divert criticism of the real lack of action. Very often in US national politics, issuing a statement or forming a committee to investigate is confused for action or is intended to co-opt more direct action.[13] Making R2P, or any action, to save life a real and meaningful alternative to politics as usual requires much more than political will. It requires an in-depth understanding of the national and international political systems and the pressures generated and responded to not only by leaders, but the public as well. In short, any prescription such as R2P must begin with a forthright understanding of how politics is involved.

Both international and national politics are messy and often lack coherence. The attempt to inject coherence into a chaotic system may lead to confusion and to an inability to deal with the complexity of those systems. For example, in his book, *Understanding International Conflicts*, Joseph Nye (2007) issues the following warning:

> The bipolar world is over, but it is not going to be replaced by a unipolar world empire that the United States controls alone. The world is already economically multipolar, and there will be a diffusion of power as the information revolution progresses, interdependence increases, and transnational actors become more important. The new world will not be neat, and you will have to live with that. (282)[14]

This includes not only genocide scholars but activists and others interested in preventing genocide.

Conclusion

All of the aforementioned reports and new approaches are in a long line of well-meaning attempts to reform the United Nations and the international state system. From World Federalism through functionalism and regionalism and arguments about the "end of history," to modern views of the impact of "cyberfeudalism" and globalism, we have seen numerous prescriptions for reform, in both the long and short run, falter as they run aground on the shoals of sovereignty and self-interest. So, we may conclude that, yes, the genocides of the last century and, one might add, the genocides of this century, have generated very good intentions from politicians, diplomats, scholars and others, but that, as the old cliché still holds: "the road to hell is paved with good intentions." When the latter are blind to the real impediments facing them and their efforts, much, if not all, may come to naught.

Despite all the "remedies" spelled out in the "prescriptions" (i.e., the reports discussed herein)—monitor the state of human rights around the world carefully; when an early warning is triggered, take action, whether it be sanctions or something more vigorous; have rules of engagement that allow a force, hopefully of sufficient numbers with adequate arms, to act as quickly as possible; be aware of the national and international politics surrounding the situation; try to make sure that humanitarian intervention does not become politicized, as Foley (2008) cautions;[15] do no harm, and be prepared to rebuild the culture and polity and society—massive human rights violations have persisted in Darfur since 2003, in the Democratic Republic of Congo even longer period, and now in the Nuba Mountains, which is entering its third month. In addition, violence and chaos continue unabated in failed states such as Somalia, Libya, Syria, Yemen, Bahrain, and other various places around the globe. As always, in complicated political circumstances, the gap between rhetoric and action is wide and often camouflaged by lies and rhetoric designed to protect national interests and sovereignty and to avoid any responsibility to protect what is not viewed as part of those national interests. Yes, good intentions do not necessarily translate into good policy.

Notes

1. Madeline K. Albright and William S. Cohen (co-chairs), *Preventing Genocide: A Blueprint for U.S. Policymakers*. Washington, DC: Genocide Prevention Task Force, 2008.
2. Madeline K. Albright and William S. Cohen (co-chairs), *Preventing Genocide: A Blueprint for U.S. Policymakers*. Washington, DC: Genocide Prevention Task Force, 2008. Since the task force report was deemed by

the editors of *Genocide Studies and Prevention* to be an important event, a symposium was also organized to be held in Washington, DC. It was co-organized by the International Association of Genocide Scholars, the International Institute for Genocide and Human Rights Studies (a division of the Zoryan Institute), and the editors of *Genocide Studies and Prevention: An International Journal.*

The objective of this one-day symposium was to assemble a group of experts in genocide and international human rights from various disciplines and countries to provide an independent, in-depth, scholarly review and assessment of its findings and implications. The commentaries consist of experts from at least four countries and provide a diversity of views. They range from in-depth scholarly analyses to editorial-style opinion pieces, reflecting different approaches to the report by the various commentators. Yet, they provide a series of stimulating views on the task force report which may, we hope, stimulate further attention and discussion. (*Genocide Studies and Prevention*, Summer 2009).

3. The Montreal Institute for Genocide and Human Rights Studies, *Mobilizing the Will to Intervene: Leadership and Action to Prevent Mass Atrocities.* Montreal: Concordia University, 2009.
4. Matthew C. Waxman, *Intervention to Stop Genocide and Mass Atrocities.* Council Special Report No. 49. New York: Council on Foreign Relations, October, 2009.
5. Sarah Sewall, Dwight Raymond, and Sally Chin, *Mass Atrocity Response Operations: A Military Planning Handbook.* Cambridge, MA: Carr Center for Human Rights Policy, Harvard Kennedy School, 2010.
6. Madeleine K. Albright and William S. Cohen, *Preventing Genocide: A Blueprint for U.S.* Policymakers (Washington, DC: Genocide Prevention task Force, 2008), http://www.usip.org/genocide_taskforce/report.html.
7. "Symposium on MARO: Mass Atrocity Response Operations," *Genocide Studies and Prevention: An international Journal.* Volume 6, No. 1 (April 2011). Edited by Herb Hirsch.
8. Gwynne Dyer, *Climate Wars: The Fight for Survival as the World Overheats* (Oxford: Oneworld Publications, 2010), p. 10.
9. John Prendergast and Lisa Rogoff, "R2P, the ICC, and Stopping Atrocities in the Real World." New York: ENOUGH Strategy Paper #13, February 2008.
10. Samantha Power, *"A Problem from Hell:" America and the Age of Genocide.* New York: Basic Books, 2002, 504.
11. *Ibid.*, 508.
12. Herbert Hirsch, *Genocide and the Politics of Memory: Studying Death to Preserve Life. Chapel Hill, NC: University of North Carolina Press, 1995.*
13. Herbert Hirsch, *Anti-Genocide: Building an American Movement to Prevent Genocide.* Westport, CT: Praeger, 2002.
14. Joseph S. Nye, Jr. *Understanding International Conflicts: An Introduction to Theory and History.* New York: Pearson/Longman, 2007, 282.
15. Conor Foley, *The Thin Blue Line: How Humanitarianism Went to War.* London: Verso, 2008.

References

Dyer, Gwynne. 2010. *Climate Wars: The Fight for Survival as the World Overheats.* Oxford: Oneworld Publications.

Foley, Conor. 2008. *The Thin Blue Line: How Humanitarianism Went to War.* London: Verso.

Genocide Prevention Task Force. 2008. *Preventing Genocide: A Blueprint for U.S. Policymakers.* Washington, DC: The United States Holocaust Memorial Museum, The American Academy of Diplomacy, and the Endowment of the United States Institute of Peace.

International Commission on Intervention and State Sovereignty. 2001. *The Responsibility to Protect: Report of the International Commission on Intervention and State Sovereignty.* Ottawa: Government of Canada.

The Montreal Institute for Genocide and Human Rights Studies. 2009. *Mobilizing the Will to Intervene: Leadership and Action to Prevent Mass Atrocities.* Montreal, Quebec: Concordia University.

Nye, Jr., Joseph S. 2007. *Understanding International Conflicts: An Introduction to Theory and History.* New York: Pearson/Longman.

Power, Samantha. 2002. *"The Problem from Hell": America in the Age of Genocide.* New York: Harper Perennial.

Prendergast, John, and Lisa Rogoff. 2008. "R2P, the ICC, and Stopping Atrocities in the Real World." *ENOUGH Strategy Paper #13*, February. Washington, DC: ENOUGH

Sewall, Sarah, Dwight Raymond, and Sally Chin. 2010. *Mass Atrocity Response Operations (MARO): A Military Planning Handbook.* Cambridge, MA: Carr Center for Human Rights Policy, Harvard Kennedy School.

Waxman, Matthew C. 2009. *Intervention to Stop Genocide and Mass Atrocities.* Council Special Report No. 49. New York: Council on Foreign Relations.

Annotated Bibliography

Reports

Genocide Prevention Task Force. *Preventing Genocide: A Blueprint for U.S. Policymakers.* Washington, DC: The United States Holocaust Memorial Museum, The American Academy of Diplomacy, and the Endowment of the United States Institute of Peace, 2008, 147 pp.

Preventing Genocide: A Blueprint for U.S. Policymakers comprises the following: Executive Summary; Defining the Challenge; chapter 1, Leadership: The Indispensable Ingredient; chapter 2, Early Warning: Assessing Risks and Triggering Action; chapter 3, Early Prevention: Engaging before the Crisis; chapter 4, Preventive Diplomacy: Halting and Reversing Escalation; chapter 5, Employing Military Options; chapter 6, International Action: Strengthening Norms and Institutions; Summary of Recommendations; and *Appendices* ([A] Task Force Members, [B] Expert Group Members, [C] Task Force Staff, [D] List of Consultations, [E] Plenary Sessions, and [F] Acronyms).

International Commission on Intervention and State Sovereignty. *The Responsibility to Protect: Report of the International Commission on Intervention and State Sovereignty.* Ottawa: Government of Canada, 2001, 91 pp.

The report's central theme is "The Responsibility to Protect," the idea that sovereign states have a responsibility to protect their own citizens from avoidable catastrophe, but that when they are unwilling or unable to do so, that responsibility must be borne by the broader community of states. The authors comment: "We hope very much that the report will break new ground in a way that helps generate a new international consensus on these issues."

The report consists of the following: (1) The Policy Challenge (The Intervention Dilemma, The Changing International Environment, The Implications for State Sovereignty, The Meaning of Intervention); (2) A New Approach: "The Responsibility to Protect" (The Meaning of Sovereignty Human Rights, Human Security and Emerging Practice, Shifting the Terms of the Debate); (3) The Responsibility to Prevent: (A Commitment to Prevention, Early Warning and Analysis, Root Cause Prevention Efforts, Direct Prevention Efforts); (4) The Responsibility to React (Measures Short of Military Action, The Decision to Intervene, Threshold Criteria: Just Cause, Other Precautionary Criteria); (5) The Responsibility to Rebuild (Post-Intervention Obligations, Administration under UN Authority, Local Ownership and the Limits to Occupation); (6) The Question of Authority (Sources of Authority under the UN Charter, The Security Council's Role—and Responsibility, When the Security Council Fails to Act); (7) The Operational Dimension (Preventive Operations, Planning for Military Intervention, Carrying Out Military Intervention, Following Up Military Intervention, A Doctrine For Human Protection Operations); (8) The Responsibility to Protect: The Way Forward (From Analysis to Action, Mobilizing Domestic Political Will, Mobilizing International Political Will, Next Steps, Meeting the Challenge); Appendix A: Members of the Commission; and Appendix B: How the Commission Worked.

The Montreal Institute for Genocide and Human Rights Studies. *Mobilizing the Will to Intervene: Leadership and Action to Prevent Mass Atrocities*. Montreal, Quebec: Concordia University, 2009, n.p.

Mobilizing the Will to Intervene: Leadership and Action to Prevent Mass Atrocities, which originates in Canada, has been ignored in the United States. While it focuses on intervention, it has not received the attention devoted to either the *Genocide Prevention Task Force* or *MARO*.

The Montreal Institute for Genocide reports that "*Mobilizing the Will to Intervene: Leadership and Action to Prevent Mass Atrocities* contains concrete policy recommendations for the governments of Canada and of the United States, as well as recommendations for journalists and civil society groups, which will advance . . . the goal of the fight against genocide by building domestic political will in Canada and the United States to prevent future mass atrocities. [The report] details the long term consequences to Canadian and American security, public health and prosperity that result from mass atrocities, which make engaging in the prevention of such atrocities in each county's national interest."

Sewall, Sarah, Dwight Raymond, and Sally Chin. *Mass Atrocity Response Operations (MARO): A Military Planning Handbook*. Cambridge, MA: Carr Center for Human Rights Policy, Harvard Kennedy School, 2010, 130 pp.

Mass Atrocity Response Operations (MARO): A Military Planning Handbook comprises the following: Executive Summary; The MARO Concept;

(A) MARO's Relation to Other Operations; (B) Distinctions of a MARO Situation; (C) Operational and Political Implications; and MARO Planning Considerations. (A) Introduction; (B) Mission Analysis; (C) Courses of Action; (D) Plan Design and Implementation. Future Research Areas and Ways Forward. (Annexes: [A] Definitions of Genocide and Mass Atrocity Crimes; [B] Draft Strategic Guidance; [C] Sample Critical Factors Analyses; [D] Assumptions; [E] Task List; [F] Intelligence Considerations; [G] Flexible Deterrent Options; [H] Selected Bibliography; [I] History of the MARO Project; [J] Contacts and Resources; and Acronyms.)

Waxman, Matthew C. *Intervention to Stop Genocide and Mass Atrocities.* Council Special Report No. 49. New York: Council on Foreign Relations, 2009, 38 pp.

This report comprises the following sections: "Deterring and Stopping Mass Atrocities: Policy Challenges"; "International Norms of Intervention and Calls for Reform"; "International Norms and Effective Strategy"; and "Recommendations."

Commentary on Various Reports

I. Genocide Prevention Task Force (2008). *Preventing Genocide: A Blueprint for U.S. Policymakers*

Feirstein, Daniel. "Getting Things into Perspective." *Genocide Studies and Prevention* 4, no. 2 (Summer 2009): 155–60.

Feirstein presents a "Latin American" perspective on the task force. He argues that it is confusing to non-Americans because it is embedded in the values of American Society. He also notes that the report leaves out the role played by the United States in supporting some of the practices discussed in the report.

Hirsch, Herb. "The Genocide Prevention Taskforce: Recycling People and Policy: An Introductory Critique." *Genocide Studies and Prevention* 4, no. 2 (Summer 2009): 153–54.

Hirsch provides a critical analysis of the report noting that it rewrites US history by leaving out the role played by the United States in allowing the genocides discussed to proceed without intervention. He also points out that the way politics works in Washington, DC does not lead to new approaches to preventing genocide since officials from previous administrations are "recycled" into the new administration and propose the same old policies.

Kuperman, Alan J. "Wishful Thinking Will Not Stop Genocide." *Genocide Studies and Prevention: An International Journal* 4, no. 2 (Summer 2009): 191–200.

Kuperman believes that the report has good intentions but ignores the most important lessons related to past failures to prevent genocide. He discusses six faulty assumptions and notes that they lead to prescriptions that are not likely to be successful.

Mennecke, Martin. "Genocide Prevention and International Law." *Genocide Studies and Prevention: An International Journal* 4, no. 2 (Summer 2009): 167–76.

Mennecke argues that the task force report deserves praise for taking a first step toward translating research into action. However, he proceeds to note that the "treatment of international law in the report remains inconsistent and insufficient."

Schabas, William A. "Definitional Traps and Misleading Titles." *Genocide Studies and Prevention: An International Journal* 4, no. 2 (Summer 2009): 177–84.

Schabas argues that the report avoids international legal definitions and, therefore, is misleading. His discussion is all about legal definitions.

Straus, Scott. "A Step Forward." *Genocide Studies and Prevention: An International Journal* 4, no. 2 (Summer 2009): 185–90.

Straus notes that the report is an important step forward and is a contribution to the debate over how to stop genocide. He believes it is a major advance on policy and academic discussions related to the question of genocide prevention.

Theriault, Henry. "The Albright-Cohen Report: From Realpolitik Fantasy to Realist Ethics." *Genocide Studies and Prevention: An International Journal* 4, no. 2 (Summer 2009): 201–10.

Theriault notes that the report rests on certain questionable assumptions. One of the primary assumptions is that if US leaders take genocide more seriously as a threat, action will be taken to prevent its occurrence. He points out how these are questionable assumptions that rely on faulty interpretations of past actions taken by the United States in not acting to stop ongoing genocides or protect human rights.

II. *Mass Atrocity Response Operations (MARO): A Military Planning Handbook*

Alvarez, Alex. "Reflections on the Mass Atrocity Response Operations Project." *Genocide Studies and Prevention: An International Journal* 6, no. 1 (Spring 2011): 70–76.

Alvarez argues that MARO is another step in the direction of protecting human rights and preventing genocide. He questions the assumptions upon which the report is based and, in particular, the unilateral nature of the proposed interventions.

Burgess, Stephen. "Comments on the Mass Atrocity Response Operations (MARO) Handbook." *Genocide Studies and Prevention: An International Journal* 6, no. 1 (Spring 2011): 66–69.

Burgess believes that MARO provides realistic scenarios but that it is unlikely it will be incorporated into US military doctrine and training. If it is distributed widely, he thinks it might have the effect of persuading states that are willing to prepare to intervene.

Feirstein, Daniel. "The Good, the Bad, and the Invisible: A Critical Look at the MARO Report." *Genocide Studies and Prevention: An International Journal* 6, no. 1 (Spring 2011): 39–44.

In this article, Feirstein argues that genocide complexity is oversimplified by this report. Simply stated, it does not provide a realistic scenario for prevention.

Genocide Studies and Prevention. "Symposium on MARO: Mass Atrocity Response Operations." *Genocide Studies and Prevention: An International Journal* 6, no. 1 (Spring). Edited by Herb Hirsch.

A collection of articles that critically evaluate the *Mass Atrocity Response Operations Handbook.* Organized according to US and non-US perspectives, the symposium presents in-depth analysis.

Hairabedian, Federico Gaitan, and Alexis Papazian. "Critical Reflections on MARO: A View from Argentina." *Genocide Studies and Prevention: An International Journal* 6, no. 1 (Spring 2011): 45–51.

As one of the non-US analyses, this article contextualizes the report within the history of US interventions and international law.

Hiebert, Maureen. "MARO as the Partial Operationalization of R2P." *Genocide Studies and Prevention: An International Journal* 6, no. 1 (Spring 2011): 52–58.

Hiebert relates MARO to the responsibility to protect. She notes that it is the operationalization of one aspect, namely the responsibility to react through military intervention.

Hirsch, Herb. "Editor's Introduction. MARO: Mass Atrocity Response Operations: A Military Planning Handbook: Selling the Mission and/or Protecting Human Rights." *Genocide Studies and Prevention: An International Journal* 6, no. 1 (Spring 2011): 1–6.

Hirsch lays out the context of MARO by placing it within US policy and notes that there are numerous problems with the report. Not the least of which is the bureaucratic jargon that renders operationalizing the recommendations questionable.

Kuperman, Alan J. "Mass Atrocity Response Operations: Doctrine in Search of a Strategy." *Genocide Studies and Prevention: An International Journal* 6, no. 1 (Spring 2011): 59–65.

Kuperman notes that MARO is a corrective to what he calls the "naïve optimism" of many past analyses. It provides a model for intervention thereby making intervention more likely.

Smith, Roger. "Utopian Goals, Unasked Questions: Reflections on a Proposed Military Planning Handbook for Response to Mass Atrocities against Civilians." *Genocide Studies and Prevention: An International Journal* 6, no. 1 (Spring 2011): 77–80.

Smith argues that the report offers valuable suggestions for military intervention. However, he notes that the major flaw is it relegates political, diplomatic, humanitarian, and reconstructive elements to the periphery.

Theriault, Henry. "The MARO Handbook: New Possibilities or the Same Old Militarism?" *Genocide Studies and Prevention: An International Journal* 6, no. 1 (Spring 2011): 7–31.

Theriault notes both positive and negative aspects of MARO. On the one hand, it raises the important issues related to intervention while, on the other, it contains numerous problems with history and interpretation.

Ungor, Ugur Umit. "Team America: Genocide Prevention?" *Genocide Studies and Prevention: An International Journal* 6, no. 1 (Spring 2011): 32–38.

Ungor places this report into the historical context of humanitarian intervention. He points out how it is naïve and raises questions about how effective it might be against large nation-states. He uses the example of Russia and Chechnya to illustrate the problems.

III. *The Responsibility to Protect: Report of the International Commission on Intervention and State Sovereignty*

Badescu, Cristina. *Humanitarian Intervention and the Responsibility to Protect.* New York: Routledge, 2010, 212 pp.

This book explores attempts to develop a more acceptable account of the principles and mechanisms associated with humanitarian intervention, which has become known as the "Responsibility to Protect" (R2P). While international actors tend to agree that killing civilians as a necessary part of state formation is no longer acceptable, nor is standing by idly in the face of massive violations of human rights, and yet, respect for the sovereign rights of states remains central among the ordering principles of the international community. How can populations affected by egregious human rights violations be protected? How can the legal constraints on the use of force and respect for state sovereignty be reconciled with the international community's willingness and readiness to take action in such instances? And more importantly, how can protection be offered when the Security Council, which is responsible for authorizing the use of force when threats to international peace and security occur, is paralyzed? The author addresses these issues, arguing that R2P is the best framework available at present to move the humanitarian intervention debate forward.

Bellamy, Alex J. *Global Politics and the Responsibility to Protect: From Words to Deeds.* London: Polity, 2009, 268 pages.

Basically point outs the path-breaking nature of R2P in finally encouraging nation-states, or at least some within the United Nations, to consider breaking, or at least talking about breaking, the barriers to prevention imposed by the doctrine of sovereignty. Anyone interested in R2P is encouraged to read the original report and to examine the United Nations' discussions over the implementation.

Evans, Gareth. *The Responsibility to Protect: Ending Mass Atrocity Crimes Once and For All [Paperback].* Washington, DC: Brookings Institution Press, 2009, 349 pp.

This is a basic explication of the doctrine.

International Coalition for the Responsibility to Protect. *International Coalition for the Responsibility to Protect.* New York: World Federalist Movement, Institute for Global Policy, 2005, 91 pp.

There have been numerous discussions of the importance and success and failure of implementing the concept of The Responsibility to Protect. Perhaps the best source of information and analysis is The International Coalition for the Responsibility to Protect (ICRtoP). According to their website it "brings together NGOs from all regions of the world to strengthen normative consensus for R2P, further the understanding of the norm, push for strengthened capacities to prevent and halt genocide, war crimes, ethnic cleansing and crimes against humanity, and mobilize NGOs to push for action to save lives."

O'Bannon, Brett, and John Roth, eds. *The Evolution of the Responsibility to Protect: Imperfect Duties?* New York: Routledge, 2011, 208 pp.

This book's primary objective is to examine the evolution of the Responsibility to Protect (R2P) norm, and to analyze the "fit" between the R2P and Africa. The book comprises the following parts and chapters: Introduction Part 1: Political, Legal, and Ethical Challenges for R2P: (1) Understanding the Gap between the Promise and the Reality of 'The Responsibility to Protect'; (2) Why the Responsibility to Protect (R2P) as a Doctrine or (Emerging) Norm Is on the Decline: Principles, Pragmatism, and International Relations; (3) The Responsibility to Protect and the Limits of International Authority; (4) Crying Out for Action: Do the Dead Say Anything about the Responsibility to Protect? Part 2: Situating R2P in the African Topography; (5) The Responsibility to Protect in the Congo: The Failure of Prevention; (6) UN Peacekeeping in Post-conflict Southern Sudan: Protecting Whom and to What End?;

(7) Endemic Conflicts and Intervention in the Horn of Africa: Implications of the End of the Cold War; (8) Africa: Implications of Statelessness for a State-Centric Human Protection Norm; and (9) Conclusion.

Serrano, Monica, and Claudio Fuentes, eds. *The Responsibility to Protect in Latin America: A New Map*. New York: Routledge, 2012, 224 pp.

This book assesses the opportunities for the normative and practical advancement of the Responsibility to Protect (R2P) in Latin America.

Thakur, Ramesh. *The Responsibility to Protect: Norms, Laws and the Use of Force*. New York: Routledge, 2011, 240 pp.

Basically point outs the path-breaking nature of R2P in finally encouraging nation-states, or at least some within the United Nations, to consider breaking, or at least talking about breaking, the barriers to prevention imposed by the doctrine of sovereignty. Anyone interested in R2P is encouraged to read the original report and to examine the United Nations' discussions over the implementation.

List of Contributors

Paul R. Bartrop is a fellow in the faculty of arts at Deakin University, Melbourne, Victoria, Australia, and for years was a member of the teaching staff at Bialik College, Melbourne, where he taught history, international studies, and comparative genocide studies. He is currently the Visiting Distinguished Professor of Holocaust and Genocide Studies at Richard Stockton College of New Jersey.

Brent Beardsley has served over twenty-five years as an infantry officer in the Royal Canadian Regiment and retired at the rank of major. Prior to and during the 1994 genocide in Rwanda, Beardsley served as the Personal Staff Officer to then-Major-General Romeo Dallaire, the Force Commander of the United Nations Assistance Mission for Rwanda. Essentially, Beardsley was an eyewitness to the horror of the genocide in Rwanda. Following the genocide, Beardsley testified for the prosecution in the case against Colonel Theoneste Bagasora, the alleged architect of the Rwandan genocide, at the International Criminal Tribunal for Rwanda (ICTR). With General Dallaire, Beardsley coauthored the stunning and extremely informative book entitled *Shake Hands with the Devil: The Failure of Humanity in Rwanda*. Beardsley continues to speak about the 1994 genocide to university classes and at other venues, and in doing so he addresses why humanity needs to avoid failing yet again in stanching genocide early on.

Kenneth J. Campbell is an associate professor of political science and international relations at the University of Delaware. His academic interests are in international security, US foreign policy, contemporary genocide, and the role of force in global governance. Campbell is the author of *Genocide and the Global Village* (Palgrave Macmillan, 2001). A recent publication, "Genocide," appeared in *The International Studies Association Compendium Project*, edited by Robert A. Denemark (Blackwell, 2010).

Christian Davenport is professor of peace studies, political science, and sociology with the Kroc Institute at the University of Notre Dame. Between 1999 and 2008, he was on the faculty of the University of Maryland, where he directed the Minorities at Risk Data Project. Among Davenport's publications are *State Repression and the Domestic Democratic Peace* (Cambridge University Press, 2007) and *Media Bias, Perspective and State Repression: The Black Panther Party* (Cambridge University Press, 2010), which won the prize for best book in "social movements and black politics" from the American Political Science Association. He also is the editor of two books: *Repression and Mobilization* coauthored with Carol Mueller and Hank Johnston (University of Minnesota Press, 2004) and *Paths to State Repression: Human Rights Violations and Contentious Politics* (Rowman & Littlefield, 2000).

His articles have appeared in *the American Political Science Review, the American Sociological Review, the American Journal of Political Science, the Annual Review of Political Science, the Journal of Politics, the Journal of Conflict Resolution, Political Research Quarterly, Comparative Political Studies,* and *the Monthly Review.* Davenport has held visiting appointments at the Transitional Justice Institute at the University of Ulster, Ireland; the Center for Advanced Study in the Behavioral Studies at Stanford University; and the Peace Research Institute in Oslo, Norway.

Maureen S. Hiebert is an assistant professor of political science and law and society at the University of Calgary, Calgary, Alberta, Canada. She currently teaches courses in comparative politics (Asia) and sociolegal studies, and has previously taught courses in comparative genocide in the Department of Political Science, University of Toronto (St. George campus), and has been a guest lecturer on the Cambodian genocide at McMaster University. Prof. Hiebert received her PhD from the Department of Political Science at the University of Toronto (March 2007), where she wrote her dissertation, *The Origins of Genocide: Political Culture, Crisis, and the Construction of Victims,* in which she explored the role played by collective identity construction in the perpetration of the Holocaust and the Cambodian genocide. Her research interests include comparative genocide theory and methodology, the Holocaust, the Cambodian genocide, comparative politics, processes of elite decision making, international humanitarian law, and international criminal law. Prof. Hiebert's publications include "The Three 'Switches' of Identity Construction in Genocide: The Nazi

Final Solution and the Cambodian Killing Fields," *Genocide Studies and Prevention* 3, no. 1 (April 2008), "Theorizing Destruction: Reflections on the State of Comparative Genocide Theory," *Genocide Studies and Prevention* 3, no. 3 (December 2008), and "Genocide in Chile? An Assessment" (coauthored with Pablo Policzer) in *State Violence and Genocide in Latin America: The Cold War Years* (2010).

Herbert Hirsch is professor of political science at the L. Douglas Wilder School of Government and Public Affairs at Virginia Commonwealth University in Richmond, Virginia, where he teaches courses on United States politics, political psychology, and the politics of war, violence, and genocide with a focus on genocide and human rights. He is the author of several books on genocide, including *Genocide and the Politics of Memory* (1995) and *Anti-Genocide: Building an American Movement to Prevent Genocide* (2002). He serves on a number of advisory boards and teaches a course every summer at the University of Toronto on genocide and human rights sponsored by the Zoryan Institute. Professor Hirsch is one of the founding coeditors of *Genocide Studies and Prevention: An International Journal*, published by the University of Toronto Press.

Cyanne E. Loyle is an assistant professor of political science and international studies at West Virginia University. Her research interests span the fields of comparative politics, international relations, and conflict studies. Dr. Loyle's current research focuses on postconflict transitional justice and the strategic use of justice processes in Rwanda and Northern Ireland. She is an East African specialist and has done field work in Rwanda, Burundi, the Democratic Republic of Congo, and Northern Ireland.

Loyle received her MA in Holocaust and genocide studies from Richard Stockton College and her MA and PhD in political science from the University of Maryland. In 2004, Dr. Loyle was part of the team that constructed the National Genocide Memorial in Kigali, Rwanda. In 2008, she was a visiting scholar at the Peace Research Institute, Oslo (PRIO), and from 2009 to 2011 she was a visiting researcher at the Kroc Institute for International Peace Studies at the University of Notre Dame. Currently, she is the Assistant Director of the Northern Ireland Research Initiative and cocreator of the Post-Conflict Justice (PCJ) database. Her research has been published with the Social Science Research Council, *Journal of Peace Research, Genocide Studies and Prevention* and *Global Public Health.*

Isabelle Macgregor is a PhD candidate at the Australian National University. Her research focuses on genocide prevention.

Henry C. Theriault is professor in and chair of the Philosophy Department of Worcester State University, Massachusetts, USA, where from 1999 to 2007 he coordinated the Center for the Study of Human Rights and helped develop the Dennis Brutus Collection. His research on genocide and human rights focuses on long-term justice and repair, denial, definition, perpetrator motivation, mass violence against women, militarization, and Western philosophy's relationship to genocide. Recent publications include "The Mass Atrocity Response Operation Handbook: New Possibilities or the Same Old Militarism," in *Genocide Studies and Prevention* 6, no. 1 (2011), "Genocidal Mutation and the Challenge of Definition," in *Metaphilosophy* 41, no. 4 (2010), "Rousseau, Plato, and Western Philosophy's Anti-Genocidal Strain," in *Metacide: In the Pursuit of Excellence* (2010), and "Genocide, Denial, and Domination: Armenian-Turkish Relations From Conflict Resolution to Just Transformation," in the *Journal of African Conflicts and Peace Studies* 1, no. 2 (2009). He is Chair of the Armenian Genocide Reparations Study Group and coauthor of its forthcoming report. Since 2007, he has served as a coeditor of *Genocide Studies and Prevention.*

Samuel Totten is a genocide scholar based at the University of Arkansas, Fayetteville. For the last eight years he has conducted research along the Chad/Darfur border and in the Nuba Mountains, Sudan.

In July and August of 2004, Totten served as one of twenty-four investigators on the US State Department's Darfur Atrocities Documentation Project, whose express purpose was to conduct interviews with refugees from Darfur in order to ascertain whether genocide had been perpetrated or not in Darfur. Based upon the data collected by the team of investigators, US Secretary of State Colin Powell declared on September 9, 2004, that genocide had been perpetrated in Darfur, Sudan, by Government of Sudan troops and the *Janjaweed.*

In 2008 (January through July), Totten was a Fulbright Scholar at the Centre for Conflict Management at the National University of Rwanda. While there he began conducting a series of interviews that was published as *We Cannot Forget: Interviews with Survivors of the 1994 Genocide in Rwanda* (Rutgers University Press, 2011).

Among the essays/articles Totten has published on the prevention and intervention of genocide are "The Intervention and Prevention of Genocide: Sisyphean or Doable?" *Journal of Genocide Research* 6, no.

2 (June 2004); "The U.S. Government Darfur Genocide Investigation" (with Eric Markusen), *Journal of Genocide Research* 7, no. 2 (June 2005); and "The UN International Commission of Inquiry on Darfur: New and Disturbing Findings" in *Genocide Studies and Prevention* 4, no. 3 (Winter 2009).

Among Totten's books are: *Genocide in Darfur: The Investigation and Findings of The Darfur Atrocities Documentation Team* (with Eric Markusen) (New York: Routledge, 2006); *Centuries of Genocide: Eyewitness Testimony and Critical Essays* (New York: Routledge, 2012); *An Oral and Documentary History of the Darfur Genocide* (Santa Barbara, CA: Praeger Security International, 2010); *We Cannot Forget: Interviews with Survivors of the 1994 Genocide in Rwanda* (New Brunswick, NJ: Rutgers University Press, 2011).

Hannibal Travis is an associate professor of law at Florida International University. He has published *Genocide in the Middle East: The Ottoman Empire, Iraq and Sudan* (Carolina Academic Press, 2010), a chapter on Sudan in *The Top Ten Global Justice Law Review Articles, 2008* (Oxford University Press, 2009), a chapter on Nigeria and Pakistan in *Untold Stories of War Crimes Trials* (Oxford University Press, forthcoming 2012), chapters on the Ottoman Assyrians in *Forgotten Genocides* (University of Pennsylvania Press, 2011) and *Hidden Genocides* (Alex Hinton, Editor, forthcoming 2012), and an article on the Ottoman Assyrians in *Genocide Studies and Prevention* 1, no. 3 (2006): 327–71.

Index